Teaching and Learning America's Christian History

"WHERE THE SPIRIT OF THE LORD IS, THERE IS LIBERTY." II CORINTHIANS 3:17

Harvard Hall.

Stoughton H.

Teaching and Learning
America's Christian
History

American Revolution Bicentennial Edition

Developed by Rosalie J. Slater

Foreword by Dr. Mark Fakkema

The Study of Basic Principles from the Text,

CHRISTIAN HISTORY OF THE CONSTITUTION OF THE UNITED STATES OF AMERICA

CHRISTIAN SELF-GOVERNMENT

Compiled by Verna M. Hall

FOUNDATION FOR AMERICAN CHRISTIAN EDUCATION

SAN FRANCISCO, CALIFORNIA

Published by Foundation for American Christian Education

2946 Twenty-Fifth Avenue, San Francisco, California

Printed by the Iversen-Norman Associates

New York, New York

Designed by John Grossman

San Francisco, California

First Printing, September 17, 1965

Second Printing, April 19, 1969

Third Printing, July 4, 1973

American Revolution Bicentennial Edition

April 19, 1975

Title Page: "A Prospect of the Colledges in Cambridge in New England"

Eighteenth Century Engraving by William Burgis

Courtesy of the Library of Congress

Eagle cast by Paul Revere for General Henry Knox

A Christian Education Guide
for the American Christian Home,
the American Christian Church,
the American Christian School

The Principle Approach

New England's First Fruits (opposite page) is the first of the "Eliot Tracts" describing the work of John Eliot (1604–1690) known as the "Apostle to the Indians."

"And though thy beginnings be small, thy latter end shall greatly encrease." Job 8:7

"The oldest extant document which, in type, clearly recognizes the existence of Harvard College is a precious pamphlet with this title, '*New England's First Fruits in respect to the Progress of Learning in the College at Cambridge, in Massachusetts Bay,*' . . . . It was published in London in 1643, the year following the graduation of our first class of nine members . . ." *Rev. George E. Ellis, 1884*

NEVV ENGLANDS FIRST FRUITS;

IN RESPECT,

First of the { Conversion of some, Conviction of divers, Preparation of sundry } of the *Indians*.

2. Of the progresse of *Learning*, in the *Colledge* at CAMBRIDGE in *Massacusets* Bay.

WITH

Divers other speciall Matters concerning that *Countrey*.

Published by the instant request of sundry Friends, who desire to be satisfied in these points by many *New-England* Men who are here present, and were eye or eare-witnesses of the same.

Who hath despised the Day of small things. Zach. 4. 10.

If thou wert pure and upright, surely now he will awake for thee : — And though thy beginnings be small, thy latter end shall greatly encrease. Iob. 8 6, 7.

LONDON,

Printed by R. O and G. D. for *Henry Overton*, and are to be sold at his Shop in *Popes-head-Alley.* 1 6 4 3.

NEW ENGLANDS FIRST FRUITS

2. In respect of the Colledge, and the proccedings of *Learning* therein.

1. AFter God had carried us safe to *New-England*, and wee had builded our houses, provided necessaries for our liveli-hood, rear'd convenient places for Gods worship, and setled the Civill Government: One of the next things we longed for, and looked after was to advance *Learning*. and perpetuate it to Posterity; dreading to leave an illiterate Ministery to the Churches, when our present Ministers shall lie in the Dust. And as wee were thinking and consulting how to effect this great Work; it pleased God to stir up the heart of one Mr. *Harvard* (a godly Gentleman, and a lover of Learning, there living amongst us) to give the one halfe of his Estate (it being in all about 1700. l.) towards the erecting of a Colledge, and all his Library: after him another gave 300. l. others after them cast in more, and the publique hand of the State added the rest: the Colledge was, by common content, appointed to be at *Cambridge*, (a place very pleasant and accommodate) and is called (according to the name of the first founder) *Harvard Colledge.*

The Edifice is very faire and comely within and without, having in it a spacious Hall; (where they daily meet at Common Lectures) Exercises, and a large Library with some Bookes to it, the gifts of diverse

---

(13)

diverse of our friends; their Chambers and studies also fitted for, and possessed by the Students, and all other roomes of Office necessary and convenient, with all needfull Offices thereto belonging: And by the side of the Colledge a faire *Grammar* Schoole, for the training up of young Schollars, and fitting of them for *Academicall Learning*, that still as they are judged ripe, they may be received into the Colledge of this Schoole: Master *Corlet* is the Mr., who hath very well approved himselfe for his abilities dexterity and painfulnesse in teaching and education of the youth under him.

Over the Colledge is master *Dunster* placed, as President, a learned consionable and industrious man, who hath so trained up, his Pupills in the tongues and Arts, and so seasoned them with the principles of Divinity and Christianity, that we have to our great comfort, (and in truth) beyond our hopes, beheld their progresse in Learning and godlinesse also; the former of these hath appeared in their publique declamations in *Latine* and *Greeke*, and Disputations Logicall and Philosophicall, which they have beene wonted (besides their ordinary Exercises in the Colledge-Hall) in the audience of the Magistrates, Ministers and other Schollars, for the probation of their growth in Learning, upon set dayes, constantly once every moneth to make and uphold: The latter hath been manifested in sundry of them by the savoury breathings of their Spirits in their godly conversation. Insomuch that we are confident, if these early blossomes may be cherished and warmed with the influence of the friends of Learning and lovers of this pious worke, they will by the help of God, come to happy maturity in a short time.

Over the Colledge are twelve Overseers chosen by the generall Court, six of them are of the Magistrates, the other six of the Ministers, who are to promote the best good of it and (having a power of influence into all persons in it) are to see that every one be diligent and proficient in his proper place.

2. *Rules, and Precepts that are observed in the Colledge.*

1. WHen any Schollar is able to understand *Tully*, or such like classicall Latine Author *ex tempore*, and make and speake true Latine in Verse and Prose, *suo ut aiunt Marte*; And decline perfectly the Paradigm's of *Nounes* and *Verbes* in the *Greek* tongue: Let him then and not before be capable of admission into the Colledge.

2. Let

---

(22)

2. Let every Student be plainly instructed, and earnestly pressed to consider well, the maine end of his life and studies is, *to know God and Jesus Christ which is eternall life*, Joh. 17. 3. and therefore to lay *Christ* in the bottome, as the only foundation of all sound knowledge and Learning.

And seeing the Lord only giveth wisedome, Let every one seriously set himselfe by prayer in secret to seeke it of him *Prov* 2,3.

3. Every one shall so exercise himselfe in reading the Scriptures twice a day, that he shall be ready to give such an account of his proficiency therein, both in *Theoreticall* observations of the Language, and *Logick*, and in *Practicall* and spirituall truths, as his Tutor shall require, according to his ability; *seeing the entrance of the word giveth light, it giveth understanding to the simple*, Psalm. 119. 130.

4. That they eshewing all profanation of Gods Name, Attributes, Word, Ordinances, and times of Worship, doe studie with good conscience, carefully to retaine God, and the love of his truth in their mindes else let them know, that (notwithstanding their Learning) God may give them up *to strong delusions*, and in the end *to a reprobate minde*, 2 Thes. 2. 11, 12. Rom. 1. 28.

5. That they studiously redeeme the time; observe the generall houres appointed for all the Students, and the speciall houres for their owne *Classis*: and then diligently attend the Lectures without any disturbance by word or gesture. And if in any thing they doubt, they shall enquire, as of their fellowes, so, (in case of *Non satisfaction*) modestly of their Tutors.

6. None shall under any pretence whatsoever, frequent the company and society of such men as lead an unfit, and dissolute life.

Nor shall any without his Tutors leave, or (in his absence) the call of Parents or Guardians, goe abroad to other Townes.

7. Every Schollar shall be present in his Tutors chamber at the 7th. houre in the morning, immediately after the sound of the Bell, at his opening the Scripture and prayer, so also at the 5th. houre at night; and then give account of his owne private reading, as aforesaid in Particular the third, and constantly attend Lectures in the Hall at the houres appointed? But if any (without necessary impediment) shall absent himselfe from prayer or Lectures, he shall bee lyable to Admonition, if he offend above once a weeke.

8. If any Schollar shall be found to transgresse any of the Lawes of God, or the Schoole, after twice Admonition, he shall be lyable, if

The Republican Form of Government Depends Upon The Principles Contained In The Holy Scriptures

"The government of the United States is acknowledged by the wise and good of other nations, to be the most free, impartial, and righteous government of the world; but all agree, that for such a government to be sustained many years, the principles of truth and righteousness, taught in the Holy Scriptures, must be practised. The rulers must govern in the fear of God, and the people obey the laws." Emma Willard, 1843

Dedication

To the Christians of the first century who lived and died for Liberty of Conscience, thus laying the foundation of the American Christian Constitution and of individual liberty. Will the American Christian of this century accept this heritage from primitive Christianity and emulate the Founding-Father Generation—to restore once again "this most sacred of all property"—Liberty of Conscience? "For I am not ashamed of the Gospel of Christ: for it is the power of God unto salvation to every one that believeth; to the Jew first, and also to the Greek." Romans 1:16

An American Christian Education

FOR OVER ONE HUNDRED YEARS *Americans have not known or learned of America's Christian History. Five generations of Americans have produced a national ignorance concerning the Providential founding of this nation and of God's hand in preserving, defending, and leading the Colonists to victory in 1775-1781—the seven long years of the American Christian Revolution. Today we have no proud heroes—no models of character, or leadership, to inspire our youth. We have no identity for courage, conscience or compassion, to cherish as part of the proud fabric which a people weaves into its character and tradition. The reason is not that we do not possess such a treasury of greatness and heroism. The reason is that we have allowed our treasury to be robbed and pillaged of its gold—the gold of Christian character. In so doing we have lost our vision of the destiny and purpose of God's America.*

One hundred years ago we took education out of the Christian home where it had raised up men and women who were God-fearing, Christ-honoring, Bible-loving people. People who were willing to count the cost of Christian liberty. Yielding to the arguments of secularism in the 1830's, 40's and 50's, we permitted our churches to relinquish their leadership of Christian education. In making this change into the government sponsored schools, we closed our Bible as the educational and political textbook, and we shifted our level of education from the building of individual Christian character to the building of a group character, conformable to society. As we shifted from a God-centered republic to a man-centered democracy—we began to flounder.

Today, while the signs of the times seem most disheartening, there is evidence that the overturning, overturning, overturning, is taking place. Our unique heritage and founding has again been brought to light and some Americans are remembering their Christian heritage. Some Christians are again raising the standard of character and xiii *conscience of our Pilgrim, Puritan and Patriot heroes and heroines. The conservative revolution of our times is in effect a Christian revolution. It will force us ultimately to awaken from our national apathy. It will inspire us to build up our individual defenses, and so to strengthen our citadel of freedom—which is the mighty fortress of Christianity itself.*

The Christian school—a direct outgrowth of our Bible-based Christian churches—has a most critical role to play in restoring Christian leadership to our nation. The anti-Christian education of the progressive state schools has produced the socialism and the communism of our times. Teachers are most vital to Christian school education—teachers who are models of Christian character and teachers who are alert to the challenge to America's freedom and the nature of that challenge. Christianity alone is the citadel of America's freedom.

The Founding Fathers of our nation had a clear conception of Christian character and Christian citizenship as part of the inseparable fabric of education. They cherished both these aspects of development as vital to the maintenance of individual liberty and the freedom of America. Samuel Adams, that devoted and intrepid Christian, known as the "Father of the American Revolution" urges teachers of the young to give careful consideration to the virtues of Christian character and knowledge of Christian self-government in the following passage, found in the opening pages of Christian History of the Constitution of the United States of America:

"Let divines and philosophers, statesmen and patriots, unite their endeavors to renovate the age, by impressing the minds of men with the importance of educating their little boys and girls, of inculcating in the minds of youth the fear and love of the Deity and universal philanthropy, and, in subordination to these great principles, the love of their country; of instructing them in the art of self-government, without which they never can act a wise part in the government of societies, great or small; in short of leading them in the study and practice of the exalted virtues of the Christian system . . ."
Christian History, *page XIV*

The record of America as a Christian nation resides in the documented history of her founding. This record has been deliberately obscured in order to deprive the individual of his Christian heritage of individual liberty. The rediscovery of the Christian foundation of our country will restore the Christian leadership of America. This knowledge needs to be part of the background of every individual engaged in the education of American youth.

As Christian teachers and parents draw upon their own love of Christ and country they will discover many new ways in which to build a living curriculum from the Christian treasury of the founding of our nation. As the student sees his own relationship to Christianity and to America he can be helped to put into practice Christianity's own form of government—Christian self-government.

Emma Willard, a Christian educator, whose biography can be found on pages 438 and 439 of Christian History, *makes the following statement in her "Abridged History*
of the United States: or Republic of America," 1843:

"There are those, who rashly speak, as if in despair of the fortunes of our republic; because, say they, political virtue has declined. If so, then is there the more need to infuse patriotism into the breasts of the coming generation. And what is so likely to effect this national self-preservation, as to give our children, for their daily reading and study, such a record of the sublime virtues of the worthies of our earliest day,— and of Washington and his compatriots, as shall leave its due impress? And what but the study of their dangers and toils,—their devotion of life and fortune, can make our posterity know, what our country, and our liberties, have cost? And what but the History of our peculiar, complicated fabric of government, by which it may be examined, as piece by piece the structure was built up, can impart such a knowledge of the powers it gives, and the duties it enjoins, as shall enable our future citizens, to become its enlightened and judicious supporters."

"The Blessings of America"

In a sermon entitled The Blessings of America, *delivered at the request of the Tammany Society, or Columbian Order in New York, 1791, "being the Anniversary of the Independence of America," the Reverend William Linn made the following statement:*

"Civil liberty is a blessing the more precious, because with it are connected the rights of conscience. Where slavery prevails these are always infringed. In this country, as they are well understood, so they are preserved inviolate."

The phrase "as they are well understood, so they are preserved inviolate" *is the purpose of the educational program contained in this* Christian Education Guide *developed so that the American Christian home, school and church, might study* Christian History of the Constitution of the United States of America, *compiled by Verna M. Hall.*

It is now apparent that if we would preserve both liberty of conscience *and* civil liberty *for every individual in America, we must begin to understand the* Principles *upon which our American Christian Constitution is constructed.*

Today there are vast amounts of literature flooding the country and, in an effort to keep abreast of the times, individuals spend a large proportion of time each week reviewing many publications and books. But there are still too few efforts to pursue, either individually, in families or in study groups, positive programs *for learning the* principles *of America's Constitutional form of government.*

Once the individual becomes informed and aware of the problems of the times, it then becomes critically important to take effective action to correct, *to* reconstruct, *to* xvi *rebuild Constitutional liberty. This cannot be accomplished by merely uncovering the problem. With awareness must come constructive knowledge in order to deal intelligently and effectively with every challenge to individual liberty and to the freedom of these United States of America. Human knowledge and human reason are not able to provide the insight and wisdom needed. Unless one understands the Christian history of this nation and the Christian Principles of our form of government, one is not equipped to deal with today's challenge to the freedom of mankind. Reverend Linn reminds us of the source of our liberties:*

"Not only do we enjoy the right of private judgment in matters of conscience, but the gospel is preached and its ordinances administered throughout a great part of our land. Without this we would be less civilized, and less free . . . What is an extensive and beautiful country, what liberty with all its concomitant blessings, destitute of the worship of our Creator. . . Though the rights of man be invaluable, yet we may successfully plead for these and be unhappy hereafter. 'This is life eternal, that they might know thee, the only true God, and Jesus Christ whom thou hast sent.' (John 17:3) The abundant means of this knowledge are within our power."

Just as Reverend Linn establishes our liberty in Christianity so must we, once again, as in the founding period of our nation, reunite our knowledge of America and the principles of her Constitution, with our knowledge of the Holy Scriptures—"the great political text-book of the patriots." (Page 375 Christian History) *In the words of the Apostle, Paul, "For we wrestle not against flesh and blood, but against principalities, against powers, against the rulers of the darkness of this world, against spiritual wickedness in high places." (Eph. 6:12)*

The battle today is for men's hearts and souls. It is not a battle for men's minds. The mind will believe only what the heart, the character, the conscience, of an individual dictates. We cannot rely alone on information, *but we must depend upon* consecration*—"as servants of Christ, doing the will of God from the heart."*

We cannot win this battle unless we first put on "the whole armour of God." This includes "the helmet of salvation" and the "sword of the Spirit, which is the word of God." Equipped thus with our spiritual armour, we are ready to deepen our knowledge of America's Christian roots. The Tree of Liberty must be nourished with our attention to what constitutes the Constitution. *It has to do with* character *and* conscience. *We must be as knowledgeable about* principles *as the enemies of freedom are knowledgeable about* issues.

We shall pursue our study of America's Christian History *by a three-fold thrust:*

1st We shall consider how the character of America is formed in the Christian home, the Christian church, the Christian school.

2nd We shall establish the Property of conscience *as the "end and purpose of government."*

3rd We shall consider how the study and embodiment of basic Christian Constitutional Principles can be delegated to every aspect of the individual's many spheres of self-government, extending from the home, into the business, school, social, and political circles.

Let us pray such a study conducted in the homes, in the churches, and in the Christian schools of our nation, may once again restore to America that liberty for which her patriots toiled so long and so bravely. May we be able to "Stand fast in the liberty wherewith Christ hath made us free" and not "be entangled again with the yoke of bondage." (Galatians 5:1)

Foreword

To educate the children of today *is to construct the foundation of the nation of tomorrow. Faithless teaching makes for unfaithful citizens.*

Shall our nation continue in the faith of our Founding Fathers or shall we veer in the direction of secularizing the citizens of tomorrow?

This is not merely one of our nation's problems. It is the problem of all problems, for as we educate our youth today so will be our nation tomorrow.

Our nation now is standing at the crossroads. Today our American youth is being trained in state schools whose educational program is committed by law to secularize the citizens of tomorrow and that at state expense!

To save our country from the dry rot of secularism we are in need of a nation-wide education that honors God and that teaches study content in the light of God's Word. To attain such a goal in the basic study of History we are in need of two Christian source books:

1) *A source book that presents the History of our country in its true God-centered light.*
2) *A teacher's guide which organizes the source material and presents it to the teacher in useable grade level form.*

It gives me real pleasure to announce that these two Christian source books are now available. I consider the publication of these books a much needed work never before attempted. I am amazed at the extensiveness of this pioneer work which has been done in the important field of Christian teaching.

The Christian history source book has already been completed. We refer to the "Christian History of the Constitution" which is compiled by Miss Verna M. Hall, and published by the American Christian Constitution Press.

The teacher's handbook is a valuable aid in "Teaching and Learning America's Christian History." This Teacher's Guide is designed to help the busy teacher to properly organize the valuable source material found in the above mentioned "Christian History of the Constitution." The author of this teacher's guide is Miss Rosalie J. Slater.

Especially during the past generation our secular and secularizing public education has lost that which is most precious in our national life. We have lost that which inspired our Founding Fathers to come to the bleak shores of our country. We as a nation have lost our former national conscience. It was for the purpose of preserving this "conscience" that our Founding Fathers came to this country.

Where is the faith in God—where is the heroic devotion to Christian conscience which characterized the founding of the Plymouth Colony in 1620?

In coming to the rocky western shore of Cape Cod Bay in south-eastern Massachusetts, the primary concern of our Founding Fathers was not financial gain or mere adventure. Like their counter-parts of the first century of Christianity, they would rather die than lose their faith. They were ready to endure every hardship, even death itself, rather than lose their faith for future generations. Even though 52 of their number died the first year, they were unperturbed. When their ship, the "Mayflower," returned to England, NOT ONE WENT BACK. What a testimony; what a manifestation of CHRISTIAN CHARACTER, CHRISTIAN SELF-GOVERNMENT, CHRISTIAN ECONOMICS, CHRISTIAN EDUCATION AND BIBLICAL CHRISTIAN UNITY!

The coming of the Christian Founding Fathers, like the coming of Christ, was by Divine Design. Both happened in the fulness of God's time.

The planting of Christianity on American soil was immortalized by the Mayflower Compact which stated that the Pilgrims were to establish themselves as a "single covenanted body of Christians, united for civil as well as spiritual purposes." Theirs was to be an "undertaking for the glory of God and for the advance of the Christian faith."

Today the national laws of our country are such that our state schools which teach seven-eighths of the nation's children are forbidden by the courts of our land to teach the faith of our fathers. To all intent and purposes they must teach an ever-growing educational program—but it must be one that disregards that which was central to our Founding Fathers—the glory of God.

May the number of schools that are true to the Faith of our Fathers ever increase. May the preparation for life fostered by these schools ever be true to the faith of our Founding Fathers and may our present day Christian schools ever be motivated as were their schools: "For the glory of God and for the advance of the Christian faith."

Dr. Mark Fakkema

Chicago, Illinois
xx March 19, 1965

Just One Christian Education Guide for the Christian Home, the Christian Church, the Christian School

Why

WHY IS THERE JUST ONE *Christian Education Guide to be used by the home, the church, the school? Because there is just one seed which built our republic—the Christian home, the Christian church, the Christian school. These comprise the basic elements or constituents of our Constitutional liberty.*

America's proud heritage and traditions have been subverted. While it is easy to point out the aggressiveness of those forces which would "divide and conquer" us, we as a people by our "falling away" have provided the means and opportunity for its accomplishment.

Can we now come to the recognition that requires our faith *and not our* fear? *Are we willing to reestablish the importance of the Christian home, the Christian church and the Christian school? Will we honestly face up to our own questions?*

1) *Have I imparted to my own family circle the understanding and knowledge of America's history and purpose and tradition? Or have I relegated this responsibility to agencies outside the home?*

2) *What am I doing to support my church in a program of Christian Americanism? Does my pastor have my support in his leadership from the pulpit in Biblical American Christian patriotism?*

3) *Am I helping my Christian school to separate from secularism—and fulfill its leadership in Christian curriculum and Christian teaching methods? Am I supporting a program which teaches* Christian History of the Constitution?

How

How can the same Guide *be used by the Christian home, the Christian church and*   **xxi** *the Christian school?*

The seed which built our Christian republic must once again restore our nation to Christ. Therefore each one of these aspects—the home, the church and the school—must function individually *so that we may have a* unity of purpose and accomplishment. *Too long we have accepted a division of these basic elements of Constitutional Government. Once again the Christian home must accept its Biblical responsibility for the building of Christian character and in kindling the love of Christ and country at its own hearthside.*

Our Bible based Christian churches must accept leadership in teaching American Christian patriotism and its relationship to Christianity. And our Christian schools must accept their unique ministry to separate from secularism and psychological atheism and to re-establish a Christian method and curriculum. They need to accept the challenge to teach Christian History *as a part of the entire school curriculum—from kindergarten through college.*

This Christian Education Guide entitled Teaching and Learning America's Christian History *embodies a Christian method and approach to the study of* Christian History of the Constitution of the United States of America *compiled by Verna M. Hall. Laying the ax at the root of modern methodology, which is evolutionary in technique and implies a "search for truth" or a "discovery of truth," we begin from the position of God's Word. Seven fundamental principles derived from God's Word are amplified and expanded through the text,* Christian History. *They become standards of reference for understanding both the founding of this nation and its maintenance as a Christian Republic.*

The Expanding Principles of America's Christian History *include two programs which cover the same content:*

1) Study Group Plan for Christian History of the Constitution *based upon the Holy Bible—"the great political text-book of the patriots"*
2) Teachers' Guide for Christian History of the Constitution *Expanding the Principles through the Grades*

In addition to these two sections of the Guide *covering the same material in* Christian History, *there is, beginning on page 303 a* Study Course for Christian History *which proceeds* sequentially *through Volume One of* Christian History.

When

Thus it is possible for the Christian home to begin at once to re-establish the family altar and to re-establish the tradition of kindling the love of Christ and country at its own hearthside. At the same time our clergy, who have in the past led us in "patriotic piety," can initiate study groups in their own churches for adults, teen-agers or the wider community outside their own congregations. And culminating this three-fold program of the home, the church and the school, our Christian schools can teach teachers in a weekly or bi-monthly study group, and then schedule time in the curriculum so that every child in every grade learns these basic principles of America's Christian History.

We do not limit the study of the Holy Scriptures to just the home, or the church, or to the school. Instead the Word of God binds our hearts together even as individually we pursue our appointed paths. Just so do we need to take unto ourselves the challenge of restoring the knowledge, love and understanding of America's Christian History to the Christian home, to the Christian church and to the Christian school. Then once again we can reconstruct "one nation under God" which, like its constitutents of liberty, is "indivisible" in Christ.

Table of Contents

The Christian Principle of American Political Union

God's Principle of Individuality

The Christian Principle of Self-Government

The Christian Form of Our Government

How the Seed of Local Self-Government is Planted

The Christian Principle of American Political Union

The Christian Principle of American Political Union

Appendix

Part IV   Christian History Study Course

The American Christian Home
The American Christian Church
The American Christian School

Constituents of Constitutional Liberty

The American Christian Home

The Educational Goal of the
American Christian Home in a Republic
is to build the Foundation of
America's Christian Character

THERE ARE FEW STATEMENTS TODAY about the opportunity and the obligation of a Christian home in a republic. Yet there is no single element in America which contributes more significantly to the success of Christian Constitutional government. It is in the home where the foundations of Christian character are laid. It is in the home where Christian self-government is learned and practised. Yet, the Christian American who is aware of the particular challenges to America's Christian character and to the Constitutional form of government still inclines to political education outside the home. Thus, while parents are active politically, educationally, religiously, it becomes necessary for other agencies—the school, the church, the community—to pick up the responsibility for making home the first sphere of government in the republic. Needless to say they cannot substitute what only the home can provide.

The following selection by Reverend S. Phillips, written in 1861, is entitled in part: "The Christian Home as it is in the Sphere of Nature and the Church—Showing the Mission, Duties, Influences, Habits, and Responsibilities of Home; its Education, Government, and Discipline . . ." It is evident that home as rightfully conceived by Christian parents includes far more than a mere Grand Central Station—accommodating travelers with food, clothing and shelter, while they entrain for separate destinations

The simplicity of these selections stands in sharp contrast with the psychological writing of today regarding the role of the home. Yet the emphasis is clear and it becomes a standard of reference for 20th century Christians who have permitted the erosion of the home by secularism and who, in few cases, present a contrast to paganism in life, manners and pursuits. For our encouragement we

3

can study the primitive Christians—their testimony in a pagan world is unsurpassed. We can learn from them of the glorious liberty which the salvation of Jesus Christ brought—especially to those who were surfeited with dissatisfaction from both their sensual and intellectual pursuits. In fact, the most noteworthy conversions were among those intellectuals who had explored thoroughly the pagan philosophers and who found their conclusions comfortless.

Today we are in a period stirring with a "great awakening"—a revival of faith and dedication and Christian commitment which will be greater than any the world has ever witnessed. This redemption must extend to the preeminence of Christ in all areas of life and living. Thus education, cultural and social life, and especially Christian government must reflect and witness to His salvation and grace.

As Christian parents restore the "family altar" to their homes they will also be able to rekindle the watchfires of an enlightened patriotism. This Christian patriotism includes a recognition and understanding of America's unique function in the Chain of Christianity and a knowledge of the Christian principles of America's Christian History.

The Christian Home
As It Is In The Sphere Of Nature
And The Church

Preface

Rev. S. Phillips,
A.M.

"It is a fact conceded by all, that the constitution of the Christian family, and its social and spiritual relations, are not as fully developed as they should be. In this age of extreme individualism, we have almost left out of view the mission of home as the first form of society, and the important bearing it has upon the formation of character. Its interests are not appreciated; its duties and privileges are neglected; husbands and wives do not fully realize their moral relation to each other; parents are inclined to renounce their authority; and children, brought up in a state of domestic libertinism, neither respect nor obey their parents as they should. The idea of human character as a development from the nursery to the grave, is not realized. Home as a preparation for both the state and the church, and its bearing, as such, upon the prosperity of both, are renounced as traditionary, and too old and stale to suit this age of mechanical progression and 'young Americanism.'

"As a consequence, the influence of home is lost; the lambs of the flock are neglected, grow up in spiritual ignorance, and become a curse both to themselves and to their parents. The vice and infidelity which prevail to such an alarming extent in the present day, may be ascribed to parental neglect of the young. The desolating curse of heaven invariably accompanies neglect of domestic obligations and duties; it was this that constituted that dreadful degeneracy which preceded the coming of the Messiah. The parents were alienated from the children, and the children from their parents. And the only way in which the Jews could avert deserved and impending ruin, was by 'turning the heart of the fathers to the children, Luke 1:17 and the heart of the children to their fathers.'

"We must adopt the same method. We need in the present day a deeper and more scriptural sense, both in the state and church, of the importance of the family, and of its position in the sphere of natural and religious life. The attention of the people should be directed to the nature, the influences, the responsibilities, the prerogatives, duties and blessings of the Christian home . . .

"The following work is an humble contribution to this important cause. It is intended to excite interest in the religious elements of family life, and to show that the development of individual character and happiness in the church and state, in time and in eternity, starts with, and depends upon, home-training and nurture . . . If this unassuming volume should be instrumental in the saving of one family from ruin, we shall feel ourself fully compensated."

The Author

Chambersburg, Pa., 1859

Home in the Sphere of the Church

"What is the Christian home? Only in the sphere of Christianity does the true idea of home become fully developed . . .

"Here the marriage union is preserved 'honorable,' held sacred, and woman is raised to her true position. In the sphere of the Christian church, home is brought fairly and completely into view. Here it rises above the measure of natural affection and temporal interest. It enters the sphere of supernatural faith, and becomes the adumbration of our home in heaven.

"The Christian home is a true type of the church. 'The husband is the head of the Ephesians 5:23 wife, as Christ is of the church.' The love of the family is self-denying and holy, like that between Christ and His church. The children are 'the heritage of the Lord;' Psalms 127:3 the parents are His stewards. Like the church, the Christian home has its ministry. Yea, the church is in the home, as the mother is in her child. We cannot separate them; they are correlatives. The one demands the other. The Christian home can have existence only in the sphere of the church . . .

"Home is a partnership of spiritual as well as of natural life. The members 5 thereof dwell 'as being heirs together of the grace of life.' 'Heavenly mindedness,' 'the hidden man of the heart,' and a 'hope full of immortality,' are the ornaments of the Christian home. Hers is 'the incorruptibility of a meek and quiet spirit;' her members are 'joint heirs of salvation;' they are 'one,' not only in nature, but 'in Christ.' They enjoy a 'communion in spirit,' that their 'joy might be full.' 'What God, therefore, hath joined together, let not man put asunder.'

"Such a home, being 'right with God,' must be 'full of good fruits, without partiality and without hypocrisy.' Here the Christian shows his real character. In the sphere of the church, the family reaches its highest excellence and its purest enjoyment. Says the learned D'Aubigne, 'Without the knowledge and the love of God, a family is but a collection of individuals who may have more or less of natural affection for one another; but the real bond,—the love of God our Father, in Jesus Christ, our Lord,—is wanting.'

"We, therefore, abuse the idea of home when we divest it of the religious element. As the family is a divine institute and a type of the church and of heaven, it cannot be understood in its isolation from Christianity; it must involve Christian principles, duties, and interests; and embrace in its educational functions, a preparation, not only for the State, but also for the church . . .

"How many Christian parents practically discard this attribute of home! While all their temporal interests cluster around their home, and their hearts are fondly wedded to it as their retreat from a cold and repulsive world, they never think perhaps that God is in their family, that He has instituted it, and given those cherished ones who 'set like olive plants around their table.' . . .

The Mission of the Christian Home

"If home is a divine institution, and includes the religious element, moving in the sphere of nature and of the church, then its calling must be of God; its mission is divine; it is designed to subserve a spiritual purpose; it has a soul-mission . . .

"What then is the mission of the Christian home? It is two-fold,—the temporal and eternal well-being of its members . . . It is the mission of home to provide for the temporal well-being of its members. As the parent sustains a physical, intellectual and moral relation to the child, it is his mission to provide for its physical, mental and moral wants. 'He that provideth not for his own house hath denied the faith, and is worse than an infidel.' Natural affection will prompt to this . . .

"That it is a part, therefore, of the home mission to provide for the physical wants of the dependents there, is very evident. To refuse to fulfill it is a crime against nature. This part of the home-mission includes the education of the body, by properly unfolding and directing its powers, and providing it with appropriate nutriment, raiment and shelter. In a word, we should make proper provision for the development and maturity of the physical life of our children. This is the mission of the parent until the child is able to provide for itself. This, says Blackstone, 'is a principle of natural law;' and, in the language of Puffendorf, is 'an obligation laid on parents, not only by nature herself, but by their own proper act in bringing them into the world.' The laws of the land also command it. The child has a legal claim upon the parent for physical sustenance and education.

"It is another part of the home-mission to provide for the intellectual wants and welfare of the child. Children have mind as well as body. The former needs nourishment and training as well as the latter. Hence it is as much the mission of the family to minister to the well-being of the mind of the child, as to that of its body. Civil law enforces this. Children have a legal as well as a natural claim to mental culture. In a word, it is the home-mission to provide for the child all things necessary to prepare it for a citizenship in the state.

"Parents abuse this mission in two ways, either when they by their own indolence and dissipation compel their children to support them; or, on the other hand, when they become the willing slaves of their children, labor to amass a fortune for them, and, in the anticipation of that, permit them to grow up in ignorance, idleness, and prodigality, fit only to abuse and spend the fruit of parental servitude. In this way the misapplied provision made by parents often becomes a curse, not only to the members of the family, but to the state and church . . .

"Parents are 'priests unto their families,' and have the commission to act for Revelation 1:6
them as faithful stewards of God in all things pertaining to their everlasting welfare. Their souls, as well as their bodies, are committed to their trust, and God says to them,—

" 'Go nurse them for the King of Heaven,
And He will pay thee hire.'

"This is their great mission, and corresponds with the conception of the Christian home as a spiritual nursery. The family is 'God's husbandry;' and this implies a 1 Corinthians 3:9
spiritual culture. As its members dwell as 'being heirs together of the grace of life,' it is the function of each to labor to make all the rest 'fellow-citizens with the saints, Ephesians 2:19
and of the household of God.' Parents should provide for the religious wants of their children. Mere physical maintenance and mental culture cannot supersede the necessity of spiritual training. Children have a right to such training.

"This religious provision is twofold; their moral and spiritual faculties should be developed; and their moral nature supplied with appropriate nutriment. All the wants of their moral nature are to be faithfully provided for. The home-mission involves the business of education of body, of mind, and of spirit;—of preparation for the state, for the church, for eternity. It is this which makes it so sacred and responsible. Strip the Christian family of its mission as a nursery for the soul; wrest from the parents their high prerogative as stewards of God; and you heathenize home, yea, you brutalize it! . . .

"Husband and wife may love each other, and live together in all the peace and harmony of reciprocated affection; yet if the religious part of their home-mission remain unfulfilled, their family is divested of its noblest attraction; its greatest interests will fall into ruin; its highest destiny will not be attained; and soon its fruits will be entombed in oblivion; while their children, neglected and perishing, will look back upon that home with a bitterness of spirit which the world can neither soothe nor extract!

"How many such homes there are! Even the homes of church members are too often reckless of their high vocation. Their moral stewardship is neglected; their dedications, formal and heartless. No prayers are heard; no Bible read; no instructions given; no pious examples set; no holy discipline exercised. Their interests, their hopes and their enjoyments; their education, their labor and their rest, are all of the world,—worldly . . .

"Many parents disqualify themselves for their home-mission by devoting too much attention to society,—by spending more time abroad, at parties, theaters and masquerade balls, in gossiping and recreation, than at home with each other and with their children. They commit their children, with all the family interests, to nurses and servants. They regard their offspring as mere playthings to be dandled upon the knee, brought up like calves in the stall, and then turned out to shape their own destiny.

"This is a sad mistake! There is no substitute for home,—no transfer of a parent's commission, no adequate compensation for a parent's loss. None can effectually take the parent's place. Their influence is overwhelming and absolute . . .

"What a folly and a sin, therefore, for Christian parents to give over their holy mission to another, while they immerse themselves in the forbidden pleasures and recreations of the world! Oh, if you are loving, faithful parents, you will love the society of your household more than the fashions and the fashionable resorts of the world; you will not substitute the 'nurse' and the 'boarding school' for the more efficient ministrations of the Christian home . . .

Family Religion

Matthew 21:13
Luke 10:42

"The Christian home demands a family religion. This makes it a 'household of God.' Without this it is but a 'den of thieves. 'It is 'the one thing needful.'

"What is 'family religion?' . . .

"Family religion includes parental Bible instruction, family prayer, and religious

Deuteronomy
6:6, 7

education, government, discipline and example . . . 'Thou shalt teach my words diligently unto thy children, and talk of them when thou sittest in thy house.' . . .

"Thus felt and acted our primitive fathers. By every winning art, they sought to fill their children with the knowledge of God's Word. The entire range of nursery instruction and amusement was comprised in Scripture pictures and hieroglyphics. They intermingled religion with all their home pursuits, and entwined it with their earliest and purest associations of childhood. If Christian parents would follow

8

their example now, in these days of parental deliquency, we would not behold so many of their children grow up in religious ignorance and indifference.

"The same may be said of the family altar and prayer. A prayerless family is an irreligious, godless family. Says Henry, 'They who daily pray in their houses do well; they that not only pray, but read the Scriptures, do better; but they do best of all, who not only pray and read the Scriptures, but sing the praises of God.'

"Besides, the religion of home implies that we 'command our children and household to keep the way of the Lord,'—that we 'bring them up in His nurture and admonition,' and 'train them up as He would have them go;' and that in things pertaining to their spiritual welfare we 'go in and out' before them as their pattern and example, bidding them to 'follow us even as we follow Christ,' and living in their midst as 'the living epistles of Christ, known and read' of them all . . .

Genesis 18:19
Ephesians 6:4
Proverbs 22:6

1 Corinthians 11:1
2 Corinthians 3:2

"Many parents seek to excuse themselves from the practice of family religion, upon the ground that they have not the capacity nor the time. If so, you should not have married. But if you are Christians, you have the capacity, and you will take the time . . .

"But some are ashamed to begin family religion. Ashamed of what? of your piety? of your children? of the true glory and greatness of your home? Then you are ashamed of Jesus! You should rather blush that you have not begun this good work.

"The great defect of family religion in the present day is, that it is not educational. Parents wait until their children have grown up, and established habits of sin, when they suppose that the efforts of some 'protracted meeting' will compensate for their neglect in childhood. They overlook the command of God to teach them His words. The influence of this defect and delusion has been most destructive . . .

"One great reason, perhaps, why there are so many such homes is, that there are now so many irreligious marriages, where husband and wife are 'unequally yoked together,' one a believer and the other not. 'How can two walk together except they be agreed?' Can there be family religion when husband and wife are traveling to eternity in opposite roads? No! There will be hindrances instead of 'helps.' If they marry not 'in the Lord,' religion will not be in their home. Says the pious Jay, 'I am persuaded that it is very much owing to the prevalence of these indiscriminate and unhallowed connections, that we have fallen so far short of those men of God, who are gone before us, in the discharge of family worship, and in the training up of our households in the nurture and admonition of the Lord.'

2 Corinthians 6:14
Amos 3:3

"Family religion is implied in the marriage relation and obligation. It is included in the necessities of our children, and in the covenant promises of God. The penalties of its neglect, and the rewards of our faithfulness to it, should prompt us to its establishment in our homes. Its absence is a curse; its presence a blessing. It is a foretaste of heaven. Like manna, it will feed our souls, quench our thirst, sweeten the cup of life, and shed a halo of glory and of gladness around our firesides. Let yours, therefore, be the religious home; and then be sure that God will delight to dwell therein, and His blessing will descend, like the dews of heaven, upon it . . .

Genesis 27:28

"Yours will be the home of love and harmony; it shall have the charter of family

9

rights and privileges, the ward of family interests, the palladium of family hopes and happiness. Your household piety will be the crowning attribute of your peaceful home,—the 'crown of living stars' that shall adorn the night of its tribulation, and the pillar of cloud and of fire in its pilgrimage to a 'better country.' . . .

The Relation of Home to the Church

"The Christian home sustains a direct relation to the church. This relation is similar to that which it sustains to the state. The nature and mission of home demand the church. The former is the adumbration of the latter. The one is in the other. 'Greet the church that is in thine house.' The church was in the house of Aquila and Priscilla, in the tent of Abraham, and in the palace of David. It must be in every Christian home, and every Christian home must be in the church. In a word, our families must be churchly.

Romans 16:5

"This relation is vital and necessary,—a relation of mutual dependence. The family is a preparation for the church, subordinate to it, and must, therefore, throw its influence in its favor, be moulded by it, and labor with direct reference to the church in the way of training up for membership in it. As the civil and political relations of home involve the duty of parents to train up their children for efficient citizenship in the state, so its moral and religious relations involve the duty of education for the church. Hence the Christian home is churchly in its spirit, religion, education, influence, and mission . . .

"Thus, therefore, we see that the relation between the Christian home and the church is one of mutual dependence . . .

Home Influence

"Home-influence is traditional. It passes down the current of life from one generation to another. Its continuity is preserved from first to last. The homes of our forefathers rule us even now, and will pass from us to our children's children. Hence it has been called the 'fixed capital' of home. It keeps up a continuous stream of home-life and feeling and interest . . .

"Let us now briefly advert to the objects of home-influence. It is exerted upon the members of home, especially upon the formation of their character and destiny. It moulds their character . . .

"Ask the strong man in the prime of life, whether the most firm and reliable principles of his character were not the inheritance of the parental home. What an influence the teachings and prayers of his mother Monica had upon the whole character of the pious Augustine! The sterling worth of Washington is a testimony to the formative power of parental instruction. John Quincy Adams, even when his eloquence thundered through our legislative halls, and caused a nation to startle from her slumber, bent his aged form before God, and repeated the prayer of his childhood . . . 'Generally,' says Dr. Cumming, 'when there is a Sarah in the house, there will be an Isaac in the cradle; wherever there is an Eunice teaching a Timothy the Scriptures from a child, there will be a Timothy teaching the gospel to the rest of mankind.' By the force of this same influence, the pious wife may win over to Christ her ungodly husband, and the godly child may save the unbelieving parent . . .

2 Timothy 1:5

"The Christian home has its influence also upon the state. It forms the citizen, lays the foundation for civil and political character, prepares the social element and taste, and determines our national prosperity or adversity. We owe to the family, therefore, what we are as a nation as well as individuals. We trace this influence in the pulpit, on the rostrum, in the press, in our civil and political institutions. It is written upon the scroll of our national glory.

"The most illustrious statesmen, the most distinguished warriors, the most eloquent ministers, and the greatest benefactors of human kind, owe their greatness to the fostering influence of home. Napoleon knew and felt this when he said, 'What France wants is good mothers, and you may be sure then that France will have good sons.' The homes of the American revolution made the men of the revolution. Their influence reaches yet far into the inmost frame and constitution of our glorious republic. It controls the fountains of her power, forms the character of her citizens and statesmen, and shapes our destiny as a people . . .

"But the family, whether Christian or heathen, exerts an overwhelming influence over the state. It is on the family altar that the fire of patriotism is first kindled, and often, too, by a mother's hand . . .

"The same, too, may be said of the influence of home on the church. It is the nursery of the church, lays the foundation of her membership, and conditions the character of her members . . .

"What a fearful responsibility must rest, therefore, upon the Christian home! If its influence is for good or for evil, for weal or for woe, for heaven or for hell; if it is either a powerful emissary of Satan for the soul's destruction, or an efficient agent of God for the soul's salvation, then how responsible are those who wield this influence!

"Are you not, Christian parents, responsible to God for the exercise of such sovereign power over the character and well-being of your dear children? And will not the day soon come when you must 'give an account of your stewardship?' . . .

Luke 16:2

Home As a Stewardship

"The Christian home is a stewardship. The parents are stewards of God. A steward is a servant of a particular kind, to whom the master commits a certain portion of his interest to be prosecuted in his name and by his authority, and according to his laws and regulations. The steward must act with what is committed to his care. Such was Eliezer in the house of Abraham; and such was Joseph in the house of Potiphar . . .

"In a religious sense, a steward is a minister of Christ, whose duty is to dispense the provisions of the gospel, to preach its doctrines and to administer its ordinances. It is required of such that they be found faithful.—1 Cor., Chap. iv.

"In its application to the Christian home, it expresses its relation of subordination to God, and the kind of services which the former must render to the latter. The stewardship of home is that official character with which God has invested the family. In this sense the proprietorship of parents is from God. They are invested only with delegated authority. Their home is held by them only in trust. It belongs to them in the same sense in which a household belongs to a steward. It is not at

their absolute disposal. It is the 'household of the Lord,' and they are to live and rule therein as the Lord directs. They are to appropriate it and dispose of its interests according to the known law and will of their divine Master, and in this sense, yield, with their whole household, a voluntary subordination to His authority.

"As a stewardship, God has entrusted the Christian home with important interests. He has committed to her trust, body and soul, talents and means of grace. He has entrusted to the parents the training of their children both for time and for eternity. These children are the heritage of the Lord; they are not at the absolute disposal of their parents; but merely entrusted to their care to be educated and dealt with according to the will of God.

"There is one great peculiarity in this stewardship of the Christian family,— the absolute identity of interest between the Master and the steward. The interest of the former is that also of the latter; and the latter, in promoting the interest of his Lord, is but advancing his own welfare. Such is the economy of the gospel, and it is this which makes the servitude of the Christian so delightful. Faithfulness to God is faithfulness to our own souls. Parents who are thus faithful to God must be faithful to themselves and to their children. Thus, then, the interest of God in our families is the welfare of all the members. When we act towards our children as God directs, we are but promoting their greatest welfare. This is one prominent feature of God's mercy towards us in all His dealings with us. He identifies His interest with the interest of His people. This is a powerful incentive to parental integrity, and is beautifully exemplified in the mother of Moses . . .

"As the stewards of God, we must be faithful, giving the souls as well as the

bodies of our children 'their meat in due season;' we must not 'waste the goods' of our Lord, but be 'blameless, not self-willed, not soon angry, not given to filthy lucre, but a lover of hospitality, sober, just, holy, temperate, holding fast the faithful word as we have been taught.' As the faithful stewards of God, we should

dedicate our household in all respects to Him, and make it tributary to His glory. 'Seek ye first the kingdom of heaven and all these things shall be added unto you.'

"The unjust steward will first seek the world and the things of the world, its gold, its pleasures and its honors; and after that seek the kingdom of heaven. But this is reversing the order of procedure as prescribed by the Master; it is running counter to His will, and, consequently, wasting His goods.

"But the greatest trust committed to parents is the souls of their children; and hence their most responsible duty, as the stewards of God, is to attend to their salvation. You should 'give them the bread of life in due season.' It will be of no avail for you to inquire, 'What shall they eat, and what shall they drink, and wherewithal shall they be clothed,' if you neglect this their highest interest and your greatest trust? 'What shall a man give in exchange for his soul?' It is not the wealth, nor the magnificence of life which will make your home happy; but souls 'fed upon the sincere milk of the word,' and 'trained up in the ways of the Lord.' The training of the soul for heaven is both the duty and the glory of our homes. What if parents lay up affluence here for their children, and secure for them all that the world calls interest, while they permit their souls to famish, and do nothing for their redemption! Will not such parents be denounced in the day of judgment as unjust and unfaithful stewards? And yet alas! how many such Christian parents there are who prostitute this highest interest of home either at the altar of mammon or of fashion! The precious time and talents with which God has entrusted them, they squander away in things of folly and of sin, leaving their children to grow up in spiritual ignorance and wickedness, while they resort to balls and theaters and masquerades, the pursuit of unhallowed amusement and pleasure.

"Such are unnatural parents as well as unjust stewards, and their homes will ere long be made desolate. Other parents prostitute the holy trust of home to money. They are 'self-willed' stewards, 'given to filthy lucre,' who, for the sake of a few dollars, will 'waste the goods' of their Lord, make their homes a drudgery, and work their children like their horses, bring them up in ignorance, like 'calves in the stall,' and contract their whole existence, and all their capacities, desires and hopes, in the narrow compass of work and money.

"We would direct the attention of parents to our last thought upon the stewardship of the Christian home, viz., that it involves the principle of accountability. It implies a settlement, a time when the Master and his steward shall meet together to close accounts . . .

"Then He will examine into your stewardship. He will ask you how you employed your talents, and to what purpose you appropriated those interests He committed to your trust; and whether you were faithful to those souls which 'hung upon your hire;' whether you 'nursed them for him,' and whether you provided them with 'their meat in due season.' And if you can answer, 'Yea, Lord, here are those talents which thou hast given me; behold I have gained for thee five other talents. Here, Lord, are those children whom thou hast given me; I have brought them up in thy nurture, and trained them in thy ways.' Your Lord will then answer, 'Well done, thou good and faithful servant, thou hast been faithful over a few things; behold I will make thee ruler over many things; enter thou into the joy of thy Lord!'

"But if you have been unfaithful as stewards, and have made your household

John 6:35
Matthew 6:31

Mark 8:37

1 Peter 2:2

Exodus 2:7–9

Matthew 25:20, 21

13

unproductive for God, then you shall hear from His lips the dreadful denunciation, 'Thou wicked and slothful servant!' 'Take the talent from him, and cast ye the unprofitable servant into outer darkness; there shall be weeping and gnashing of teeth; for unto every one that hath shall be given, and he shall have abundance; but from him that hath not shall be taken away even that which he hath!' . . .

Responsibilities of the Christian Home

"From the potent influence and moral stewardship of the Christian home, we may infer its responsibility. The former is the argument for the latter. The extent of the one is the measure of the other . . . God will hold us accountable for the achievements we make by the abilities he has given us. If he gives us a field to cultivate, seed to sow, plants to train up, then we are responsible for the harvest, just in proportion to our agency in its production. If there is not a harvest of the right kind, because we neglected to cultivate the soil, to sow the proper seed, and to train up the plants, then He will hold us accountable, and 'we shall not come out thence till we have paid the uttermost farthing.'

"This is an evident gospel principle. Who will doubt its application to the Christian home? The family is such a field; the seed of good or evil the parents can sow therein; their children are young and tender plants, entrusted to their care; their mission from God is to 'bring them up in his nurture' and to 'train them in his ways.' And where God gives the command, He also gives the power to obey . . .

Ephesians 6:4
Proverbs 22:6

Galatians 6:6–10

"Home-responsibility may be inferred from the relation of the family to God as a stewardship. We have seen that parents are stewards of God in their household, and that as such they are placed over their children, invested with delegated authority. God entrusts them to the care of their parents. Their nature is pliable, fit for any impression, exposed to sin and ruin, entering upon a course of life which must terminate in eternal happiness or misery, with bodies to develop, minds to educate, hearts to mould, volitions to direct, habits to form, energies to rule, pursuits to follow, interests to secure, temptations to resist, trials to endure, souls to save! Oh, how the parental heart must swell with emotions too big for utterance, when they contemplate these features of their important trust. What a mission this, to superintend the character and shape the destiny of such a being! Such is the plastic power you exert upon it, that upon your guidance will hinge its weal or its woe; and yours, therefore, will be the lasting benefit or the lasting shame . . .

"Thus, therefore, you see, Christian parents, how your responsibility is measured by the magnitude of those interests committed to your care, by the kind of influence you exert over them, and by the enormity of that guilt and woe which are consequent upon your unfaithfulness. Let this be an incentive to parental integrity . . .

The Family Bible

"The family Bible! What sweet and hallowed memories cling like tendrils around that book of books! . . . Who can forget the family Bible? It was the household oracle of our grandfathers and grandmothers,—of our dear parents . . .

"That old family Bible! Do we not love it? Our names and our children's names are drawn from it. It is the message of our Father in heaven. It is the link which connects our earthly with our heavenly home; and when we open its sacred page, we gaze upon words which our loved ones in heaven have whispered, and which dwell even now upon their sainted lips; and which when we utter them, there is joy in heaven! . . . John 20:31 Deuteronomy 17:19

"The old family Bible! What an inheritance from a Christian home! Clasp it, child, to thy heart; it is the gift of a mother's love! . . . John 5:39

"Every Christian home has a family Bible. It is found in the hut as well as in the palace. It is an indispensable appendage to home. Without it the Christian home would be in darkness; with it, she is a 'light which shineth in darkness.' It is the chart and compass of the parent and the child in their pilgrimage to a better home . . . Acts 17:11 Romans 15:4

"The Bible is adapted to the Christian home. It is the book for the family. It is the guardian of her interests, the exposition of her duties, her privileges, her hopes and her enjoyments. It exposes her errors, reveals her authority and government, sanctions her obedience, proclaims her promises, and points out her path to heaven. It makes sacred her marriages, furnishes names for her children, gives the sacrament of her dedication to God, and consecrates her bereavements. It is the fountain of her richest blessings, the source of her true consolation, and the ground of her brightest hope. It is, therefore, the book of home. She may have large and splendid libraries; history, poetry, philosophy, fiction, yea, all the works of classic Greece and Rome, may crowd upon her shelves; but of these she will soon grow wearied, and the dust of neglect will gather thick upon their gilded leaves; but of the Bible the Christian home can never become weary. Its sufficiency for all her purposes will throw a garland of freshness around every page; its variety and manifoldness; its simplicity and beauty; its depth of thought and intensity of feeling, adapt it to every capacity and to every want, to every emergency and to every member, of the household. The little child and the old man, hoary with the frost of many winters, find an equal interest there. The rich and the poor, the learned and the ignorant, the high and the low, are alike enriched from its inexhaustible treasury. Luke 21:33

"It is a book for the mind, the heart, the conscience, the will and the life . . . It is simple, yet grand; mysterious, yet plain; and though from God, it is nevertheless, within the comprehension of a little child. You may send your children to school to study other books, from which they may be educated for this world; but in this divine book they study the science of the eternal world. Deuteronomy 11:19

"The family Bible has given to the Christian home that unmeasured superiority 15 in all the dignities and decencies and enjoyments of life, over the home of the heathen. It has elevated woman, revealed her true mission, developed the true idea and sacredness of marriage and of the home-relationship; it has unfolded the holy mission of the mother, the responsibilities of the parent, and the blessings of the child. Take this book from the family, and she will degenerate into a mere conventionalism, marriage into a 'social contract;' the spirit of mother will depart; natural affection will sink to mere brute fondness, and what we now call home would become a den of sullen selfishness and barbaric lust!

"The Bible should, therefore, be the text-book of home-education. Where it is not, parents are recreant to their duty. It is the basis of all teaching, because it reveals 'the truth, the way and the life,' because it is God's testimony and message, and is 'profitable for doctrine, for reproof, for correction, for instruction in righteousness,' and was written 'for our learning, that we, through patience and comfort of the scriptures, might have hope,' and be made 'wise unto salvation.' . . .

John 14:6
2 Timothy 3:16

"Here in these sacred pages is a beauty ever fresh, and a sublimity which towers in dazzling radiance far beyond the reach of human genius. This is evident from the fact that tributes of admiration have been paid to the Bible by the most eminent poets, jurists, statesmen, and philosophers, such as Milton, Hale, Boyle, Newton and Locke. Erasmus and John Locke betook themselves solely to the Bible, after they had wandered through the gloomy maze of human erudition. Neither Grecian song nor Roman eloquence; neither the waters of Castalia, nor the fine-spun theorisms of scholastic philosophy, could satisfy their yearnings. But when they wandered amid the consecrated bowers of Zion, and drank from Siloah's brook, the thirst of their genius was quenched, and they took their seats with Mary at the feet of Jesus, and like little children, learned of him!

Colossians 2:6–10

"Even deists and infidels have yielded their tribute of praise. What says the infidel Rousseau? Hear him: 'The majesty of the Scriptures strikes me with astonishment. Look at the volumes of the philosophers, with all their pomp, how contemptible do they appear in comparison with this! Is it possible that a book at once so simple and sublime, can be the work of men?' . . .

"How often is this precious book abused! In many would-be Christian homes, it is used more for an ornament of fashion than for a lamp to the Christian's path . . .

"You may buy them splendid Bibles, gilt and clasped with gold, and have their names labeled in golden letters upon its lid; but if the good old family Bible is neglected, and the yellow covered literature of the day substituted in its stead; if you permit them to buy and read lovesick tales in preference to their Bible, and they see you do the same, you are but making a mock of God's Word, and must answer before Him for your children's neglect of its sacred pages.

Psalms 50:17
Isaiah 5:24

"Let me, therefore, affectionately admonish you to be faithful to that precious book you call the family Bible. Read it to your children every day. From its sacred pages teach them the way to live and the way to die. Let it be an opened, studied family chart to guide you and them in visions of untold glory to the many mansions of your Father's offered home in heaven . . .

Home as a Nursery

"To nurse means . . . to protect, to foster, to supply with appropriate food, to cause to grow or promote strength, to manage with a view to increase . . . In horticulture, a shrub or tree is the nurse or protector of a young and tender plant. We are said to nurse our national resources . . .

1 Thessalonians 2:7

Isaiah 5:17

"In the same sense and for the same reason, the Christian home is the nursery of the young . . . The nursery is that department of home in which the mother fulfils her peculiar mission. This is her special sphere. None can effectually take her place there. She is the center of attraction, the guardian of the infants' destiny; and none like she, can overrule the unfolding life and character of the child. God has fitted her for the work of the nursery. Here she reigns supreme, the arbitress of the everlasting weal or woe of untutored infancy. On her the fairest hopes of educated man depend, and in the exercise of her powers there, she sways a nation's destiny . . . The nursery is that department of home in which the formation of our character is begun. . . .

"The nursery is moral and spiritual. The first moral and religious training of the child belongs to the nursery, and is the work of the mother. Upon her personal exhibition of truth, justice, virtue, &c., depends the same moral elements in the character of her child. In the nursery we receive our first lessons in virtue or in vice, in honesty or dishonesty, in truth or in falsehood, in purity or in corruption. The full-grown man is the matured child morally as well as physically and intellectually. The same may be said of the spiritual formation and growth of the child. Spiritual culture belongs eminently to the nursery. There the pious parent should begin the work of her child's salvation . . .

John 21:15

Family Prayer

. . . "A prayerless home is destitute of religious sympathy. The family demands prayer. Its relation to God, its dependence and specific duties, involve devotion. Communion with God constitutes a part of the intercourse and society of home. The necessity of family prayer arises out of the home-constitution and mission. Family mercies and blessings; family dangers and weaknesses; family hopes and temptations,—all bespeak the importance of family worship. If you occupy the responsible station of parent; if God has made you the head of a religious household, and you profess to stand and live on the Lord's side, then, tell me, have you not by implication vowed to maintain regular family worship? Besides, the benefits and

Matthew 21:13

privilege of prayer develop the obligation of the family to engage in it. Is not every privilege a duty? And if it is a duty for individuals and congregations to pray, is it not, for a similar reason, the duty of the family to establish her altar of devotion? As a family we daily need and receive mercies, daily sin, are tempted and in danger every day; why not then as a family daily pray?

"But what is family prayer? It is not simply individual prayer, not the altar of the closet; but the home-altar, around which all the members gather morning and evening, as a family-unit, with one heart, one faith and one hope, to commune with God and supplicate his mercy. 'In the devotion of this little assembly,' says Dr. Dwight, 'parents pray for their children and children for their parents; the husband for the wife, and the wife for the husband' . . .

"And yet the neglect of family prayer is a very general defect of the Christian home. No home-duty has indeed been more grossly neglected and abused. Some attend to it only occasionally; some only in times of affliction and distress, as if then only they needed to pray to God; some only on the Sabbath, as if that were the only day to commune with Him. Some perform it in a formal way, having the form without the spirit of prayer, as if God did not require the fervent, in order to

James 5:13-16 the effectual, prayer that availeth much . . .

"Let me, therefore, urge upon you, Christian parents, to make prayer a prominent element of your home. You should be a priest unto your family,—a leader in home-communion with God. Your children have a right to expect this from you. If you are a church member, how strange and startling must be the ennunciation in heaven, that you are a prayerless Christian, and your home destitute of the altar! . . . Oh

Matthew 6:1-15 then, make your home a house of prayer; lead your little flock in sweet communion with God. Establish in them the habit of devotion: Shape their consciences by prayer. In this way you shall secure for yourself and them the blessing of God: His smile shall ever rest upon your household: Salvation shall be the heritage of your children; they will grow up in the divine life; and will live amid the blessings of prayer, and be faithful to its requisitions . . .

The Character of Home Education

"We come now to consider one of the most important features of the Christian home, viz., as a school for the education of character . . . We there receive a training for good or for evil. There is not a word, nor an emotion, nor an act, nor even a look there, which does not teach the child something. Character is ever being framed and moulded there . . .

"Home-education must be intellectual. Much of human character and happiness depends upon the education of the mind, both as respects the development of its faculties and the application of legitimate truth . . .

18   "Home-education must be moral. The family should develop the moral nature

of the child. The will should be educated; the sense of right and wrong trained; the emotions cultivated; the passions and desires ruled; the conscience and faith developed . . .

"Home-education should be religious. As the child has a religious nature, religious wants, and a religious end to accomplish, it should receive from its parents a religious training. Religion is educational. We are commanded to teach religion to our children. The admonition to 'train up a child in the way he should go,' and to Proverbs 22:6 'bring him up in the nurture and admonition of the Lord,' is a scripture sanction of Ephesians 6:4 religious education . . .

"Childhood is the period in which the principles of Christianity can be the most effectually engrafted in our nature. Its pliability at that period insures its free assimilation to the spirit and truth of religion . . .

"To the mother especially, is committed the religious education of the child at home. She is eminently adapted, if herself a Christian, for such a work. Her love, her piety, which breathes in every word, in every look, makes her instructions effectual and pleasing . . .

"To encourage Christian parents to give their children a good religious education, God has given them numerous examples, from both sacred and profane history, of conversion and eminent piety in the age of childhood, as the direct fruit of early parental instruction. Look, for instance, at the child Samuel worshiping the Lord. Look, too, at the case of Moses and of David, of Joseph and of John the Baptist . . .

"The aged Polycarp, when under arrest during the persecution under Marcus Aurelius, in reply to the injunction of the pro-consul, 'Swear, curse Christ, and I release thee!' exclaimed, 'Six and eighty years have I served Him, and He has done me nothing but good; and how could I curse Him, my Lord and Saviour?' Thus showing himself to have been a Christian at the early age of four years! It was through the instructions of his grandmother Lois, and his mother Eunice, that young Timothy 'knew from a child the holy scriptures, which made him wise unto 2 Timothy 3:14–17 salvation.'

"And what an effectual antidote are such instructions against vice and temptation! How many have by them been arrested from the devouring jaws of infidelity and ruin! Thus it was with John Randolph, who said that in the days of the French revolution, when infidel reason took the place of God and the Bible, and infidelity prowled unmolested throughout France, he would have become an infidel himself, had it not been for the remembrance of his childhood days, when his pious mother taught him to kneel by her side, and to say, 'Our Father, who art in heaven!' Thus, too, with the pious and learned J. Q. Adams, who daily repeated the little prayers his mother taught him when a child.

"Thus, then, we see that parents are encouraged by the most brilliant examples of history, to teach their children religion at the home-fireside, 'when thou liest Deuteronomy 6:6, 7 down and risest up'. Oh, let the gentle courtesies and sweet endearments of home engrave the Word and Spirit of God upon their tender hearts. Wait not until they are matured in rebellion, and sin lay beds of flinty rock over their hearts; but let them breathe from infancy the atmosphere of holiness, and drink from the living fountains of divine truth. See that your homes become their birth-place in the spiritual kingdom of Christ.

"Such religious training will be the guardian of their future life, and will fortify them against impending evil. What made Daniel steadfast amidst all the efforts to heathenize him during his captivity in Babylon? His early religious culture. It was the means of his preservation. The truth had been deeply engraven upon his heart when young, and nothing could ever efface it. His early home-impressions glowed there with pristine freshness and power amid all the terrors which surrounded him in the den and before the throne of his implacable foe. These home-instructions may be silenced for a time, but never destroyed. They may be over-shadowed, but not annihilated. Says Dr. Cumming, 'The words spoken by parents to their children in the privacy of the home are like words spoken in a whispering-gallery, and will be clearly heard at the distance of years, and along the corridors of ages that are yet to come. They will prove like the lone star to the mariner upon a dark and stormy sea, associated with a mother's love, with a father's example, with the roof-tree beneath which they lived and loved, and will prove in after life to mould the man and enable him to adorn and improve the age in which he is placed.'

Isaiah 28:10

1 Corinthians 3:6–8

"Be faithful, therefore, in the spiritual culture of your children. Give them 'line upon line and precept upon precept, here a little and there a little.' Lead them on by degrees to Christ until each indelible impression becomes an established habit. In the morning of their life sow the seed; and God will give the increase; and then in the day of judgment your children will rise up and call you blessed.

Neglect and Abuse of Home-Education

"Home-education in all its parts is most sadly neglected and abused at the present day. Many parents think that the office of teacher is not included in the parental character and mission. The neglect of home-training seems to arise out of an existing prejudice against it. . . .

Deuteronomy 6:4, 5

"If you do not educate your child in the truths of nature and religion, be assured he will become trained in falsehood and in the ways of Satan. 'Uneducated mind is uneducated vice.' A proper education is a divine alchemy which turns all the baser parts of man's nature into gold . . . Dr. Johnson was once asked, 'Who is the most miserable man?' He replied, 'That man who cannot read on a rainy day!' It has well been said by Edmund Burke that 'Education is the cheap defense of nations.' Why? Because it prevents vice, poverty, misery, and relieves the state of the support of paupers and criminals. 'A good education,' says Miss Sedgwick, 'is a young man's best capital.' . . . Crates, an ancient philosopher, used to say that if he could reach the highest eminence in the city, he would make this proclamation:

'What mean ye, fellow-citizens, to be so anxious after wealth, but so indifferent to your children's education? It is like being solicitous about the shoe, but neglecting entirely the foot that is to wear it!' . . .

"One great abuse of home-education is to substitute the boarding school for home-culture,—to send our children to such school at an age when they should be trained by and live under the divine influence of the parent . . .

"If we would not abuse home-education we must not separate the moral from the mental,—the secular from the religious; for in doing so, we expose the child to rationalism and infidelity on the one hand, and to superstition and spiritualism on the other. This course is generally taken by parents when they educate their children for mere worldly utility and fashion, when they have not the welfare of the soul in view, and look only to the advantage of the body.

"The duty then of Christian parents to give their children a true home-education may be seen from the consequences of its neglect and abuse on the one hand, and from its value and importance on the other. They should furnish them with all the necessary means, opportunities, and directions, of a Christian education. Give them proper books. 'Without books,' says the quaint Bartholin, 'God is silent, justice dormant, science at a stand, philosophy lame, letters dumb, and all things involved in Cimmerian darkness.' Bring them up to the habit of properly reading and studying those books. 'A reading people will soon become a thinking people, and a thinking people must soon become a great people.' Every book you furnish your child, and which it reads with reflection is 'like a cast of the weaver's shuttle, adding another thread to the indestructible web of existence.' It will be worth more to him than all your hoarded gold and silver. Make diligent use of those great auxiliaries to home-education, which the church has instituted, such as Sabbath schools, Bible classes and catechisation. . . . 2 Timothy 2:15

"Christian parents! be faithful to this duty. Magnify your office as a teacher; be faithful to your household as a school. Diligently serve your children as the pupils that God has put under your care. Educate them for Him. Teach them to 'walk by faith, not by sight.' . . . You are encouraged to do so by the assurance of God 'that when they grow old they will not depart from it.' 2 Corinthians 5:7

Family Habits

"Much of the character, usefulness and happiness of home depend upon home habits. No one is without habits, good or bad. They have much to do with our welfare here and hereafter. Hence the importance of establishing proper habits . . . There are habits of the body, of the mind, of action; physical, mental, moral and religious habits. All these are included in the term home-habits . . .

"Home-habits are easily formed and established. Some kind, either good or bad, are being established every day. They are often secretly and unconsciously formed.

All the principles and rules of conduct there introduced become at once the nuclei of future habits. These increase in power and supremacy as they are formed. We see this in the use of tobacco and intoxicating drink. These are, at first, disagreeable, and the victim has the power of repelling and overcoming them; but soon the habit is formed, when their use becomes pleasant, and he is made a willing slave to them.

2 Peter 1:4-11

"The same may be said of the habits of industry, of study, of frugality, yea, of all the moral and religious acts of the Christian. It is easy to form such habits in children. Evil habits are more easily established, because we are naturally inclined to all evil; and when once formed, no parental interposition can break them up. Hence the importance of an early training up to good. If parents but leave their children to their own ways, they will run into evil habits; for sin is an epidemic. Profanity and falsehood and all other outrages against will soon become the controlling habits of their lives. But when taken early, parents have complete power over their offspring.

Philippians 4:8, 9

"It is, therefore, a gross abuse of the Christian home when parents become indifferent to the formation of habits. It is their duty to crush every evil habit in its incipient state . . . That indulgence which the misguided sympathy of too many parents prompts to, and which does away with all parental restraint, is the cause of children coming under the curse of evil habits. In this way parents often contribute to the temporal and eternal ruin of their offspring. This indulgence is no evidence of tender love, but of parental infatuation. It shows a blind and unholy love,—a love which owns no law, which is governed by no sense of duty, and which excludes all discipline; and hence unlike the love of God, who 'chastiseth every one whom He loveth and receiveth.'

"The force and influence of home-habits will teach us the importance of establishing such only as receive the sanction of God. Habits, as we have seen, are much more easily formed than broken. When once established they enslave us to them, and subject our character to their iron despotism. They become the channel through which our life flows. The stream of our existence first forms the channel, and then the channel rules, guides and controls the current of the stream. The deeper the channel is wrought, the greater is its moulding and controlling influence over the stream. Thus our habits become our masters, and are the irrevocable rulers of our life. This is true of good as well as of bad habits. We come into voluntary subjection to them, until we shrink from the first proposal to depart from them . . .

"It should never be forgotten by Christian parents, and they cannot be too careful to impress it upon their children, that habit engenders habit,—has the power of reproducing itself, and begetting habits of its own kind, increasing, according to the laws of growth, as it is thus reproduced . . . And shall any other kind save Christian habits, be found in the Christian home? These we cannot give in detail. It is plain that those habits only are Christian, which receive the sanction of God's Word and Spirit, and find a response in the Christian faith and conscience. Here, for instance, is a habit being formed,—a habit of thought: is it pure? Here is a habit of conversation: is it holy? Here is a habit of action: is it godly? And if not, it does not belong to the Christian home.

"See, then, ye members of the Christian home, to the habits you are forming. Form the habit of 'doing all things decently and in order.' Let the work and duties of each day be done according to method. This is essential to success in your pursuits and aims. Without this, your Christian life may be blustering and stormy, but you will accomplish little, and will be as unstable as water. One duty will interfere with another. You may have family prayer and instruction to-day, but something will prevent it to-morrow. Establish the habit of Christian industry. Be diligent; not slothful in business. Industry must be the price of all you obtain. You must be instant in season. The Christian home cannot be an indolent, idle home. Whatsoever thy hand findeth to do, do it with all thy might. Press forward . . .

1 Corinthians
14:40

Romans 12:11

"Establish the habit also of perseverance in well-doing. 'Be steadfast, immovable, always abounding in the work of the Lord.' 'Be not weary in well-doing.' Let the strata of your home be made up of the immovable Rock. He only that continueth unto the end shall be saved. Having done all, stand! Let your motto be, Perseverando vinces. Form the habit of contentment with your home and condition in life. 'Godliness with contentment is great gain.' If your home is humble, and not adorned with the embellishments and luxuries of life, yet it may be holy, and hence, happy. Avoid all castle-building. Do not fancy a better home, and fall out with the one you enjoy. Never permit the flimsy creations of a distorted imagination to gain an ascendancy over your reason and faith. Live above all sentimentalism and daydreaming; and in all the feelings and conduct of your household, submit to the guidance of a superintending Providence, walking by faith and not by sight, assured that your present home is but probationary and preparatory to a better home in heaven.

1 Corinthians
15:58

Galatians 6:9

1 Timothy 6:6

Home-Government

"Home is a little commonwealth jointly governed by the parents. It involves law. The mutual relation of parent and child implies authority on the one hand, and obedience on the other. This is the principle of all government. Home is the first form of society. As such it must have a government. Its institution implies the prerogatives of the parent and the subordination of the child. Without this there would be no order, no harmony, no training for the state or the church . . .

"The principle of home-government is love,—love ruling and obeying according to law. These are exercised, as it were, by the instinct of natural affection as taken up and refined by the Christian life and faith. This government implies reciprocity of right,—the right of the parent to govern and the right of the child to be governed. It is similar in its fundamentals to the government of the state and church. It involves the legislative, judicial and executive functions; its elements are law, authority, obedience, and penalties. The basis of its laws is the Word of God. We may consider the whole subject under two general heads, viz., parental authority,

Ephesians 6:1–17

and filial obedience.

"1. Parental authority is threefold, legislative, judicial and executive. The two latter we shall more fully consider under the head of home-discipline. The legislative authority of the parent is confined to the development of God's laws for the Christian home . . . It does not, as in the old Roman law, concede to the parent the power over the life of the child. This would not only violate the law of natural affection, but would be an amalgamation of the family and state. Neither is the parental authority merely conventional, given to the parent by the state as a policy. It is no civil or political investiture, making the parent a delegated civil ruler; but comes from God as an inalienable right, and independent, as such, of the state. It does not, therefore, rest upon civil legislation, but has its foundation in human nature and the revealed law of God; neither can the state legislate upon it, except in cases where its exercise becomes an infringement upon the prerogatives of the state itself.

"Parents are magistrates under God, and, as His stewards, cannot abdicate their authority, nor delegate it to another. Neither can they be tyrants in the exercise of it. God has given to them the principles of home-legislation, the standard of judicial authority, and the rules of their executive power. God gives the law. The parent is only deputy governor,—steward, 'bound to be faithful.' Hence the obligation of the child to obey the steward is as great as that to obey the Master. 'Where the principal is silent, take heed that thou despise not the deputy.'

"Here, then, we have the extent of the parent's authority, and the spirit and manner in which it should be exercised. . . . According to the vagaries of some religious sentimentalists and fanatics, it is supposed that religion supersedes the necessity of parental government. They think that such authority runs counter to the spirit and requisitions of the gospel. But this is asserted in the broad face of God's Word. The promptings of such sentimentalism are to permit children to do as they please, and to bring them up under the influence of domestic libertinism. Honor thy father and thy mother, is a command which explodes such a gaudy theory; and he who does not obey it, brutalizes human nature, dishonors God, subverts the principles of constitutional society, throws off allegiance to the prerogatives of a divinely constituted superior, and overthrows both church and state. Hence the severe penalties attached, in the Mosaic law, to disobedience of parental authority. 'He that curseth his father or mother, shall surely be put to death.' 'The eye that mocketh at his father, and despiseth to obey his mother, the ravens of the valley shall pick it out, and the young eagles shall eat it.' And hence also that affectionate obedience which Joseph yielded to his aged father, and that profound veneration with which he kneeled before him to receive his dying blessing.

"2. Filial obedience is the correlative of parental authority. If parents have authority, children must yield obedience to it. This is not only necessary to home-government, but also to the proper formation of the character of the child. It must be trained up under law and authority to prepare it for citizenship in the state. This must be the obedience of confidence and love. It does not imply the sub-

Isaiah 33:22

Romans 13:1–8

Exodus 20:12

Exodus 21:17

Proverbs 30:17

24

ordination of the slave.

"As the father's authority is not that of the despot, so the obedience of the child is not that of the servile, trembling subject. It is not unnatural,—no infringement upon the rights and liberties of the child. His subordination to the parent is the law of his liberty. He is not free without it. The home in which filial obedience is not yielded to parental authority is 'a marvel of permitted chaos,' and will soon become desolate, a scene of anarchy and strife. The members live in a state of lawlessness, destitute of reciprocated affection,—the parent unhonored, the father and mother despised and cursed, and the child untrained, uncared for, lawless, and unfit for the state or the church.

"If, therefore, God has constituted governmental relations in the Christian home, and invested the parent with authority over his children, who will deny the co-ordinate obligations of the child to yield reverence, submission and gratitude to the parent? 'Children, obey your parents in all things; for this is well pleasing unto the Lord.'

"This is called the first commandment with promise. It is one of promise both to the parent and the child. Children are bound to obey their parents in all things, that is in all things lawful and in accordance with the revealed will of God. The child is not bound to obey the parent's command to sin,—to lie, steal, or neglect the means of grace; because these are express violations of God's law; and in such instances the authority of God supersedes that of the parent. Obey God rather than man.

"But, on the other hand, the obligation of the child is, to obey the parent in all things lawful and Christian. Where this is not done the Christian home becomes a curse . . . We may neglect and abuse the home-government in two ways, either by over-indulgence, or by the iron rod of tyranny. When we make it lax in its restraints and requisitions, it becomes merely nominal, and its laws are never enforced and obeyed. Often parents voluntarily relinquish their right and duty to rule their household; and as a consequence, their children abandon the duty of obedience, and grow up in a lawless state; or if they do command, they never execute their commands, but leave all to the discretion of their children. They violate their laws with impunity, until all influence over them is lost, and the child becomes the master of the parent. The self-will of the former takes the place of the authority of the latter, until at last the home-government becomes a complete farce and mockery. Such parents are always making laws and giving commands; but never enforce them; they complain that they cannot get their children to obey them; and this is but the utterance and exponent of their unfaithfulness and disgrace.

"The opposite abuse of home-government is parental despotism,—ruling with a rod of iron, making slaves of children, acting the unfeeling and heartless tyrant over them, assuming towards them attitudes of hard taskmasters, and making them obey from motives of trembling, fear and dread.

"There is no Christianity in all this. It engenders in them the spirit of a slave; it roots out all confidence and love; their obedience becomes involuntary and me-

Exodus 20:1–18

Matthew
22:35–40

Colossians
3:20–24

Genesis 27:8

1 Samuel 12:15

Acts 5:29

chanical. They shrink in silent dread from the presence of their parents, and long for the time when they can escape their galling yoke. The parental rod destroys the filial love and confidence. Hence the obedience of the latter is servile; and home loses its tender affections and sympathies, and becomes to them a work-house, a confinement; its restrictions are a yoke; its interests are repulsive, and all its natural affinities give way to complete alienation. The children of such homes, when grown up, are the most lawless and reckless, ready at once to pass over from extreme servitude to libertinism.

1 Timothy 1:9

"The government of the Christian home lies in a medium between these two extremes. It is mild, yet decisive, firm; not lawless, yet not despotic; but combines in proper order and harmony, the true elements of parental authority and filial subordination. Love and fear harmonize; the child fears because he loves; and is prompted to obedience by both. 'But give thy son his way, he will hate thee and scorn thee together.'

1 Peter 1:13–16

"Christian parents! be faithful to the government of your household . . .

Home-Discipline

"Discipline involves the judicial and executive functions of the home-government. It is the method of regulating and executing the principles and practice of government. It includes the rein and the rod, the treatment of offences against the laws of home, the execution of the parental authority by the imposition of proper restraints upon the child. It involves a reciprocity of duty,—the duty of the parent to correct, and the duty of the child to submit. God has given this discipline; He has invested the parent with power to execute it, and imposed upon the child the obligation to live submissively under it . . . It is necessary because God commands it; and He commands it because it is indispensable to the security and well-being of the child, and, we might add, of the state and the church . . .

Proverbs 13:24

"There are two false systems of home-discipline, viz., the despotism of discipline, or discipline from the standpoint of law without love; and the libertinism of discipline, or discipline from the standpoint of love without law.

"Home-discipline from the standpoint of law without love, involves the principle of parental despotism. It is extreme legal severity, and consists in the treatment of children as if they were brutes, using no other mode of correction than that of direct corporeal punishment. This but hardens them, and begets a roughness of nature and spirit like the discipline under which they are brought up. Many parents seek to justify such mechanical severity by the saying of Solomon, 'he that spareth the rod spoileth the child.' But their interpretation of this does not show the wisdom of the wise man. They suppose the term rod, must mean the iron rod of the unfeeling and unloving despot. Not so: God has a rod for all His children; but it is the rod of a compassionate Father, and does not always inflict corporeal

Romans 13:10

punishment. It is exercised because He loves them, not because He delights in revenge and in their misery. He uses it, not to have them obey Him from fear of punishment, not to force them into a slavish service, and to cause them to shrink with trembling awe from His presence; but to correct their faults by drawing them to Him in fond embrace, in grateful penitence and hopeful reformation, under the deep conviction that every stroke of His rod was the work of love, forcing from them a kiss for His rod, and a blessing for His hand, the utterance of a sanction for His deed, 'It was good for me that I was afflicted!'

Psalms 119:67

"This rod is very different, however, from that of the despot beneath whom the child crouches with trembling dread, and under the influence of whom he becomes, like the down-trodden subject, servile, brutish and rebellious. You will reap bitter fruits from such a discipline, which is but the scowl and the frown and the cruel lash. You might as well seek 'to gather grapes from thorns, or figs from thistles,' as to reap from it a true reformation and religious training. Your child will be trained to hate the law, to despise authority, and to regard his obedience as a compromise of true liberty. He will, therefore, seek liberty only in the usurpation of law and government. He will contemn love, because where it should have been disinterested, and shown in its greatest tenderness and purity,—in the parent's heart, it was abused and silenced.

Matthew 7:16

"That discipline, therefore, which is ever magnifying trifles, finding fault, scolding and storming, and threatening and whipping, and falling upon the child, like the continual dropping of rain in a winter day, casts a withering gloom over home, makes it repulsive to the child, gives to the parent a forbidding aspect, until the children become provoked to wrath, and regard their home as a prison, their life as a slavery, and long for the time when they may leave home and parents forever. Such discipline makes the reign of the parent a reign of terror . . .

"Home-discipline from the standpoint of love without law, is the second false system which we have mentioned, and involves the principle of parental libertinism. It does not consist so much in the want as in the neglect and abuse of discipline. The restraints may be sufficient, and the threats abundant, but they are never executed. When the children disobey, the parents may flounder and storm, loud and long, but all ends in words, in a storm of passion or whining complaint, and the child is thus encouraged to repeat the misconduct, feeling that his parents have no respect for their word. Such a home becomes a scolding, but not an orderly home . . .

2 Timothy 3:5

"That parent who cannot restrain his children, does not bear rule in his house, and as a consequence, cannot bless his household. That parental tenderness which withholds the proper restraints of discipline from an erring child, is most cruel and ruinous. It is winking at his wayward temper, his licentious passions and growing habits of vice. And these, in their terrible maturity, will recoil upon the deluded parent, 'biting like a serpent and stinging like an adder.' Nothing is more ruinous to a child and disastrous to the hopes and happiness of home, than such relaxation of discipline . . .

Proverbs 23:32

"Abraham instituted in his household a model system of home-discipline. 'I know him,' says God, 'that he will command his children and his household after him, and they shall keep the ways of the Lord to do justice and judgment.' He was not a tyrant; his comrades did not bear the rough sternness of a despot, neither did his power wear the scowl of vengeance. But these bore the firmness and decision of love tempered and directed by the law of Christian duty and responsibility. They showed his station as a father; they wore the exponent of his authority as a parent, whose love was a safeguard against tyranny on the one hand, and whose accountability to God was a security against anarchy, on the other. Hence, his children respected his station, venerated his name, appreciated his love, confided in his sympathy, and yielded a voluntary obedience to his commands; for they discerned in them the blessing; and when offenses came, they bent in the spirit of loving submission and pupilage, under his rod of correction, and kissed it as the means of their reformation and culture.

"Thus does home-discipline involve the firmness of parental authority united with the mildness of parental love. Love should hold the reins and use the rod. Then it will purify and elevate natural affection, and develop in the child a sense of proper fear, without either disrespectful familiarity or mechanical servitude . . .

"Home-discipline should be steady, uniform, consistent and reasonable. Both parents and children should be guided by the dictates of reason and religion. It should not be administered by the caprice of passion, nor received in the spirit of insubordination. It should be prompted by a parent's heart, and inflicted by a parent's hand. Convince the recreant child that you correct him from motives of love, and for his own good. Let reason and love be at the bottom of every chastisement; let them hold the reins and guide the rod; and when the latter is used, let it be from necessity. Lay no injunction upon your child without the ensurance of a compliance . . .

"In home-discipline, parents should act harmoniously and cooperate with each other. They should be of one mind and of one heart, and equally bear the burden. The one should not oppose the discipline which the other is administering. This destroys its effect, and leaves the child in a state of indecision, leading to prejudice against one or the other of the parents. It too often happens that parents thus take opposite sides,—the father too severe perhaps, and the mother too indulgent. Thus divided, their house must fall. Nothing is more ruinous to the child than for the mother to counteract by soothing opiates, the admonitions of the father. Children soon see this, and will soon hate their father. When one parent thus holds the reins without the rod, and the other uses the rod without the reins, the very ends of discipline are frustrated . . .

"Discipline should be administered with impartiality. Never make one child a favorite. Favoritism and consequent indulgence, will produce prejudice against the other children. It will introduce dissension among them. This is unworthy the Christian parent and his home. The history of Jacob and Joseph, as regards both the subject and the victim of parental favoritism, is a warning against such partiality. It produces pride, envy, jealousy, family broils and strife, in which even the parents take a part, and by which the husband is often set against his wife, parents against children, and children against each other.

"Correction is an essential element of true discipline. 'The rod and the reproof give wisdom.' There are two things in correction,—the reins and the whip, or the command and the chastisement. The one should not take the place of the other. The scepter must not be converted into a whip. If the reins are properly held and used, the whip need scarcely ever be required. If the child is timely and properly trained, commanded and chided, he will not require much chastisement,—perhaps no corporeal punishment. It is better to prevent crimes than to punish them; for prevention is more than cure.

"Hence the first thing in discipline is timely and wholesome command. Guide and train your child properly, and you need seldom resort to coercion. Training and leading are better than forcing. By the former you establish a habit of systematic obedience which will soon become a pleasure to the child. By the latter you jade and vex and burden him . . .

"In the discipline of home, whether by guidance or by forcing, whether by the rein or the rod, much depends upon the manner in which it is administered. It should always be adapted to the peculiar character and offense of the child. You can restrain some children better by kind words and promises than by rough admonitions and threats. Study, therefore, the peculiarities of your child, and prudently apportion the correction to the offense. If there are sincere penitence and confession, the correction should be purely moral. Let the object be to produce penitence and reformation of heart as well as of conduct, and a hatred of the offense. Always execute your threats and fulfill your promises at the time and on the occasion designated. Threaten as little as possible, and be not hasty in your threats. Treat your children as rational and moral beings . . . Always examine the offense before you punish. See whether it is of ignorance or not,—whether of the head or the heart,—whether intentional or accidental. Examine his motives in committing the offense . . .

"Never correct in a state of anger. Some correct only when they are in a violent passion. This is ruling from passion, not from principle . . . A mild rebuke in the season of calmness, is better than a rod in the heat of passion. Let your children know and see that all your discipline is for their own good,—to arrest them from danger and ruin, and to train them up in the way God would have them go.

Home-Example

"Example has much to do with the interests of home. It plays an important part in the formation of character; and its influence is felt more than that of precept. Our object in this chapter is to show the bearing of example upon the well-being of 29 the Christian home. Example may be good or bad. Its power arises out of the home-confidence and authority. Children possess an imitative disposition. They look up to their parents as the pattern or model of their character, and conclude what they do is right and worthy of their imitation. Hence the parental example may lead the child to happiness or ruin . . .

1 Peter 2:21, 22

"The power and influence of the home-example are incalculable. Example is teaching by action. By it the child inherits the spirit and character of the parent. Such is its influence that you can estimate the parent by the child. Show me a child, polite, courteous, refined, moral and honorable in all his sentiments and conduct; and I will point you to a well-conducted nursery, to noble and high-minded parents, faithful to their offspring. Theirs is a holy and a happy home; and the blessing of God rests upon it. But on the other hand, in the wayward, dissolute child I discern unfaithful parents who have no respect for religion, and who take no interest in the spiritual welfare of their children. Thus the child is a living commentary upon its home and its parents. The fruits of the latter will be seen in the character of the former. The child is the moral reproduction of the parent. Hence the pious parent is rewarded in his child. Whatsoever thou sowest in thy child, that shalt thou also reap.

2 Corinthians 3:2

"The precepts of home are unavailing unless enforced by a corresponding example. Nothing is so forcible and encouraging as the 'Follow me.' . . . We learn from example before we can speak. Hence if we would have our children walk in the way of God's commandments, we must go before them; we must take the lead; we must exemplify in our action what we incorporate in our oral instructions; our light must shine not only upon, but before them; they must see our good works as well as hear our good precepts. Said a man once to J. A. James, 'I owe everything under God, to the eminent and consistent piety of my father. So thoroughly consistent was he, that I could find nothing in the smallest degree at variance with his character as a professor of religion. This kept its hold upon me.' It was the means of his conversion to God.

Luke 9:23

"Thus children readily discern any discrepancy between a parent's teaching and example. If we are professors of religion, and they see us worldly-minded, grasping after riches, pleasures and honors; the dupes of ungodly fashion, manifesting a malicious spirit, indolent, prayerless, and indifferent to their spiritual welfare, what do they infer but that we are hypocrites, and will our precepts do them any good? No. 'Line upon line and precept upon precept' will be given to no purpose. Hence the necessity of enforcing our precepts by Christian deportment. Speak in an angry tone before your child; and what will it avail for you to admonish him against anger? Many parents express surprise that all they can say to their children does no good; they remain stubborn, self-willed and recreant.

Isaiah 28:10

"But if these parents will look at what they have done as well as said, they will perhaps be less surprised. They may find a solution of the problem in their own capricious disposition, turbulent passions and ungodly walk. The child will soon discard a parent's precepts when they are not enforced by a parent's example.

Hence that parent who ruins his own soul can do but little for the soul of his child. The blasphemer and sabbath-breaker is unfit to correct his child for swearing and sabbath-breaking. He alone who doeth the truth can teach his children truth. He only who has good habits can teach his children good habits . . . 'Thou that teachest another, teachest thou not thyself?' Hence parents should say to their children, 'Be ye followers of me, even as I also am of Christ.' Their example should include all their precepts. In this way they both hear and see religion in its living, moving and breathing form before them . . .

"If such, then, are its influence and necessity, we can easily infer the duty of parents to show their children a Christian example. If they form their character upon the approved model of their parents, then the duty to give them a Christian model is very obvious . . . That family is happy as well as holy, where the parents rear up their children under the fostering influence of a Christian example . . .

The Home-Parlor

"The Christian home includes the parlor. This department we must give but a brief and passing notice. Yet it is as important and responsible as the nursery. In it we have a view of the relations of home to society beyond it. The parlor is set apart for social communion with the world . . . the mind and heart are impressed and moulded there; the cob-web lines of etiquette are drawn there; a panorama of social fascinations pass before the youthful eye there,—these make the parlor the most dangerous department of home. There the young receive their first introduction to society . . . There, too, they make choice of companions; there they form matrimonial alliances; there their hearts are developed, their minds trained for social life, their affections directed, and influence brought to bear upon them, which will determine their weal or their woe.

"If such be the influence of the home-parlor, should it not be held sacred, and made to correspond in all the uses for which it is set apart, with the spirit and character of a Christian family; and should not its doors be effectually guarded against the intrusion of spurious and demoralizing elements of society? . . .

"One of the most dangerous periods of life is, when we leave the nursery and school, and enter the parlor. With what solicitude, therefore, should Christian parents guard their parlors from social corruption. They should prepare their children for society, not only by teaching them its manners and customs, how to act in company, how to grace a party, and move with refined ease among companions there, but also by teaching them the dangers and corruptions which lurk in their midst and follow in the train of rustling silks and fashionable denouement. They should never permit their parlor to become the scene of fashionable tyranny. It should be sacred to God and to the church. It should be a true exponent of the social elements of Christianity. It should not be a hermitage, a state of seclusion from the world; but should conform to fashion, yet so far only as the laws of a sanctified taste and refinement will admit.

"These laws exclude all compromise and amalgamation with the ungodly spirit and customs of the world. Allegiance to the higher and better law of God will keep us from submission to the laws of a depraved taste and carnal desire. We must keep ourselves unspotted from the world. Whenever we submit with scrupulous exactness to the laws of fashion; whenever we yield a servile complaisance to its forms and ceremonies, wink at its extremes and immoralities and absurd expenditures, seek its flatteries and indulge in its whims and caprices, by throwing open our parlors as the theatre of their denouement, and introducing our children to their actors and master-spirits, we prostitute our homes, our religion and those whom God has given us to train up for Himself, to interests and pleasures most unworthy the Christian name and character.

2 Corinthians 6:16-18

"There is much danger now of the Christian home becoming in this way slavishly bound to the influence and attractions of society beyond the pale of the church, until all relish for home-enjoyment is lost, and its members no longer seek and enjoy each other's association . . . The children . . . become disgusted with each other's company, and sacrifice their time and talents to a thousand little trifles and absurdities. Taste becomes depraved, and loses all relish for rational enjoyment. The heart teems with idle fancies and vain imaginations. Sentimentalism takes the place of religion; filthy literature and fashionable cards shove the Family Bible in some obscure nook of their parlor and their hearts. The hours devoted to family prayer are now spent in a giddy whirl of amusement and intoxicating pleasure, in the study of the latest fashions and of the newly-published love adventures of some nabob in the world of refined scoundrelism. The parental solicitude, once directed to the eternal welfare of the child, is now expended in match-making and setting out in the world.

Proverbs 4:23

"Thus does the Christian home often become adulterated with the world by its indiscriminate association with unfit social elements . . . It is, therefore, beneath the dignity of the Christian to permit his home to become in any way a prey to immoral and irreligious associations and influences. Like the personal character of the Christian, it should be kept unspotted from the world; and no spirit, no customs, no companions, opposed to religion, should be permitted to enter its sacred limits . . .

2 Timothy 2:22

"Here is indeed the great fault of many Christian parents in the present day. They do not exert that guardian care they should over the social relations and interests of their children. They are too unscrupulous in their introduction to the world, and leave them in ignorance of its snares and deceptions. What results can they look for if they permit their parlor tables to become burdened with French novels, and their children to mingle in company whose influence is the most detrimental to the interests of pure and undefiled religion? Can they reflect upon their daughters for forming improper attachments and alliances? Can they wonder if their sons become desperadoes, and ridicule the religion of their parents? No! They

Titus 2:11-15

permitted them to dally with the fangs of a viper which found a ready admittance into their parlor; and upon them, therefore, will rest the responsibility,—yea, the deep and eternal curse! . . .

"Guard your parlor, therefore, from the corrupting influence of all immoral associations. Be not carried away by the pomp and glare of refined and decorated wickedness. Let not the ornaments and magnificence of mere outward life divert your attention from those hidden principles which prompt to action. In the choice of companions for your children in the parlor, look to the ornaments of the heart rather than to those of the body. Be not allured by the parade of circumstance and position in life . . . Ever remember that the future condition of your children, their domestic character and happiness, will depend upon the kind of company you admit in your parlor.

Match-Making

"Having considered some of the false standards of judgment in the choice of a companion for life, we now revert to those true tests which are given us in the Word of God. There we have the institution and true idea of marriage, and the principles upon which we should proceed in making the marriage choice.

"We are taught in the holy scriptures, the primary importance of judicious views of the nature and responsibilities of the marriage institution itself. We should apprehend it, not from its mere worldly standpoint, not as a simple legal alliance, not only as a scheme for temporal welfare and happiness, but as a divine institute, a religious alliance, involving moral responsibilities, and momentous consequences for eternity as well as for time, for soul as well as for body. We are commanded to look to its religious elements and duties; and to regard it with that solemnity of feeling which it truly demands . . .

Mark 10:9

"In the days of our forefathers, marriage was thus held sacred, as a divine institution, involving moral and religious duties and responsibilities; and their celebration of it was, therefore, a religious one. They realized its momentous import, and its bearing upon their future welfare . . .

"As true, mutual love is the basis of marriage, so also should it be a standard of our judgment in the marriage choice. Without it, neither beauty, wealth nor rank will make home happy. True love should be such as is upheld in scripture. It is above mere passion. It never faileth. It is life-like and never dies out. It is an evergreen in the bosom of home. It has moral stamina, is regulated by moral law, has a moral end, contains moral principle, and rises superior to mere prudential considerations. It is more than mere feeling or emotion; it is not blind, but rational, and above deception, having its ground in our moral and religious nature. It extends to the whole person, to body, mind, and spirit, to the character as well as to the face and form. It is tempered with respect, yea, vitalized, purified, directed and elevated

Isaiah 54:5

33

by true piety. Such love alone will survive the charms and allurements of novelty, the fascinations of sense, the ravages of disease and time, and will receive the sanction of heaven.

"Mutual adaption of character and position is another scripture standard of judgment. Is that person suited for me? Will that character make my home happy? Could I be happy with such an one? Are we congenial in spirit, sentiment, principle, cultivation, education, morals and religion? Can we sympathize and work harmoniously together in mind and heart and will and taste? Are we complemental to each other? These are questions of far greater importance than the question of wealth, of beauty, or of rank.

Ruth 1:16

"Fitness of circumstances, means, and age should be also considered. Am I able to support a family? Can I discharge the duties of a household? Where there is ignorance of household duties, indolence, the want of any visible means of supporting a family, no trade, no education, no energy, and no prospects, there is no reason to think there can be a proper marriage. Thus, then, mutual love, adaptation of character, of means, of circumstances, of position, and of age, should be considered in the formation of a marriage alliance.

"But the standard of judgment to which the scriptures especially direct our attention is that of religious equality, or spiritual adaptation. 'Be not unequally yoked together with unbelievers.' The positive command here is, that Christians should marry only in the Lord. Here is a test in the selection of a companion for life, from which neither parents nor children should ever depart. It evidently forbids a matrimonial union with those who have no sympathy with religion. We should make more account of religious equality than of equality of rank and wealth. Is not true piety of more importance than education, affluence or social distinction? When husband and wife are unequally yoked together in soul and grace, their home must suffer spiritually as well as temporally. The performance of religious duties and the enjoyment of religious privileges, will be impossible. The unbeliever will discourage, oppose, and often ridicule, the pious efforts of the believer. Partiality will be produced, and godliness will decline; for, says Peter, unless we dwell as heirs together of the grace of life, our prayers will be hindered. The pious one cannot rule in such a home. Thus divided and striving with each other, their house must fall. Where one draws heavenward and the other hellward, opposite attractions will be presented, and the believer will find constant obstructions to growth in grace, to the discharge of parental duty, and to the cultivation of Christian graces in the heart. How can the unbeliever return, like David, to bless his household? How can he bring up his children in the nurture and admonition of the Lord? Can he be the head of a Christian home? And, tell me, does the true Christian desire any other than a Christian home? 'How can two walk together, except they be agreed?' And are you, then, in your marriage, agreed to walk with the unbeliever in the broad road of sin and death? You are not, if you are a true Christian!

2 Corinthians 6:14

1 Peter 3:7

34

"We see, therefore, the importance of a rigid adherence to the scripture standard,

'Be not unequally yoked together with unbelievers.' . . .

"But how much more important that they be united in their pilgrim walk to eternity,—united in the Lord Jesus Christ, by a common life and faith and hope! We believe that Christians commit a sin when they violate this law of religious equality, and unite themselves in matrimony with those who pay no regard to religion . . . Parents encourage their pious children to marry unbelievers, though they are well aware that such unholy mixtures are expressly forbidden, and that spiritual harmony is essential to their happiness. 'She is at liberty to be married to whom she will, only in the Lord!' Those who violate this cardinal law of marriage, must expect to suffer the penalties attached to it. History is the record of these. The disappointed hopes, and the miseries of unnumbered homes speak forth their execution. This great scripture law has its foundation in the very nature of marriage itself . . .

1 Corinthians 7:39

"Shall the Christian parent and child disregard this prohibition of God? Will you ridicule this fundamental principle of Christian marriage? Will the children of God not hesitate to marry the children of the devil? Can these walk together in domestic union and harmony? Can saint and sinner be of one mind, one spirit, one life, one hope, one interest? Can the children of the light and the darkness, opposite in character and in their apprehension of things, become flesh of each other's flesh, and by the force of their blended light and darkness shed around their home-fireside the cheerfulness of a mutual love, of a common life and hope, and of a progressive spiritual work? . . .

Amos 3:3

"Such unequal matches are not made in heaven. 'God's hand is over such matches, not in them.' 'What fellowship hath light with darkness?' . . . Both the old and the new testaments give explicit testimony to the law of spiritual harmony in marriage. Thus the law of Moses forbid the children of Israel to intermarry among heathen nations . . . Paul upholds this law when he exhorts the Corinthians to marry 'only in the Lord.' . . .

"The primitive Christians developed this law in their families. They forbade marriage with Jews, Pagans, Mohammedans, and ungodly persons. With them piety was the first desideratum in marriage. The sense of the Christian church has ever been against religious inequality in marriage. It has always been felt to be detrimental to personal piety and to the general interests of Christianity. It limits and neutralizes the influence of the church, brings overwhelming temptations to lukewarmness in family religion, and is, in a word, in almost every instance, the fruitful cause of spiritual declension wherever it is practiced.

"Let me, then, exhort you to marry only in the Lord. Such an union will be blessed. Daughter of Zion! marry such a man as will, like David, return to bless his household. Son of the Christian home! marry no woman who has not in her heart the casket of piety. Make this your standard; and your home shall be a happy, as well as a holy home . . .

1 Chronicles 16:43

The Antitype of the Christian Home

"The Christian home on earth is but a type of his better home in heaven . . . Heaven is the antitype of the Christian home. There the latter reaches its consummation, and reaps the rich harvest of its great reward. The Father; the Mother of us all; our Brethren; our inheritance; our all sufficiency are there. Yea, all that is included in the dear name of home, is treasured up there, for the child of God . . .

1 Corinthians
13:12

"There you shall not see through a glass darkly, but shall behold all things face to face. You shall not merely know in part, but even as you are known . . .

Isaiah 33:24
Revelation
7:16, 17

"In heaven 'sighing grief shall weep no more,' and we 'shall hunger no more, neither shall we thirst any more; and we shall not say I am sick; and there shall be no night, nor sorrow, nor tears, nor sighing, nor death; for the former things are passed away.' Love will then be perfect; there will be no heart-burnings and disappointments there. There you shall enjoy the honey without the sting, and the rose without the thorn. 'Earth hath no sorrows that heaven cannot heal.' . . .

Psalms 73:25

"Christ is the great center of heaven's glory and attraction. 'Whom have I in heaven but thee?' It would not be heaven if He were absent . . .

1 John 2:1

"There is a living union between the Christian's home on earth, and his home in heaven. Christ represents our nature and advocates our cause . . .

2 Corinthians
5:1, 2

"And as there is a living union of the Christian's home on earth and in heaven, so also will there be a conscious union and recognition of the members of the Christian home, when they enter that better land. When the tent-home is broken up, and its members take their place and enter upon their joys in the heavenly home, they will recognize each other, and exchange congratulations. The bonds of natural affection which bound them together here will bind them also there. They will possess the same home-feeling and sympathy; they will love each other as members of the same household; the parents will know and love their children as parents; and the children will feel towards their parents as children. Thus in the clear light of that blessed land we shall see and know our kindred, and shall be recognized and known by them. All family ties will be re-knit; all home-relationships will be restored; all the links of affection will be renewed . . .

Revelation 19:9

"And oh, what a glorious meeting in heaven that will be, when all the members of the Christian household shall unitedly surround the marriage supper of the Lamb! It will be joyful beyond conception. There they 'shall meet at Jesus' feet,—shall meet to part no more!' No one is absent. Bright faces will meet there; bounding hearts will meet there; and on the banks of the river of life they will walk hand in hand, as they did unitedly in this vale of tears. 'There is hereafter to be no separation in that family. No one is to lie down on a bed of pain. No one to wander away into temptation. No one to sink into the arms of death . . .',

"Gentle reader! seek that better land. Let your home be a preparation for, and a pilgrimage to, a home in heaven. You are now in the wilderness beset on every side by enemies. Go forward! You are now in the deep vale,—in the low retreats of

36

pilgrim life. 'Friend, go up higher!' 'Be thou faithful unto death, and you shall receive a crown of life.' Be patient in tribulation . . . Remember that 'the sufferings of the present time are not worthy to be compared with the glory that shall be revealed in us.' In a few years at most the conflict shall end, and sighing grief shall weep no more; the wormwood and the gall will be exchanged for the cup of salvation; the armor and the battle-field will be exchanged for the whole garment, the crown and the throne. Soon your typical homestead shall be exchanged for your antitypical home; and we shall unite in the homesong of everlasting joy,—the song of 'unto Him that loved us and washed us in His own blood, to Him be praise and glory and dominion forever.' . . .

"We have now enumerated some of the elements of the Christian home—its constitution, its ministry, its trials, its joys, and its relation to a better home in heaven. . . ."

Revelation 2:10
Romans 8:18

Revelation 1:5, 6

The American Christian Church

The Educational Goal of the American
Christian Church in a Republic is
to build the foundation of
America's Christian Conscience.

PATRIOTISM IN THE PULPIT was the American way of life during the founding of our nation. This fact Miss Verna M. Hall is fully documenting in the compilation of *The Christian History of the Constitution*. In her study of the sermons of the clergy —north, south, middle colonies—there has been abundant evidence of the concern and the leadership of the clergy in stating and defining the *principles* of Christian government, of the obligations of the governors and those governed.

In addition to leadership for the lay leaders our patriotic preachers continued to challenge their own brethren—those ministers of the Gospel whom they wished to remind held their role of leadership only by virtue of their fidelity to the Holy Scriptures.

The following selection is from Nathanial Appleton, A.M. Pastor of the First Church in Cambridge, preaching before His Excellency the Governour, on May 26, 1742, being the day for "electing His Majesty's Council" for the Province of the Massachusetts-Bay:

"As for you my *Fathers* and *Brethren* in the *Ministry* . . . surely it concerns us to be *ready Scribes, well instructed in the Law of our* GOD, *and in the Gospel of his Son* . . . Surely then, It is absolutely necessary for *Ministers* to be well acquainted with the *holy Scriptures*. Not only to have some certain Portions of Scripture by rote, to use upon all Occasions, but to understand the Meaning of Scripture, and to be able to give the Meaning of it to others—And it was a Concern for a *learned* as well as *godly Ministry*, that stirred up such an early Care in our Fathers, to encourage Schools, and to erect a College, which has now for a *Century of* Years, conferred academical Honour upon the learned Youth, that have been trained up in it. GOD forbid, that an ignorant, and unlearned Ministry should ever rise up in this Land, especially a Ministry that should be ignorant of the Holy Scriptures; or that should think or speak disparagingly of them, or that should insinuate the *Uselessness* of them to *unconverted Men;* Especially when we are told that the *Law of the Lord is perfect, converting the Soul; the Testimony of the Lord is sure, making wise the Simple.* Psal. 19:7. And no less dangerous is it to insinuate, as if the *Bible* was not very necessary for the *Saints,* by Reason of their having the Spirit to inlighten and direct them. *If the Foundations be destroyed, what can the Righteous do?* The Scripture is that *sure Word of Prophecy, to which we must take heed, as to a Light that shineth in a dark Place.* And once we neglect this Light, to follow the supposed Dictates of the Spirit, or a *Light within,* I verily fear that the *Light,* which such fancy to be in them, will prove but *Darkness.*

"Accordingly we who are the *Ministers of Christ,* and have the glorious Gospel committed to our Trust, should be upon the *Watch-Tower,* to spy out every Thing of such a dangerous Tendency, that we may give seasonable Warnings thereof."

This selection is dedicated to those courageous clergy of our times who, remaining faithful to the Gospel and from the "Watch-Tower" of Scripture, give faithful warning of the "dangerous tendencies" of Satan.

The Church And The Republic

"I have in my library a volume bearing this title: 'Historical and Patriotic Addresses, Centennial and Quadrennial.' The American flag forms its frontispiece and American History constitutes the contents of its pages. The book has over one thousand pages . . . It is the intention of the book to give the steps of American progress and set forth the elements of our Republic's strength. In the book are national odes by Whittier and Holmes, and orations by Webster and Adams and Evarts and Curtis and Depew and Winthrop and kindred spirits, and patriotic sermons by loyal divines, closing with a sermon delivered in this pulpit. When I took up this book and turned its pages, this was the one thing which I noticed: looking through the book was like looking over an American landscape or over an American city; the chief thing which caught the eye was the Christian church. In every ode and oration and sermon of the book rises the tapering church spire, tipped with a glittering cross or with a blazing star. Here is a book composed of the deepest thoughts and observations of America's foremost thinkers,—poets, jurists, statesmen, merchants, ministers,—and it represents all classes of Americans as saying, The Christian church has been one of the most potent factors in the construction of the American Republic and one of the greatest bulwarks of its magnificent

David Gregg, D.D., *Makers of the American Republic*

principles and institutions.

"That book set me thinking. It gave me also my topic for this morning. It started such questions with me as these: Is its teaching true? Ought the church spire to shoot up in every patriotic ode and oration and sermon? If the Christian church be the national power which these patriotic men represent it to be, what constitutes its power? How does the church serve the Republic? . . .

"I affirm that the teaching of this book concerning the Christian church is true . . . The very first house of any importance which our Pilgrim fathers built on this continent was the house of God . . . The *Mayflower*, which brought our Pilgrim fathers to the Plymouth Rock, was simply the old church of Scrooby Manor afloat and heading its way to a great future. And Plymouth Rock, where the prow of the *Mayflower* touched and where the Scrooby church landed, was simply a fragment of the Alps, broken off at Geneva, the home of John Calvin. Plymouth Rock stands in history as the symbol of Calvinism. The covenant of the Mayflower, which every American should write in his memory, shows all this. It shows the play of religion in the origin of American national life. Before the Pilgrim fathers set foot on American soil they took America for God and the Christian religion, and entered into a religious compact with one another. This is the way that covenant opens:

" 'In the name of God, amen. We whose names are underwritten, having undertaken for the glory of God and the advancement of the Christian faith, do solemnly and mutually, in the presence of God and of one another, covenant and combine ourselves together into a civic body politic.'

"Do we wonder that, in beginning to construct our nation in accordance with this *Mayflower* compact, the first building of note which the Pilgrim fathers constructed was a Christian church? There was no other way of beginning for them, and as there was no other way of beginning for them, there is no other way of continuing for us. In taking possession of new territory we must run up the church, and we must run it up in the very beginning. The Christian church must be there in the new territory to help formulate the character of its institutions, and to breathe the soul of Christ into its gathering society, and to incarnate God and conscience in all its history and in all its progress. That is the way it was in the beginning. That is the way Plymouth Rock was taken possession of. It is good to keep near to the Plymouth Rock type of life. Take Plymouth Rock out of the Republic, and the Republic will fall to pieces in the very first storm upon the sands of infidelity.

"So imbedded in the life of our early civic fathers was the Christian church that we cannot think of them apart from the Christian church. The church was the real morning of the state with them. They saw to it that every infant settlement had its sanctuary, until ten thousand spires pointed upward to the Source of their national prosperity. With them this was the method of their political building: the people made the laws, and the churches made the people . . . Their churches were the incarnation of federalism and so prophecies of the coming American Union.

They built into New England general intelligence, reverence for law, and faith in God. These were the triple foundations which they put underneath the young Republic. When, in after ages, the sons of New-Englanders moved out of New England and sought the West in the conquest of new territory, they belted this whole continent with a zone of New-Englandism and built this triple foundation under our whole political fabric. Into the great West they carried with them their churches, and these continued what they were in the beginning, centers of political intelligence and of patriotic devotion and of hope for the future. The holy and everlasting principles taught in the churches wove new stars and stripes to float over new homes, and added new State luminaries to the galaxy which dotted the blue in our national banner. Some one has said, 'Education and religion are at home wherever our flag shakes out its folds,' and this is true; but there is a truth prior to this and greater than this, and that truth is, the stars and stripes are at home wherever Christian education and the Christian religion pioneer and take the land and fill it with churches . . .

"I will indicate two ways in which the Christian church serves the American Republic. The first way is this:

1. *It protects and fosters those institutions which have proved a blessing to the Republic.*

"I will center my thought here upon one institution, viz., the Christian Sabbath. The rule is, where there is no church and no church-going there is no Sabbath, and where there is no Sabbath and no Sabbath-keeping there is no religion, and where there is no religion there is no God, and where there is no God there is no conscience, and where there is no conscience there is no respect for the rights of man, and where there is no respect for the rights of man there is no security for life or property. Now take religion, God, conscience, respect for the rights of man, and protection of life and property out of the American Republic, and just how much of what is left would be worth having? . . .

"There is a second way in which the Christian church serves the American Republic. It is this:

2. *It keeps before the people the true idea with regard to national greatness and national strength* . . .

"The church, in teaching American citizens begins with God. The first essential is to get into right relation with God, to get His law written on the heart and incorporated in the life. Institutions must harmonize with His will, and so must rulers, and so must voters. The church, in instructing American citizens, set Jesus Christ before men as the pattern after which to model. His views of man, man's dignity, man's rights, man's needs, must be held. His principles and His views of doctrines concerning God must be adopted. The divine love which shines out of His cross must be allowed to dominate all the affairs of human life. His hopefulness must be granted an entrance into the souls of men. His manhood must be reproduced in our citizens, and the nation must wheel itself into line with the purposes of His coming kingdom of righteousness and peace and love . . .

"Do I properly magnify and represent the Christian church, this institution of God which announces the law of God, and which guards the day of God, and which labors to make the nation Christian? Is it the power in this land of ours which I have represented it to be? If so, then duty is plain, and there is no escape from duty. What is duty? It is duty to give the Republic Christian churches . . . When we have church bells everywhere, from Alaska to New Mexico, and from Maine to California, then we can challenge them to do their God-assigned work for the American Republic . . ."

America For Christ

"In one of his glowing letters Paul the Hebrew writes to his fellow-countrymen, 'Brethren, my heart's desire and prayer to God for Israel is, that they might be saved.'

"These burning words introduce Paul as a citizen. They photograph him as he appears in a supreme patriotic moment, and the result is a magnificent personage—a Christian patriot. The camera of inspiration catches the picture just as an intense prayer leaps from his intense soul. Although the prayer is condensed into one brief sentence, yet it is a prayer of magnificent sweep. It seeks the grandest display of the glory of the true God and the greatest good of a whole nation . . .

"From Paul we wish to learn our duty to our country. We wish his patriotism to relive in us; we wish to bring before our souls the two objects which he brought before his soul,—Christ and Country,—that we may pray as he prayed. It is our privilege to see Christ as Paul saw Him; more than this, it is our privilege to look at the march of Christ through nineteen centuries. The centuries transfigure Him and give Him an added glory. They reveal Him as the mighty force in history. History reveals that the ruling nations of the age are the nations in which He is honored . . .

"As patriotic Christians there is only one cry in our souls, and that is, 'America for Christ! Christ for America!'

"I mean to push this motto; I push it on three grounds: for America's sake, for the world's sake, for Christ's sake.

"1. We demand America for Christ for America's sake.

"We know what Christ does for an individual when he yields himself up to Him; He fills him with His own life and makes him one of the luminaries of the world . . . Now, what Christlessness and Christfulness are in the individual man, Christlessness and Christfulness are in the nation. A nation is only an aggregation of individual men. Christ deals with nations. In His sight nations are moral personalities.

They perform all the functions of a moral person, and He treats them according to their character. Divorce your nation from Christ and you ring its death-knell; you link its fate to the fate of Judas. Marry your nation to Christ and you open for it a door into a new future and secure for it a place among the nations of the world like that which Paul occupied among men. Tell me how the American Republic will treat Christ and I will tell you the future of the American Republic. Because the destiny of this nation depends upon its relation to Christ, I stand at the portals of the nation and as a loyal citizen cry, "Lift up your heads, O ye gates; and be ye lifted up, ye everlasting doors; and the King of glory shall come in.' . . .

"As American patriots we should not allow ourselves to be blind to facts by a foolish optimism . . . With all our greatness, the God of nations could break us in pieces with a single stroke. Our only protection is loyalty to Christ. We must make our land and keep our land a gospel land. Whenever America becomes a Sahara of infidelity it will be as worthless as any other moral sand-heap. Whenever the citizens of our Republic allow the sirocco of atheism to sweep it, then, so far as I am concerned, farewell, Republic; whoever wishes may claim the old, withered, shriveled, blasted, lifeless thing which the sirocco leaves.

"But is our view on these matters the view universally held? No; men who have no practical interest in Christ and His religion ignore Him and His as factors in the upbuilding of nations. For example, an infidel science sees the elements of a nation's destiny solely in its physical environment . . . as if character were the product of outward circumstances . . .

"The majority of men attribute our greatness as a nation to our natural resources and to the width and richness of our land; the *Mayflower* and Plymouth Rock are ignored. But that is not the true explanation, and facts show it. The North American Indian possessed these natural and material resources ages and ages before our Pilgrim fathers set foot on this continent. There is not a river nor a mine nor a field that was not here when they owned the land. Why did not God unlock these natural resources to them? This is the reason: He kept them that He might give them to those who were in true relation with Himself. Our Pilgrim fathers came to these shores for His glory, and gave themselves to Him in the *Mayflower* covenant as a preparation for taking possession of the land. They were consecrated to His cause, and this is the reason He opened the treasures to them and to their children. My fellow-countrymen, it required the magic inspiration of spiritual life to transmute the natural resources of the United States into wealth. Our territory, every inch of it breadthwise and lengthwise, is in the hand of God, and He can lock up its mines, and stop the flow of its rivers of oil, and blight its more fertile soil . . .

"I wish, in treating this point that America needs Christ, that the nation should be taken for Christ for America's sake—I wish to hew close to the line of history and to build only with historical facts. History shows that the Christ-men and the Christ-women have always been the loyal men and women of the land, and the men and women who have inaugurated great and beneficial movements. Our national

43

liberties were bought with their blood. This is an open and fearless statement, but it has as many verifications as there are races in our American nationality. Each race has contributed its heroes. Some of you have come down the line of the Pilgrim history, and you have the verification of the statement on that line. Some of you came to America in the loins of the French Huguenots, and in the history of these noble refugees you have a verification of the statement. Some of you are Dutch, your ancestors were the true-minded Hollanders who gave America primitive New York and you have a verification of the statement on that line.

"I know the verification which the statement receives on the line of the history of the Covenanters of America, and I am proud to be able to speak of this verification. Scotland is not the only land of Covenanter heroism. America has its stories of Covenanter heroism. The Covenanters were here before the American Republic, and they held the principles of the American Revolution long before the American Revolution was inaugurated. Bancroft tells us that two years before the American Declaration of Independence was issued in Philadelphia, 1776, the Covenanters in Mecklenburg, N.C., in 1774 issued the Mecklenburg declaration, and it contained the very same principles which are in the Philadelphia Declaration. Two years in advance? Yes. All honor to the Covenanters of America. When the Revolutionary War was declared that old church almost to a man fell into rank, and the report of the Covenanter's rifle was heard in the very forefront of the battle. But why single these men out? To show that wherever there were true Christians there were true warriors for American liberty. Through Christian men and women of all races the gospel worked itself into our civil life. The Pilgrims of Massachusetts, the Covenanters of the Carolinas, the Huguenots of New Jersey, the Hollanders of New York, the Episcopalians of Virginia, all were loyal. The story of their loyalty to country and of their sacrifice for country is one. The type of men who built the nation in the past, and the principles with which they built, are the men and the principles which alone can devlop and preserve the nation.

"Allow me to push this point just a little further. Give our country men who fear God and God only, and who live perpetually in His sight, and who feel that God has commissioned them to carry on reform and incorporate Christ into the national life, and you give it the men who become the heroes of the country. They are the men of courage . . .

"America needs Christ—the rule of Christ, the truth of Christ, the spirit of Christ, the gospel of Christ, and the men of Christ.

"2. We demand America for Christ for the world's sake.

"It is well known that America is the great cosmopolitan nation of the world; it is a fusion of nationalities. Hence the eyes of all nations are upon it; hence all the nations claim kinship with it . . .

"The work of America . . . is different. Instead of sending out her colonies to
44 distant lands, and bringing other peoples under her sway by conquest, she has

opened her vast territory to be colonized. She has invited all nations and races to meet and mingle here and make one composite family, thus forming a world's republic, and thus illustrating the world's humanity . . . On her own soil, she gathers the children of the nations, and in her homes and churches and schools she trains them to be teachers of the world. This is an opportunity such as is given to no other nation on the face of the earth. These polyglot populations are thrown upon her to be fused into one nationality by one culture and one faith and one liberty . . .

"The responsibility laid upon her, therefore, is a double one; first and supremely, to keep the fountains of her own intelligence and virtue and religion pure for the sake of the native-born in the land; and, second, to ply with all the forces of Christian learning and religion the thousands of the unevangelized who have come to her shores, that they may send back to their old homes, in the form of letters and newspapers and earnest appeals, the blessed gospel of the Son of God to work as a regenerating and converting power in the different fatherlands across the sea.

"All this being true, it is the veriest truism to say that America taken for Christ means the nations of the world far and near taken for Christ; America a Christian nation means a mighty witness for God among all lands of the earth . . .

"My fellow-men, our country is the battle-ground on which the conflicts of the ages are to be fought and decided. It is the valley of decision, filled with multitudes and multitudes. Every instinct of our being ought to say, 'Let that nation be saved, and saved at once, which carries the world's largest hopes and the world's final destinies.' In the Christianizing of our nation the Republic has its life at stake, society its order, labor its reward, home its happiness, and the world its future."

Patriotic Piety Of 1776

"The original chart of American Liberty was drawn and signed in the cabin of the Mayflower. It was a civil compact, based on republican principles and sanctioned by religious faith. Such men as Carver, Bradford, Brewster, and Winslow, blessed our nation in its cradle, and patriotic teachers of religion have ever fostered its growth. At an early day, the acute and subtle Cotton, the erudite and energetic Hooker, and their associates, replenished the beacon-fires of learning, patriotism and piety along our 'rock-bound coast.' Not a little did these men of God contribute to produce that state of things which prospectively seemed propitious, and in view of which they greatly rejoiced . . . Hooker was an apostolic hero, whose eye, voice, soul, gesture, and whole form were animated with the vital energy of primitive zeal. . . . His contemporaries . . . praised him as 'the one rich pearl, with which Europe more than repaid America for the treasures from her coast' . . .

E. L. Magoon,
*Orators of the
American
Revolution*

45

A Patriotic and Conservative Ministry

"A careful perusal of our primitive annals will induce a high appreciation of the patriotic piety and mutual sympathy between preachers and their flocks that then prevailed. Devoted ministers of religion, like Eliot and Wilson, shared in the hardships and dangers consequent on the early Indian Wars. And when news first arrived in Boston of the menacing attitude assumed by England, prompt consultations were held for the common weal, and the boldest measures were projected. The fathers in Israel were all assembled, and 'discovered their minds to one another.' They voted unanimously against submission, and publicly declared, says Winthrop, 'We ought to defend our lawful possessions, if we are able; if not, to avoid and protract.' Six hundred pounds were immediately raised in the poor settlements of the northern colony, and the fortifications were hastened by every kind of popular aid. The influence of the ministry was patriotic and conservative, at the South as well as around Plymouth rock.

A Confederation of Patriotism and Piety

"The Revolutionary War was a struggle imposed on our fathers, not sought by them; injustice was in their esteem a legitimate cause for resistance, and all willingly shared in the discharge of a duty which none could doubt. Those who led in the church, and those who led in the field, were impelled by one conviction and labored together with the same design. One taught the law of justice, the other defended it; one was the voice of God, the other was His arm. Thus, the American Colonies, confederated by patriotism and piety long before they were united under a written constitution, felt that their resistance to oppression was a common cause, and simultaneously grasped a sword which had been tempered in the fires of suffering and bedewed with the tears of the sanctified. Then were laity and clergy distributed to all the posts of defence—the chamber of council and the field of battle,—the rural church and the martial camp,—and from each station of trust and solicitude, fervent prayer ascended to heaven for favor on our arms.

"Burke said: 'The Americans augur misgovernment at a distance, and snuff the approach of tyranny in every tainted breeze.' The sense here described was most acute in those whose faculties had been educated and refined in the school of the Prophets. As a hunter, standing armed, listens at the foot of a tree to see whence comes the wind, so they stood by the altars they were appointed to guard, and listened attentively in that direction whence wrong approached. Considerations of time, place, peril, or calling, impeded no one. Men of the greatest dignity, largest wealth, and most sacred functions did not stop to compute profit and loss: blood was poured out freely and poured for all. The sainted Robinson had magnanimously said to the voyagers in the Mayflower, that he would not foreclose his mind to the truth of God, even if it were new. The new light and liberties which our fathers had here learned to enjoy, were deemed of too much value to be lightly surrendered to injustice or the miserable expediency of false mercy. Conscience was their only compensation on earth, and God on high. Hands consecrated to sacred service, breaking the bread of life and soothing penitential sorrow, from the pulpit scattered profusely in moral and martial tempests, seeds of patriotic piety whose glorious harvests the whole world is yet destined to reap in peace . . .

Rev. Samuel Davies—Virginia

"Reverend Samuel Davies, for some time a pastor in Virginia, and afterwards President of Nassau Hall, deserves especial notice. He was born in Delaware, Nov. 3d, 1724, and received his education in Pennsylvania. His grand characteristic, as a patriot and preacher, was boldness. This is a valuable attribute in every public agent. The great Lord Verulam declared, that 'if he were asked what is the first, second, and third thing necessary for success in business, he should answer, boldness, boldness, boldness.' Timid and effeminate efforts in the pulpit are as inefficient and more destructive than elsewhere. The stupid soul is startled into attention only by bold blows. Ministers may describe for ever the beauties of nature, the pleasures of virtue, the dignity of self-respect and the vulgarity of vice, but until more exalted motives are urged, and more potent influences are employed, few effects will follow that are either great or good.

"Davies was the ablest Dissenter in the southern provinces. His custom was to study his discourses with great care. Being pressed to preach on a certain occasion without his usual preparation, he replied: 'It is a dreadful thing to talk nonsense in the name of the Lord.'

Davies' Defence of Religious Liberty

"But he was as prompt and fearless in any sudden emergency, as he was habitually deliberate and studious. Thanks to the movements in behalf of religious liberty made at the North, England granted the Toleration Act in favor of all the Colonies. Virginia, however, ruled by her Episcopal establishment, refused to admit that the Dissenters of their territory were included. Davies withstood all their forces alone, with Peyton Randolph at their head. He had made himself a thorough master of English law, civil and ecclesiastical, and always chose to meet every persecuting indictment in the highest courts with his own plea. So powerful was he in the capacity which the law of necessity compelled him to assume, that many of his friends, and even his foes were wont to exclaim, 'What a lawyer was spoiled when Davies took the pulpit!' Spoiled, forsooth! As if the pulpit, with all its themes of eternal interest, was not the sublimest field for the development and exercise of eloquence ever vouchsafed to man.

47

"Not satisfied with establishing his religious rights at the bar of colonial power, he went to England and obtained the explicit sanction of the highest authority with respect to the extension of the Toleration law to Virginia. It was during this mission that he gave another striking instance of his boldness. George II. and many of his court were in the congregation of this American Dissenter. His majesty, struck with admiration, or forgetting the proprieties of the occasion, spoke several times to those around him and smiled. Davies paused a moment, and then looking sternly at the king, exclaimed, 'When the lion roars, the beasts of the forest all tremble; and when King Jesus speaks, the princes of earth should keep silence.'

"Mr. Davies was tall, manly and dignified. A distinguished character of the day, on seeing him pass, said: 'he looked like the ambassador of some great king.' His understanding was strong, his elocution graceful, and his address on some occasions was overwhelming. Patrick Henry was his neighbor and ardent admirer. It is believed that the renowned pupil was greatly indebted to this patriotic preacher, both for his sentiments and the invincible manner with which he enforced them . . .

Prophecy Concerning Washington

"On the 10th of July, 1755, General Braddock sustained his memorable defeat, and the remnant of his army was saved by the courage and skill of Colonel Washington, then but twenty-three years old. On the 20th of the same month, our moral hero preached a sermon, 'On the defeat of General Braddock, going to Fort Du Quesne.' In this sermon, he calls on all his hearers, in the most impassioned and patriotic term, to show themselves men, Britons, Christians, and to make a noble stand for the blessings they enjoyed. In the same year, he delivered a sermon before Captain Overton's company of volunteers, under the title of 'Religion and patriotism, the constituents of a good soldier.' It was in the discussion of this subject that his famous prophecy occurred. Speaking of the encouraging fact, that God had 'diffused some sparks of martial fire through the country,' said he, 'as a remarkable instance of this, I may point out to the public that heroic youth, Colonel Washington, whom I cannot but hope Providence has hitherto preserved, in so signal a manner, for some important service to his country.'

Sacred Eloquence

"Sacred eloquence, in revolutionary times, is the chief conservative of order and the grand solace of the popular mind. While it fortifies the patriot in his rebellion against tyranny, it exhorts him to a patient endurance of unavoidable wrongs. It alleviates as much as possible the pressure of the chain, by opening before the sufferer celestial horizons, fragrant with immortal amarynths, and teeming with infinite beatitudes. Davies was of this stamp, a bold patriot and a bold Christian . . . True eloquence, like true religion is a movement of sensibility as well as an act of reason. If one has 'thoughts that breathe,' you may be sure he will have 'words that burn.' If one is truly a patriot, in the pulpit or out of it, his conduct will comport with his professions, and his life will be at the service of his country as well as of his God.

"Illustrious examples abound in every direction, but we will take our next in a region farther north. It was fitting that the first battle of the Revolution should be fought under the eves of the church at Lexington. It was in that vicinity that the Genius of Patriotism had long dwelt with her enthusiastic devotee.

Rev. Jonas Clark—Lexington, Mass.

"The town records of Lexington contain many important documents which discussed the great questions involved in the national struggle for Independence. In 1765, the citizens vindicated the popular movement in respect to the Stamp-Act. In 1767, they unanimously concurred with the resolution of Boston, to prevent the consumption of foreign commodities. In 1768, they argued with great force against the right of Great Britain to tax America. In 1772, they resolved, in most thrilling terms, to seek redress for daily increasing wrongs; and in 1774, they took measures to supply themselves with ammunition, arms and other requisites for military defence. What hero drew those masterly papers, defended their principles, and fired the people at all hazards to defend them? History has recorded the fact, the Reverend Jonas Clark was their author and chief defence. He was one of the many patriotic clergy of New England, who instructed their beloved flock in peace, and guarded them amid the dread necessities of war. 'Mr. Clark,' says Edward Everett, 'was eminent in his profession,—a man of practical piety,—a learned theologian,—a person of wide, general reading,—a writer perspicuous, correct, and pointed, beyond the standard of the day,—and a most intelligent, resolute, and ardent champion of the popular cause. He was connected by marriage with the family of John Hancock.

"Their connection led to a portion of the interesting occurrences of the 19th of April, 1775. The soul-stirring scenes of the great tragedy which was enacted on this spot, were witnessed by Mr. Clark, from the door of his dwelling hard by. To perpetuate their recollection, he instituted, the following year, a service of commemoration. He delivered himself a historical discourse of great merit, which was followed on the return of the anniversary, till the end of the Revolutionary war, in a series of addresses in the same strain, by the clergy of the neighboring towns.

Rev. John Witherspoon—New Jersey

"A happy combination of piety and patriotism, constituting the most useful private and public virtue, we have already found in different sections of our   49 common country during the Revolution. We have only to turn to the highest council of our infant nation, the most august assembly of men that ever congregated to declare themselves free, and we shall find another illustrious example in the person of John Witherspoon.

"He was lineally descended from John Knox, the moral hero of Scotland, was born near Edinburgh, 1722, and from the time he adopted America as his country, was as much distinguished as a preacher as a patriot. Dr. Witherspoon was one of the signers of the Declaration of Independence, which he eloquently defended; through a trying period of congressional responsibility he was a very efficient legislator; and for many years performed the duties of a laborious, erudite, and eminently successful president of Princeton College. On taking his seat in Congress, he surprised his associates, as his brother Davies, had surprised the courts of Virginia, with his wonderful knowledge and skill as a civilian. He was associated with Richard Henry Lee and John Adams on several important committees and himself drew many valuable State papers . . . As soon as the liberties of the country were won, Dr. Witherspoon gladly resumed his classical pursuits and the work of the ministry . . .

Dr. Samuel Stillman—Boston

"Dr. Samuel Stillman of Boston, distinguished patriot and divine, was born in Philadelphia, but was removed early to Charleston, South Carolina, where he was educated, and where he was ordained, in 1759. He removed to Boston, 1763, and remained there until his death, 1806, the universally admired pastor of the First Baptist Church . . .

"The respect which this admirable preacher won was most comprehensive and of the highest kind. Among refined gentlemen, liberal scholars, and eloquent divines, he ranked second to none of any section or name. Standing in the presence of armed foes, he preached with a power that commanded respect, even when he could not create compunction.

"When the British took possession of Boston, and desecrated its sacred edifices some of the more skillful of their number, who had recoiled under Stillman's patriotic appeals, illustrated their spite by drawing a charcoal outline of the great divine on the plastered wall of his own pulpit, in all the freedom of expressive gesture and eloquent denunciation.

"It will not seem strange that Dr. Stillman's own church was habitually thronged, or that whenever he visited other cities his instructions were sought with avidity by the most exalted minds . . .

"The best orators of every age have been created by the oppressive circumstance, in the midst of which they have suddenly arisen with resistless power, as if they gathered strength and inspiration from the terrors of the storm. When the age needs great men it will find them—heroes not of the timid mimosa kind, who 'fear the dark cloud, and feel the coming sound.' Preachers in Revolutionary times are eminently practical; nature supplies them with abundant ammunition, and necessity teaches them expressly to load and fire. They are the flying artillery of 'the sacramental host of God's elect.' They are inspired by no fictitious goddess of the Aonian Mount, but by that Eternal Spirit who directed the pen of Moses, the fingers of David, and the tongue of Paul; they drink of no fancied Pierian spring, but at a purer and more exalted source . . . The most highly endowed among men are the chosen medium of communications from heaven. Such spirits are most numberous when most needed, and most powerful in the tempests which they are born to rule . . . While Providence thunders in portentous events they fulminate with divine inspirations, and it is thus that celestial instruction is perpetuated and rendered intelligent to mankind. This was the mission which our patriotic fathers were raised up to perform; in every dread emergency, heroes like them are placed by Jehovah on the watch-towers of Jerusalem, and they are silent neither day nor night . . .

"It is not to be understood, however, that Dr. Witherspoon, or his distinguished co-patriots in the pulpit, were religious or political fanatics. When a clergyman transforms himself into a phrenzied partizan, the dupe or champion of a local faction, he renders himself the more odious in contrast with the exalted profession he has disgraced . . . What can be more sacrilegious and fatal to human hopes than to place an earthly passion or human interest on the altar by the side of Christ, and sometimes even in Christ's own place? But the appropriate functions of a religious teacher do not forbid the duties of a patriot—they imperiously demand them. God designed that the minister of the Gospel should be the man of the people, the confidant of their miseries, the balm of their secret griefs, the depositary of their tears, the interpreter of their necessities, their protector, friend and father, a living providence to all who hunger and thirst, a light to guide the benighted, and a beacon to warn those in danger of destruction.

"Every kingdom of nature, every department of science, and every production of art—philosophical research and patriotic disquisition,—whatever history has bequeathed, imagination invented, or fancy embellished,—may be appropriately employed in the foundation of the preacher's work. To him, at the head of all speakers, most legitimately belong the richest treasures of earth, air, and sea, the peculiar tint and tone of each clime, the mental wealth of each nation, and the accumulated wonders of the whole universe."

The American Christian School

The Educational Goal of the American
Christian School is to build a
Christian Curriculum upon the foundation of
Christian Character and Christian Conscience.

It is evident that the de-Christianization of America has received its greatest impetus through the *secularization* of education. From a people proud of a great heritage founded upon the Bible as *the textbook of liberty* we have become a people who today permit the *legislation of atheism* into our schools under the pretext that the "open Bible" and prayer—*"the weapons of our warfare"*—might offend. Yet Paul the great Christian patriot of the first century establishes the standard by which we can be true to ourselves and thus to others when he states: "*And herein do I exercise myself, to have always a conscience void of offence toward God, and toward men.*" Acts 24:16

America—the only nation in history ever to establish a government and a Constitution upon principles of Christian liberty derived from the Word of God—America forgot.

But the subversion of Christianity through education did not occur easily in a nation so dedicated to fulfilling God's purpose for America. And while we might be tempted to believe that the accomplishment of this secularization of education occurred when the highest court in our land—the Supreme Court—ruled on the Prayer Case of 1962, it is not so. One cannot legislate Christianity out of a nation through the courts—it must occur first through *individual acceptance* of an educational system without God or Christ as its foundation. Thus, the records show, that when individuals, churches, communities yielded up to the state the control and direction of education it was then that the Bible became *"as the words of a book that is sealed"*.

In the years 1837–1848 Horace Mann, whom John Dewey designated as "*the father of progressive education*", made a series of Annual Reports to the Massachusetts Board of Education of which he was Secretary. These Reports paved the

52

way for a state financed, state directed, and ultimately a state controlled education program superseding local control through the demand for "standardization" of school structures, textbooks, curriculum, and teacher training and certification. But even this might not have proved so effective in the "secularization" of education had we not deliberately removed the Bible as the basis of our Christian character and substituted for salvation and regeneration of heart a *psychological atheism* which found man innately "good" and society "bad".

There were many alert clergymen of the time of Horace Mann who were aware of his "condition" for the drive to achieve "universal public education." This "condition" was that Christianity be *neutralized* for the larger goal of building, not Christian character and conscience, but *humanitarians* with *benevolent inclinations* toward mankind. And for those individuals who wished the schools to teach a patriotism which indicated how great was "the faith of our fathers" there was substituted a bland form of *non-controversial democracy* and "citizenship in the state". Thus the public school was able to accomplish that which the hired European mercenaries of England never could—namely to separate our patriotism from our Christian conviction.

The threat of "control" of both the *degree* and *amount* of Christianity in the schools is foreshadowed in this statement by the Reverend Mathew Hále Smith— one of the fundamental clergy whose challenges to Horace Mann in print were rewarded by labels of *extremism:*

"The principles of piety, as you illustrate and enforce them, exclude all that treats of human depravity—salvation by the blood of Jesus Christ—the atonement and the sanctions to a good life, drawn from the world to come. All these common truths, held by nine-tenths of all in this State, who profess any form of Christian faith, are ruled out of schools by the high authority of the Secretary of the Board of Education; they are declared to be sectarian and unconstitutional. You have settled by the authority of the Board, or without that authority, what Piety *is, according to the statute. Your influence is derived from the Legislature; through you, the people are told what they must receive and be satisfied with, as a construction of the Constitution. All towns must hear—all districts obey, else incur the penalty of forfeiture of their portion of the school money."*

A Rich Treasury of Documentation

The fact of America's establishment as a Christian nation—"reserved by God"— as the early historians indicated—can be richly documented in the work of Miss Verna M. Hall, compiler of *Christian History of the Constitution*. Returning to "original" sources of the Journals of Congress, the Journals of the Colonies, governmental proclamations, diplomatic correspondence, letters, speeches, sermons, newspapers of the times, a veritable "treasure house" of evidence has been uncovered.

There is no doubt that the *temper* and *character* of our nation was Christian beginning with the steadfast Pilgrims of Plymouth who came to these shores "for ye propagating & advancing ye gospell of ye kingdom of Christ". For one hundred and fifty years and more, up to the time of our Revolution, the seven years of that long struggle, and through the ratification of our Constitution—even through the perilous years of the French Revolution—we maintained our Christian character as a nation. Then began our period of *"falling away"* when we worshipped the "effect" of our great success—and forgot the "cause". This vacuum was readily filled with *man-centered* philosophies which replaced the internal battles of conscience with the social, economic and political struggles of society.

Thus we veered from a period when, even our governmental proclamations were filled with the language of salvation and the recognition that Christ alone could change the hearts of men, to a pre-occupation with educational, social, economic, and eventually political arrangements, which claimed to insure progress and improvement for society and hence for man.

But even as the Christian influence in education began a sharp decline and the "progressives" made their inroads, the Christian schools endeavored to maintain a Christian standard of education. In an effort to off-set the secularism of the publicly financed schools, the Christian schools made sure that the theme of salvation was uppermost in their curriculums. But even the American Christian School felt the inroads of subversion for with the importation of the elements of modernism and liberal theology the case against the Christian piety of the founding fathers was constructed. Patriotism and Christianity were divorced and with the gradual disappearance of the primary sources in the sermons, the official documents, the early historians of our country, the climate for the "rewriting" of American history was created.

Christian schools remained the citadel of Christian liberty. But as the seminaries and Christian colleges found their early sources of American history replaced with modern interpretations cast in the "socialization" of America, so teachers learned the new history and passed it along to their students. The following quotation indicates the degree to which this subversion pervaded American scholarship:

Veritas
Foundation,
The Great Deceit,
Social
Pseudo-Sciences
"The first problem was to change the attitude of Americans toward the history of their own country and the ideals of the Founding Fathers of the American Republic.

"This was not an easy task. The American people have been brought up to believe that George Washington, John Adams, Thomas Jefferson, James Madison, Alexander Hamilton, and other statesmen of their time were men of patriotism and principle. Hundreds of authoritative books had praised the heroic stature and noble purpose of the heroes who had defied the British Empire and founded a new nation based upon individual freedom.

"History had been picked out as the vanguard of the 'social sciences' in picturing socialism as an inevitable development. But first the image of the Founding Fathers as men of high purpose had to be destroyed. This done, the socialists had a ready-made Marxian formula to replace the traditional patriotic account of American history.

"Charles Beard had co-authored with James Harvey Robinson 'The Development of Modern Europe' in 1907. This was a highly successful work which popularized the socialistic teachings of Karl Marx. It achieved a wide acceptance as a textbook in American colleges.

"Beard at this time became associated with the Intercollegiate Socialist Society (known today as the League for Industrial Democracy). The Intercollegiate Socialist Society had organized Fabian socialist branches in scores of universities and colleges in America.

"With this socialist background Beard was in a position not only to write but also to find a market for his books.

"In 1913, he wrote 'An Economic Interpretation of the Constitution of the United States'. This was heavy artillery designed to demolish the lofty reputations of the Founding Fathers. It was one of the most audacious pieces of historical deceptions of all time. James Madison, one of the framers of the United States Constitution, and the fourth President of the United States, was caricatured as an exponent of a Marxist type of economic interpretation of history 21 years before Marx was even born . . . In the portion that Beard extracted out of context from Madison's writings he tries to show that Madison attributed a purely economic and selfish motivation to the building of the American Republic . . .

"Beard's slant was calculated to undermine not only the heroic picture of the founders of our nation, but also to denigrate those features of independence, individualism and self-reliance that characterized the pioneer era . . . ."

"The socialistic theme outlined by Beard in 'An Economic Interpretation of the Constitution of the United States' was carried through all his subsequent works. Some eleven million copies of his 47 books have been sold.

"As Beard's interpretations have dominated the teaching of history in American schools, there is hardly an American alive who has not been exposed to this leftist virus.

"Since Beard's death (1948) the socialistic slant on history has been continued by such persons as Carl Becker, Max Lerner, and the two Schlesingers.

"The historical perversions of Beard and his successors are not their own personal idiosyncracies, but are linked with the massive Fabian socialist movement in this country. The eleven million copies of Beard's works are a small part of the flood of socialistic material which has discolored American history. His followers and imitators have issued many millions more that are slowly corroding our people's veneration for the wise statesmen who conceived and made viable our constitutional form of government, the envy of all mankind.

"This degrading process is not only reflected in college textbooks, but lurks in the pages of historical novels, in motion pictures and in television programs. . . . The socialist game of 'debunking history' has become a popular literary pastime." 55

The Challenge of the Christian School

The documentation of the perversion of American History and the de-Christian-ization of CHRIST HIS STORY of America is today an accomplished fact. The state and federal programs which provide these textbooks to school districts make no effort to question the accuracy of the historical scholarship which either omits our Found-ing Fathers or questions their position politically. Yet this "changing" of our American history and the subversion of our Founding Fathers could not have oc-curred had not the citadel of America's Christian character—the Christian schools, yielded to *secularism of the curriculum.*

Christian educators of the nineteenth and twentieth century have been incon-sistent. While they have been aware of the many foreign importations as Biblically incorrect and have rejected them theologically, they have permitted the *"modern-ism" of the philosophies of progressive education* to infiltrate their educational programs. Today there is hardly a Christian college or university in America whose education department does not closely approximate the education departments of those secular colleges, universities and liberal seminaries who attack the Bible. The same quality of progressive education is represented in course content, teacher training programs, philosophy and methodology.

The Christian school in America—from kindergarten through the college level—has a most critical role of leadership. If America is to restore her path to CHRIST HIS STORY then Christians must lead the way. The question is not *can* the Christian school restore a true Christian education in America—but *will* the Christian school accept the challenge?

Unless the Christian school in America *separates* itself from the *evolutionary* philosophy which has *formed* and *shaped* the *character of atheism* and *socialism* in our land—unless the Christian school will teach from a basis of *Christian Philosophy of Education* and through *Christian Methods* produce a *Christian Curriculum*—we shall soon be inundated in the flood-tides of *federal secularism.*

Today in *educational modernism* we are dealing with a conception of man which is totally and diametrically opposed to Biblical Creation. The choice becomes our educational position. We either believe that man was created by God as a *"living soul"*. Or we believe that man *evolved* as a physical, emotional, social *organism*—upon whom learning and behavior is *impressed*. We cannot defeat the Pavlovian *stimulus-response* theory of education which determines learning and behavior through the environmental approach, except we once again turn to Scripture for our pattern and program. The Apostle Paul enjoining the Galatians to be *"formed"* from within indicates his concern *"until Christ be formed in you"*.

Just as the Christian of the first century had to seek Christian methods to successfully plant Christianity in the hearts of men surrounded by a pagan world, so today the Christian educator must employ only those methods which are fundamentally Christian in their conception. The real conspiracy of our times is the successful deception of Christians especially in the area of education where socialism has successfully achieved the secularism of America. The Apostle, Paul, warns us that we need to *"beware lest any man spoil you through philosophy and vain deceit, after the tradition of men, after the rudiments of the world, and not after Christ."* Colossians 2:8

If we would restore the American Christian Constitution to its original "end and purpose", we need to re-unite the American Christian home, the American Christian Church, the American Christian School in their individual efforts to construct the elements of Constitutional Liberty.

Part

II

Study Group Plan for *Christian History*

Teacher's Guide for *Christian History*

Teaching and Learning America's Christian History

Study Group Plan for Christian History

Based Upon the Holy Bible,
"the great political text-book of the Patriots"

The Purpose of the Study Group Plan

1. To *identify* the Principles of America's *Christian History* from their source
2. "The Bible, the great political text-book of the patriots"

What Is the Study Group Plan for Christian History?

1. The *chart* on page 63 *Expanding Principles of America's Christian History* indicates seven basic principles which this Study Group Plan will cover systematically through the text, *Christian History of the Constitution of the United States of America*, compiled by Verna M. Hall.
2. Each *Principle* is introduced and defined through pages in this *Guide*. The principles are then *expanded* through the text, *Christian History*.
3. Each *Study Group* may determine for itself how long a period of time is needed for a thorough documentation of each *Principle*.

How Is the Content of Christian History Studied and Read?

1. It is desirable that each individual member of a *Study Group* "*do his homework*" and study and read the text material related to each principle. This leaves more time for discussion.
2. It is valuable to spend some time during each *Study Group* meeting in *specific reading* from the *Bible* and the text, *Christian History*. This may be accomplished   61

TEACHING
AND
LEARNING
AMERICA'S
CHRISTIAN
HISTORY
during an individual report, through summarizing, pin-pointing or high-lighting specific passages which emphasize the *Principle*.

3. *Study Group* meetings need a balance of *study* and *discussion*. Reading should be specifically directed to clarification, identification and documentation of *Principles*.

When Can Discussion Be Profitable in the Study Group Plan?

It is suggested that *discussion* of the *Principles* be related to the following two aspects of the study of *Christian History of the Constitution*.

1. *Historical discussion* of the *Principles*
2. *Current discussion* of the *Principles*

These can be defined as follows:

1. Historical Discussion
Discussion of the *Principle* as it is identified *historically*. The *Study Group Plan* represents the use of the *Bible* as the American Political Textbook. Each *Principle* is *documented* in the Bible and *expanded* historically. *Discussion* should bring forth *America's* individual function in the *Chain of Christianity*.

2. Current Discussion
This represents the challenge to relate the *Principles* of America's *Christian History* as "*measuring rods*" for current problems. Discipline is required on the part of each *Study Group* when a small portion of time is allotted to this aspect because:
a) We are used to discussing *issues* today.
b) We fail to *define* and *identify* basic *principles* when we discuss current issues and problems
c) We are well-informed on the *ever-changing detail* of current issues but
d) We are not yet *well-grounded* on the *changeless fundamental principles* of America's *Christian History*.

Our Founding Father generation was alert to detect the slightest infraction of their liberties, freedoms, rights. This was because they were knowledgeable on *principles*. This enabled them to *stand fast* despite every effort to insinuate legislation which would threaten their right of Christian self-government, their property of conscience, their initiative and enterprise. We, too, need to become so knowledgeable about the *principles* of our *American Christian Constitution* that we can once again restore its *spirit* and *purpose* in the *preservation* of our "*Lives, Liberties and Estates*".

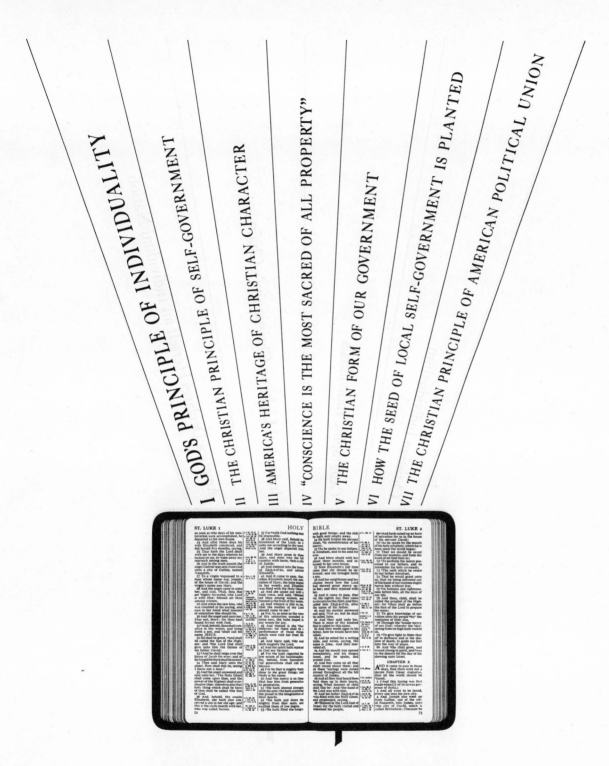

I GOD'S PRINCIPLE OF INDIVIDUALITY

II THE CHRISTIAN PRINCIPLE OF SELF-GOVERNMENT

III AMERICA'S HERITAGE OF CHRISTIAN CHARACTER

IV "CONSCIENCE IS THE MOST SACRED OF ALL PROPERTY"

V THE CHRISTIAN FORM OF OUR GOVERNMENT

VI HOW THE SEED OF LOCAL SELF-GOVERNMENT IS PLANTED

VII THE CHRISTIAN PRINCIPLE OF AMERICAN POLITICAL UNION

Expanding Principles
of America's Christian History

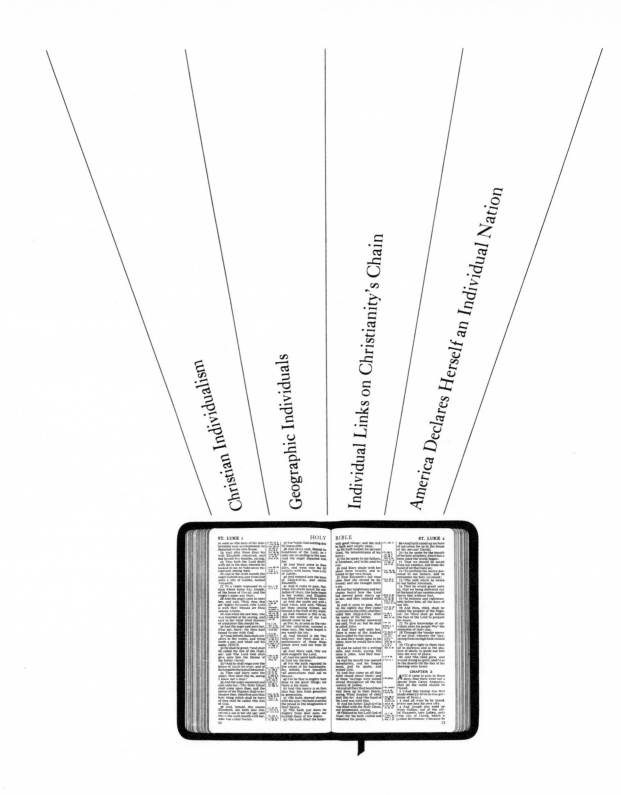

Christian Individualism

Geographic Individuals

Individual Links on Christianity's Chain

America Declares Herself an Individual Nation

God's Principle of Individuality

God's Principle of Individuality

Expanding the First Principle

Statement of the Principle	Everything in God's universe is revelational of God's infinity, God's diversity, God's individuality. God creates distinct individualities. God maintains the identity and individuality of everything which He created.	See Key, pages 141–183
Words related to INDIVIDUALITY	ONENESS, INDIVISIBILITY, WHOLENESS, INTEGRITY, COMPLETENESS. That which is DISTINCT, UNIQUE.	
BIBLICAL *Index*	GENESIS, Chapter One; JOHN 1:3; I CORINTHIANS 12:4–11	

Expanding the Principle
Christian Individualism

The Christian idea of man and government	CHRISTIAN HISTORY: Pages I–XIV CHRISTIAN EDUCATION GUIDE: Page 155
Two political concepts of man: Pagan or Christian	CHRISTIAN HISTORY: Pages 1, 2, 6, 11, 12

65

TEACHING
AND
LEARNING
AMERICA'S
CHRISTIAN
HISTORY

Individual sovereignty	CHRISTIAN HISTORY: Pages 148–;150 270C, 270E.
The representative principle	CHRISTIAN HISTORY: Pages 13–15; 135, 136.

Bible Research

Why is *individualism* separate from *Christ* as dangerous to mankind as any form of *collectivism?*
Where and how does the *Bible* document the following?
1. God's principle of individuality
2. Human individualism
3. The lack of Christian individualism

"Geographic Individuals"

"Each continent has, therefore, a well defined individuality, which fits it for an especial function."

Christian Geography	CHRISTIAN EDUCATION GUIDE: Pages 156, 157 CHRISTIAN HISTORY: Page 6A
"The Continents of History"	CHRISTIAN HISTORY: Pages 3–5
America reserved by God	CHRISTIAN EDUCATION GUIDE: Pages 143, 153 CHRISTIAN HISTORY: Pages 5–16
One indivisible republic	CHRISTIAN HISTORY: Pages 380–390

Individual Links on Christianity's Chain

The Chain of Christianity	CHRISTIAN HISTORY: Page 6A
The Law: "In tables of stone"	CHRISTIAN EDUCATION GUIDE: Page 158 CHRISTIAN HISTORY: Page 270C

The Gospel: ". . . in fleshly tables of the heart"	CHRISTIAN EDUCATION GUIDE: Page 159 CHRISTIAN HISTORY: Page 270C
The Pagan nations and Christianity	CHRISTIAN EDUCATION GUIDE: Pages 159–160
The character of the Greeks	CHRISTIAN EDUCATION GUIDE: Pages 160–162
The character of the Romans	CHRISTIAN EDUCATION GUIDE: Pages 162–165
Roman Civil Law	CHRISTIAN EDUCATION GUIDE: Pages 165–166
John Wycliffe: To place the Bible in the heart of the individual	CHRISTIAN EDUCATION GUIDE: Pages 166–168
Martin Luther: A Bible for the German people	CHRISTIAN EDUCATION GUIDE: Pages 168–170
John Calvin: "The City of God" at Geneva	CHRISTIAN EDUCATION GUIDE: Pages 170–172
The King James Bible: The WORD *free from notes and interpretation*	CHRISTIAN EDUCATION GUIDE: Page 173 Christian History Study Course: Lesson V—"The Bible in English" GUIDE: Page 332
Magna Charta: "From the age of traditional rights . . . to the age of written legislation . . ."	CHRISTIAN EDUCATION GUIDE: Pages 173–175
English Bill of Rights	Christian History Study Course: Lesson VI—"Christian Rights and English Law" GUIDE: Page 343
John Locke: Individual sovereignty in civil government	CHRISTIAN EDUCATION GUIDE: Page 175
Charles de Montesquieu: "The title deeds of humanity"	CHRISTIAN EDUCATION GUIDE: Page 175

TEACHING
AND
LEARNING
AMERICA'S
CHRISTIAN
HISTORY

William Blackstone: Individual rights as the law of the land	CHRISTIAN EDUCATION GUIDE: Page 176
Jamestown: The English representative principle	CHRISTIAN EDUCATION GUIDE: Page 177
Plymouth: Christianity the basis of local self-government	CHRISTIAN EDUCATION GUIDE: Page 178
The Mayflower Compact: "For the glory of God, for the advance of the Christian faith . . ."	CHRISTIAN EDUCATION GUIDE: Page 179

America Declares Herself an Individual Nation

CHRISTIANITY: *Internal liberty produces external freedom*	CHRISTIAN EDUCATION GUIDE: Pages 179–180
The DECLARATION OF INDEPENDENCE	CHRISTIAN EDUCATION GUIDE: Pages 180–183

68

The Christian Principle of Self-Government

Expanding the Second Principle

Statement of Principle

"He knows not how to rule a kingdome, that cannot manage a Province; nor can he wield a Province, that cannot order a City; nor he order a City, that knows not how to regulate a Village; nor he a Village, that cannot guide a Family; nor can that man Govern well a Family that knows not how to Govern himselfe; neither can any Govern himselfe unless his reason be Lord, Will and Appetite her Vassals: nor can Reason rule unlesse herselfe be ruled by God, and (wholy) be obedient to Him."
HUGO GROTIUS, 1654

See Key, pages
184–209

BIBLICAL *Index*   PROVERBS 16:32; I TIMOTHY 3:5

Expanding the Principle
Learning Christian Self-Government

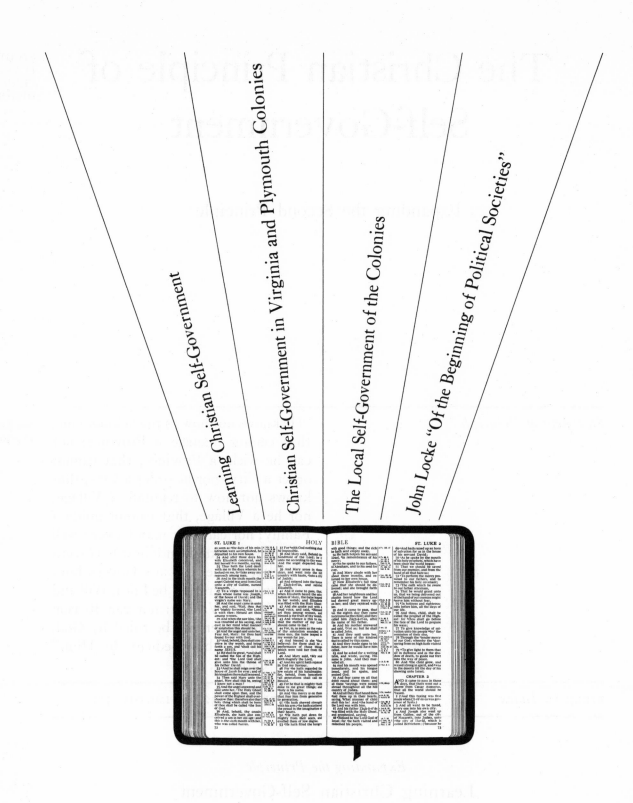

Learning Christian Self-Government

Christian Self-Government in Virginia and Plymouth Colonies

The Local Self-Government of the Colonies

John Locke "Of the Beginning of Political Societies"

The Christian Principle of Self-Government

Defining the term SELF-GOVERNMENT	CHRISTIAN EDUCATION GUIDE: Pages 184–186
Local self-governing congregations	CHRISTIAN HISTORY: Pages 16–28
The BIBLE *as the American political text-book*	CHRISTIAN EDUCATION GUIDE: Study Course, Lesson V, "The Bible in English" page 332

Christian Self-Government in Virginia and Plymouth Colonies

| *Representative government in Virginia Colony* | CHRISTIAN EDUCATION GUIDE: Pages 190–194 |
| *Christian self-government in Plymouth Colony* | CHRISTIAN EDUCATION GUIDE: Pages 194–198 |

The Local Self-Government of the Colonies

New England Township: Congregational form of church government	CHRISTIAN EDUCATION GUIDE: Pages 198–200
Virginia county system: Episcopal form of church government	CHRISTIAN EDUCATION GUIDE: Pages 200–201
Pennsylvania established as a Christian colony	CHRISTIAN EDUCATION GUIDE: Pages 201–203

John Locke "Of the Beginning of Political Societies"

| *John Locke: Christian philosopher of the American Revolution* | CHRISTIAN HISTORY: Pages 50B–56 |
| *Christianity and the importance of individual consent* | CHRISTIAN EDUCATION GUIDE: Pages 204–206 |

TEACHING
AND
LEARNING
AMERICA'S
CHRISTIAN
HISTORY

Locke examines the beginnings of politi-cal societies	CHRISTIAN EDUCATION GUIDE: Study Course, Lesson VII "A Biblical-Politi-cal Index to John Locke", page 353
In a republic the MAJORITY *represents each individual*	CHRISTIAN EDUCATION GUIDE: Pages 206–208
In a democracy the MAJORITY *represents the group*	CHRISTIAN EDUCATION GUIDE: Pages 161, 208–209

Bible Research

When did Israel provide opportunities for self-government which made it *unlike* "all the nations"?

What are some examples of the principle of Christian self-government for individual nations, individual men and women?

How do the two commands of our Lord reveal the principles of the separation of church and state?

America's Heritage of Christian Character

Expanding the Third Principle

Statement of the Principle

"This divine power of the gospel revealed itself to the heathen in the lives of Christians, which showed forth the virtues of Him who had called them out of darkness into his marvellous light, and enabled them to walk as the children of God, in the midst of a perverse generation, among whom they shone as lights in the world! . . . The whole life of the Christian, from the beginning to the end, is a conflict with the world and the powers of darkness, a conflict within and without . . ." NEANDER "MEMORIALS OF A CHRISTIAN LIFE," 1852

See Key, pages
210–224

BIBLICAL *Index*

MATT. 7:24–29; 2 TIM. 4:7; PHIL. 4:13; ACTS 24:16

Expanding the Principle
Faith and Steadfastness

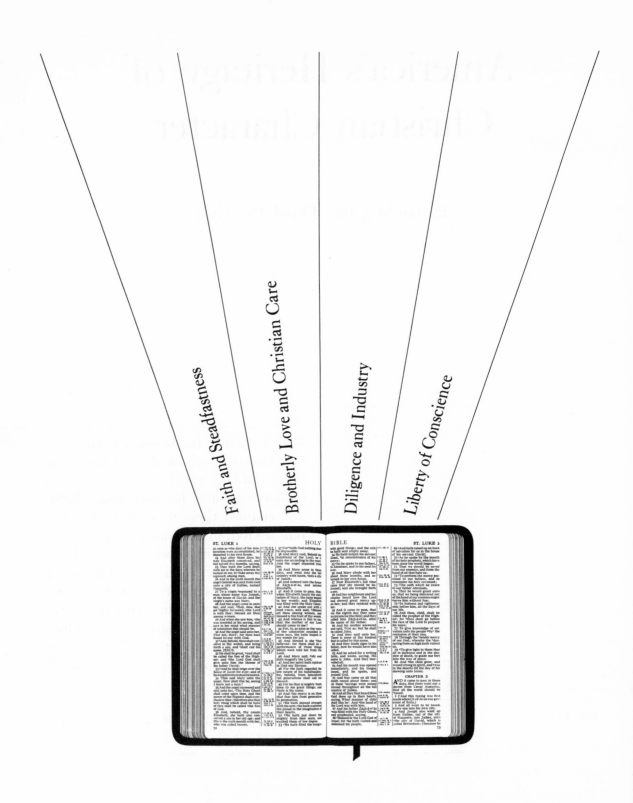

Faith and Steadfastness

Brotherly Love and Christian Care

Diligence and Industry

Liberty of Conscience

America's Heritage of Christian Character

Christian character of the first century	CHRISTIAN EDUCATION GUIDE: Pages 210–212
Life of a Christian contrasted with paganism	CHRISTIAN EDUCATION GUIDE: Pages 212–215
"God's children are like stars" and "like the chamomile"	CHRISTIAN HISTORY: Page 183
The FAITH *and* STEADFASTNESS *of the Pilgrims*	CHRISTIAN EDUCATION GUIDE: Pages 215–219

Brotherly Love and Christian Care

The standard for Christian conduct toward others	CHRISTIAN EDUCATION GUIDE: Pages 219–221

Diligence and Industry

"Christian behavior under persecution"	CHRISTIAN EDUCATION GUIDE: Pages 221–223

Liberty of Conscience

The power of the Gospel in the lives of the Pilgrims	CHRISTIAN EDUCATION GUIDE: Page 224

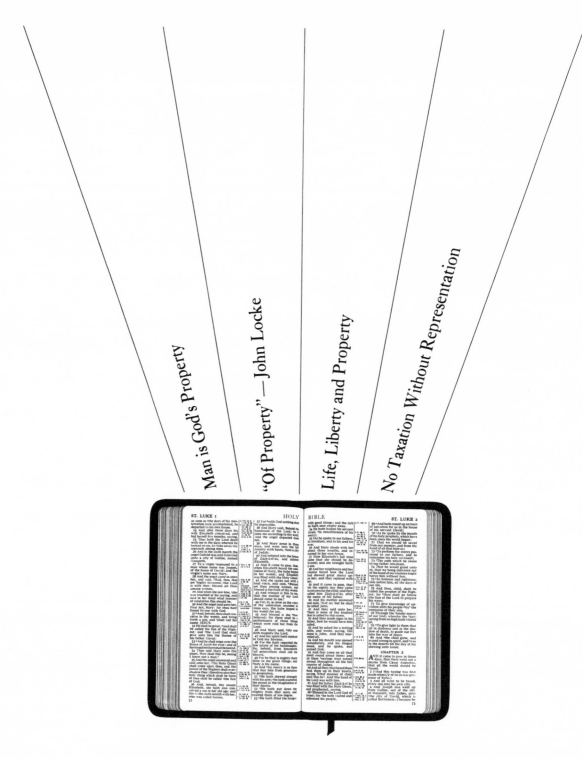

Man is God's Property

"Of Property" —John Locke

Life, Liberty and Property

No Taxation Without Representation

"Conscience is the Most Sacred
of All Property"

"Conscience is the Most Sacred of all Property"

Expanding the Fourth Principle

Statement of the Principle

"For men being the Workmanship of One Omnipotent, and infinitely wise Maker: All the Servants of one Sovereign Master, sent into the World by his Order, and about his Business, they are his Property, whose Workmanship they are, made to last during his, not one anothers Pleasure . . ." "Of Civil-Government" JOHN LOCKE, 1689

See Key, pages 225–239

BIBLICAL *Index*

GENESIS 1:1; ISAIAH 43:7; EPHESIANS 2:10; REVELATION 4:11

Expanding the Principle
Man is God's Property

Blackstone on property

CHRISTIAN EDUCATION GUIDE: Pages 225–227
CHRISTIAN HISTORY: Pages 139–146

TEACHING
AND
LEARNING
AMERICA'S
CHRISTIAN
HISTORY

Christian stewardship and ownership	CHRISTIAN EDUCATION GUIDE: Pages 227–232

"Of Property"—John Locke

The title to property	CHRISTIAN EDUCATION GUIDE: Pages 232–236

Life, Liberty, and Property

"The Blessings of Liberty"	CHRISTIAN EDUCATION GUIDE: Pages 236–238

No Taxation without Representation

Property and representation	CHRISTIAN EDUCATION GUIDE: Pages 238–239

The Christian Form of Our Government

Expanding the Fifth Principle

Statement of the Principle	"As men we have God for our King, and are under the Law of Reason: as Christian, we have Jesus the Messiah for our King, and are under the Law reveal'd by him in the Gospel . . ." "The Reasonableness of Christianity" JOHN LOCKE, 1695	See Key, pages 240–249
BIBLICAL *Index*	DEUTERONOMY 1:9–18: ISAIAH 33:22; MATTHEW 22:35–40	

Expanding the Principle
The Christian Idea of Man and Government

The Christian form of our government	CHRISTIAN EDUCATION GUIDE: Pages 240–245

The Law and the Gospel as the Basis of our Government

The Christian Idea of Man and Government

The Law and the Gospel as the Basis of Our Government

A Government Resting on Moral Principles

The Pulpit and American Independence

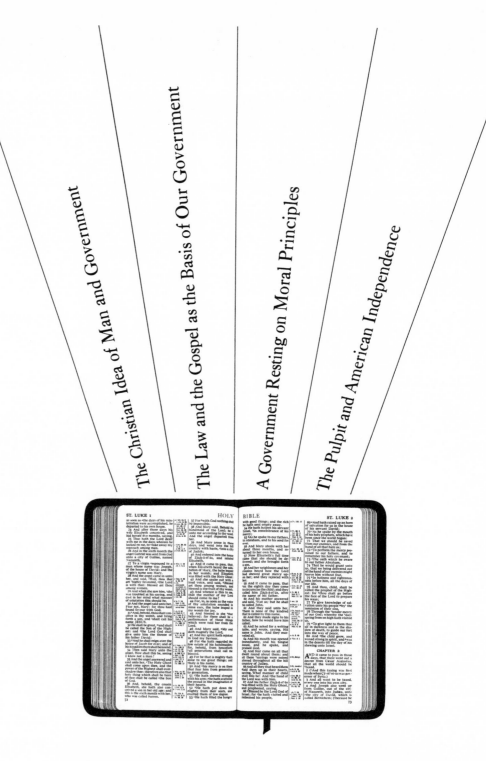

The Christian Form of Our
Government

Our Christian heritage	CHRISTIAN EDUCATION GUIDE: Pages 245–246
Christianity and education	CHRISTIAN EDUCATION GUIDE: Pages 246–247
Representation	CHRISTIAN HISTORY: Pages 13–15; 135–136; 254–257; 270C, 270E
The Separation of Powers: the three branches of government	CHRISTIAN HISTORY: Pages 93–98; 134, 135, 138
Our Dual Form of government	CHRISTIAN HISTORY: Pages 148, 149, 358

"A Government Resting on Moral Principles"

Christian leadership	CHRISTIAN EDUCATION GUIDE: Pages 247–248

The Pulpit and American Independence

Patriotic piety	CHRISTIAN EDUCATION GUIDE: Pages 248–249

81

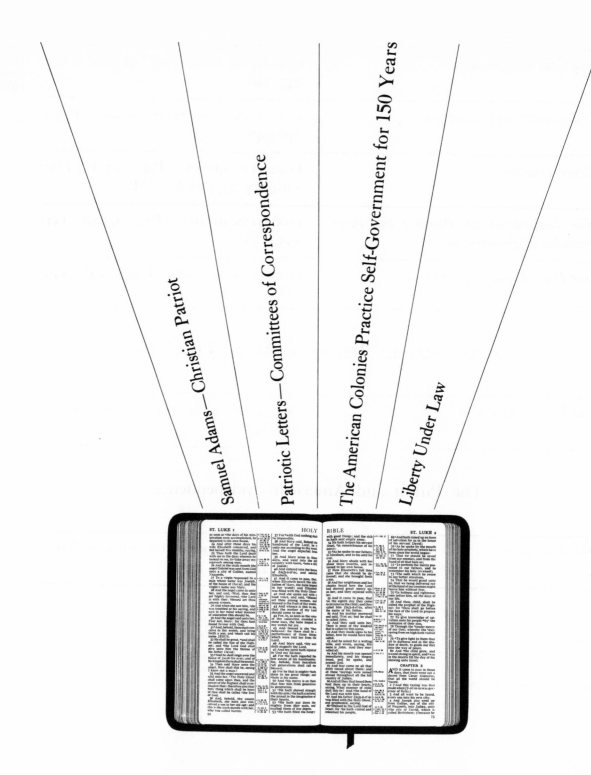

Samuel Adams—Christian Patriot

Patriotic Letters—Committees of Correspondence

The American Colonies Practice Self-Government for 150 Years

Liberty Under Law

How the Seed of Local
Self-Government is Planted

How the Seed of Local Self-Government is Planted

Expanding the Sixth Principle

Statement of the Principle

"The government of the United States is acknowledged by the wise and good of other nations, to be the most free, impartial, and righteous government of the world; but all agree, that for such a government to be sustained many years, the principles of truth and righteousness, taught in the Holy Scriptures, must be practised. *The rulers must govern in the fear of God, and the people obey the laws.*" EMMA WILLARD, 1843

See Key, pages 250–261

BIBLICAL *Index*

DEUTERONOMY 10:12–14; ISAIAH 9:6; LUKE 9:6

Expanding the Principle
Samuel Adams—Christian Patriot

Samuel Adams works for liberty

CHRISTIAN EDUCATION GUIDE: Pages 251–254

TEACHING
AND
LEARNING
AMERICA'S
CHRISTIAN
HISTORY

The Christian character of Samuel Adams	CHRISTIAN EDUCATION GUIDE: Pages 255–257

Patriotic Letters—Committees of Correspondence

Committees to educate in principles	CHRISTIAN EDUCATION GUIDE: Pages 257–259

The American Colonies Practice Self-Government for 150 Years

"Self-government increases the dignity of the man"	CHRISTIAN EDUCATION GUIDE: Pages 259–260

"Liberty Under Law"

The rule of Gospel principles	CHRISTIAN EDUCATION GUIDE: Page 261

The Christian Principle
of American Political Union

Expanding the Seventh Principle

Statement of the Principle	"Till we all come in the unity of the faith, and of the knowledge of the Son of God, unto a perfect man, unto the measure of the stature of the fulness of Christ . . ." EPHESIANS 4:13	See Key, pages 262–268
BIBLICAL *Index*	I CORINTHIANS I:IO; PSALMS 133:I; EPHESIANS 4:1–3	

Expanding the Principle
Boston Patriots and the Tea Act

Christians "Stand Firm"	CHRISTIAN EDUCATION GUIDE: Pages 263–264

Boston Port Closed—A Day of Fasting and Prayer

Public humiliation, fasting and prayer	CHRISTIAN EDUCATION GUIDE: Pages 264–265

85

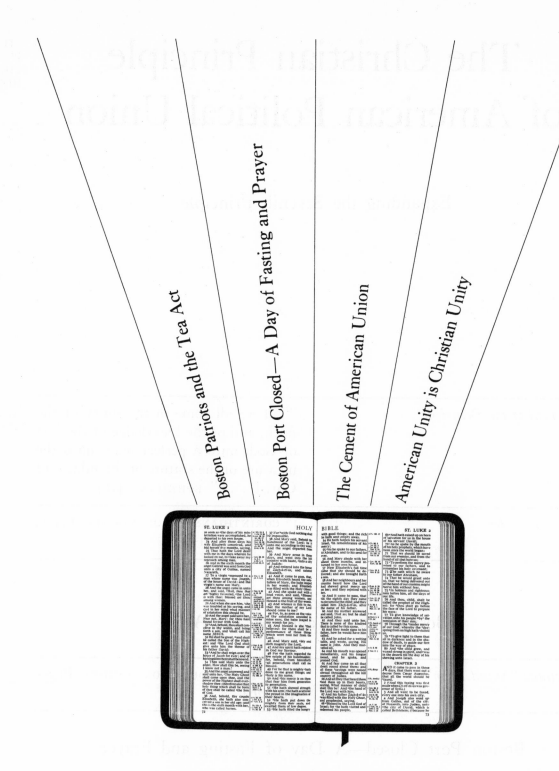

Boston Patriots and the Tea Act

Boston Port Closed—A Day of Fasting and Prayer

The Cement of American Union

American Unity is Christian Unity

The Christian Principle
of American Political Union

The Cement of American Union

The Town-Meeting as a school of self-government	CHRISTIAN EDUCATION GUIDE: Pages 265–266

"In ye fellowship of ye Gospell"	CHRISTIAN EDUCATION GUIDE: Page 267

American Unity is Christian Unity

"Unity of the Spirit"	CHRISTIAN EDUCATION GUIDE: Page 268

Teacher's Guide
for Christian History

The Principle Approach to American Christian Education

THE PRINCIPLE APPROACH is America's historic Christian method of Biblical reasoning which makes the Truths of God's Word the basis of every subject in the school curriculum.

The Principle Approach begins by restoring the 4 R's to teaching and learning:

1st R: the RESEARCHING of God's Word to identify basic principles

2nd R: the REASONING from these Biblical principles to their identification in the subjects of the curriculum

3rd R: the RELATING of Biblical principles to each student, to Christian character, to Christian self-government, to the stewardship of God-given talents

4th R: the RECORDING or the written record by each student of the individual application of the principles

Does the Bible provide us with any precedent for reasoning from principles? Consider the following passages:

Acts 17:2 "*And Paul, as his manner was, went in unto them, and three sabbath days reasoned with them out of the scriptures.*"

Acts 24:25 "*And as he reasoned of righteousness, temperance, and judgment to come, Felix trembled, and answered, Go thy way for this time; when I have a convenient season, I will call for thee.*"

1 Peter 3:15 "*But sanctify the Lord God in your hearts: and be ready always to give an answer to every man that asketh you a reason of the hope that is in you with meekness and fear.*"

The Pilgrims learned Biblical reasoning from Pastor John Robinson during their twelve years in Holland. Thus they were prepared to extend Christian principles into civil government and to deal with the problems that confronted them in the

88

New World. Challenged on the *Mayflower* by rebellious "strangers," they wrote the *Mayflower Compact*, so that every man might voluntarily share in making and keeping the laws. Confronted with distrustful Indians, they made a mutual pact and maintained a long-lasting peace. Faced with starvation, William Bradford, Governor of Plymouth Plantation, "had the courage and wisdom" to shift from "labor in common" to the responsibility of individual enterprise and private property. For more than twenty years the Pilgrims labored to repay their original debt to the venture capitalists in England who had financed the voyage of the *Mayflower*. There were many opportunities to escape from this responsibility but they held to the obligation as a matter of Christian conscience. The Pilgrims were consistent because of their application of Christian truths or principles.

The ability to reason from the Word of God and to relate its principles to every area of life was characteristic of the American clergy prior to the American Revolution. The ministers of the Gospel understood civil government because they knew church government. Their election and artillery sermons identified "the principles of civil government with the principles of Christianity."

At the time of the *Declaration of Independence* the quality of education had enabled the colonies to achieve a degree of literacy from "70% to virtually 100%." This was not education restricted to the few. Modern scholarship reports "the prevalence of schooling and its accessibility to most segments of the population." Moses Coit Tyler, historian of American Literature, indicates the colonist's "familiarity with history . . . extensive legal learning . . . lucid exposition of constitutional principles, showing, indeed, that somehow, out into that American wilderness had been carried the very accent of cosmopolitan thought and speech." When the American State Papers arrived in Europe they surprised and astonished the "enlightened men." Americans had been dismissed as "illiterate backwoodsmen" as, perhaps, "law-defying revolutionists." But when these papers were read they were found to contain "nearly every quality indicative of personal and national greatness."

Dr. Lawrence A. Cremin in his study of American Education from 1607 to 1789, credits the high quality of American education to the Bible, "the single most important cultural influence in the lives of Anglo-Americans." The Bible "contained the means to salvation, the keys to good and evil, the rules by which to live, and the standards against which to measure the conduct of prince and pastor."

After the establishment of our American Republic, young Noah Webster began to write American Christian textbooks consistently teaching the Principle Approach. Why was the "blue-backed" speller an all-time best seller in American Education? It set forth the principles of spelling which provided educational independence for each individual who mastered the principles. So successful was this method of teaching and learning that the Bible and Webster's speller continued across the continent as Christianity expanded westward.

America's Biblical Education produced America's Christian History and Constitution. The method was the Principle Approach. Let us restore the foundation of American Independence.

89

TEACHING
AND
LEARNING
AMERICA'S
CHRISTIAN
HISTORY

The Need for Christian Method in American Christian Education

'The whole life of the Christian from beginning to the end, is a conflict with the world and the powers of darkness, a conflict within and without.' Neander

The Apostle, Paul, has reminded us of the ceaseless activity of the Devil and urges us to *"resist steadfast in the faith"*:

Be sober, be vigilant: because your adversary the devil, as a roaring lion, walketh about, seeking whom he may devour. (1 Peter 5:8)

As the new Federal Aid programs are calculated to include Christian schools, we recognize how, despite the tremendous growth of these schools in the last decade, there is real danger that they will indeed be *devoured*. If secular educators can now—once and for all—establish the fact that the Christian school and the state school are alike in their curriculum, choice of textbooks, use of method—we shall indeed become officially a part of the political program which is building the modern city and tower of Babel. It is significant that God in His infinite wisdom destroyed Babel and refuted man's efforts to establish conformity and uniformity—thus defying God's infinity, diversity, and immensity. In the New Testament the Day of Pentecost exemplified the unity of the Spirit through the diversity of Spirit wherein every man heard in his own tongue *"the wonderful works of God."*

But if Christian education is truly devoted to building for God and is not devoted to "aggrandizing the state"—then we must now be prepared to *"give an answer to every man that asketh you a reason of the hope that is in you."* (1 Peter 3:15)

Christians of the first century, concerned lest their children be corrupted with eastern heathen philosophy, were careful to instruct them in the doctrines of their holy religion. But the intellectual temptation to investigate and explore all knowledge led to the attempt to mix philosophy and religion. This "alienated the minds of many in the following centuries from Christianity itself."

We may have been tempted to measure Christian Education by man's standards but today the demand is upon us to *"give an answer"* as to how and why Christian Education must fulfil its special ministry for Christ. As we understand that the conquest of our nation is being achieved through secularization—and as we realize that secularization works most specifically through education, we must begin to evaluate the Christian school by Christian standards. In this age of atheism, materialism, and socialism, we may fall into the very net which is laid, and become ensnared *"through philosophy and vain deceit, after the tradition of men, after the rudiments of the world, and not after Christ."* (Colossians 2:8)

90

Progressive Education Is Political Not Educational

As educators in Christian schools we need to become aware of the fact that progressive education is not *educationally oriented*. Progressive education is *politically oriented* to produce both the *philosophy* and the *character* of socialism. It is also quite evident that even Christian schools have been permeated with the evolutionary philosophy—particularly in the use of evolutionary and progressive methods of teaching. Our purpose here, however, is neither to document nor to debate about the degree to which Christian schools are using secular methods, texts, or teachers. Our purpose is, instead, to ask ourselves how and to what degree can we establish Christian standards so that the *philosophy*, the *curriculum* and the *methods* "testify of me"—Christ.

The Christian History of America

There may be those who state that America is pluralistic, Judeo-Christian, or non-Christian. America's Christian founding, the Christian character of her people, and the Christian principles which formed the basis of her Christian Constitution —all of this has been fully documented in Miss Verna M. Hall's compilation *Christian History of the Constitution of the United States of America*. The Third Volume which Miss Hall has compiled, dealing with the American Revolution, abundantly demonstrates how completely the Christian character and conviction of Americans can be discovered in the primary sources of her history. America's *Christian History* is evident in the provincial and congressional journals, in the letters of her statesmen and in the sermons of her clergymen, in the governmental proclamations, in the newspapers, diaries and archives written at the period when CHRIST HIS STORY of America was being recorded. Because the documentation is so rich and so abundant it is our purpose to demonstrate through the development of an *American Christian Educational Program* how present-day Christians can once again teach Christian principles which relate to every subject in the school curriculum.

The Need to Practice Christian Method

While there are few textbooks written from the standpoint of Christian philosophy it is still possible for Christian Schools to establish a school curriculum which is Christian in content. Like the widow of old whom Elisha questioned "Tell me, what hast thou in the house?" we must look at what God hath already provided. In returning the documentation of *America's Christian History*—a documentation

TEACHING
AND
LEARNING
AMERICA'S
CHRISTIAN
HISTORY

which has been deleted from our educational systems, our seminaries and our Christian colleges for over one hundred years—we can begin with what we have in our own house.

This *Christian Education Guide* for *Teaching and Learning America's Christian History* is the effort to establish *Christian Method* in the curriculum of the Christian School. While it might look as if we were dealing with the subject of Christian government—actually, we are teaching *principles* which are basic to every Christian in every area of life. For what *constitutes* the *Constitution* is what *constitutes* the life and character of our people. If the American character has been shaped, moulded, and formed by the *environmental* approach to life and living—we shall be *externally* or *materially* oriented and educated. If instead, as we understand Christian education to begin with *salvation*—the internal commitment of heart and mind to the saving grace of JESUS CHRIST—then we are concerned as to whether we are extending the Christian approach—internal—to our methods of teaching.

Psychological Atheism

Secular methods have a *psychological* and *behavioral* base and they deal with the individual as though he were a higher order of animal. There are certain recognizable aspects to this approach to learning which need to be pointed out if the Christian educator is not going to use these same methods and thus contribute to the development of a *socio-psycho-politico* individual whose behavior will be responsive to the *socialistic atheistic* demands of our times.

Many of the once distinct systems of psychology such as behaviorism or conditioned response, Gestalt or Organismic psychology, Connectionism or Stimulus Response psychology, today find themselves *in agreement* concerning the basic assumptions about man. Ernest R. Hilgard of Stanford University, one of America's most eminent psychologists, in an article "Learning Theory and its Applications" summarizes the major principles as contained within the following three fields:

"*A. Principles emphasized within S-R theory; B. Principles emphasized with cognitive theory; C. Principles from personality theory. I believe these principles to be in large part acceptable to all parties, and the affiliation with one or another source is a matter of emphasis rather than of controversy.*" Stanford Institute for Communication Research, 1960

Pavlov and the Non-Reflective Response

There are a number of identifiable steps to what can be essentially described as *behavioral conditioning* through Stimulus-Response. These stem from the most notable experiment of our time in its influence upon educational programs in Russia and the United States. Pavlov's experiment with a dog *conditioned* the animal to produce saliva with the ringing of a bell. The *learning* progressed to the point where the bell-stimulus would produce saliva without the presence of the food. There is much evidence to indicate that we in America have created a society in which a majority of individuals respond as they have been *conditioned* to specific stimuli—whether there is evidence of reality or fact. We note the *immediate* and *non-reflective* response to terms such as "extremist", "radical right", "hate groups" and others. These stimuli represent the more obvious cues to the triggering of response. Far more dangerous are the hidden stimuli in much of the provocative advertising which Ernest Dichter, President of the Institute for Motivational Research, has documented in his volume, *The Strategy of Desire*, an authoritative description of the science of persuasion. (Doubleday, 1960) We shall characterize four steps used to *"change the behavior"* of organisms which are implicit in the evolutionary doctrine of "learning":

1. STIMULATE: To excite, rouse, goad, or provoke into action, through physical or psychological stimuli. Organism's desires justified as needs—legitimate to his status.

2. MOTIVATE: Organism not committed to *"subdue"* the environment to the demands of conscience. Organism is compelled to *submit* to external environment—in spite of diminishing conscience.

3. ENCULTURATE: Satisfaction achieved or "learned" through successful adaptation and adjustment to the environment—physical, social, religious, economical, political.

4. INDOCTRINATE: Conviction reinforced through satisfaction of physio-psychological desires. *Truth* is what is true—what works. *Knowledge* is discovered through *experience*. It is not established by authority.

What is the result of such psychological and political "conditioning"? Let us briefly compare psychological atheism as a basis for building teaching methods with the Christian approach to learning and behavior:

Pavlov	Christ
Conditioned Learning and Behavior	*"Keep thy heart with all diligence; for out of it are the issues of life."*
Externally oriented. Organism *acted upon*—provoked. Impression.	Internally oriented. Individual action proceeds from within. Expression.

93

TEACHING
AND
LEARNING
AMERICA'S
CHRISTIAN
HISTORY

Man is a physio-psychological organism, sensitive to his physical, social, political environment.

1. STIMULATE the organism to need, want, desire.

2. MOTIVATE the organism to satisfy needs externally. Consumer oriented.

3. ENCULTURATE the organism to conform and shape desires and their satisfaction to society-approved behavior.

4. INDOCTRINATE. Deny doctrine of authority of God or His Word. Validate truth through sense knowledge.

Man is a *"living soul"* responsive to the demands of *Conscience.*

1. INSPIRE the heart to *"Commit thy way unto the Lord."*

2. CONSECRATE the individual to CHRIST. *"He shall give thee the desires of thy heart."* Production oriented.

3. CULTIVATE *"the new man"*. *"Bring every thought into conformity with Christ."*

4. INSTRUCT in *"knowledge of salvation"*. *"But continue thou in the things which thou hast learned and hast been assured of, knowing of whom thou hast learned them; And that from a child thou hast learned the holy scriptures, which are able to make thee wise unto salvation through faith which is in Christ Jesus."* (2 Tim. 3:14, 15)

A Christian "Environment" for Learning

How does the Christian Educator evaluate whether he or she is basing teaching methods upon a secular or upon a Christian philosophy? Must the Christian Educator "scrap" all use of the "environment" in the arrangement of classroom displays and in the presentation of lessons? How should the Christian Educator regard the use of Audio-Visual Aids? Should they be "discarded" inasmuch as they are particularly geared to learning through the senses?

These and many other like questions must be viewed from the position of God's Word. In the Genesis account of Creation earth is *secondary* because God commands man to "subdue" the earth and "have dominion" over "every living thing that moveth upon the earth". Thus the "environment" was not to shape man, already created by God, but, instead man was, according to God's command, to "be fruitful, and multiply, and replenish the earth, and subdue it".

94

The secular educator creates a *causative environment* to which the student must become *responsive*. He becomes *conditioned* to look to the *external environment*—social, economic, religious, political—before he determines how he will act. Secular education helps each student construct *an individual radar system* oriented to the external and enabling him to *read* his universe—to become *sensitized* to the environment. The result of this method of education has indeed created a generation of individuals who can "discern the face of the sky" but cannot "discern the signs of the times".

The Christian Educator from the position of God's Word must *subdue* the environment rather than *submit* to it. In teaching students his use of the environment should emphasize the *internal demands of conscience* as *causative* of behavior and action and the external environment as *effect*. Just as the heavens and the earth mirror forth or reflect the Divine Original, God, so the classroom environment reflects or mirrors forth God as Creator, Preserver, Legislator. For in themselves the heavens and the earth and man are nothing. They have significance only as they "*declare the glory of God*". Thus the Christian learns to *subdue* the earth for God's purpose and according to His will.

God's Creation begins when there is "no form" to the heavens and the earth. Into this empty, dark void, the Spirit of God moves bringing light, order, identity and blessing. So must the Christian Educator, allowing the Holy Spirit to work in him, bring "form" and "shape" to subjects with the light of God's Word. Perhaps the following three directional statements of the Creator may suggest a criteria for the Christian Educator—a standard by which the classroom "environment" may be evaluated:

Biblical Standards for Christian Education

1. "*Let there be light*" Let the light of God's Word appear in every subject.

2. "*Let there be a firmament in the midst of the waters, and let it divide the waters from the waters*" Let God's Truth be the fixed principle or "firmament"—separating the waters above from those which were under.

3. "*Let the waters under the heaven be gathered together unto one place, and let the dry land appear*" Let the basic elements of every subject appear clearly identified and clearly named.

Because the Christian Educator does believe in *absolutes* it is impossible to take *relativistic* positions in regard to the psychological basis of learning which regards man as an *organism evolved* through the animal stages of development to his present position. God commanded man to have dominion over "every living thing". Are the behavior and learning abilities of man to be derived from the study of animals? 95

TEACHING
AND
LEARNING
AMERICA'S
CHRISTIAN
HISTORY
This the Christian Educator must determine from his own position of the inerrancy of Holy Scripture.

The increase of rioting and "mob" activity in our nation is indicative of the kind and quality of behavior which is produced when man classifies himself as a "higher order" of animal—needing not the salvation of a Saviour to determine his behavior —but instead psychological analysis. Man's depravity has only one avenue of redemption—and even as the *saving grace of* JESUS CHRIST redeems him from animality it also enables him to walk on two feet like man whom God created "in the image of God". The posture of humility for a Christian is not that of a beast in the mud—but of a man on his knees in prayer.

As we continue to sharpen these two positions of learning we may not be exhaustive but we shall be definitive.

Characteristics of a Classroom Environment

PAVLOV	CHRIST
Goal for learning:	Goal for learning:
To change human/animal behavior.	To provide for the growth of Christian character.

Bulletin Boards, Charts, Diagrams, Maps, etc.

Purpose: To motivate for learning.	Purpose: To teach the knowledge of God in all subjects.
To arouse, to provoke, to stimulate attitudinal response to projections of subject areas.	To impart exact knowledge of God's Word—basic principles, specific rules and facts. To establish the elements and the fixed boundaries for each subject.

Use of Audio-Visual Aids

Purpose: Impression through sensory avenues.	Purpose: Expression of ideas.
Stimulus through eye-ear to provoke impression and response in the organism. Establish a "neural circuit" through S-R.	Develop "critical faculties". Films etc. evaluated for their accuracy of content, historical emphasis, philosophy and psychological premises for learning.

Less dependence upon films—wider use of many texts and references for individual search to verify and amplify a subject and to discuss and debate a position.

Records:
Language labs for foreign language learning. Audio recall and reproduction of sound patterns. Continuous feedback. Repetition.

Records:
For study of cultural fields of literature, music, drama. Not for imitation but for information and inspiration.

Tachistoscope: Quantitative
Speed Reading to accelerate eye movement. Paced exercises. Reading becomes a visual skill. Quantitative response—speed & accuracy.

Qualitative Reading Skills:
Teaching for mastery of "idea" skills—outlining, re-phrasing summarization, etc.

Teaching Machines or Programmed Learning

Teacher-perfect machine. "Bite sized" subject. Individualized with mechanical monitor. Correct learning reinforced or rewarded. Immediate correction of errors. Complete mechanization, regimentation and control of teacher, subject, student.

Teacher response to challenge of subject. Greater dependence upon the inspiration of the Holy Spirit less dependence upon textbook teaching. Appeal to individual hearts, minds and souls of students. Horizons of thought, and imagination expanded.

Expanding God's Principle of Individuality to Basic School Subjects

Arithmetic and Mathematics

Research in the changes which have occurred in the Arithmetic curriculum indicate that the pendulum swung from abstract problems and excessive drill to the "incidental, experience approach" wherein the only arithmetic students learned 97

TEACHING
AND
LEARNING
AMERICA'S
CHRISTIAN
HISTORY
arose from their own *"concrete experiences"*. This was coincidental with the entire thrust to make learning *"environmental"*—of the senses and emotions, rather than *"academic"*—of the mind and heart. This was also the change from *qualitative* to *quantitative* thinking.

Today we are being subjected to more political tampering with our educational system by the introduction of *"new math,"* or the *collective* approach to learning—*grouping, set theory, association.* The emphasis is again less and less upon mental skill and academic competence—but rather upon *perception* and *comprehension* of *quantitative* aspects of number. The breakdown of the integrity of whole numbers and their identity is related to the breakdown of the integrity and identity of the individual in our society. Many will challenge this statement! Verify for yourself the increasing emphasis upon the constant changing of values, even the basic number system itself. Ask yourself where does the student learn absolutes or fixed principles upon which he can rely? We are told today that *absolutes* are *relative* to given situations—mathematical or otherwise.

How can the Christian educator relate the teaching of arithmetic or Mathematics to *God's Principle of Individuality?* Perhaps the following questions might prove helpful as you determine if this subject is making a contribution to Christian conviction in your curriculum.

1. Do my students think of arithmetic or Mathematics as *revelational of God's universe* or as revelational of man's world? Do I teach this subject as revealing the following aspects of God?
   a) Dr. Mark Fakkema in his *Christian Philosophy and Its Educational Implications*, Book Three, indicates that Mathematics proclaim that
      1) "God is unchangeable"
      2) "That God is a God of order"
      3) "That God is a God of system"
      4) "That God is a God of precision"
      5) "That dependability is one of God's attributes"
      6) "That God's infinitude is perhaps more clearly revealed in Mathematics than in any other school subject"
2. Do my students learn to recognize and identify *basic principles* from the arithmetical processes which I teach?
3. Do I teach *specific rules* or *laws* which my students can depend upon to occur in arithmetic? Do they relate these to the *order, system* and *precision* of God's universe?
4. Do I depend completely upon *grouping* to teach *number facts*—such as the addition facts, subtraction facts, multiplication tables etc.?
5. Am I producing the *politically* and *academically* *"free and independent"* student —who is less and less dependent upon "concrete tools" of learning and more and more independent in his ability to mentally perform arithmetical processes with speed and accuracy?

6. Do I constantly recall that arithmetic or Mathematics is an academic subject and should produce mental competence on the part of my students? Am I gearing it more to the professional fields than to the technological alone?
7. To what extent do I recognize mathematical skill as an *individual* not a *social skill*—to be employed to fulfil God's purpose in His Plan not merely as an asset for the Great Society? See *Christian History*, page 6 paragraph "Individual benefit".

Reading and Literature

American education spends more time, money and technique endeavoring to teach reading than any other subject in the school curriculum. If our efforts and our knowledge of this field were consistent with our success we should not be suspicious. But we have a higher proportion of non-readers or inadequate and incompetent readers than at any time in our history. We have the means of success but we are not successful. Why? One teacher knew when she said "The purpose is to take away our ability as a nation to read the WORD OF GOD". That statement is not inconsistent with the political developments concerning the position of the Bible and prayer in our educational systems.

Today with a system of fundamental phonics it is possible to teach children to read within the first few years of primary schooling. At the end of two, or at the most three years, students should be able to read, first of all, the Holy Bible, second, worthwhile classics, third, begin to deal with *ideas* and *ideals*. We prolong, through psychological justification, the mastery of basic reading skills thus closing the doors to individual satisfaction and individual challenge through reading.

God's Principle of Individuality, with its demand for distinction and identification, should function as teachers in Christian schools begin to break the *"lock-step"* of mediocrity and literally enable their students to take wing again. It might also prove to be a means of *widening the gulf* between the state school and the Christian school—enabling parents to see more visible evidence that the Christian school places a true value upon the *liberation of the individual*—spiritually, academically and politically.

The Cultivation of Reading

Only a word can be said here about the need for Christian schools to give serious scrutiny to the *content* of their reading curriculum. Again, the *collective* approach of grouping reading content within graded Readers has watered down both *context* and *content*. Individual books and individual authors are given decreasing attention.

TEACHING
AND
LEARNING
AMERICA'S
CHRISTIAN
HISTORY

Selection is not as qualitative as the selection of foods to be fed a family and often the *putrid*, the *sordid and rotting*, the *poisonous* articles are not eliminated. Again the BIBLE needs to become the standard of judgement and books dealing with *character*, *conscience* and *country* once again brought into focus.

Reading is a subject whose many facets can best be appreciated through *constant* and *specific cultivation*. Does every classroom have a *reading period* where teacher and students experience together rich moments of inspiration, excitement and joy? There are many wonderful books of content and character which should be introduced by the adult teacher to the students that they may *savour* fine writing and inspiring literature. This habit of what used to be called the *family reading hour* has never been equalled as an educational tool for building and cultivating the love of fine books. It should be continued through college and presents the teacher with invaluable opportunities for the development of critical skills, understanding and appreciation.

Individualization of Literature

Today is the day of the *blur*, the *blend* the *blob*. There are no distinctions—only gray. This is evident in the de-emphasis of study on the characteristics of specific literature forms. The *essay*—particularly suited to the definition and development of *ideas*, is not taught for individual achievement. *Biography*, or the *identification of character*, has been viewed from an "existentialist" position and, like much of the subjective modern art, is only identified in terms of "*sensitivity to feelings*". It does not represent the content of individual character. Shakespeare, *bard of the Bible*, is slipping away—for he is too clear and distinct in his portrayal of good and evil, too demanding of the student and the teacher. Again, education must be regarded as part of the total philosophy of life which one accepts. Our secular schools are an integral part of the political, social, economic, psychological indoctrination of man as *evolution's climax*. Therefore education is not devoted to the Christian idea of man—man whom God created and endowed and for whom God has planned. The preparation for the world to come must not *preclude* Christ's pre-eminence in the here and now of today's world. There cannot possibly be two worlds—that of God and that of man. God is the alone—Creator and it is His universe with which we wish to deal. Man's tower of Babel fell once—and it always will when he attempts to build without God.

Language

Noah Webster in his extensive research on the origin of language opposed the evolutionary concept that language *evolved* along with the progressive development of animal life—from grunts to groans. This statement occurs in his *Introduction to an American Dictionary of the English Language*, 1856: "An Introductory Disser-

tation on the Origin, History, and Connection, of the Languages of Western Asia,
and Europe, and with an Explanation of the Principles on Which Languages are
Formed":

Origin of Language

" . . . *We further read, that God brought to Adam the fowls and beasts he had made,
and that Adam gave them names; and that when his female companion was made, he
gave her a name. After the eating of the forbidden fruit, it is stated that God addressed
Adam and Eve, reproving them for their disobedience, and pronouncing the penalties
which they had incurred. In the account of these transactions, it is further related that
Adam and Eve both replied to their Maker, and excused their disobedience.*

"*If we admit, what is the literal and obvious interpretation of this narrative, that vocal
sounds or words were used in these communications between God and the progenitors
of the human race, it results that Adam was not only endowed with intellect for understanding his Maker, or the signification of words, but was furnished both with the faculty
of speech and with speech itself, or the knowledge and use of words as signs of ideas,
and this before the formation of the woman. Hence we may infer that language was
bestowed on Adam, in the same manner as all his other faculties and knowledge, by
supernatural power; or, in other words, was of* divine origin. *It is, therefore, probable,
that* language, *as well as the faculty of speech, was the* Immediate Gift of God."

Spelling

It is no longer necessary to confound this subject by the *incidental, accidental*
approach of the "*activity unit*". Nor is it necessary to confine spelling to the mean-
ingless memorization of unrelated word lists. There are methods of teaching spelling
which include for the student a systematic approach in which specific word-
construction skills are learned and specific rules mastered. Thus, again, God's
Principle of Individuality can direct the basic spelling program so that the individual student can be provided with the needed tools for competence in writing and
reading.

How is God revealed in this subject? Does spelling enable us to understand God's
"*speech and language*" and to "*speak the mystery of Christ*" and "*to write*" the
things which we learn of God? Spelling is a distinct subject—not to be blurred nor
blended as a part of the language arts. It has a unique and individual function to
play in communicating—not man's needs, desires, aims, ideas—but, primarily, to
communicate the specifics of God's will to man.

Gospel from the Saxon means *god-spell*. "God, good, and *spell*, history, relation,
narration, word, speech, that which is uttered, announced, sent, or communicated;
answering to the . . . L. *evangelium*, a good or joyful message."

TEACHING
AND
LEARNING
AMERICA'S
CHRISTIAN
HISTORY

Handwriting

In an age when man has neglected the *Word of God*, he also neglects to accept stewardship of the ability to use a pen or pencil.

"Millions of dollars are lost by American businesses each year because of illegible handwriting." Handwriting Foundation, Washington, D.C.

But this statement alone reveals a far greater loss than merely the dollars and cents resulting from indecipherable handwriting. It reflects the loss of Christian character —the loss of care and attention to detail—the loving care which must characterize clear, concise handwriting. The marvel of our Founding Father period when they wrote voluminously with scratching quills, is that these letters, diaries, state papers, are legible and bespeak an attitude towards life which regards each act as revelational of one's Christian conviction.

The word *character* has a most interesting meaning. It refers externally to "letters" or *"distinctive quality of any kind strongly marked"*. Internally it refers to distinctive aspects of character. Thus, as we learn the identification and re-production of individual letters, we shall also be *imprinting the mark* of our Christian character. God's attention to detail and to its perfection can be seen in all of His creation and His infinite attention may be likened to "small rain upon the tender herb".

Let us perfect our ministry as Christian teachers in Christian schools. Let us be willing to honestly evaluate and appraise our curriculum, our methods and our basic philosophy. Never was there a time in the history of Christianity than this time in America when Christian schools have a challenge placed before them to *"come out and be separate"*.

Extending Christian Self-Government to Christian Classroom Control

One of the first concerns of the teacher is classroom control. When this is established the teacher can perform successfully as a teacher. When classroom control is not achieved, the teacher becomes a policeman—imposing harsh measures of discipline to counteract inconsistency, laxness, or poor classroom management. In the absence of good classroom government the teacher also becomes a fireman—sirening about to handle small fires of insurrection or helplessly fanning flagrant conflagrations of disobedience.

The Christian Educator has a tremendous responsibility in the area of classroom government for the secularism of the times has invaded the first area of parental authority, the home. In teachers' colleges the influence of the behavioral fields of psychology, anthropology, sociology, have promoted methods of classroom control, which put the criteria for judgement of action in society. This becomes socialism. The Christian Educator needs to teach students first, that the source of all authority, law and government are found in GOD and defined in His Word; second, that Christian self-government makes God's Law the requirement of the heart— internal—and this is the basis of our American Christian Constitution.

Today we see the decline of regard for, or obedience to, God's commands. With the rise of "*sociological jurisprudence*" in our courts the State has been substituted for God and conformity to its provisions take priority over obedience to God.

"A worldly or non-Christian philosophy of law is equally expressed by those people who say that the Supreme Court has spoken, and its voice is the law of the land. Whatever the government decrees, that we must do, say they . . . Christian governments have no such tyrannical license. They, rather, are limited in their power and can enforce only God's laws. All modern socialist states, which are established on the proposition that the Father of Jesus Christ is no longer God, have had to repeal the laws based upon the Ten Commandments and erect a tyrannous system whose only consistent threat is that nobody can challenge or question the power of the government. In Soviet Russia, we are told, there is no capital punishment. There is no punishment at all. One is simply eliminated for crimes against "the people" (the Communist Party) In Russia men die for crimes against the state—but not for crimes against God.

"The socialist system has reverted to the most degenerate of all the forms of ancient paganism, recalling Israel's bondage in Egypt and the savagery of Carthage. The American flyer, Francis Powers, whose trial was a vast propaganda move to establish the socialist principle of human law, was not tried as a military agent of an enemy power but as a criminal. Spying was not treated as the act of war which it is, thus deserving whatever penalty the warring power deems fit, but as a crime. The meaning of that trial was that the world was informed of the new pattern of law to be imposed upon it: that crime is an offense against world government—not against God."

Rev. T. Robert
Ingram, *The
World Under
God's Law*

The classroom has successfully been used as the agent for the *transmission* of new *"cultural values"*—values which are diametrically opposed to those which built our Christian republic. These so called values are not derived from the changelessness of God's Word and authority but are being codified from the shifting sands of man's social, economic, religious and political environment. How can the Christian educator become aware of "*the net that they have laid privily for me*"?

The *currciculum makers* of our times are those *anthropologists*, those *sociologists* and those *psychologists*, who are "*defining*" for us the values and goals of society and thus determining the kind of "*cultural man*" which education should develop. The following summary of Dr. George D. Spindler of Stanford University, psychi-

TEACHING
AND
LEARNING
AMERICA'S
CHRISTIAN
HISTORY

atrist, anthropologist and educator, indicates the direction in which he believes school and society must move together.

"It is the shifts in what I believe are the core values in American culture, and the effect of these shifts on education, that I wish to discuss. I will present these shifts in values as the conditions of life to which education and educators—whether progressives, experimentalists, conservatives or in-betweeners must adapt—and to which they are adapting —albeit confusedly . . .

Traditional Values	*Emergent Values*
Puritan Morality. (*Respectability, thrift, self-denial, sexual constraint; a puritan is someone who can have anything he wants, as long as he doesn't enjoy it!*)	Sociability. (*As described above. One should like people and get along well with them. Suspicion of solitary activities is characteristic.*)
Work-Success ethic. (*Successful people worked hard to become so. Anyone can get to the top if he tries hard enough. So people who are not successful are lazy or stupid, or both. People must work desperately and continuously to convince themselves of their worth.*)	Relativistic moral attitude. (*Absolutes in right and wrong are questionable. Morality is what the group thinks is right. Shame, rather than guilt-oriented personality is appropriate.*)
Individualism. (*The individual is sacred, and always more important than the group. In one extreme form, the value sanctions egocentricity, expediency, and disregard for other people's rights. In its healthier form the value sanctions independence and originality.*)	Consideration for others. (*Everything one does should be done with regard for others and their feelings. The individual has a built-in radar that alerts him to other's feelings. Tolerance for the other person's point of view and behaviors is regarded as desirable, so long as the harmony of group is not disrupted.*)
Achievement orientation. (*Success is a constant goal. There is no resting on past glories. If one makes $9,000 this year he must make $10,000 next year. Coupled with work-success ethic, this value keeps people moving, and tense.*)	
Future-time orientation. (*The future, not the past, or even the present, is most important. There is a 'pot of gold at the end of the rainbow'. Time is valuable, and cannot be wasted. Present needs must be*	Hedonistic, present-time orientation. (*No one can tell what the future will hold, therefore one should enjoy the present— but within the limits of the well-rounded, balanced personality and group.*)

104

denied for satisfactions to be gained in the future.)

Conforming to the group. (*Implied in the other emergent values. Everything is relative to the group. Group harmony is the ultimate goal. Leadership consists of group-machinery lubrication.*)

NOTE: *Spindler. "I have been particularly influenced by the writings of David Riesman and particularly his* The Lonely Crowd, *now available in a Doubleday Anchor Book Edition, 1953, with Nathan Glazer and Reuel Denney."*)

The Christian Educator can read the derision for the *traditional* position and the effort made to ridicule the individual Christian who demands of himself, not only *respectability* but *integrity*. The subversion of our private enterprise system is evident when seen in the breakdown of individual habits of *thrift* and *self-denial* —with the move away from *hard work* as the means to *success*. The focus upon the *group* as the arbiter of *morality*, and *sociability* as the criteria for behavior has produced an age of social legislation where more and more emphasis upon "the law" is compelling compliance. But lawlessness is on the increase. There has never been a period in the history of the world when man's inhumanity to man has been as great—and this in an age when education has been directed to *consideration for others*.

With the appearance of our Lord there was set forth the only cause for individual action which would ever produce real *consideration for others*. Christ Jesus in *"fulfilling the law"* commanded the Christian to make the law not *cause*—but *effect* —the effect of his individual, internal salvation. This is the reason why our American Republic and our American Christian Constitution cannot function from a position of law enforcement. While the Ten Commandments form a foundation for our laws they cannot compel obedience. The law cannot make a man "do that which is good". The Christian obeys the law because he has already accepted the *saving grace of* JESUS CHRIST as his redemption from sin and lawlessness. The *cause* of his obedience—that which "fulfills all the law and the prophets"—is his acceptance of Christ. The *effect* of his salvation is expressed in the citizen who *fulfills* the law rather than *abides* by the law. This position is that of the New Testament Christian. *"For the law of the Spirit of life in Christ Jesus hath made me free from the law of sin and death."* (Romans 8:2).

Thus while dealing with crowded classrooms of students the Christian Educator is actually teaching each individual student to become internally governed through his commitment to Christ. This is Christian self-government. Without Christ it would be man governing himself through *relativistic moral attitudes*. The great strength of our republic becomes evident when it is seen that the founders put the responsibility for local, state and national government, not upon the group but upon the *integrity of individual action*. Thus the cause and purpose for right action begins with individual fulfillment of the first commandment of the New Testament. If love for God and Christ becomes the dominant theme of an individual's life then

TEACHING
AND
LEARNING
AMERICA'S
CHRISTIAN
HISTORY

the second commandment of our Lord will follow in its rightful place and society will benefit far more than when concern for the group takes precedence over love for, and obedience to, our precious Saviour.

Summary of Criteria for Classroom Government

1. Christian classroom government or control begins with the recognition of the authority of Christ in each life. The teacher as God's steward, accountable to Him, never relinquishes his position of authority in the classroom—even during sessions of student government.

2. Nations and individuals must learn *self-government*. First, comes the *"school-master"* of the law. Each individual must learn to *"abide"* by the law and recognize its place in society. As individuals accept more and more of the internal law of the Gospel, they may depend less and less upon external law for their control. So classrooms which begin with much external control by the teacher may achieve that position where more and more responsibility can be *delegated* to each individual member as each individual member learns to accept the responsibility for individual Christian self-government—thus *"fulfilling"* the law.

3. The class "group" may need to discuss the government of the classroom and clarify the *absolute standards* for behavior *from* GOD'S WORD. But the *opinion* of the group never determines the standard, its infraction, nor the punishment of individuals.

4. Thus classroom control in a Christian school begins with the decision of the teacher to accept God's stewardship of the classroom. More and more classroom control becomes the responsibility of each individual for his or her own behavior as that behavior approximates the standard set forth in God's Holy Word.

Primary Teachers Construct the Character of the Constitution

It may surprise Primary teachers to find that *Teaching and Learning America's Christian History of the Constitution of the United States of America* begins in the kindergarten. It is America's Christian character which *constitutes* our Constitution. Therefore, the principles dealing with America are principles dealing with the testimony of Christian character. Primary teachers help to lay the foundation of Christian character as they continue the work which parents have already started in the Christian home. A nation which is humble enough to begin with its children in the constructing of its foundations for liberty may once again have the opportunity to lead nations to Christ. In Isaiah's beautiful prophecy of the Saviour to come he pictures Him as a "little child" who can dwell with the most ferocious and bestial elements of the world and concludes *"a little child shall lead them"*.

As we survey the wreckage of our nation in Christian character and in the understanding of Constitutional government we can see what two generations of Deweyism and over one hundred years of state education have accomplished. As the state has grown in importance and in control the Christian has become less significant in ability and independence. At a time when man's intelligence is more and more in bondage to his Frankenstein of the computer, individuals are less able to undertake individual research or independent scholarly pursuits. Today most research is subsidized and indeed there is little initiative to begin projects which are not underwritten. Yet, as we toboggan in competition with the anti-Christ in scientific fields, where are the Christians who are willing or able to follow the Lord's leading? There are too few and we in Christian schools are not feeding that supply of scientific Christians who should continue what was initially American Christian research.

This is why Primary teachers can do much to help turn back our *educational design for socialism*—the development of a *dependent mentality* which can literally do nothing. Our students can accomplish more and they are hungry for the opportunity. As we liberate them from the *Dick and Jane* of *fun learning* we can open up realms of thought and exploration—an ever unfolding horizon of achievement. But we must furnish them first, with the tools of study, observation, and research, and second, with a curriculum which will offer them a genuine and significant challenge and spur them on to greater self-study and individual enterprise.

On page 434 of *Christian History of the Constitution* there is an interesting account of the life of John Fiske. It relates the following:

"From early boyhood he showed signs of exceptional talents. By the age of four he had taught himself to read haltingly. By the time he was six, he was able to read proficiently enough to dip into all the books in the family library, just 'to see what they were like'. At six he also began the study of Latin, followed later by French, Italian, German, Hebrew, and Sanscrit. He was graduated from Harvard in 1863 (at 21) and from Harvard Law School in 1865 (23)."

Today we take as our model, not individual excellence or capability, but the *median* of the *mediocre*, and we reduce ability to the level of the least common denominator. Yet if we seek to glorify not the intelligence of the brain cell but the Author and Creator of all wisdom and knowledge should it be thought impossible that once again we could raise up a generation of intelligent Christians witnessing to Christ's preeminence in all things?

TEACHING
AND
LEARNING
AMERICA'S
CHRISTIAN
HISTORY
Thus we dedicate this Christian Education Guide to those teachers who see this vision and regard their ministry in Christian education as an *educational ministry* as well as a Christian testimony. There was never a greater need for educational redemption than exists today in America with its base of socialism and psychological atheism which permeates texts, teaching methods and teachers. And here in the Primary Grades where so much of the "attitude" toward education is set, here the Primary Teacher can contribute to the Christianization of the school curriculum.

As dedicated Primary teachers, who must work independently of books, teaching tools and many of the "aids" which upper grade teachers depend upon—as they lift their hearts in prayer, may the Lord lead them to bring forth the "First Fruits" of lives consecrated and dedicated for Christ. May they be able to say with the Apostle Paul, "*I have laid the foundation, and another buildeth thereon.*" In the laying of this "*sure foundation*" Primary teachers have a unique and precious opportunity "*For other foundation can no man* lay than that which is *Jesus Christ.*" (1 Cor. 3:11).

How Can the Same Principle be Taught in Every Grade?

Why this Approach?

The message of salvation is not presented in an evolutionary manner by degrees, or part by part, nor progressively. The means by which the youngest may "*also obtain the salvation which is in Christ Jesus*" is presented full and complete from the first. The "*little child*" learns the same Gospel as the advanced student of theology. This message is amplified and expanded as the individual heart, mind and understanding opens more and more fully to CHRIST.

In secular evolutionary teaching we break up the subject areas in the curriculum and teach them progressively from one grade to another with the assumption that the parts make up the whole. In Christian education beginning from the *wholistic* position of CHRIST as the center and source of all subjects we proceed to find the unity of all knowledge in Him. "*That in all things he might have the preeminence. For it pleased the Father that in him should all fulness dwell.*" (Col. 1:18, 19).

The word *principle* goes back to its root meaning of *beginning, cause, source, origin, element.* The subject of America's *Christian History* has not been taught from the position of its Christian origin, or beginning. It is CHRIST HIS STORY of America which we wish to teach and learn. What is the particular function or part which this nation has to play in the redemption of mankind? What does the Chain of Christianity signify to the study of history?

Built into this program for teaching and learning America's *Christian History* is a change of base away from progressive techniques and methods which have a psychological, sociological and atheistic base. The use of these methods by the Christian teacher limits the opportunity for the Holy Spirit to work through his teaching. There is a need for Christian methods which permit *"the diversity of gifts"* of individual teachers, individual classes, individual students to be expressed in this study—all testifying to *"the same Spirit"*. This is why the word *Guide* has been selected for this program of study for Christian schools. It is intended to "point" or "lead the way" in the direction of a Christian approach to teaching and to permit individuals to follow as the Lord leads them.

How are the Principles Presented?

The chart following entitled *Expanding Principles of America's Christian History* indicates the seven principles which are the basis of study for all grades from kindergarten through college.

The next chart entitled *Principles Expanded Through the Grades* shows each principle expanded to include aspects or elements for four grade levels. The effort has been made to preserve the unity of the subject and not to break it down into specific grades. The grade levels are broad and include *Primary, Elementary, Junior High*, and *Senior High* subdivisions. Ideally, a teacher should learn the entire program and thus be in the position of selecting for an individual grade what appeals to his own leading and inspiration.

The four grade levels, *Primary, Elementary, Junior High*, and *Senior High* have been provided the *same background* material on the *identification* and *definition of the principles*. But in order to aid teachers to get into *Christian History* through the *principles* each of the four levels has *specific* material designated.

Thus a school can be teaching the same principles in every grade and at every grade level. Because the subject is studied from the basis of *principles* every teacher can teach the program and it will have its unique and distinct aspects. Thus while the material for the levels—*Primary, Elementary, Junior High* and *Senior High*, include a number of grades within each level—there will never be a repetition of content for each teacher will bring out different aspects of the principles as they expand and amplify in meaning and in application. A principle must be defined clearly but it cannot be confined within a single subject, or grade level, and it will have universal application as it is understood.

It is our hope that this program of *Teaching and Learning America's Christian History* will begin to restore to teachers the vision of their unique and special ministry as a Christian teacher teaching in a Christian school in America. We hope

109

TEACHING
AND
LEARNING
AMERICA'S
CHRISTIAN
HISTORY also that they will begin to recognize the challenge built into this program to enable them to take steps to free themselves from the bondage and limitation of secular reasoning which would limit both the inspiration of the Holy Spirit in their teaching and keep them from expanding their own teaching talents and abilities.

Samuel Adams on page XIV of *Christian History of the Constitution* admonishes those responsible for the education of our youth to teach and learn "the art of self-government" by "leading them in the study and practice of the exalted virtues of the Christian system". We wish to work from a Christian position—from the basis of God's Word. This Light is our center and our circumference—our Christian method:

"For God, who commanded the light to shine out of darkness, hath shined in our hearts to give the light of the knowledge of the glory of God in the face of Jesus Christ." 2 Cor. 4:6

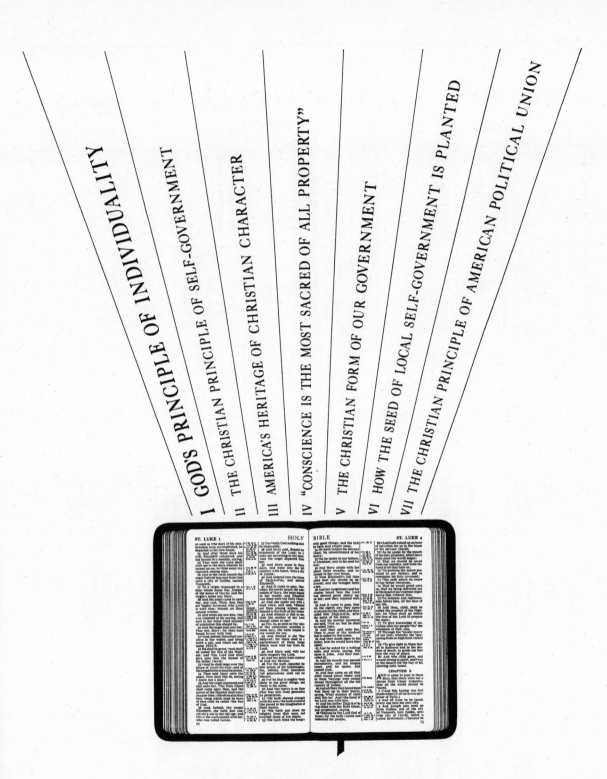

I GOD'S PRINCIPLE OF INDIVIDUALITY

II THE CHRISTIAN PRINCIPLE OF SELF-GOVERNMENT

III AMERICA'S HERITAGE OF CHRISTIAN CHARACTER

IV "CONSCIENCE IS THE MOST SACRED OF ALL PROPERTY"

V THE CHRISTIAN FORM OF OUR GOVERNMENT

VI HOW THE SEED OF LOCAL SELF-GOVERNMENT IS PLANTED

VII THE CHRISTIAN PRINCIPLE OF AMERICAN POLITICAL UNION

Expanding Principles
of America's Christian History

III

TEACHING
AND
LEARNING
AMERICA'S
CHRISTIAN
HISTORY

Principles Expanded Through the Grades

Basic Principles from Volume I—Christian History of the Constitution of the United States

I	II	III	IV	V	VI	VII
God's Principle of Individuality	Christian Principle of Self-Government	America's Heritage of Christian Character	"Conscience is the Most Sacred of all Property"	The Christian Form of Our Government	How the Seed of Local Self-Government is Planted	Christian Principle of American Political Union
Primary						
Christian Individualism	Learning Christian Self-Government in the Classroom	Faith and Steadfastness in Plymouth Plantation	Man is God's Property	The Christian Idea of Man and Government—Representation 3 Branches Dual Form	Samuel Adams Christian Patriot	Boston Patriots and the Tea Act
Elementary						
Geographic Individuals	Christian Self-Government in Virginia and Plymouth	Brotherly Love and Christian Care in Plymouth Plantation	"Of Property" John Locke Foundation of Title to Property	The Law and the Gospel as the Basis of Our Government—Christianity and Education	Patriotic Letters—Committees of Correspondence	Boston Port is Closed—Day of Fasting and Prayer, June 1, 1774
Junior High						
Individual Links on Christianity's Chain	Government of the Parent Colonies Township and County Systems Pennsylvania	Diligence and Industry in Plymouth Plantation	"Life, Liberty and Property", Boston Platform of Christian Civil Rights 1772	"A Government Resting on Moral Principles" Christian Morality in Leadership	The American Colonies Practice Self-Government for 150 Years	The Cement of American Union
Senior High						
America Declares Herself an Individual Nation	Locke—"Of the Beginning of Political Societies" Government by Consent Majority Rule	Liberty of Conscience in the Plymouth Plantation	"No Taxation Without Representation" Property Rights	The Pulpit and American Independence	"Liberty Under Law"	American Unity is Christian Unity

God's Principle of Individuality

TEACHER'S
GUIDE FOR
CHRISTIAN
HISTORY

Expanding the First Principle Through the Grades

Statement of the Principle	Everything in God's universe is revelational of God's infinity, God's diversity, God's individuality. God creates distinct individualities. God maintains the identity and individuality of everything which He created.	See Key, pages 141–183
Words related to INDIVIDUALITY	ONENESS, INDIVISIBILITY, WHOLENESS, INTEGRITY, COMPLETENESS. That which is DISTINCT, UNIQUE.	
BIBLICAL *Index*	GENESIS, Chapter One; JOHN 1:3; I CORINTHIANS 12:4–11	

Expanding the Principle
Christian Individualism

The Christian idea of man and government	CHRISTIAN HISTORY: Pages I–XIV CHRISTIAN EDUCATION GUIDE: Page 155	*Primary Grades*
Two political concepts of man: Pagan or Christian	CHRISTIAN HISTORY: Pages 1, 2, 6, 11, 12	

113

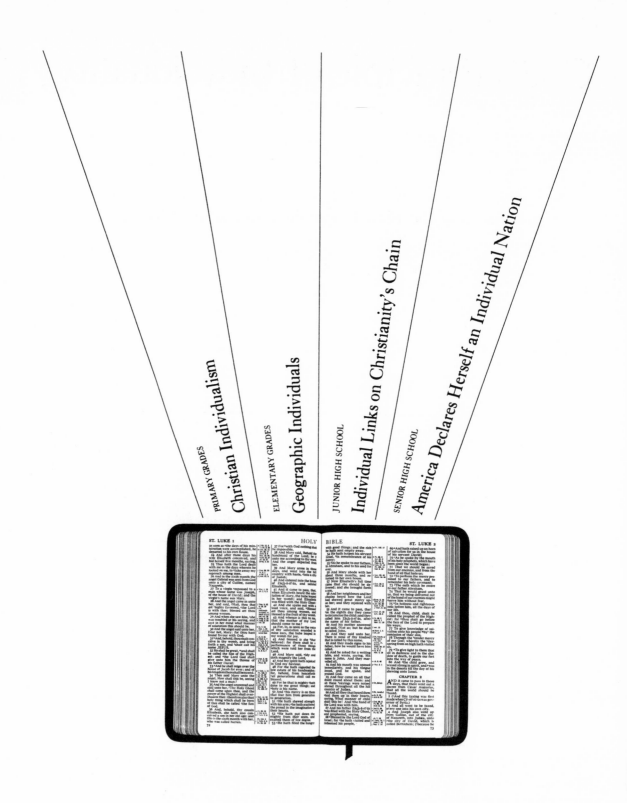

God's Principle of Individuality

Individual sovereignty	CHRISTIAN HISTORY: Pages 148–;150 270C, 270E.
The representative principle	CHRISTIAN HISTORY: Pages 13–15; 135, 136.

Bible Research

Why is *individualism* separate from *Christ* as dangerous to mankind as any form of *collectivism?*
Where and how does the *Bible* document the following?
  1. God's principle of individuality
  2. Human individualism
  3. The lack of Christian individualism

"Geographic Individuals"

"Each continent has, therefore, a well defined individuality, which fits it for an especial function."

Christian Geography	CHRISTIAN EDUCATION GUIDE: Pages 156, 157 CHRISTIAN HISTORY: Page 6A	*Elementary Grades*
"The Continents of History"	CHRISTIAN HISTORY: Pages 3–5	
America reserved by God	CHRISTIAN EDUCATION GUIDE: Pages 143, 153 CHRISTIAN HISTORY: Pages 5–16	
One indivisible republic	CHRISTIAN HISTORY: Pages 380–390	

Individual Links on Christianity's Chain

The Chain of Christianity	CHRISTIAN HISTORY: Page 6A	*Junior High*
The Law: "In tables of stone"	CHRISTIAN EDUCATION GUIDE: Page 158 CHRISTIAN HISTORY: Page 270C	

TEACHING
AND
LEARNING
AMERICA'S
CHRISTIAN
HISTORY

The Gospel: ". . . in fleshly tables of the heart"	CHRISTIAN EDUCATION GUIDE: Page 159 CHRISTIAN HISTORY: Page 270C
The Pagan nations and Christianity	CHRISTIAN EDUCATION GUIDE: Pages 159–160
The character of the Greeks	CHRISTIAN EDUCATION GUIDE: Pages 160–162
The character of the Romans	CHRISTIAN EDUCATION GUIDE: Pages 162–165
Roman Civil Law	CHRISTIAN EDUCATION GUIDE: Pages 165–166
John Wycliffe: To place the Bible in the heart of the individual	CHRISTIAN EDUCATION GUIDE: Pages 166–168
Martin Luther: A Bible for the German people	CHRISTIAN EDUCATION GUIDE: Pages 168–170
John Calvin: "The City of God" at Geneva	CHRISTIAN EDUCATION GUIDE: Pages 170–172
The King James Bible: The WORD *free from notes and interpretation*	CHRISTIAN EDUCATION GUIDE: Page 173 Christian History Study Course: Lesson V—"The Bible in English" GUIDE: Page 332
Magna Charta: "From the age of traditional rights . . . to the age of written legislation . . ."	CHRISTIAN EDUCATION GUIDE: Pages 173–175
English Bill of Rights	Christian History Study Course: Lesson VI—"Christian Rights and English Law" GUIDE: Page 343
John Locke: Individual sovereignty in civil government	CHRISTIAN EDUCATION GUIDE: Page 175
Charles de Montesquieu: "The title deeds of humanity"	CHRISTIAN EDUCATION GUIDE: Page 175

William Blackstone: Individual rights as the law of the land	CHRISTIAN EDUCATION GUIDE:	Page 176
Jamestown: The English representative principle	CHRISTIAN EDUCATION GUIDE:	Page 177
Plymouth: Christianity the basis of local self-government	CHRISTIAN EDUCATION GUIDE:	Page 178
The Mayflower Compact: "For the glory of God, for the advance of the Christian faith . . ."	CHRISTIAN EDUCATION GUIDE:	Page 179

America Declares Herself an Individual Nation

CHRISTIANITY: *Internal liberty produces external freedom*	CHRISTIAN EDUCATION GUIDE:	Pages 179–180
The DECLARATION OF INDEPENDENCE	CHRISTIAN EDUCATION GUIDE:	Pages 180–183

Senior High

PRIMARY GRADES
Learning Christian Self-Government in the Classroom

ELEMENTARY GRADES
Christian Self-Government in Virginia and Plymouth Colonies

JUNIOR HIGH SCHOOL
The Local Self-Government of the Colonies

SENIOR HIGH SCHOOL
John Locke "Of the Beginning of Political Societies"

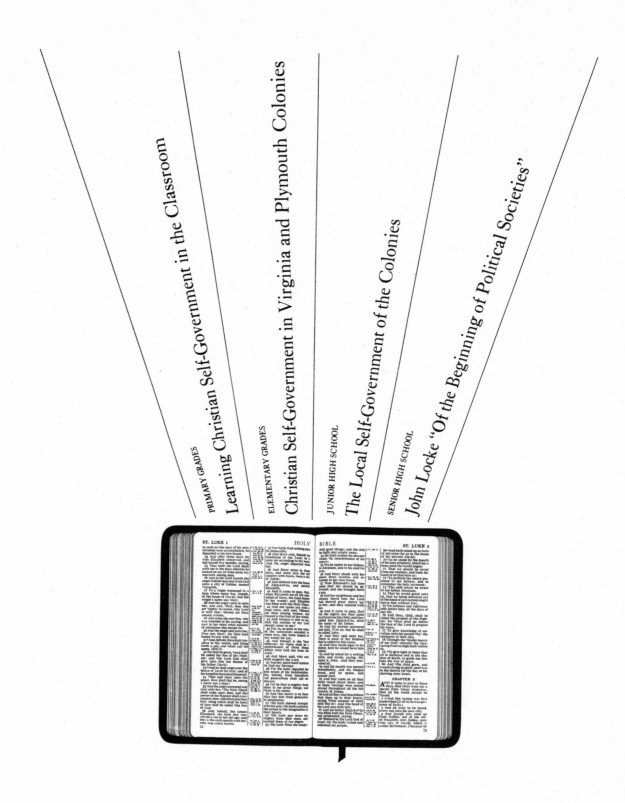

The Christian Principle of Self-Government

The Christian Principle of Self-Government

Expanding the Second Principle Through the Grades

Statement of Principle

"He knows not how to rule a kingdome, that cannot manage a Province; nor can he wield a Province, that cannot order a City; nor he order a City, that knows not how to regulate a Village; nor he a Village, that cannot guide a Family; nor can that man Govern well a Family that knows not how to Govern himselfe; neither can any Govern himselfe unless his reason be Lord, Will and Appetite her Vassals: nor can Reason rule unlesse herselfe be ruled by God, and (wholy) be obedient to Him."
HUGO GROTIUS, 1654

See Key, pages
184–209

BIBLICAL *Index*   PROVERBS 16:32; I TIMOTHY 3:5

Expanding the Principle
Learning Christian Self-Government in the Classroom

Primary Grades

TEACHING
AND
LEARNING
AMERICA'S
CHRISTIAN
HISTORY

Defining the term SELF-GOVERNMENT	CHRISTIAN EDUCATION GUIDE: Pages 184–190
Local self-governing congregations	CHRISTIAN HISTORY: Pages 16–28
The BIBLE *as the American political text-book*	CHRISTIAN EDUCATION GUIDE: Study Course, Lesson V, "The Bible in English" page 332

Christian Self-Government in Virginia and Plymouth Colonies

Elementary Grades

Representative government in Virginia Colony	CHRISTIAN EDUCATION GUIDE: Pages 190–194
Christian self-government in Plymouth Colony	CHRISTIAN EDUCATION GUIDE: Pages 194–198

The Local Self-Government of the Colonies

Junior High

New England Township: Congregational form of church government	CHRISTIAN EDUCATION GUIDE: Pages 198–200
Virginia county system: Episcopal form of church government	CHRISTIAN EDUCATION GUIDE: Pages 200–201
Pennsylvania established as a Christian colony	CHRISTIAN EDUCATION GUIDE: Pages 201–203

John Locke "Of the Beginning of Political Societies"

Senior High

John Locke: Christian philosopher of the American Revolution	CHRISTIAN HISTORY: Pages 50B–56
Christianity and the importance of individual consent	CHRISTIAN EDUCATION GUIDE: Pages 204–206

120

Locke examines the beginnings of political societies	CHRISTIAN EDUCATION GUIDE: Study Course, Lesson VII "A Biblical-Political Index to John Locke", page 353
In a republic the MAJORITY *represents each individual*	CHRISTIAN EDUCATION GUIDE: Pages 206–208
In a democracy the MAJORITY *represents the group*	CHRISTIAN EDUCATION GUIDE: Pages 161, 208–209

Bible Research

When did Israel provide opportunities for self-government which made it *unlike* "all the nations"?

What are some examples of the principle of Christian self-government for individual nations, individual men and women?

How do the two commands of our Lord reveal the principles of the separation of church and state?

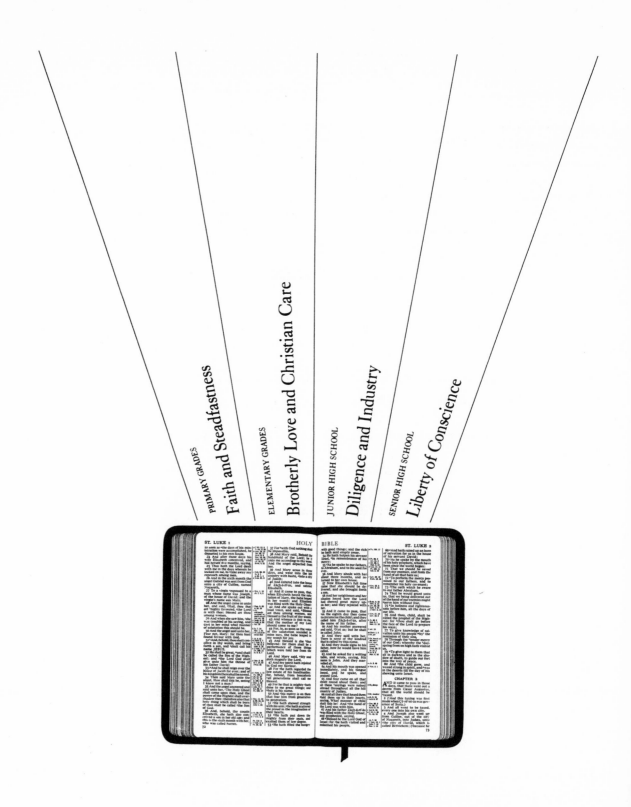

PRIMARY GRADES
Faith and Steadfastness

ELEMENTARY GRADES
Brotherly Love and Christian Care

JUNIOR HIGH SCHOOL
Diligence and Industry

SENIOR HIGH SCHOOL
Liberty of Conscience

America's Heritage of Christian Character

America's Heritage of
Christian Character

Expanding the Third Principle Through the Grades

Statement of the Principle

"This divine power of the gospel revealed itself to the heathen in the lives of Christians, which showed forth the virtues of Him who had called them out of darkness into his marvellous light, and enabled them to walk as the children of God, in the midst of a perverse generation, among whom they shone as lights in the world! . . . The whole life of the Christian, from the beginning to the end, is a conflict with the world and the powers of darkness, a conflict within and without . . ." NEANDER "MEMORIALS OF A CHRISTIAN LIFE," 1852

See Key, pages 210–224

BIBLICAL *Index*

MATT. 7:24–29; 2 TIM. 4:7; PHIL. 4:13; ACTS 24:16

Expanding the Principle
Faith and Steadfastness

Primary Grades

TEACHING
AND
LEARNING
AMERICA'S
CHRISTIAN
HISTORY

Christian character of the first century	CHRISTIAN EDUCATION GUIDE: Pages 210–212	
Life of a Christian contrasted with paganism	CHRISTIAN EDUCATION GUIDE: Pages 212–215	
"God's children are like stars" and "like the chamomile"	CHRISTIAN HISTORY: Page 183	
The FAITH *and* STEADFASTNESS *of the Pilgrims*	CHRISTIAN EDUCATION GUIDE: Pages 215–219	

Brotherly Love and Christian Care

Elementary Grades	*The standard for Christian conduct toward others*	CHRISTIAN EDUCATION GUIDE: Pages 219–221

Diligence and Industry

Junior High	*"Christian behavior under persecution"*	CHRISTIAN EDUCATION GUIDE: Pages 221–223

Liberty of Conscience

Senior High	*The power of the Gospel in the lives of the Pilgrims*	CHRISTIAN EDUCATION GUIDE: Page 224

"Conscience is the Most Sacred of all Property"

Expanding the Fourth Principle Through the Grades

Statement of the Principle	"For men being the Workmanship of One Omnipotent, and infinitely wise Maker: All the Servants of one Sovereign Master, sent into the World by his Order, and about his Business, they are his Property, whose Workmanship they are, made to last during his, not one anothers Pleasure . . ." "Of Civil-Government" JOHN LOCKE, 1689	See Key, pages 225–239
BIBLICAL *Index*	GENESIS 1:1; ISAIAH 43:7; EPHESIANS 2:10; REVELATION 4:11	

Expanding the Principle
Man is God's Property

Blackstone on property	CHRISTIAN EDUCATION GUIDE: Pages 225–227 CHRISTIAN HISTORY: Pages 139–146	*Primary Grades*

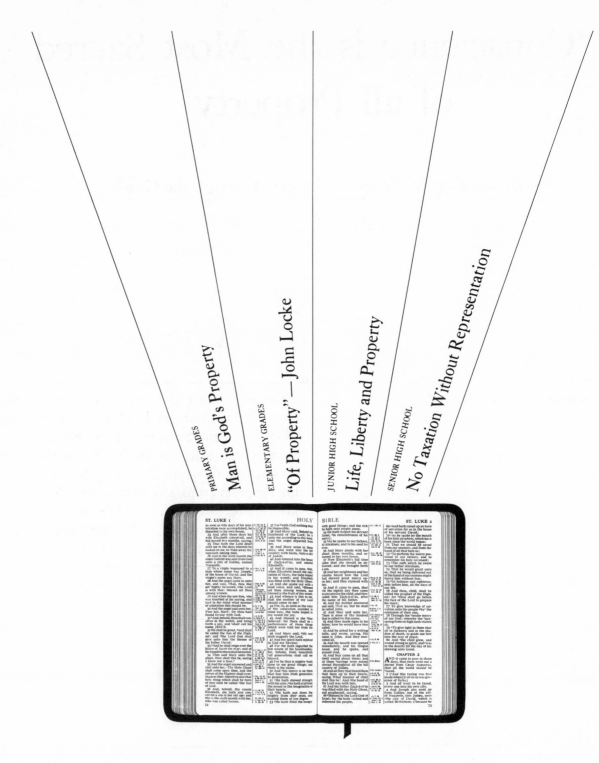

PRIMARY GRADES

Man is God's Property

ELEMENTARY GRADES

"Of Property" —John Locke

JUNIOR HIGH SCHOOL

Life, Liberty and Property

SENIOR HIGH SCHOOL

No Taxation Without Representation

"Conscience is the Most Sacred
of All Property"

Christian stewardship and ownership	CHRISTIAN EDUCATION GUIDE: Pages 227–232

"Of Property"—John Locke

The title to property	CHRISTIAN EDUCATION GUIDE: Pages 232–236	*Elementary Grades*

Life, Liberty, and Property

"The Blessings of Liberty"	CHRISTIAN EDUCATION GUIDE: Pages 236–238	*Junior High*

No Taxation without Representation

Property and representation	CHRISTIAN EDUCATION GUIDE: Pages 238–239	*Senior High*

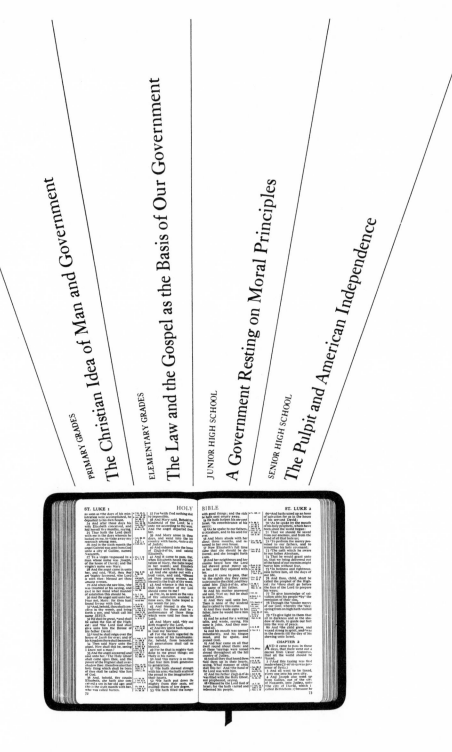

The Christian Form of Our Government

The Christian Form of Our Government

TEACHER'S
GUIDE FOR
CHRISTIAN
HISTORY

Expanding the Fifth Principle Through the Grades

Statement of the Principle	"As men we have God for our King, and are under the Law of Reason: as Christian, we have Jesus the Messiah for our King, and are under the Law reveal'd by him in the Gospel . . ." "The Reasonableness of Christianity" JOHN LOCKE, 1695	See Key, pages 240–249
BIBLICAL *Index*	DEUTERONOMY 1:9–18: ISAIAH 33:22; MATTHEW 22:35–40	

Expanding the Principle
The Christian Idea of Man and Government

The Christian form of our government	CHRISTIAN EDUCATION GUIDE: Pages 240–245	*Primary Grades*

The Law and the Gospel as the Basis of our Government

Elementary Grades

129

TEACHING
AND
LEARNING
AMERICA'S
CHRISTIAN
HISTORY

Our Christian heritage	CHRISTIAN EDUCATION GUIDE: Pages 245–246
Christianity and education	CHRISTIAN EDUCATION GUIDE: Pages 246–247
Representation	CHRISTIAN HISTORY: Pages 13–15; 135–136; 254–257; 270C, 270E
The Separation of Powers: the three branches of government	CHRISTIAN HISTORY: Pages 93–98; 134, 135, 138
Our Dual Form of government	CHRISTIAN HISTORY: Pages 148, 149, 358

"A Government Resting on Moral Principles"

Junior High *Christian leadership*	CHRISTIAN EDUCATION GUIDE: Pages 247–248

The Pulpit and American Independence

Senior High *Patriotic piety*	CHRISTIAN EDUCATION GUIDE: Pages 248–249

How the Seed of Local Self-Government is Planted

Expanding the Sixth Principle Through the Grades

Statement of the Principle

"The government of the United States is acknowledged by the wise and good of other nations, to be the most free, impartial, and righteous government of the world; but all agree, that for such a government to be sustained many years, the principles of truth and righteousness, taught in the Holy Scriptures, must be practised. *The rulers must govern in the fear of God, and the people obey the laws*." EMMA WILLARD, 1843

See Key, pages 250–261

BIBLICAL *Index*

DEUTERONOMY 10:12–14; ISAIAH 9:6; LUKE 9:6

Expanding the Principle
Samuel Adams—Christian Patriot

Samuel Adams works for liberty

CHRISTIAN EDUCATION GUIDE: Pages 251–254

Primary Grades

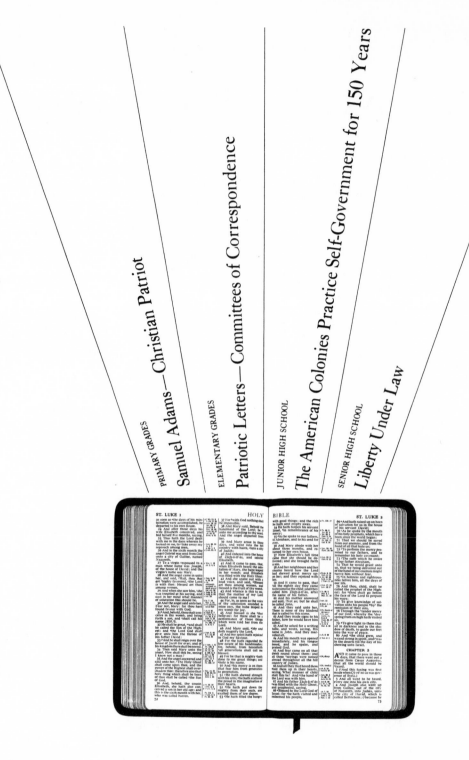

PRIMARY GRADES
Samuel Adams—Christian Patriot

ELEMENTARY GRADES
Patriotic Letters—Committees of Correspondence

JUNIOR HIGH SCHOOL
The American Colonies Practice Self-Government for 150 Years

SENIOR HIGH SCHOOL
Liberty Under Law

How the Seed of Local
Self-Government is Planted

The Christian character of Samuel Adams	CHRISTIAN EDUCATION GUIDE: Pages 255–257

Patriotic Letters—Committees of Correspondence

Committees to educate in principles	CHRISTIAN EDUCATION GUIDE: Pages 257–259	*Elementary Grades*

The American Colonies Practice Self-Government for 150 Years

"Self-government increases the dignity of the man"	CHRISTIAN EDUCATION GUIDE: Pages 259–260	*Junior High*

"Liberty Under Law"

The rule of Gospel principles	CHRISTIAN EDUCATION GUIDE: Page 261	*Senior High*

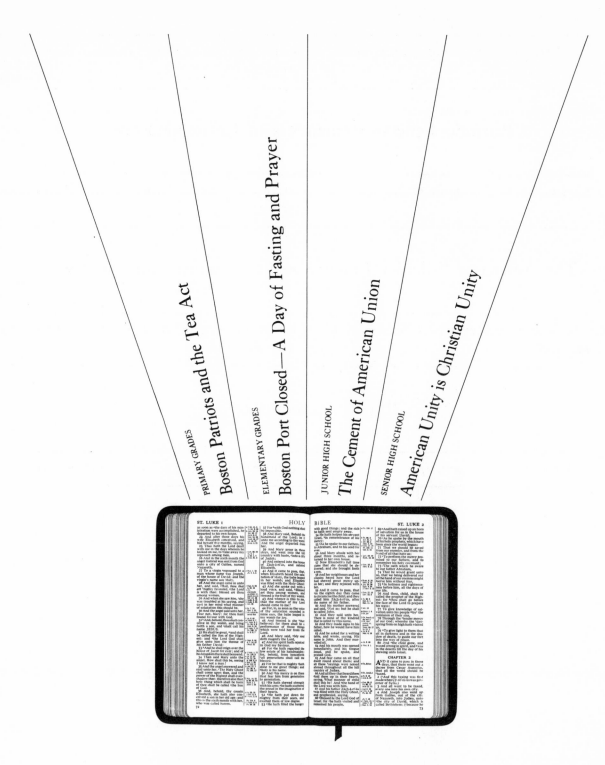

PRIMARY GRADES
Boston Patriots and the Tea Act

ELEMENTARY GRADES
Boston Port Closed—A Day of Fasting and Prayer

JUNIOR HIGH SCHOOL
The Cement of American Union

SENIOR HIGH SCHOOL
American Unity is Christian Unity

The Christian Principle
of American Political Union

The Christian Principle
of American Political Union

Expanding the Seventh Principle Through the Grades

Statement of the Principle	"Till we all come in the unity of the faith, and of the knowledge of the Son of God, unto a perfect man, unto the measure of the stature of the fulness of Christ . . ." EPHESIANS 4:13	See Key, pages 262–268
BIBLICAL *Index*	I CORINTHIANS I:IO; PSALMS I33:I; EPHESIANS 4:I–3	

Expanding the Principle
Boston Patriots and the Tea Act

Christians "Stand Firm"	CHRISTIAN EDUCATION GUIDE: Pages 263–264	*Primary Grades*

Boston Port Closed—A Day of Fasting and Prayer

Public humiliation, fasting and prayer	CHRISTIAN EDUCATION GUIDE: Pages 264–265	*Elementary Grades*

TEACHING
AND
LEARNING
AMERICA'S
CHRISTIAN
HISTORY

The Cement of American Union

Junior High	*The Town-Meeting as a school of self-government*	CHRISTIAN EDUCATION GUIDE: Pages 265–266
	"In ye fellowship of ye Gospell"	CHRISTIAN EDUCATION GUIDE: Page 267

American Unity is Christian Unity

Senior High	*"Unity of the Spirit"*	CHRISTIAN EDUCATION GUIDE: Page 268

Principles One Through Seven

Key to Expanding Principles

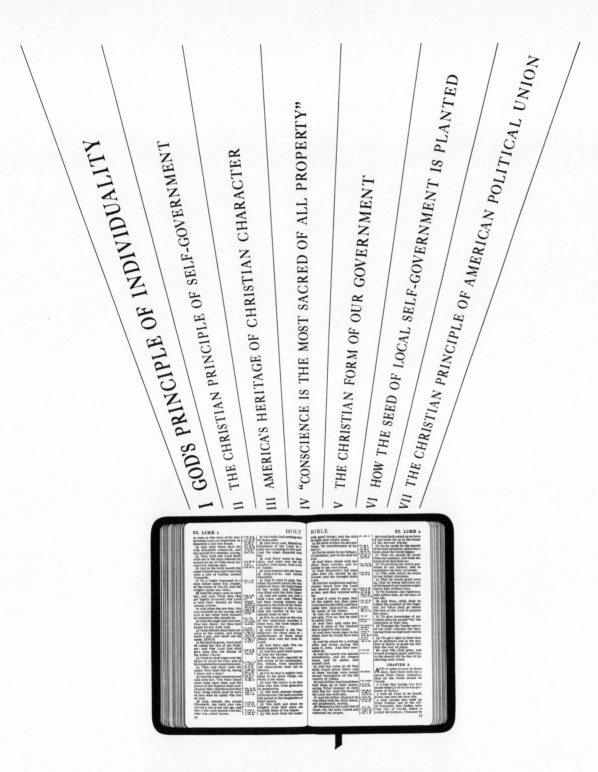

I GOD'S PRINCIPLE OF INDIVIDUALITY

II THE CHRISTIAN PRINCIPLE OF SELF-GOVERNMENT

III AMERICA'S HERITAGE OF CHRISTIAN CHARACTER

IV "CONSCIENCE IS THE MOST SACRED OF ALL PROPERTY"

V THE CHRISTIAN FORM OF OUR GOVERNMENT

VI HOW THE SEED OF LOCAL SELF-GOVERNMENT IS PLANTED

VII THE CHRISTIAN PRINCIPLE OF AMERICAN POLITICAL UNION

Expanding Principles
of America's Christian History

139

God's Principle of Individuality

Key to the First Principle

The subjects of our school curriculum have become *collectivised*—grouped together into Social Studies, Language Arts, Physical Education, and other such anonymous clusterings. This has resulted in the loss of the *identity* and *importance of individual subjects* such as *History, Geography, Grammar, Composition, Gymnastics,* etc.

One subject which has become integrated into the social history of the Social Studies program is *Geography*—a subject of endless fascination, information and knowledge of the globe—theater of man's activities. Again, what has happened in the curriculum of our state schools is part of the political philosophy which teaches that to achieve one world we must eliminate differences of individuality. By removing *Geography* as a distinct subject the students of today do not study God's world—they study the world of man.

The Apostle Paul warns us, however, that we cannot condemn—and then become guilty of that which we condemn:

"And thinketh thou this, O man, that judgest them which do such things, and doest the same, that thou shalt escape the judgement of God?
"Or despisest thou the riches of his goodness and forebearance and longsuffering; not knowing that the goodness of God leadeth thee to repentance?" Romans 2:3, 4.

God in His Goodness has given us a way to escape. Today we have the appearing of the documentation and evidence of America's Christian History. What a contribution teachers in Christian schools can make to the understanding of our Christian heritage, by teaching these simple principles of *Christian Geography* which Guyot has set forth.

141

Christian Geography

See Text, Christian History, *pages 3–5; 436.*

"But, gentlemen, it is not enough to have seized, in this point of view, entirely physical as yet, the functions of the great masses of the continents. They have others, still more important, which, if rightly understood, ought to be considered as the final end for which they have received their existence. To understand and appreciate them at their full value, to study them in their true point of view, we must rise to a higher position. We must elevate ourselves to the moral world to understand the physical world: the physical world has no meaning except by and for the moral world . . .

". . . it is correct to say that inorganic nature is made for organized nature, and the whole globe for man, as both are made for God, the origin and end of all things . . . It is as the abode of man, and the theatre for the action of human societies; it is as the means of the education of entire humanity, that we shall have to consider them, to appreciate the value of each of the physical characters which distinguish them . . .

"It belongs not to man to read in the future the decrees of Providence. But science may attempt to comprehend the purpose of God, as to the destinies of nations, by examining with care the theatre, seemingly arranged by Him for the realization of the new social order, towards which humanity is tending with hope. For the order of nature is a foreshadowing of that which is to be.

"Such, gentlemen, are the great problems our study lays before us. We shall endeavor to solve them by studying, first, the characteristic forms of the continents, the influence of these forms on the physical life of the globe; then, the historical development of humanity. We shall have succeeded, if we may have shown to you,

1. That the forms, the arrangement, and the distribution, of the terrestrial masses on the surface of the globe, accidental in appearance, yet reveal a plan which we are enabled to understand by the evolutions of history.
2. That the continents are made for human societies, as the body is made for the soul.
3. That each of the northern or historical continents is peculiarly adapted, by its nature, to perform a special part corresponding to the wants of humanity in one of the great phases of its history.

God's plan
revealed in the
harmony of
nature and
history

"Thus, nature and history, the earth and man, stand in the closest relations to each other, and form only one grand harmony . . .

"For him who can embrace with a glance the great harmonies of nature and of history, there is here the most admirable plan to study; there are the past and future destinies of the nations to decipher, traced in ineffaceable characters by the finger of Him who governs the world. Admirable order of the Supreme Intelligence and Goodness, which has arranged all for the great purpose of the education of man, and the realization of the plans of Mercy for his sake!"

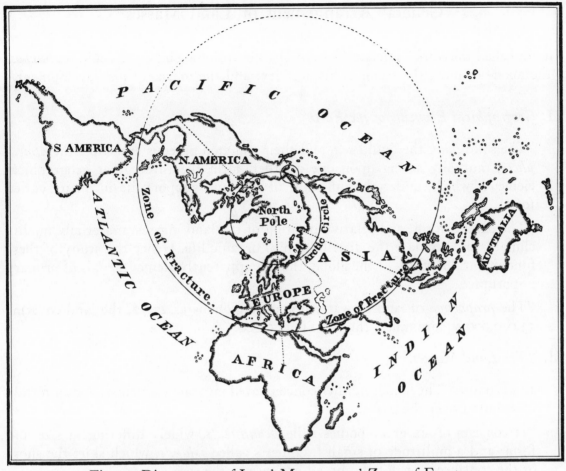

Arnold Guyot,
*Physical
Geography*

Fig. 1. Divergence of Land Masses, and Zone of Fracture

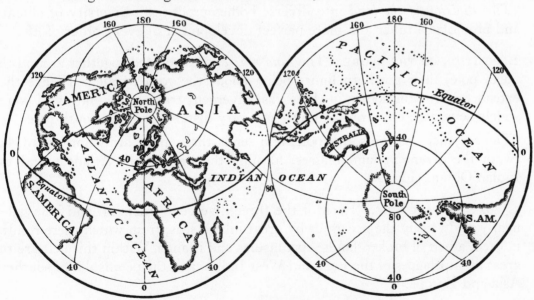

Fig. 2. Land and Water Hemispheres

General Arrangement of Land Masses

Guyot called the *earth* "a masterpiece of Divine workmanship" . . . and its *purpose* "the abode of man, the scene of his activity, and the means of his development."

Arnold Guyot,
*Physical
Geography*

I. *Geographical Elements of the Earth*

"The solid *land*, the liquid *sea*, and their common gaseous envelope, the *atmosphere*, mutually acting upon one another, form the three great geographical elements which, under the influence of the Sun, support life in all its varied forms.

"The extent, form, and relative position of the land masses, materially modify climate, and regulate the distribution of organic life. Hence the study of these fundamental features of the globe, though apparently elementary, is of primary importance.

"The *proportion* of land to water upon the globe is as 27:72, the land covering 53,000,000 square miles, the sea 144,000,000.

II. *"The Land Masses"*

1. DIVISION. "The land is neither concentrated into one vast mass, nor uniformly distributed over the globe.

"It consists of six great bodies called *continents*, widely differing in size and form; and a multitude of small fragments called *islands*, which skirt the shore of the continents or dot the broad expanse of the sea.

"This *division of the land* into diverse bodies produces a diversity of climate, and promotes a fuller and more perfect development of every order of life.

2. POSITION ON THE GLOBE. "The *land masses* are crowded together around the north pole, their northern limits being about the 70th parallel. Thence they extend towards the south, in three vast divergent tracts, terminating in points widely separated one from another, and very distant from the south pole.

"The *sea* encircles the south pole, and sends three great arms northward, between the divergent land masses, forming the Pacific, the Atlantic, and the Indian Ocean. (Fig. 2.)

3. ZONE OF FRACTURE. "Each of the three divergent tracts of land is invaded nearly midway by the ocean, or by great inland seas, from which there results, in each, a belt of broken lands—peninsulas and islands. Within this belt are the great archipelagoes of the East and West Indies, and the peninsulas of southern Asia and Europe.

"These regions form part of a broad transverse zone which may properly be designated the central *zone of fracture*. Its position can be traced by describing a circumference upon the globe, from Behring Strait as a centre, with a meridian arc of 80° as a radius.

"Figure 1 exhibits the divergent arrangement of the land masses, and the zone of fracture. The latter passes over the Carribean Sea, in the New World; and the Mediterranean Sea and East Indian Archipelago in the Old."

Contrast of the Three Continents of the North and the Three Continents of the South

"We have now to consider our continents . . . which I hope will disclose to us some of the hidden influences they seem to exercise upon the life of man; or rather, which will enable us to observe one of those admirable harmonies of nature and history, arranged by the Creator himself for the improvement of this privileged being, for whom all nature seems made . . . Arnold Guyot, *The Earth and Man*

". . . each northern continent has south of it a southern continent, more or less connected with it, whether materially by an isthmus or a chain of islands and an archipelago, or by the proximity of their extreme lands. The two continents, thus brought near together, make always a pair, the individuals being at once connected and opposite in nature. Such are the two Americas,—a perfect type of the kind; such, again, are Europe and Africa, Asia and Australia.

"This arrangement, then, gives us three continents in the North and three in the South. Now, combining in this point of view the prevailing features of their physical configuration, of their situation and of their climate, I would show you: The Continents

1. That the continents composing each of the two groups have common characters, the three in the North resembling each other, and the three in the South presenting equally strong analogies.
2. That these characters are different and opposed in the two groups, and constitute a contrast.
3. That this dissimilar nature assigns to the one a very different part from the others in the progress of human society.

"Let us see, first, how they are distinguished by their general forms and by their configuration . . .

"The continents of the North are more indented, more articulated; their contours are more varied. Gulfs and inland seas cut very deep into the mass of their lands, and detach from the principal trunk a multitude of peninsulas, which, like so many different organs and members, are prepared for a life, in some sort, independent. A great number of continental islands are scattered along their shores, and are a new source of wealth to them . . . Form and configuration

"The southern continents, on the other hand, are massive, entire, *without* indentations, with inland seas or deep inlets, scanty in articulations of every kind, 145 and in islands . . .

"Already, then, by the forms of their contours and of their relief, the continents of the North are more open to maritime life, to the life of commerce; they are more richly organized; they are better made to stimulate improvement.

"The relative situations of the continents of the two groups are equally dissimilar.

"The northern continents are brought nearer together, more consolidated. United, they form the central mass of all the lands of the globe, whence the others appear to radiate in all directions, losing themselves as they taper off in the ocean. For this reason, they have a more continental character. Owing to this greater nearness, to the facility of communication between one continent and another, to the analogy of their climate, which we shall speak of by-and-by, the three northern continents have a mutual relationship not to be mistaken . . .

"The continents of the South are more remote from each other than the foregoing. Broad oceans separate them even to isolation . . . Shut up in themselves, incapable of reacting upon each other and of modifying their respective natures, these continents are excluded from all community of life. What is there astonishing, then, in seeing their differences carried to an extreme, their characters exaggerated? . . .

Climate

"But if the northern continents are evidently favored by their forms and their grouping, is it the same also with their climate?

"The astronomical situation of these two groups is, in reality, quite different. In consequence of the general arrangement of the lands, crowding them in a mass toward the North, the three continents of the North are situated almost entirely in the temperate zone, in the middle latitudes . . .

Tropical climate "The southern continents, on the contrary, expose their principal and most important mass to the rays of the equatorial sun . . .

"Thus, taken as a whole, and in their prevailing character, the three northern continents are temperate, the three southern continents are tropical.

"Which are the most favored? Which are those we consider superior to the others?

"The answer would be easy, if the existence of the continents had no other definite end than the exhibition of the whole physical life of nature. But let us not forget that they are to serve a much higher end still; they are to serve the development of man, and of human societies. It is in this two-fold point of view that we ought to consider them.

"In the order of nature, and at the first approach, we cannot deny to the tropical continents a marked superiority . . .

"But it is in the hot region of the tropics that the life of nature displays its fullest energy, its greatest diversity, its most dazzling splendors . . .

146 "The animal kingdom is no less developed, as we already know, in this privileged

zone. The boundless variety of species, the vivacity of the colors, the diversity of the shades, strike us in the insects and the birds . . . It is true, gentlemen, here Nature triumphs; here she displays herself in all her brilliancy.

"Such is the law in the physical world. Nature goes on adding perfection to perfection, from the temperate zones to the region of the greatest heat. Animal life grows in strength and development . . . man makes here a wonderful exception.

"In the temperate climates all is activity, movement. The alternations of heat and cold, the changes of the seasons, a fresher and more bracing air, incite man to a constant struggle, to forethought, to the vigorous employment of all his faculties. A more economical nature yields nothing, except to the sweat of his brow; every gift on her part is a recompense for effort on his. Less mighty, less gigantesque, even while challenging man to the conflict, she leaves him the hope of victory; and if she does not show herself prodigal, she grants to his active and intelligent labor more than his necessities require; she allows him ease and leisure, which give him scope to cultivate all the lofty faculties of his higher nature. Here, physical nature is not a tyrant, but a useful helper; the active faculties, the understanding and the reason, rule over the instincts and the passive faculties; the soul over the body; man over nature . . .

"Thus, if the tropical continents have the wealth of nature, the temperate continents are the most perfectly organized for the development of man."

Distribution of the Human Races

"If the distribution of the human races on the surface of the globe does not follow the law of the rest of nature, what, then, is the law that regulates it? . . .

"While all the types of animals and of plants go on decreasing in perfection, from the equatorial to the polar regions, in proportion to the temperatures, man presents to our view his purest, his most perfect type, at the very centre of the temperate continents, at the centre of Asia-Europe . . . In proportion as we depart from the geographical centre of the races of man, the regularity diminishes, the harmony of the proportions disappears . . .

"The distribution of man over the surface of the globe, and that of the other organized beings, are not then founded on the same principle. There is a particular law which presides over the distribution of the human races and of civilized communities, taken at their cradle, in their infancy; a different law from that which governs the distribution of plants and animals.

"In the latter, the degree of perfection of the types is proportional to the intensity of heat, and of the other agents stimulating the display of material life. The law is of a physical order.

"In man, the degree of perfection of the types is in proportion to the degree of intellectual and moral improvement. The law is of a moral order.

147

"Thus the geographical march of the perfection of the species from the poles to the equator, is suddenly broken when man appears, to recommence on a plan wholly new.

"This difference between the two laws has its principle in the profound differences existing between the nature and destination of these distinct beings. The plant and the animal are not required to become a different thing from what they already are at the moment of their birth. Their *idea*, as the philosophers would say, is realized in its fulness by the fact alone of their material appearance, and of their physical organization. The end of their existence is attained, for they are only of a physical nature. But with man it is quite otherwise. Man, created in the image of God, is of a free and moral nature. The physical man, however admirable may be his organization, is not the true man; he is not an aim, but a means; he is not an end, like the animal, but a beginning. There is another, new-born, but destined to grow up in him, and to unfold the moral and religious nature until he attain the perfect stature of his master and pattern, who is Christ. It is the intellectual and the moral man, the spiritual man.

The Law of a moral order

"The law of development, if I may say so, is the law of man, the law of the human race, and of human societies; now, the free and moral being cannot unfold his nature without education; he cannot grow to maturity, except by the exercise of the faculties he has received as his inheritance.

The cradle of mankind in northern continents

"Here is the reason, gentlemen, that the Creator has placed the cradle of mankind in the midst of the continents of the North, so well made, by their forms, by their structure, by their climate, as we shall soon see, to stimulate and hasten individual development and that of human societies; and not at the centre of the tropical regions, whose balmy, but enervating and treacherous, atmosphere would perhaps have lulled him to sleep the sleep of death in his very cradle . . .

How has man fallen?

"Now, if man came from the hands of the divine Author of his being, pure and noble, it was in those privileged countries where God placed his cradle, in the focus of spiritual light, that he had the best chance to keep himself such. But how has he fallen elsewhere so low? It is because he was free, of a perfectible nature, and consequently capable also of falling. In the path of development, not to advance is to go back; it is impossible to remain stationary. The animal does not degenerate, because the form of his existence is necessary; he is not required to add anything. But man, who should grow in perfection by the constant exercise of the higher faculties of his nature, by struggling against the evil inclinations of a perverted will, man descends evermore, and proceeds from fall to fall, if he neglects those divine gifts, and abandons himself to the low instincts of his animal nature. He goes down to the life of the brute, whose form and semblance he takes. And what will come to pass if, separated from his God, and forgetting Him, he voluntarily stops the sources of the higher life, and moral life? Remote from the focus of tradition, where he might renew the temper of his faith, he remains unarmed in combat with that mighty nature that subjugates him; he yields in the struggle, and, vanquished, bears soon upon his figure the ineffaceable mark of bondage. Thus, perhaps, might

148

one, I do not say explain, but conceive, the incontestable influence of each continent, and each region of the earth, on the physical forms, the character and the temperament of the man who dwells in it, and the degeneracy of his type in proportion as he is removed from the place of his origin, and the focus of his religious traditions. Renouncing moral liberty, which exists only in goodness, man gives to nature power over himself . . .

"Since man is made to acquire the full possession of his faculties by toil, and by the exercise of all his energies, no climate could so well minister to his progress in this work as the climate of the temperate continents . . . The man of the temperate regions is the . . . most favored. Invited to labor by everything around him, he soon finds, in the exercise of all his faculties, at once progress and well-being.

"The result of the comparison we have made between the northern continents and the southern continents, in their most general characteristics, has convinced us, if I do not deceive myself, that what distinguishes the former is, not the wealth of nature and the abundance of physical life, but the aptitude which their structure, their situation, and their climate, give them, to minister to the development of man, and to become thus the seat of a life much superior to that of nature . . ."

In his volume entitled *Physical Geography*, 1873, Guyot concludes his contrasts of the Northern and Southern Continents by these two statements:

"*The Southern Continents*,—lying mainly in the tropical zone, where all the conditions that stimulate physical life are the most powerful, and where, with few exceptions, man has remained at the bottom of the social scale,—may be designated the *continents of nature*. Each has its own especial character, wherein the influence of every distinguishing feature of the continent is seen . . .

"*The Northern Continents*, may properly be designated the *continents of history*. Less richly endowed with those elements which foster the life of nature, they possess all the conditions most favorable for the development and progress of the races inhabiting them; and each was apparently designed, from the beginning, for the performance of a peculiar part in the education of mankind".

Conclusion of
contrast

"The Continents of History"

"The first glance we cast upon the annals of the nations, enables us to perceive a singular but incontestable fact, that the civilizations representing the highest degree of culture ever attained by man, at the different periods of his history, do not succeed each other in the same places, but pass from one country to another, from one continent to another, following a certain order. This order may be called *the geographical march of history*. We now proceed to set this forth by a rapid review of the great phases through which human societies have passed in their gradual improvement . . .

*Arnold Guyot,
The Earth and
Man*

"Asia . . . the Continent of Origins"

"*Western Asia* is not only the geographical centre of the human race, but it is, moreover, the spiritual centre; it is the cradle of man's moral nature. Was it not there that those divine teachings were proclaimed, which the most cultivated communities in the world regard as their dearest treasure, and every man who loves the true, acknowledges to be Truth itself? Was it not there that the chosen people lived, to whom they were given in trust to preserve for the world until the time appointed by the Supreme Wisdom? Was it not there that the Saviour of all the members of the human family appeared, and the gospel of grace and liberty was preached, in the lowly valleys of Judea—that gospel which recognized neither Jew, nor Greek, nor Gentile, nor barbarian, and which invites all the races of the earth to salvation, without distinction? Is it not from the height of the sacred mount where He died upon the cross for all, that Christ bids every human soul, whatever be the ephemeral form of its earthly covering, to a spiritual union which he will consummate in his glory? And these great facts, gentlemen, interesting to every human being, these facts whose blessed consequences surround us on all sides at the present day, belong not to the number of those that any historical unbelief can ever strike out of the annals of mankind. Nor are they of secondary importance, considered merely in the results already accomplished; for who will maintain that, even in the future, man will ever witness an event more important for him than the appearance of the Saviour, and the proclamation of the universal gospel destined to unite all men and at the same time to bind them all to their common Creator?

"Europe . . . the Continent of Development"

"*Europe* is thus the most favored continent, considered with respect to the education of man, and the wise discipline it exercises upon him . . . Christian Europe beholds poetry, the arts, and the sublimest sciences, successively flourish, as in the bright days of pagan Greece; but, enriched already with the spoils of the past, culture is far more comprehensive, more varied, more profound; for it is not only affluent with the wealth of days gone by, but Christianity has placed it on the solid foundation of truth. The spirit of investigation ranges in all directions; it adds to this brilliant crown a new gem, the science of nature, growing with a speed of which the Ancient World has not even a forecast. Unriddled by the spirit of man, nature has yielded up to him her secrets; her untiring forces are enlisted in the service of intellect, which knows how to guide their action for its own purposes . . . The ocean has lost its terrors; with the help of steam the sailor braves opposing winds and waves; the compass and the stars conduct him with unerring precision to the end of his voyage. Space is annihilated by railroads; the word of man, borne on the wings of electricity, outruns in its course the sun himself; distances vanish, obstacles are smoothed away. Man thus disposes at will with the forces of nature, and the earth at last serves her master.

"Such is the spectacle presented by European civilization. Looking upon it only under this brilliant aspect, and in itself, the progress of man seems to be almost touching its final goal. Nevertheless, the plan traced by the Divine Founder of the Christian church is much more vast; the goal which He sets up is much higher. These precious gifts of culture are not to remain the exclusive property of a small number of privileged men, nor of a single society, of one continent alone; the Christian principle is broader; it is universal, like the love of Christ. An important work remains, then, to be done; the work of diffusion and of propagation . . .

"Yes . . . a new work is preparing, and a grave question is propounded. To what people shall it belong to carry out this work into reality? The law of history replies, to a new people. And to what continent? The geographical march of civilization tells us, to a new continent west of the Old World—to America.

"America . . . the Most Complete Expression of the Christian Civilization"

"And what is the vital principle we find at the very root of this nation? It is the gospel. Not the gospel disfigured and cramped by the iron fetters of a powerful hierarchical church, like that the Christian Germanic world received while in its cradle, but the gospel restored by the Reformation, with its life-giving doctrines, and its regenerative power. Luther drew the Bible forth from the dust of libraries, where it lay forgotten, at the moment when Columbus discovered the New World. Will any one believe that here was only an accidental coincidence? . . .

"The founders of social order in America are indeed the true offspring of the Reformation—true Protestants. The Bible is their code. Imbued with the principles of civil and religious liberty they find written in the gospel, and for which they have given up their former country, they put them in practice in this land of their choice. They are all brethren, children of the same Father—this is equality, independence, liberty. They submit from the heart to their Divine Leader, and to his law; this is principle of order. Now the union of these two terms is free obedience to the divine will, which is the condition of a normal development, the supreme end of the education of man.

"These, you will agree, gentlemen, are the sublime doctrines whence flow the religious, political, and social forms that distinguish America at the present time, from all the other countries on the globe . . .

"Finally, the oceanic position of the American continent secures its commercial prosperity, and creates, at the same time, the means of influence upon the world. It commands the Atlantic by its ports, while Oregon and California open the route of the Pacific Ocean and the East. America, also, is so placed as to take an active part in the great work of the civilization of the world, so admirably begun by Europe . . .

"The new society ought to receive entire the inheritance of those which have gone before; for nothing good or beautiful should perish. It ought to be rooted in that living faith which nourishes nations and keeps up in them the freshness of life; its instruments should be the sciences and industry; its ornaments, literature and the fine arts; its end, the happiness of all, by training them up to moral perfection, and by spreading the gospel throughout the world, to the glory of the Redeemer.

"You see, gentlemen, this picture transports us into the future. *There* stands the goal, and we are only now at the starting point. But this lofty goal may serve as a guiding star for the present, to preserve it from losing its way. In what measure and through what perils it shall be given to mankind, and to America in particular, to attain it, is known to God alone, and future ages will teach the issue to the world; but what we do know is, that it will be in proportion as man shall be faithful to the law of his moral nature, which is the divine law itself.

Conclusion: Asia, Europe, America
"The Continents of History"

"Asia, Europe, and North America, are the three grand stages of humanity in its march through the ages. *Asia* is the cradle where man passed his infancy, under the authority of law, and where he learned his dependence upon a sovereign master. *Europe* is the school where his youth was trained, where he waxed in strength and knowledge, grew to manhood, and learned at once his liberty and his moral responsibility. *America* is the theatre of his activity during the period of manhood; the land where he applies and practises all he has learned, brings into action all the forces he has acquired, and where he is still to learn that the entire development of his being and his own happiness are possible only by willing obedience to the laws of his Maker.

"Thus lives and prospers, under the protection of the Divine Husbandman, the great tree of humanity, which is to overshadow the whole earth. It germinates and sends up its strong trunk in the ancient land of Asia. Grafted with a nobler stalk, it shoots out new branches, it blossoms in Europe. In America only, it seems destined to bear all its fruits. In these three we behold at once, as in a vast picture, the past, the present, and the future. . . .

"Before closing let us cast back a glance upon the long way we have travelled over. The geographical march of history must have convinced us, if I am not mistaken,—

1. That the three continents of the North are organized for the development of man,

and that we may rightfully name them preeminently the historical continents.

2. That each of these three continents, by virtue of its very structure, and of its physical qualities, has a special function in the education of mankind and corresponds to one of the periods in his development.

3. That in proportion as this development advances and civilization is perfected, and gains in intensity, the physical domain it occupies gains in extent and the number of cultivated nations increases.

4. That the entire physical creation corresponds to the moral creation, and is only to be explained by it."

America . . . "In the Order of Providence"

"That there shall exist on this continent one Republic, great and indivisible"

"In observing the United States, there is much to convince us, that an Almighty, Overruling Providence, designed from the first, to place here a great, united people."

Emma Willard, *History of the United States or, Republic of America*

★   ★   ★

"Although the vast country which we have been describing was inhabited by many indigenous tribes, it may justly be said, at the time of its discovery by Europeans, to have formed one great desert. The Indians occupied, without possessing it. . . . Those coasts, so admirably adapted for commerce and industry; those wide and deep rivers; that inexhaustible valley of the Mississippi; the whole continent, in short, seemed prepared to be the abode of a great nation, yet unborn.

"In that land the great experiment was to be made by civilized man, of the attempt to construct society upon a new basis; and it was there, for the first time, that theories hitherto unknown, or deemed impracticable, were to exhibit a spectacle for which the world had not been prepared by the history of the past."

Alexis de Tocqueville, *American Institutions and their Influence*

★   ★   ★

"The vast region which the flag of the United States protects was, two centuries and a half ago, the roaming ground of tribes of Indians . . . Neither the exuberance of the soil, nor the magnificence of the rivers, nor the influence of climate, nor the geographical conditions that stimulate commerce, roused in them the capacity to develop the resources of this splendid country; and it is a just inference, that their successive generations passed away with hardly more heed to any divine command to subdue and replenish the earth than is evidenced in the falling of the autumnal leaves. The wonderful riches of the land which they pompously called their own, were an untouched treasury. It was virtually a waste, awaiting, in the order of Providence, the magic influence of an incoming race, imbued with the spirit of a new civilization."

Richard Frothingham, *The Rise of the Republic of the United States*

153

How Do We Relate God's Principle of Individuality to America's Christian Form of Government and to Our Constitution?

For sixteen hundred years the *Chain of Christianity* had been travelling westward bearing within itself the seed of the freedom of man. To the degree that *Christ* was acknowledged as the basis of all liberty to that extent did the status of man in civil society improve. But it was only in 1620 that *Christian Liberty* was acknowledged as the basis of *political freedom*. This conviction brought the tiny settlement of Pilgrims to our shores to establish a nation on the rock of *Christian Conscience*—*internal* liberty—the source of *external* freedom and power.

In 1787—one hundred and sixty-seven years after the Pilgrims landed—this seed of *Individual Liberty* blossomed into the American Christian Constitution, which, in the words of the great constitutional lawyer, James A. Beck, "threw around the individual the solemn circle of the law."

Today, it is vital that Christian teachers lay this foundation-stone of *Christian individualism* early in the grades. *Collectivism*—that political term which indicates group or government determination of the amount and extent of individual freedom —permeates every fiber of our society. No wonder our nation becomes more *socialistic* daily when there is no clear-cut extension of this basic Christian principle of individualism into every aspect of our lives—social, educational, political and economic. We can begin as individual teachers to overturn the trend to be just *a part of the whole*—and instead teach *God-given individuality*.

As each student learns to love and cherish God's principle of individuality in all things, we will do much towards stemming the tide which is sweeping the earth, endeavoring to annihilate the individuality of men and nations. One has only to look at nature to see the infinite diversity and distinctness of individuality which is revelational of God. If we look within the Holy Bible we can see that though the theme is the same the individual who speaks, inspired by the Holy Spirit, has identity. Reverend A. B. Simpson writes, speaking of the individuality of the prophets:

"We know that they acted with perfect individuality, and that each man's message was colored by the complexion of his own mind, so that we know the writings of Isaiah from those of Jeremiah; we know the voice of Elijah from that of Elisha; we know the style of John from that of Paul. The Book of God is like a beautiful garden, where all the flowers grow upon the same soil and are watered from the same heaven, but each has its own unique colors, forms, fragrance and individuality."

Even as the *'very hairs of your head are all numbered"*, so is your own individual and inspirational teaching of America's Christian History of value and importance in helping restore to our nation its vision of Constitutional government and individual liberty based upon *Christian individualism*.

Christian Individualism

Starting with Me
God made me special—
Like no one else you see.
God made me a witness
To His diversity.

What Shows That I Am "Me"?

Outward Identification

My *profile* or *silhouette*, shows that the shape of my face is my very own. It is not like any other face in the whole wide universe.

God shaped my *hands*—my *right hand*, and my *left hand*, to serve Him. My two *hands* are not the same. My hands do not look like any other hands.

My *thumb-print* has a very beautiful *design*. There is no other *thumb-print* just like mine. Even though my thumb will get bigger—my *thumb-print* will always be the same *design*. God knows me. God made me. God made just one "me".

My *name* is my own. Sometimes some one else is called by the same name— but when I *write* it—it looks just like my name.

And my *picture* is a *picture* of me. God doesn't need a picture because God always knows me. He never mistakes me for some one else. God made me for Himself. God made me special. God made *only one* just like me.

Inward Identification

What *qualities* of thought, feeling, or talent, has God entrusted to me?

Every quality of Christian character is a *reflection* of God since man is "*Image* and *likeness*" of God.

"*Man looketh on the outward appearance, but the Lord looketh on the heart.*" I Samuel 16:7

"*the inward man is renewed day by day*" and it is this "inward man" which we must cultivate and let God give the "increase" of heart, mind and soul.

What is my "well defined individuality" and how can I play my part in the "definite plan of the all-wise Creator"?

Everything in God's universe is revelational of God's infinity, God's diversity, 155

God's individuality. *"The earth is the Lord's and the fulness thereof . . ."* Psalms 24:1. *"The heavens declare the glory of God; and the firmament sheweth his handywork"* Psalms 19:1.

Plants: trees, flowers, grass etc. Does not every blade of grass, every flower, and each leaf express God's principle of individuality? They are distinct, unique, individual.

Minerals: rocks, crystals, metals etc. Each crystal is unique and maintains its individual characteristics and can be identified.

Animals: No two animals are alike—even baby animals have distinctions and individuality.

Let us look at God's universe very carefully. Let us discover the many unique and wonderful things which He has created. Let us pray that God will open our heart and our eyes to see and understand God's principle of individuality in all things.

Geographic Individuals

Everything in God's universe is revelational of God. The earth was shaped to fit God's purpose and God's plan. Therefore it is not surprising to learn that the continents—those six land masses—which comprise the terrestrial surface of the earth—each have a shape and a size—*an individuality*—to fit the purpose of God.

Guyot, the Christian Geographer found on pages 3 through 5 in *Christian History*, calls the continents *"Geographic Individuals"*.

Read Text, Christian History, *page 4, last paragraph*

Guyot refers to the three *Northern Continents* as the *Continents of History*. These are the three with which we are concerned in our study of America's Christian History.

"Asia . . . The Continent of Origins". Asia's Special Function in the Westward Movement of Christianity

Where do we learn that *Western Asia* is the geographical center of the human race?

Where do we learn that *Western Asia* is the *'spiritual centre'* of mankind?

Read Text, Christian History, *page 3, first paragraph*

How did *Asia's* physical characteristics and her geographic individuality help her to fulfil her special function in God's plan?

What was *Asia's* historic function for mankind?

"Europe is Emphatically the Continent of Development"

What was the *"solid foundation of truth"* which Europe was able to add to the arts and sciences?

Read Text, Christian History, *page 3, 2nd paragraph*

Name some of the specific ways in which *Europe* proved to be the *"continent of development"* for mankind.

How did *Europe's* geographic individuality—her physical characteristics—help in fulfilling her historic function for mankind?

What special preparations in the *Old World* were God's ways of preparing mankind for the westward move to *America?*

Read Text, Christian History, *pages 1 and 2.*

"America seems Destined to Furnish the Most Complete Expression of the Christian Civilization"

Read Text, Christian History, *page 4*, America

What are some of the characteristics of the *American* continent which would make possible the great Christian principle of *unity with diversity?*

How is Guyot's concept of the individualism of the continents created and formed by God for His purpose, distinguished from the *environmental* approach?

How are cause and effect reversed when you compare *geographic individualism* with *environmental determinism?*

What isolates *America* from the rest of the world and kept her separate until God found mankind ready to come to her shores? What same fact also puts her in the pathway of history?

Why does the Gospel lie at the heart of *America's* discovery, settlement and special function for all mankind?

Read Text, Christian History, *pages 5–9*

America is known as the continent where occurs the highest development of the individual. How does the idea of individuals working to improve themselves bless the whole community and actually promote the best growth and welfare of all?

Why is this *Christian individualism?*

What must be fundamental to the idea of *individual freedom?*

Individual Links on Christianity's Chain

Read Text, Christian History, *pages 3–9*

Map on page 6A of *Christian History* shows some important links on the *Chain of Christianity*. We shall be identifying these links in order to determine just how they contributed to the westward movement of Christianity. Just what part was America destined to play; in what way would she use what had gone before; what new elements would she add? Why did God reserve her for "the completed structure"?

The Ten Commandments—The Law

"But before faith came, we were kept under the law, shut up unto the faith which should afterwards be revealed. Wherefore the law was our schoolmaster to bring us unto Christ, that we might be justified by faith." Galatians 3:23, 24

Rev. L. T.
Townsend,
*The Bible and
Law*

"Of the world's judgment respecting the two tables of commandments, there is no ground for question. Perhaps an intelligent person cannot be found who will dissent from this statement, that these two tables recorded in the writings of Moses contain in a general form the vital principles of all modern legal science, judicial, national, and international. Is not that a fact upon scientific grounds worthy of careful study"?

David Hoffman,
*A Course of
Legal Study*

"But the religion and morals of the Scriptures by no means constitute the only claim which this inestimable volume possesses on the earnest attention of the legal student. There is much *law* in it . . . Political science is certainly indebted to it for an accurate account of the origin of *society*, *government*, and *property* . . . This view of Scriptures is strongly entertained by the late Dr. Campbell, who in his lectures on ecclesiastical history, remarks that, 'When we consider attentively the institutions of Moses, we perceive that they comprehend every thing necessary for forming a civil establishment; not only precepts regarding the morals of the people, and the public and private offices of religion, but also laws of jurisprudence . . . I may add, they comprehend, also a sort of law of nations, for the use of that people, in adjusting the terms of their intercourse with other states and kingdoms, prescribing rules for the making and conducting of war and peace, entering into public treaties, and the like.'

"In *Leviticus*, *Numbers* and *Deuteronomy*, we have the ritual, moral, and civil law of the Jews."

Christianity—The Gospel

Christianity alone brings true liberty and it establishes as the basis of government—the Christian idea of man. The Gospel brings forth a higher standard of liberty than *external law*—rather that *internal law* of the Two Commandments of our Lord. Christianity's government is self-government—and he that accepts the Gospel is willing *"to bring into captivity every thought to the obedience of Christ"* (2 Cor. 10:5).

For centuries men sought freedom from slavery and tyranny. They believed their liberation to be dependent upon *external* circumstances. But it was not until the Saviour of mankind appeared that men learned that external freedom was achieved by internal liberty—*"the liberty wherewith Christ hath made us free"*.

"The greatest and most dangerous of despotisms is that beneath which the depraved inclination of human nature, the deadly influence of the world, namely, sin, miserably subjects the human conscience. There are, no doubt many countries, especially among those which the sun of Christianity has not yet illumined, that are without civil liberty, and that groan under the arbitrary rule of powerful masters. But, in order to become free outwardly, men must first succeed in being free inwardly. In the human heart there is a vast country to be delivered from slavery—abysses which man cannot cross alone, heights he cannot climb unaided, fortresses he cannot take, armies he cannot put to flight. In order to conquer in this moral battle, man must unite with One stronger than himself—with the Son of God."

J. H. Merle
D'Aubigne, D.D.,
*History of the
Reformation in
Europe*

Christianity moved Westward—each move bringing forth the evidence that freedom and progress for man rests only with the achievement of spiritual liberty—*"the glorious liberty of the children of God"* (Rom. 8:21). Thus the Christian idea of man and government had to take shape through the centuries as men grasped the idea of Christian self-government.

Read Text, Christian History, *page XIII*

The Pagan Nations—Greece and Rome

Read Text, Christian History, *pages 5-16*

"The first thing that presents itself to our notice here will be, the difference between the two great individualities of national character, out of which proceeded the civilization of those times,—the Greek and the Roman. In the Greek predominated the activity of the intellect,—the scientific, speculative element. Greece was, in fact, the birth-place of philosophy. The Roman character, on the other hand, was

Dr. Augustus
Neander, *General
History of the
Christian Religion
and Church*

159

less mobile. It was more fixed and inclined to be tenacious of old usages;—its tendency was to the practical. Both these mental characteristics will mark the peculiar shaping of Christian doctrine and theology,—will in different circumstances operate favorably or unfavorably on the process of their development; since both these individualities of character correspond to the peculiar main tendencies above described; and it was most desirable, that they should so act as mutually to balance and check each other . . .

"And while it was necessary that the influence of Judaism should penetrate into the heathen world, in order to prepare the way and open a point of communication for Christianity, so was it needful also, that the stern and repulsive stiffness of Judaism should be softened and expanded by the elements of Hellenic culture, in order to become recipient for what was new in the presentations of the Gospel.

"The three great historical nations had to contribute, each in its own peculiar way, to prepare the soil for the planting of Christianity,—the Jews on the side of the religious element; the Greeks on the side of science and art; the Romans, as masters of the world, on the side of the political element. When the fulness of time was arrived, and Christ appeared,—when the goal of history had thus been reached, —then it was, that through him, and by the power of the spirit that proceeded from him,—the might of Christianity,—all the threads, hitherto separated, of human development, were to be brought together and interwoven in one web."

Greece

Extremes of Tyranny and Democracy

"When we contemplate Greece, and especially when we fix our eyes on Athens, our admiration is strongly, I had almost said, is irresistibly excited, in reflecting, that such a diminutive spot concentrated within itself whatever is great and eminent in almost every point of view; whatever confers distinction on the human intellect; whatever is calculated to inspire wonder, or communicate delight. Athens was the pure well-head of poetry:

'*Hither, as to their fountain, other stars
Repairing, in their golden urns draw light.*'

"It was the theatre of arms, the cradle of the arts, the school of philosophy, and the parent of eloquence.

"To be regarded as the masters in learning, the oracle of taste, and the standard of politeness, to the whole civilized world, is a splendid distinction. But it is a pestilent mischief, when the very renown attending such brilliant advantages becomes the vehicle for carrying into other countries the depraved manners by which these pre-eminent advantages are accompanied. This was confessedly the case of

Greece with respect to Rome. Rome had conquered Greece by her arms; but whenever a subjugated country contributes, by her vices, to enslave the state which conquered her, she amply revenges herself . . .

"Many of the Athenian vices originated in the very nature of their constitution; in the very spirit of that turbulent democracy which Solon could not restrain, nor the ablest of his successors control . . .

"This unsettled government, which left the country perpetually exposed to the tyranny of the few, and the turbulence of the many, was never bound together by any principle of union, by any bond of interest, common to the whole community, except when the general danger, for a time, annihilated the distinction of separate interests. The restraint of laws was feeble; the laws themselves were often contradictory; often ill administered; popular intrigues, and tumultuous assemblies, frequently obstructing their operation . . .

"By this light and capricious people, acute in their feelings, carried away by every sudden gust of passion, as mutable in their opinions as unjust in their decisions, the most illustrious patriots were first sacrificed, and then honored with statues; their heroes were murdered as traitors, and then reverenced as gods . . .

"While we observe that Greece first became powerful, rich, and great, through the energy of her people, and the vigour of her character, and that this very greatness, power, and riches, have a natural bias towards corruption; that while they happily tend to produce and nourish these arts, which in their just measure are the best embellishments of a nation; yet carried to excess, and misapplied to vicious purposes, tend to weaken and corrupt it; that Athens, by her public and private vices, and by her very refinement in politeness, and her devotedness to the arts, not only precipitated her own ruin,—but by the transplantation of those arts, encumbered with those vices, ultimately contributed to ruin Rome also . . .

"Among the numberless lessons which *we* may derive from the study of Grecian history, there is one which cannot be too often inculcated, more especially as it is a fact little relished by many of our more refined wits and politicians,—we mean the error of ascribing to arts, to literature, and to politeness, that power of softening and correcting the human heart, which is, in truth, the exclusive prerogative of *religion*. Really to mend the heart, and purify the principle, is a deeper work than the most finished cultivation of the *taste* has ever been able to effect . . .

"Every description of men, who know how to estimate public good or private happiness will joyfully acknowledge the visible effect which Christianity has had (independently of its influence over its real votaries) in improving and elevating the general standard of morals, so as considerably to rectify and raise the conduct of those who are not directly actuated by its principles. And, lastly, to say nothing of a pure church establishment, so diametrically the reverse of the deplorably blind and ignorant rites of Athenian worship (Acts, Chapter 17)—who can contemplate, without thankful heart, that large infusion of Christianity into our national laws, which has set them so infinitely above all comparison with the admired codes of Lycurgus and of Solon?"

KEY TO
EXPANDING
PRINCIPLES

Revs. W.
Conybeare and
J. S. Howson,
*The Life and
Epistles of
St. Paul*

Greek character
used for spread
of the Gospel

Greek becomes
the language of
theology

"If we think of the civilization of the Greeks, we have no difficulty in fixing on its chief characteristics . . . We have only to do with this national character so far as, under divine Providence, it was made subservient to the spread of the Gospel.

"We shall see how remarkably it subserved this purpose, if we consider the tendency of the Greeks to trade and colonization. Their mental activity was accompanied with great physical restlessness. This clever people always exhibited a disposition to spread themselves . . . At the earliest period at which history enables us to discover them, we see them moving about in their ships on the shores and among the islands of their native seas; and three or four centuries before the Christian era, Asia Minor, beyond which the Persians had not been permitted to advance, was bordered by a fringe of Greek colonies . . . To all these places they carried their arts and literature, their philosophy, their mythology, and their amusement. They carried also their arms and their trade . . .

"Of all the Greek elements . . . the spread of the language is the most important. That language, which is the richest and most delicate that the world has seen, became the language of theology. The Greek tongue became to the Christian more than it had been to the Roman or the Jew . . . It was not an accident that the New Testament was written in Greek, the language which can best express the highest thoughts and worthiest feelings of the intellect and heart, and which is adapted to be the instrument of education for all nations: nor was it an accident that the composition of these books and the promulgation of the Gospel were delayed, till the instruction of our Lord, and the writings of His Apostles, could be expressed in the dialect of Alexandria. This, also, must be ascribed to the foreknowledge of Him, who 'winked at the times of ignorance,' but who 'made of one blood all nations of men for to dwell on all the face of the earth, and determined the times before appointed and the bounds of their habitation.' "

Rome

Centralization Through Law

Read Text, Christian History, *pages 12 and 13*

Revs. W.
Conybeare and
J. S. Howson,
*The Life and
Epistles of
St. Paul*

"We have to describe in a few words the characteristics of this new dominion, and to point out its providential connection with the spread and consolidation of the Church.

"In the first place, this dominion was not a pervading influence exerted by a restless and intellectual people, but it was the grasping power of an external government. The idea of law had grown up with the growth of the Romans; and wherever they went they carried it with them. Wherever their armies were marching or encamping, there always attended them, like a mysterious presence, the spirit of the City of Rome. Universal conquest and permanent occupation were the ends at which they aimed. Strength and organization were the characteristics of their sway. We have seen how the Greek science and commerce were wafted, by irregular winds, from coast to coast; and now we follow the advance of legions, governors, and judges along the Roman Roads, which pursued their undeviating course over plains and mountains, and bound the City to the furthest extremities of the provinces.

"There is no better way of obtaining a clear view of the features and a correct idea of the spirit of the Roman age, than by considering the material works which still remain as its imperishable monuments. Whether undertaken by the hands of the government, or for the ostentation of private luxury, they were marked by vast extent and accomplished at an enormous expenditure. The gigantic roads of the empire have been unrivalled till the present century. Solid structures of all kinds, for utility, amusement and worship, were erected in Italy and the provinces, amphitheatres of stone, magnificent harbours, bridges, sepulchres, and temples. The decoration of wealthy houses was celebrated by the poets of the day. The pomp of buildings in the cities was rivalled by astonishing villas in the country. The enormous baths, by which travellers are surprised, belong to a period somewhat later than that of St. Paul: but the aqueducts, which still remain the Kampagna, were some of them new when he visited Rome. Of the metropolis itself it may be enough to say, that his life is exactly embraced between its two great times of renovation, that of Augustus on the one hand, who (to use his own expression) having found it a city of brick left it a city of marble, and that of Nero on the other, when the great conflagration afforded an opportunity for a new arrangement of its streets and buildings.

Monuments of the Roman age

"These great works may be safely taken as emblems of the magnitude, strength, grandeur, and solidity of the empire; but they are emblems, no less, of the tyranny and cruelty which had presided over its formation, and of the general suffering which pervaded it. The statues, with which the metropolis and the Roman houses were profusely decorated, had been brought from plundered provinces, and many of them had swelled the triumphs of conquerors on the Capitol. The amphitheatres were built for shows of gladiators, and were the scenes of a bloody cruelty, which had been quite unknown in the licentious exhibitions of the Greek theatre. The roads, baths, harbours, aqueducts, had been constructed by slave-labour. And the country-villas, which the Italian traveller lingered to admire, were themselves vast establishments of slaves.

Monuments as emblems of magnitude, tyranny, cruelty

"It is easy to see how much misery followed in the train of Rome's advancing greatness. Cruel suffering was a characteristic feature of the close of the republic. Slave wars, civil wars, wars of conquest, had left their disastrous results behind them. No country recovers rapidly from the effects of a war which had been conducted within its frontier; and there was no district of the empire which had not been the scene of some recent campaign. None had suffered more than Italy itself. Its old stock of freemen, who had cultivated its fair plains and terraced vineyards,

Misery follows Rome's greatness

163

was utterly worn out. The general depopulation was badly compensated by the establishment of military colonies. Inordinate wealth and slave factories were the prominent features of the desolate prospect. The words of the great historian may fill up the picture:

" '*As regards the manners and mode of life of the Romans, their great object at this time was the acquisition and possession of money. Their moral conduct, which had been corrupt enough before the social war, became still more so by their systematic plunder and rapine. Immense riches were accumulated and squandered upon brutal pleasures. The simplicity of the old manners and mode of living had been abandoned for Greek luxuries and frivolities, and the whole household arrangements had become altered. The Roman houses had formerly been quite simple, and were built either of brick or peperino, but in most cases of the former material; now, on the other hand, every one would live in a splendid house and be surrounded by luxuries. The condition of Italy after the Social and Civil wars was indescribably wretched. Samnium had become almost a desert; and as late as the time of Strabo, there was scarcely any town in that country which was not in ruins . . .*'

"It would be a delusion to imagine, that when the world was reduced under one sceptre, any real principle of unity held its different parts together . . . The Empire was only the order of external government, with a chaos both of opinions and morals within . . . The old severity of manners, and the old faith in the better part of the Roman religion, were gone. The licentious creeds and practices of Greece and the East had inundated Italy and the West; and the Pantheon was only the monument of a compromise among a multitude of effete superstitions. It is true that a remarkable religious toleration was produced by this state of things; and it is probable that for some short time Christianity itself shared the advantage of it. But still the temper of the times was essentially both cruel and profane; and the Apostles were soon exposed to its bitter persecutions. The Roman Empire was destitute of that unity which the Gospel gives to mankind. It was a kingdom of this world; and the human race was groaning for the better peace of '*a kingdom not of this world.*'

"Thus in the very condition of the Roman Empire, and the miserable state of its mixed population, we can recognize a negative preparation for the Gospel of Christ. This tyranny and oppression called for a *Consoler*, as much as the moral sickness of the Greeks called for a Healer: a Messiah was needed by the whole Empire as much as by the Jews, though not looked for with the same conscious expectation. But we have no difficulty in going much farther than this, and we cannot hesitate to discover in the circumstances of the world at this period, significant traces of a positive preparation for the Gospel.

"It should be remembered, in the first place, that the Romans had already become Greek to some considerable extent, before they were the political masters of those eastern countries, where the language, mythology, and literature of Greece had become more or less familiar . . . Is it too much to say, that the general Latin conquest was providentially delayed till the Romans had been sufficiently imbued with the language and ideas of their predecessors, and had incorporated many parts of that civilization with their own?

"And if the wisdom of the divine pre-arrangements is illustrated by the period of the spread of the Greek language, it is illustrated no less by that of the completion and maturity of the Roman government. When all parts of the civilized world were bound together in one empire,—when one common organization pervaded the whole,—when channels of communication were everywhere opened—when new facilities of travelling were provided,—then was 'the fulness of time' (Gal. 4:4), then the Messiah came. The Greek language had already been prepared as a medium for preserving and transmitting the doctrine; the Roman government was now prepared to help the progress even of that religion which it persecuted. The manner in which it spread through the provinces is well exemplified in the life of St. Paul; his right of citizenship rescued him in Judea and in Macedonia; he converted one governor in Cyprus, was protected by another in Achaia, and was sent from Jerusalem to Rome by a third. The time was indeed approaching, when all the complicated weight of the central tyranny, and of the provincial governments, was to fall on the new and irresistible religion. But before this took place, it had begun to grow up in close connection with all departments of the Empire."

Roman Civil Law

"The Romans developed social control through law, as we understand it today. But the Roman law with which the formative era of the later Middle Ages came in contact was the codified law of the eastern Roman empire—the codification under Justinian. It was the codification of the law of the empire in which all the power of the magistrates, and so of judging, of issuing edicts, and of proposing laws, and in consequence complete lawmaking, law-interpreting, and law-applying authority, were concentrated in an autocratic ruler . . .

"Of the two chief systems of law in the world of today one, the modern Roman or civil law, is characteristically judicial. In antiquity, while originally the ultimate lawmaking power was theoretically in the Roman people, the Roman law grew chiefly through the edicts of the magistrates, and the writings of the juris-consults. . . . In legal theory the emperor was the first citizen of Rome to whom the whole power of all the magistrates had been delegated by a statute. Thus the theory of the legal order was administrative . . .

"Whereas in the final Roman theory law proceeded from the emperor—was made by him—in the English theory it was pre-existing and was found by the king or by his justices and applied to the cases before them as something binding on them no less than on the parties.

"As a result of this difference of attitude towards the law, the one system thinking of it as wholly the product of the government, the other thinking of a fundamental law binding the agencies of government, there is a characteristic difference as to declaration of rights and guarantees of liberties in the two systems."

"Render therefore unto Caesar the things that are Caesar's; and unto God the things that are God's." Matthew 22:21

"Render therefore to all their dues: tribute to whom tribute is due; custom to whom custom; fear to whom fear; honour to whom honour." Romans 13:7

John Wycliffe: "Morning Star of the Reformation" 1320 (?)-1384

Read Text, Christian History, *pages 28A, 28B, 29, 47*

More than one hundred years before Luther, rose the *"morning-star of the Reformation"*, John Wycliffe, first in the line of evangelical reformers to whom the Gospel was the precious measure of reform. With Wycliffe's first beams in a dark age of anti-Christian idolatry occurred "the earliest break" with Latin Christianity. An important part of his ministry was to place the Bible in the heart of the individual. To do this, Wycliffe made one of the earliest translations of the Scriptures from the Latin into English.

Prof. G. V.
Lechler, D.D.,
*John Wycliffe
and His English
Precursors*

"The principle that God's Word should be preached to the people, he expanded into the principle that Scripture must become the common property of all. As a means to this end, he saw the necessity of the Bible being translated into the language of the country, with the view of giving it the widest possible diffusion among the population . . .

"It must have been a heartfelt joy and deep satisfaction for Wycliffe when the translation of the whole Bible was completed, and the great plan accomplished which he had so long cherished and pushed forward with so warm a zeal. This, in all probability, took place in the year 1382. Wycliffe, however, was not the man to betake himself to rest as soon as he had attained any single object, and least of all in this sacred cause. To him the translation of the Bible was not an end in itself, but only a means to an end—that end being to place the Bible in the hands of his own countrymen, and to bring home the Word of God to the hearts of the English people. For this purpose copies of it were now made and circulated, not only of the whole Bible, but also of portions, and even of single books . . .

The Wycliffe
translation of
the Bible

"If we compare Wycliffe's Bible, not with his own English writings, but with English literature in general before and after his time, a still more important result is revealed. Wycliffe's translation of the Bible marks an epoch in the development of the history of the English language just as much as Luther's translation does in the history of the German tongue. The Luther Bible opens the period of the new High German; Wycliffe's Bible stands at the head of the Middle English. It is usual, indeed, to represent not Wycliffe, but Chaucer—the father of English

poetry—as the first representative of the Middle English literature. But later philologists—such as Marsh, Koch, and others—rightly recognize Wycliffe's Bible
prose as the earliest classic Middle English . . .

"During the last years of Wycliffe's life his opponents evidently cherished the
hope that his chief followers, already enfeebled and intimidated, would be hope-
lessly scattered after his death, and that the whole party would become extinct.
Soon, however, it became plain that there was a life in the movement not at all
dependent on the personality of Wycliffe. He was removed from the earthly scene;
but his adherents continued his work with no appreciable diminution of energy.
It was in the year succeeding the death of Wycliffe that the name of *Lollards*
came into general use as a designation of his followers . . . Its use by the hierarchy
to characterize his followers is a proof to us that the 'Wycliffites' had become an
independent sect, large enough to attract public attention, and formidable enough
to arouse ecclesiastical animosity.

"The Lollard party, in the years immediately following Wycliffe's death, consisted, so to speak, of an inner and an outer circle. The former was composed of
enthusiastic and able men, who in the first instance through the preaching of the
Itinerants, and subsequently through their own reading and study, had been led to
the adoption of evangelical principles. Thus it seemed to them all the more necessary, after the death of their venerated, strong-souled leader, to maintain the closest
bonds of alliance for mutual encouragement and a common defence against their
enemies.

"The outer and far larger circle comprised men and women, in different grades
of society, who listened and read, learned and often believed. Many of these naturally passed into the inner circle, and became themselves the teachers of others.
So numerous had the adherents of Wycliffe become during the period between his
death and the close of the century that, according to the testimony of opponents, at
least half the population had ranged themselves on the side of the Lollards. 'You
could scarcely meet two persons in the road, but one of them would be a disciple
of Wycliffe' . . .

"If we inquire concerning the inner life of the Lollard community, we learn little
or nothing from Church history, but much from the incidental references of the
chroniclers. They were, above all, characterized by a striving after holiness, a zeal
for the spread of Scriptural truth, for the uprooting of prevalent error, and for
Church reform. Even the common people among them were men who *believed*; and
they communicated, as by a sacred contagion, their convictions to those around
them. Thus they became mighty.

"Religious tracts had much to do with the dissemination of their doctrines. Besides Wycliffe, Hereford and others prepared many of these short treatises which
were copied and widely distributed. But above all the translation of the Bible became a power. It was largely circulated not only in a complete form, but in separate
books; and wherever it was known an impulse was given to the Lollard doctrines.

Among the MSS. of the Wycliffe Bible that have survived the ravages of time and come into the hands of the most recent editors, no fewer than twelve are of an earlier date than 1400. Some of these are very costly, showing that the precious volume was sought by the richer classes.

"The Bible being thus made a comparatively familiar book, great stress was laid upon the exposition of its contents by preaching. Staff in hand, the preachers journeyed on foot from place to place, and paused wherever they could obtain hearing from gentle or simple . . .

Gospel preachers "The preaching, be it remembered, was in English; and the preachers were mainly of the same class as their hearers: their homely expositions of Scripture went home to the heart; they spoke, moreover, of prevailing sins and evils, as luxury and the like; they called by their right names the misdeeds of the clergy, while for themselves they sought nothing. It is no wonder that these travelling preachers stirred the land, and that the minds of men were attracted to them in a continually augmenting degree.

"Besides these open-air gatherings, assemblies were convened in halls and cottages, in chapels, in gardens. Here and there a little company would assemble to converse on Divine things, to build one another up in faith and knowledge. At such meetings the Bible in Wycliffe's translation would be read aloud, or a tract by Wycliffe or Hereford, explaining the sacred text. Even the art of reading would be taught on such occasions. It was thus that William Smith of Leicester first learned his alphabet. Many others, men and women, anxious to read the Scriptures for themselves, would follow his example. Knighton bitterly complains that the Word of God translated into English 'becomes more accessible and familiar to laymen and to women able to read than it had hithertofore been to the most intelligent and learned of the clergy . . .'

The wrath of
man praises God "The decree of the Council of Constance in regard to Wycliffe's bones was carried out after long delay . . . the remains of the great Englishman were not only torn from their resting-place, but burned to ashes and cast into the little river Swift, that runs by Lutterworth on its course to the Avon. Thus, in the often-quoted words of Thomas Fuller, 'the little river conveyed Wycliffe's remains into the Avon, the Avon into the Severn, Severn into the narrow seas, they to the main ocean. And thus the ashes of Wycliffe are the emblem of his doctrine, which now is dispersed all the world over.'"

Martin Luther—1482–1546

Read Text, Christian History, *page 47*

"With Luther began the awakening of the human conscience. Terrified at the sin
he discovered in himself, he found no other means of peace but faith in the grace

of Christ Jesus. This starting-point of the German reformer was also that of every other Reformation."

Luther appealed to the authority of the Scriptures to challenge the divine right of papacy at the Diet of Worms in 1521.

Henry C. Sheldon,
*History of the
Christian Church*

" 'I am,' he pleaded, 'but a mere man, and not God; I shall therefore defend myself as Christ did, who said, 'If I have spoken evil, bear witness of the evil' . . . For this reason, by the mercy of God I conjure you, most serene Emperor, and you, most illustrious electors and princes, and all men of every degree, to prove from the writings of the prophets and apostles that I have erred. As soon as I am convinced of this, I will retract every error, and will be the first to lay hold of my books, and throw them into the fire . . . I cannot submit my faith either to the Pope or to the councils, because it is clear as the day that they have frequently erred and contradicted each other. Unless, therefore, I am convinced by the testimony of Scripture, or by clear reasoning, unless I am persuaded by means of the passages I have quoted, and unless my conscience is thus bound by the Word of God, I cannot and will not retract; for it is unsafe and injurious to act against one's own conscience. Here I stand, I can do no other: may God help me! Amen.'

"One of the sublimest scenes in history! No battle ever fought or won has been worth more to the cause of human liberty than this act of the peasant's son in asserting the claims of conscience before the dignitaries of Church and empire . . .

"By far the most important task, however, which occupied his leisure, was the translation of the Bible. The first draft of the New Testament was produced here. The work of the translation was continued at Wittenberg, until at length, in 1534, the complete Lutheran Bible was given to the people. The enterprise may well be regarded as marking an epoch in the national history. It is true that other translations into the vernacular had preceded this of Luther. But none of them had any thing like the same adaptation to the people; none of them were such homelike products to the German mind; none so brought out the riches of the German tongue; none were so true at once to the German and to the original; for, while it was a maxim with Luther that a translation must express the sense of the original, it was equally a maxim with him, that it must express that sense in the national idiom . . . 'A genuine son of his own people, gifted with all the wealth and depth of the German mind, he could enter into that age of simple national faith; he made its spirit and language his own, and thus acquired the power of translating into German the religious-poetic and poetic-religious mode of expression.' It is scarcely necessary to add, that the copies of the new German Bible, issued as fast as the hard-worked presses could supply them, became powerful instruments for the spread of evangelical truth . . .

"Luther passed away (Feb. 18, 1546). His departure, as far as his personal fortunes were concerned, was in peace and unshaken faith. Among his last words was the thrice-repeated sentence: 'Father, into thy hands I commend my spirit. Thou hast redeemed me. Thou faithful God.' So ended a stormy life; so passed away one

Luther's
translation of
the Bible

Luther was the
man of Germany

169

of the great men of history . . . We see in him a marked individuality, an heroic temper, a consummate genius, a deeply religious spirit, a peculiarly faithful embodiment of strong national traits. As David was the man of Israel, so Luther was the man of Germany. As David embodied the chivalry, the patriotism, the lyric talent, the domestic affection, and the religious ardor of Israel, so Luther embodied the leading features of the German heart and mind. His words thrilled the men of his time, and to-day are in large part fresh and living . . . Heart and mind of the Germans were in his hand like the lyre in the hand of the musician. Moreover, he has given to his people more than any other man in Christian ages has ever given to a people, language, manual for popular instruction, Bible, hymns of worship; and every thing which his opponents in their turn had to offer or to place in comparison with these, showed itself tame and powerless and colorless by the side of his sweeping eloquence. They stammered: he spoke with the tongue of an orator; it is he only who has stamped the imperishable seal of his own soul alike upon the German language and upon the German mind; and even those Germans who abhorred him as the powerful heretic and seducer of the nation cannot escape; they must discourse with his words, they must think with his thoughts."

John Calvin—1509–1564

Read Text, Christian History, *page 47*

"The times of Luther were followed by those of Calvin. He, like his great predecessor, undertook to search the Scriptures, and in them found the same truth and the same life; but a different character distinguishes his work.

"The renovation of the individual, of the Church, and of the human race, is his theme. If the Holy Ghost kindles the lamp of truth in man, it is (according to Calvin) 'to the end that the entire man should be transformed.'—'In the kingdom of Christ,' he says, 'it is only the new man that flourishes and has any vigor, and whom we ought to take into account.'

"This renovation is, at the same time, an enfranchisement; and we might assign, as a motto to the reformation accomplished by Calvin, as well as to apostolical Christianity itself, these words of Jesus Christ: *The truth shall make you free.* John 8:32 . . .

"The reformation of the sixteenth century restored to the human race what the middle ages had stolen from them; it delivered them from the traditions, laws, and despotism of the papacy; it put an end to the minority and tutelage in which Rome claimed to keep mankind forever; and by calling upon man to establish his faith not on the words of a priest, but on the infallible Word of God, and by announcing to every one free access to the Father through the new and saving way—Christ Jesus, it proclaimed and brought about the hour of Christian manhood.

"An explanation is, however, necessary. There are philosophers in our days who regard Christ as simply the apostle of political liberty. These men should learn that, if they desire liberty outwardly, they must first possess it inwardly . . .

"There are, no doubt, many countries, especially among those which the sun of Christianity has not yet illumined, that are without civil liberty, and that groan under the arbitrary rule of powerful masters. But, in order to become free outwardly, men must first succeed in being free inwardly . . .

"The liberty which the Truth brings is not for individuals only: it affects the whole of society. Calvin's work of renovation, in particular, which was doubtless first of all an internal work, was afterwards destined to exercise a great influence over nations.

"In intellect, Calvin was undoubtedly one of the most remarkable men of the sixteenth century. The mere amount of work which he accomplished in the space of about thirty years attests extraordinary capacity. His routine duties as a teacher, preacher, and administrator, were such that it is difficult to conceive how there could have been time or strength for other tasks. In fact, however, the additional labors were of great compass. He carried on an extensive correspondence, responding with much pains-taking to the manifold inquiries which came from the great multitude that owned him as the master mind among all the leaders in the religious revolution. He assisted in preparing the translation of the Bible which passed into general use among the French Protestants, though his work in this line was of much less significance than that of Luther. His commentaries, distinguished for lucidity, terseness, and rational attention to the trend of each writing, covered the larger part of the Bible. Not a few controversial treatises came from his pen. Crowning all, was his great work in systematic theology, to which he gave the finishing touch five years before his death. As one surveys this list of achievements, he can readily credit Calvin with that mental trait of which Beza makes special note,—memory of wonderful tenacity and promptness, which brought under control all the acquisitions gained through years of industrious research. Along with this was associated great keenness, logical vigor, and firmness of mental grasp . . . Everyone must allow that he laid hold upon a wide circle of truth with great vigor and precision . . .

"Whatever the dogmatic defects or merits of Calvin's Institutes, it was well qualified to exert a powerful influence . . . 'No writing of the Reformation era was more feared by Roman Catholics, more zealously fought against and more hostilely pursued, than Calvin's Institutes.' . . .

"As already indicated, Protestants in different countries felt that he was a pillar of strength to their cause; and Romanists feared his pen as one of the most formidable foes with which they had to contend. Geneva, under his hand, became a citadel and an arena, a refuge to which the fugitive might flee from persecution, and a training-school in which he might be equipped for heroic service. Philip II expressed what many among the foes of the Reformation felt, when he wrote to the French King, respecting Geneva: 'This city is the source of all mischief for France, the

GOD'S
PRINCIPLE OF
INDIVIDUALITY

Henry C. Sheldon,
*History of the
Christian Church*

Calvin remarkable
in intellect

The influence of
Geneva

171

most formidable enemy of Rome. At any time I am ready to assist, with all the power of my realm, in its overthrow.' The French Government on its part threatened to destroy the city if it did not keep its evangelists at home, and sent an ambassador to give notice to that effect. The evangelists, however, continued to pour forth; Calvin having assured the magistrates, that, inasmuch as the city depended upon the omnipotent God alone for protection, the highest prudence consisted in the most perfect obedience to His Will. The scale on which Geneva exercised the function of a training-school may be estimated from the fact that at one time, according to the report of a contemporary, Calvin had regularly a thousand hearers for his theological lectures; and also by the fact that the Academy of Geneva, which was opened in 1559, enrolled during its first year nine hundred students. As far as into the eighteenth century, the academy was an important factor in educating the clergy of the Reformed Church in France and the Netherlands, as well as in Switzerland.

Calvin's influence
on history

"The reasons for the wide and penetrating influence of Calvin have been indicated in the account of his character and work. He organized an intellectual system for the reform movement, and gave incisive expression to the ideas which were struggling in the minds of his contemporaries. The masculine tone to his writings took a strong hold upon a great multitude of men, and infused into them something of his own energy and resoluteness of spirit. Having the temper of the lawgiver, as well as that of the logician, he gave an unique stress to the ethical demands of Christianity, and urged powerfully the need of realizing the truth of God in practice, as well as acknowledging it in theory. Not a little of that stern practical energy, that readiness to carry out convictions, which has been manifested in various sections of the Reformed Church, was born of Calvin's spirit and teaching . . .

"The immense labors of Calvin involved premature exhaustion of body . . . He passed away in peace on the 27th of May, 1564.

J. H. Merle
D'Aubigne,
*History of the
Reformation in
Europe*

". . . the characteristic element of the Genevese Reform is liberty . . . The necessity of liberty for the Gospel and of the Gospel for liberty is now acknowledged by all thoughtful men; but it was proclaimed by the history of Geneva three centuries ago . . . It is in this small republic that we find men remarkable for their devotion to liberty, for their attachment to law, for the boldness of their thoughts, the firmness of their character, and the strength of their energy . . . The great movements in the way of law and liberty effected by the people in the sixteenth and seventeenth centuries, have certain relations with the Reformation of Calvin, which it is impossible to ignore . . . What chiefly distinguishes the Reformation of Calvin from that of Luther is, that wherever it was established, it brought with it not only truth but liberty . . .

"Lastly, Calvin was the founder of the greatest of republics. The 'pilgrims' who left their country in the reign of James I and, landing on the barren shores of New England, founded populous and mighty colonies, are his sons, his direct and legitimate sons; and that American nation which we have seen growing so rapidly boasts as its father the humble reformer on the shores of the Leman."

King James Bible 1611

Read Text, Christian History, *pages 28A–36*

The Conference at Hampton Court in 1604, called by James I, began the work of the Authorized Version. The committee of revisers included the most capable linguists, theologians and Bible scholars of the times. Efforts were made also, to draw from the lesser clergy, so that all might know of the work of translation and make such contribution as his talents indicated.

Particular significance was given to the individual study by each member of the six companies which comprised the organization of the revisers. Then the individual companies met together to consider the work of their individual members. Each company sent on its work to the other companies and points of "special obscurity" were sent to "any learned man in the land for his judgement."

The following quotation from *Christian History* indicates the importance of the Christian character of these men whom God raised up for this important work:

The importance
of the Authorized
Version

"*In the first place, then, the King's Bible was indebted for its success to the personal qualifications of the revisers. They were the picked scholars and linguists of their day. They were also men of profound and unaffected piety. Let them speak for themselves. 'In what sort did these assemble? In the trust of their own knowledge, or of their sharpness of wit, or deepness of judgement? At no hand. They trusted in Him that hath the key of David, opening and no man shutting; they prayed to the Lord, O let Thy Scriptures be my pure delight; let me not be deceived in them, neither let me deceive by them . . .'*"

This version of the Bible has particular significance for the course of Christian History and the advancement of Christianity. We note the predominance of Saxon words as compared with Latin words. And, again, in the fulness of God's time, the English language had reached that peak of its richness—its full flowering. So did God's word crown this period of the blossoming of English literature.

Most important, however, was the fact that this was the *freest* and *purest* of Bible translations since Wycliffe's first work. This edition had no notes and "the interpretation of it was therefore left perfectly free." A Bible relying wholly on the power of the Word to reveal its holy message!

Individual Rights and the Law of the Land

Read Text, Christian History, *pages 37–41*

This document is important because it marks the appearing of specific rights of individuals—spelled out into the written law of the land. The Englishman of the **173**

13th Century called these rights *Natural Rights*. The American Colonist of the 18th Century recognized these rights as "*Unalienable Rights*" which were "endowed" to all men "by their Creator."

The *Magna Charta* marked a landmark in the limitation of monarchy and represented a *limitation* of the power of government. To the American Christian who recognized sovereignty as "found in the free and independent man" the God-given Rights of the individual were to be *preserved* by government. In the words of John Locke, the Philosopher of the American Revolution, men unite in civil government "for the mutual *Preservation* of their Lives, Liberties and Estates, which I call by the general Name, *Property*." 1690.

Read Text, Christian History, *pages 42–44*

The right to petition against grievances and encroachments upon individual liberty became a method of constitutional redress. As specific rights became part of the law of the land, men resorted to further clarification through written legislation—as opposed to political action which might merely exchange external sovereigns. Gradually sovereignty—the power of government—was transferred to "the free and independent man" and appeared finally in the republican form of government of the United States of America.

Read Text, Christian History, *pages 44–47*

Richard L. Perry,
Editor, *Sources
of Our Liberties*

"This is the British Act of December 16, 1689 . . . entitled: 'An act for declaring the rights and liberties of the Subject, and Settling the Succession of the Crown.' It became law as part of the agreement under which William and Mary succeeded to the British throne after the fall of James II . . .

"The Bill of Rights and the other documents constituting the Revolution Settlement represented the triumph of principles for which the recently formed Whig Party had struggled against Charles II (1660–85) and James II. These documents asserted the supremacy of Parliament over the claimed divine right of kings. The royal prerogative was sharply curtailed, and even the possession of the crown became a statutory right, not a hereditary right. Toleration for Protestant dissenters was assured, and a number of individual liberties, insisted upon as among the rights of the subject, were given formal recognition as part of the law of the land."

England did much to establish the rights of the individual as a vital part of the law of the land. These rights, however, had always to be *granted* to the subject of the realm, or *agreed to* by the monarch. America was the first nation to establish and declare the rights of man to be *God-granted*—thus indicating that external government can never confer on man that which is his God-given endowment. The *rights of the individual* were considered to be the *sacred property* of the individual. The *preservation* of this property was defined as the "chief end and purpose of government."

The colonists adapted specific guarantees to life and limb from the English Bill of Rights. These were expressed in the respective state constitutions. The first ten amendments to our federal constitution can be traced to the English Bill of Rights.

John Locke 1632–1704

Read Text, Christian History, *pages 50B–56; 57–125*

John Locke can justly be described as one of the most brilliant of political writers. Two years after the Glorious Revolution of 1688, Locke published "Two Treatises on Government" in which he successfully vindicated the principles upon which the revolution was founded. In these essays he refuted the doctrine of the divine right of kings as being contrary to God's law.

John Locke was widely read in America by the clergy and by the Founding Fathers. His development of political theory was found in many of the sermons, newspapers, and educational writing of the period for about seventy-five years preceding the American Christian Revolution. His recognition of the internal sovereignty of Christianity is expressed in the following statement:

"*As men we have God for our King, and are under the Law of Reason: as Christians, we have Jesus the Messiah for our King, and are under the Law reveal'd by him in the Gospel.*" From "The Reasonableness of Christianity", 1695.

Charles de Montesquieu 1689–1755

Read Text, Christian History, *pages 131–138*

Montesquieu was of interest to our American Colonists because of his philosophic inquiry into history to examine the basis of law and government. His work, *The Spirit of Laws*, published in 1748, became more successful in England, than in his native France, due largely to his study of and admiration for the British Constitutional system of government.

Montesquieu provides us with valuable reflections on "the political liberty of the subject" in relation to the balance of the three powers of government—legislative, executive, and the judiciary. His discussion of the republican form of government as being more truly representative of the individual, as opposed to the direct power of the people in a democracy, is important.

As Christian educators we note with interest his statement relating education and the principles of government, indicating their inseparability:

"*That the Laws of Education ought to be relative to the Principles of Government*" 175

Montesquieu, as did Locke, relates law to its primary source—God. In his opening statements of *The Spirit of Laws* he states:

"God is related to the universe, as Creator and Preserver; the laws by which He created all things are those by which He preserves them."

William Blackstone 1723–1780

Read Text, Christian History, *pages 139–146*

In 1765 Blackstone published his *Commentaries on the Laws of England*. This study represented the first collection of the common law of England with detailed explanations as to how this law functioned specifically in a constitutional monarchy—with its heritage of Magna Charta, Petition of Rights and the Bill of Rights. This digest of English common law represented also a remarkable commentary on the philosophy of law, particularly as it related to the rights of individuals in society. Blackstone is specific and detailed in his analysis, and thus became a basic part of the study of the course of Law by English and American students.

*Roscoe Pound,
The Development
of Constitutional
Guarantees of
Liberty*

"Lawyers who had 'read law' had read Coke's *Institutes*, published between 1628 and 1644, the authoritative systematic exposition of the common law down to Blackstone's *Commentaries*, published 1765–69. Thus they were brought up on ideas of 'the law of the land,' of the immemorial rights of Englishmen guaranteed by Magna Carta. Blackstone at once became the first book to be studied by American lawyers and held that place till the beginning of the present century. The *Commentaries* had an exceptionally large sale in the colonies. We are told that twenty-five hundred copies were bought in America before the Revolution. A subscription reprint was published in Philadelphia in 1771–72. The list of subscribers is headed by 'John Adams, Esq, barrister at law, Boston'. Blackstone set forth Coke's doctrine in readable form."

Blackstone, as did Locke, defined the Law of Nature as "will of his Maker". The following quotation is from his introductory article, "The Nature of Laws".

"As man depends absolutely upon his Maker for everything, it is necessary that he should, in all points, conform to his Maker's will. *This will of his Maker is called the law of nature . . . This law of nature*, being coeval with mankind, and dictated by God himself, *is of course superior in obligation to any other*. It is binding over all the globe, in all countries, and at all times: no human laws are of any validity (i.e. in the forum of conscience), if contrary to this; and such of them as are valid derive all their force, and all their authority, mediately or immediately, from this original."

Thus we find, through *Locke, Montesquieu* and *Blackstone*, the establishment of a Christian philosophy of government and law, which aided our American colonists to write an American Christian Constitution.

The Pilgrims and the Puritans

Read Text, Christian History, *pages 20–27; 48–50; 182*

"The great Reformation in the sixteenth century was an attempt to recover the primitive Gospel . . . Then began that age-long conflict in the Church of England between the government Protestantism, on the one hand, completed and immovable, and the demand, on the other hand, for a more thorough reformation that should carry the National Church and the national Christianity back to the original purity portrayed in the Scriptures."

On the one side stood the Puritans, demanding reformation of church and state by compulsion. A Scripturist of the Old Testament law and letter, the *Puritan* refused to separate his own conscience from that of the national church.

The *Pilgrim* had accepted individual reformation as he had individual salvation. He felt the urgency of reformation "without tarrying for any". He was willing to separate from the Church of England for he regarded this "ecclesiastico-political institution" as incompatible with the New Testament church of Christ.

Jamestown 1607

Read Text, Christian History, *pages 150A-175*

As one of the two Original, Parent Colonies, setting a pattern which other colonists imitated, Virginia was settled in 1607 as a Royal Province. Virginia was established for commercial enterprise and "the enriching of commerce by new commodities".

Virginia colony transplanted the seed of *representative government* as a direct continuation of English society and custom. In fact the seed of monarchial government here introduced long influenced the development of her history and accounts for many struggles against the truer strain of Christian self-government representing all men. The Virginians were Royalists, members of the Established Church of England—and thus firm supporters of church and state.

As Englishmen, the Virginians were accustomed to certain rights and privileges, among these the law-making or legislative function. Accordingly, in the year 1619, Sir George Yeardly called the first legislative assembly held in Virginia. This gave the Virginians the satisfaction of beholding "among themselves an image of the English constitution, which they reverenced as the most perfect model of free government."

Read Text, Christian History, *pages 270D, and 270E*

Virginia's episcopal form of church government produced the county system as the unit of representation for the individual in the civil government. The county system was more removed from the direct control of the entire population as its offices were generally appointive and self-perpetuating. Virginia, however, produced many distinguished statesmen and patriots—men like Washington, Jefferson, Henry, Madison and Marshall—who contributed much to the founding of this nation—and who cherished the tradition of representative government.

Plymouth 1620

Read Text, Christian History, *pages 176–183*

The Pilgrim Separatists established the beginnings of our Christian Republic— the United States of America. They came to New England for *liberty of conscience* —and because "they had a great hope and inward zeall" for "ye propagating and advancing ye gospell of ye kingdom of Christ in those remote parts of ye world".

Fleeing both ecclesiastical and civil tyranny, the valiant Pilgrims of Plymouth Plantation brought to these shores Primitive Christianity. Like their counterparts of the first century of Christianity, they witnessed by their lives the consistency of their faith. *Not one went back.* In the record of Plymouth Colony we find the parenthood of our Republic. Here can be found the seed of all our important institutions. Here begins our precious record of *Christian Character, Christian Self-Government, Christian Economics, Christian Education* and *Biblical Christian Unity.* For it is what constitutes the character of individual Americans that determines whether our government, economics, education and unity are Christian or pagan.

Read Text, Christian History, *pages 270B, 270C*

New England's Congregational form of church government—local self-government of the church—was expressed also in the society. Each local township was a "small, self-governing republic".

"Of the various kinds of government to be found in the United States, we may begin by considering that of the New England township . . . It is in principle of all known forms of government the oldest as well as the simplest . . . In a New England township the people directly govern themselves; this government is the people . . . Jefferson said, 'Those wards, called townships in New England, are the vital principles of their governments, and have proved themselves the wisest invention ever devised by the wit of men for the perfect exercise of self-government, and for its preservation.' . . .

". . . in the history of Massachusetts during the Revolution we are chiefly impressed with the wonderful degree in which the mass of the people exhibited the kind of political training that nothing in the world except the habit of parliamentary discussion can impart." *Christian History*, pages 271, 279, 280

178

Read Text, Christian History, *pages 150, 204, 205*

The tradition of Christian self-government which the Pilgrims on the Mayflower carried with them, culminated in America's first document of Christian self-government—the *Mayflower Compact*.

"The document represents the application to the affairs of civil government of the philosophy of the church covenant which was the basis of Puritan theology. This theology found in the Scriptures the right of men to associate and covenant to form a church and civil government and to choose their own officers to administer both religious and civil affairs. Each member of the congregation had a vote in the election of officers, and each congregation was considered as independent and autonomous of every other and not subject to the authority of any centralized church hierarchy."

Richard L. Perry, Editor, *Sources of Our Liberties*

The purpose of the *Compact*, expressed in its original wording, was "to covenant and combine ourselves togeather into a civill body politick, for our better ordering and preserving and furtherance of ye ends aforesaid; and by vertue hereof to enacte, constitute, and frame such just and equall lawes, ordinances, acts, constitutions, and offices, from time to time, as shall be thought most meete and convenient for ye general good of ye Colonie, unto which we promise all due submission and obedience . . . solemnly and mutualy in ye presence of God, and one of another . . ."

By the signing of the *Compact* the Pilgrims established themselves as a *"single covenanted body of Christians, united for civil as well as spiritual purposes."* They also established their mission as "Undertaken *for the glory of God, for the advance of the Christian faith*, and for the honor of their king and country."

The *Mayflower Compact* became firmly established as the earliest example of Christian self-government to be found in America. It was the first written document of American representative government.

America Declares Herself an Individual Nation

Read Text, Christian History, *pages 346B–359*

"Yet Christianity nowhere began with outward revolutions and changes, which, in all cases where they have not been prepared from within, and are not based upon conviction, fail of their salutary ends. The new creation to which Christianity gave birth, was in all respects an inward one, from which the outward effects gradually, and therefore more surely and healthfully, unfolded themselves to their full extent.

Dr. Augustus Neander, *General History of the Christian Religion and Church*

It gave servants first the true, inward freedom, without which the outward and earthly freedom is mere show, and which, wherever it exists, can be cramped by no earthly bond, no earthly yoke. The apostle Paul says, 'He that is called in the Lord, being a servant, is the Lord's freeman.' "

When can a
Christian
participate
in revolution?

For one hundred and fifty years prior to the American Revolution, the clergy of the north, south and middle colonies had been wrestling spiritually with Romans, Chapter 13:1–7. The Bible admonition to *"obey magistrates"* was clear and explicit. Was there ever a time when a Christian should consider it a *duty* to resist the magistrate?

One of the outstanding clergymen of the revolutionary period was Samuel West, pastor of a church in Dartmouth. In his sermon of May 29, 1776, he discusses the relation of the Christian to government:

"But though I would recommend to all Christians, as part of the duty that they owe to magistrates, to treat them with proper honor and respect, none can reasonably suppose that I mean that they ought to be flattered in their vices, or honored and caressed while they are seeking to undermine and ruin the state; for this would be wickedly betraying our just rights, and we should be guilty of our own destruction. We ought ever to persevere with firmness and fortitude in maintaining and contending for all that liberty that the Deity has granted us.

"The love of our country, the tender affection that we have for our wives and our children, the regard we ought to have for unborn posterity, yea, everything that is dear and sacred, do now loudly call upon us to use our best endeavors to save our country. We must beat our ploughshares into swords, and our prunninghooks into spears, and learn the art of self-defense against our enemies. To save our country from the hands of our oppressors ought to be dearer to us even than our own lives, and, next to the external salvation of our own soul, is the thing of greatest importance,—a duty so sacred that it cannot justly be dispensed with for the sake of our own secular concerns . . .

"Does it not, then, highly concern us all to stand fast in the liberty wherewith Heaven hath made us free, and to strive to get the victory over the beast and his image—over every species of tyranny? Let us look upon a freedom from the power of tyrants as a blessing that cannot be purchased too dear, and let us bless God that he has so far delivered us from that idolatrous reverence which men are so very apt to pay to arbitrary tyrants . . ."

The Declaration
of Independence

A study of the *Declaration of Independence* brings to our attention the careful wording used by the American Colonists. Consider the following phrases and words with meanings derived from the first American Dictionary, Webster, Third Edition, 1856:

"*Dissolve* the Political Bands which have connected them"

DISSOLVE = "To melt, to loose, to free"

"to *alter* or to *abolish* it"

ALTER = "To make some change in; to make different in some particular; to vary in some degree, without an entire change."

ABOLISH = "To make void; to annul; to abrogate; applied chiefly and appropriately to established laws, contracts, rites, customs and institutions; as, to *abolish* laws by a repeal, actual or virtual."

The entire tenor of the term *Revolution* in 18th Christian America meant *change* as opposed to "violent overthrow". One definition of the word has an interesting connotation:

REVOLUTION = "In *physics*, rotation; the circular motion of a body on its axis; a course or motion which brings every point of the surface or periphery of a body back to the place at which it began to move; as the *revolution* of a wheel; the diurnal *revolution* of the earth."

The People of the United Colonies by the Declaration of Independence Declare Themselves a Sovereign Nation Composed of Free and Independent States.

There is no document or declaration concerning the individuality of a nation which so expresses, in a Christian manner, the reasons for its existence. What better statement of God's principle of individuality concerning nations could we find than the opening paragraph of our own *Declaration of Independence*, see page 346B.

The Colonists recognize and admit "that Governments long established should not be changed for light and transient Causes" and thus they take great care to identify the reasons for their serious step of separation.

As you study the long list of *"abuses"* and *"usurpations"* see if you can place them in the following categories:

Against individual rights of the Colonists	*Against property rights of the Colonists*	*Against the right of self-government*

Which list is longest?

What specific acts do the "Representatives of the *United States of America*, in *General Congress*" define as indicating their full status as a sovereign nation?

Congress postponed the vote on the Independence of the Colonies until the members of Congress requested their local assemblies in each colony to express their sentiments on independence. Check out on the following chart the vote of each of the colonies as it acted *individually* on the vital question of *independence:*

181

The Vote for Independence by Each Individual State

Independence in 1776 in Colony of	Influential Leaders Active	Opposition by Loyalist or Proprietary Government	New Delegates Chosen	Vote Taken Directly to the People	Delegates Instructed to Vote *for* Independence	Delegates Instructed *not* to Vote for Independence
Massachusetts						
Connecticut						
Rhode Island						
Delaware						
New Jersey						
New York						
Pennsylvania						
New Hampshire						
Maryland						
North Carolina						
South Carolina						
Virginia						
Georgia						

This was the second time in the Christian History of America that she had *separated* herself from England. What concept of *America's mission* expressed at the time of the *Declaration* was the same as that expressed by the Pilgrim Separatists?

How did *Christian Geography* determine America's identity as a nation? Does *Christian Geography* relate solely to the *physical world*, or is *Christian Geography* more concerned with the *moral world?*

What part did "public virtue" play in the struggle for Independence?

What part did Christian faith play in the attitude of the Colonists towards their action against Great Britain?

What were the *"two orders of trusts"* which the American people intended always to keep in proper balance?

How did the United States achieve *internal sovereignty?*

At what local level does Christian self-government begin?

The Christian idea of man and government as expressed in the *Declaration of Independence* recognizes *"the individual as the unit of society"*. Discuss how this represents God's principle of individuality in government.

The Christian Principle of Self-Government

Key to the Second Principle

Read Text, Christian History, *pages I–VI*

Defining the term *Government*

Some of the meanings of the word *govern* from the *1856 Webster:*

Govern:
1. To direct and control, as the actions or conduct of men, either by established laws or by arbitrary will; to regulate by authority; to keep within the limits prescribed by law or sovereign will. Thus in *free* states, men are *governed* by the constitution and laws; in *despotic* states, men are *governed* by the edicts or commands of a monarch. Every man should *govern* well his own family.
2. To regulate; to influence; to direct. This is the chief point by which he is to *govern* all his counsels and actions.
3. To control; to restrain; to keep in due subjection; as to *govern* the passions or temper.
4. To direct; to steer; to regulate the course or motion of a ship. The helm or the helmsman *governs* the ship.

Government:
1. Direction; regulation. These precepts will serve for the *government* of our conduct.
2. Control; restraint. Men are apt to neglect the *government* of their temper and passions.
3. The exercise of authority; direction exercised over the actions of men in communities, societies, or states; the administration of public affairs, according to established constitution, laws, and usages, or by arbitrary edicts.

184

4. The exercise of authority by a parent or household. Children are often ruined by a neglect of *government* in parents.

   "Let family government be like that of our heavenly Father, mild, gentle, and affectionate." Kollock

5. The system of polity in a state; that form of fundamental rules and principles by which a nation or state is governed, or by which individual members of a body politic are to regulate their social actions; a constitution, either written or unwritten, by which the rights and duties of citizens and public officers are prescribed and defined; as, a *monarchial* government, or a *republican* government.

Governor:
1. He that governs, rules, or directs; one invested with supreme authority. The Creator is the rightful *governor* of all his creatures.
2. One who is invested with supreme authority to administer or enforce the laws; the supreme executive magistrate of a state, community, corporation, or post.

Self-government in the dictionary is simply defined as: *"The government of oneself."*

Christian History of the Constitution of the United States of America traces Christianity as the basis of the American idea of Local Self-Government, beginning in the first century with the government of the primitive churches, as local, independent bodies. This concept of government only became possible with the advent of our Lord whose gospel of salvation began with the redemption of individuals and challenged the *external* law to be superseded by the *internal* law. The history of Christianity, moving westward, reveals the progress of man beginning only with individual salvation and individual responsibility. *Christian Liberty* is both *evangelical* and *political*.

Government
defined as
individual

Read Text, Christian History, *pages XIII, "The Christian Idea of Man and Government"*

Local Self-Government Defined:

This definition from Part Three of the text, *Christian History*, beginning on page 149, includes these words:

"*Local self-government*—The self-government which developed and is recognized in the Republic is not simply a custom, in the units termed municipalities or States, of managing their local affairs; but a degree of freedom in the individual to engage in the various pursuits of life, unrecognized elsewhere at the period when the Republic was formed, and yet unknown where centralization prevails, whether he chooses to act by himself or in association for civil or religious purposes; and this

185

self-government exists in union with the fulfillment of every obligation demanded by the nation."

Scripture is full of the precepts of Christian Self-Government. The following two quotations are taken from the Old Testament and the New Testament:

"He that is slow to anger is better than the mighty; and he that ruleth his spirit than he that taketh a city." Proverbs 16:32

"For if a man know not how to rule his own house, how shall he take care of the church of God?" I Timothy 3:5

Hugo Grotius, who wrote many treatises concerning the law of nations, paraphrases Paul's statement in 1654:

"He knows not how to rule a kingdome, that cannot manage a Province; nor can he wield a Province, that cannot order a City; nor he order a City, that knows not how to Regulate a Village; nor he a Village, that cannot guide a Family; nor can that man Govern well a Family that knows not how to Governe himselfe: neither can any Govern himselfe unless his reason be Lord, Will and Appetite her Vassals: nor can Reason rule unlesse her selfe be ruled by God, and (wholy) be obedient to Him."

Learning Christian Self-Government
in the Classroom

"For it is written, As I live, saith the Lord, every knee shall bow to me, and every tongue shall confess to God. So then every one of us shall give account of himself to God." Romans 14:11, 12

The recognition of individual responsibility to God came to America with the Pilgrims who had learned that each individual must give account of himself to God—and thus cannot "tarry for any".

"Men were beginning to learn that there might be individual and personal reformation, voluntary conformity to the rules and principles given in the New Testament, without waiting for a reformation of the National Church by the National Government . . . 'by the travail and diligence of some godly and zealous preachers . . . many became enlightened by the word of God, and had their ignorance and sins discovered by the word of God's grace, and began to reform their lives and make conscience of their ways.' In other words, they began to be conscientious in all things, and were earnest to know the will of God that they might obey it. This was

186

nothing else than private judgment in religion—the practical recognition of individual responsibility to God—the first stage of 'reformation without tarrying for any.' Individuals, one by one, were beginning to reform themselves under the guidance of the Scriptures." *Christian History*, page 24

Classroom Government

When a teacher and a class of students discuss the government of the classroom it is easy to fall into the socialistic concept of good government. Under a man-based form of government, such as socialism, each individual is but a part of the state—and the state is made up of the parts. In a Christian Republic, because the individual Christian accepts Jesus Christ as his Lord and Saviour—whole and complete—each individual is whole and complete in Christ.

"For as the body is one, and hath many members, and all the members of that one body, being many, are one body: so also is Christ." I Corinthians 12:12

Socialism's government is the *external* control of the parts, as opposed to Christianity's *internal* control of the individual.

Navigation of the seas, especially of the tremendous oceans of God's earth, was a particular challenge for the Christian Navigator. After men discovered the *North Star* or the *Pole Star* and recognized it as a fixed position in the heavens—they invented the compass—the unerring needle which always points *North* to the North Star. With this guide—this assurance of God's direction—they ventured across the trackless oceans and seas. Because there was so little to depend upon *externally* in those days the navigator had to depend on God. Perhaps this is why the illustration of sailing a ship presents many good examples of learning how to become Christianly self-governed. Each one in the Christian tradition, eventually must sail his own ship, relying wholly on his faith in God. But while there are many lessons of faith and of personal responsibility to be learned first before an individual is entrusted with his own self-government—it can be practiced in the everyday events and activities of the classroom.

Each student can learn to be a good *steersman*—whether this be in learning work habits which will enable him to be an effective student, or in conducting himself in a Christian manner in every activity. The Pilgrims taught us many qualities which enabled them to survive in a wilderness. They had to learn to do things which they had never done before in England. That is how they learned to govern themselves. Socialism today makes the individual more and more dependent on things and other people and less and less able to be independent and self-reliant.

The manner in which students conduct themselves—and especially what they learn in the home and in the school—determines whether they will need a "king" or "state" to tell them how to live—or whether they will rely wholly on God and learn to be directed from within. In a Christian home Father and Mother are God Magistrates. It is their duty to teach their children God as the source of authority. In a Christian school this duty is *delegated* to teachers—who must account to God for their stewardship of the children. But Christian government relies less and less on the *external* forms of authority—but instead more and more on the *internal* government of God as Christ becomes a living presence in each heart and mind.

It is important for children to learn the difference of *being controlled*, or learning to *accept* God's authority in their lives by learning how God governs our hearts, our feelings, our thoughts and our actions if we are in the Will of God. They need to be taught that the external authority of parents and teachers will grow less as they become more and more responsible for what they do.

To help children determine how they are progressing, many stories from the Bible will teach them how individuals let God govern their hearts. This enabled Samuel, David, Joseph, Moses and many others to fulfill God's purpose in their lives. It is also useful to let each child evaluate his own growing ability to be self-governed in classroom activities and playground conduct by having a series of charts which change from time to time as new occasions arise or as the teacher wishes to convey certain specific points. The following are suggestions for relating daily activities to the learning of self-government:

I am learning self-government

Classroom charts

I come in quickly when the bell rings—without being reminded.

I get to work by myself without having to be told.

I finish the work I have been given to do.

I like to do a good job.

I am learning to be self-governed in everything I do.

I need a "Ruler" to tell me what to do.

I am not sure what my teacher wants me to do.

I have to ask my neighbor for help.

I never get my work done.

I talk a lot. I get out of my seat often.

188   I can do what I want.

Areas of self-government

Compose your own individual charts for areas which your class needs to learn: always emphasize the items as an individual challenge and accomplishment rather than a collective or group enterprise. In this way all will be blessed. See *Christian History*, page 6, read paragraph "Individual benefit."
Faithful fulfillment of responsibility which one has accepted as one's own is "*Bearing one's own burden*". Gal. 6:5

Obedience to the *internal* demands of conscience brings greater freedom than mere compliance with the *external* law. We are learning a change of base from "*Thou shalt not*" to "*Thou shalt . . .*"

The following qualities are suggestions for study and application in the classroom. Many others can be used to teach the important qualities of character which it takes to help an individual to gain the ability to govern himself. Our American National government begins at the local level of each individual's ability to be self-governing. Self-governing, God-fearing, Christ-honoring citizens cannot be controlled easily when they have developed the habit of thinking and acting independently—for the glory of God and not for the glory of man.

Pilgrim Self-Government

Thrift—Economy: Learning to make good use of time, supplies and all things that God gives us. Self-government requires us to learn how to be good stewards and manage or take care of whatever is given us.

Waste and consumption help to destroy the accumulation of capital—whether that capital be goods, money, or the saving of time and talent.

Industry & Initiative: Industry means "habitual diligence in any employment"—It also means "steady attention to business or study". Bodily or mental activity. Idleness and slothfulness are its opposites. *Initiative* refers to the ability to begin on one's own—to initiate action when one is convinced that it is worthy action. This is a quality that belongs to free men and women. It is a quality which is disappearing with the constant effort of government to plan and advise the individual in his every enterprise.

Industry and frugality basic to our form of government

Self-Reliance & Confidence: The Christian says "*I can of mine own self do nothing.*" But "*I can do all things through Christ which strengtheneth me.*"

When the state is supreme the individual grows less and less able to manage his own affairs and make his own decisions. This produces the uncertainty and insecurity of our times. A Christian learns to be self-reliant by accepting responsibility as God gives him stewardship of talents and opportunities for using these talents. He is confident because of his faith in God to reveal His purpose and His will. *Self-reliance* and *Confidence* enabled the Pilgrims to establish their local church, govern their local township, make treaties with the Indians and conduct all their affairs without interference from any other church, colony or ruler.

In a sermon, preached in Roxbury, Mass., on the day of the General Fast, April 6, 1769, Amos Adams, Pastor of the First Church of Roxbury, made the following statement:

"I have often and earnestly recommended industry and frugality, as virtues absolutely necessary to public happiness . . . It is the happiness of New England that property is more equally divided than in any other part of the world; and, I believe, the poor have advantages for acquiring a comfortable subsistence, and, even, for laying up estates, beyond almost any country whatsoever. But without industry and 189 frugality, no people in the world can flourish. If families live in idleness, if people go beyond their abilities in living, building, dress, equipage, and the like; if children are not carefully brought up to industry, there is no doubt they will be miserable, with the greatest and best advantages. It is therefore highly necessary, if considered only as the means of present public happiness, that children be trained up to useful business, that we retrench superfluities, that we content our selves with the effects of our own industry. These things I urge, not merely or chiefly as being at this time peculiarly necessary for answering political purposes in Great Britain, but as now and always necessary to the life and prosperity of a people."

Christian Self-Government in Virginia Colony and Plymouth Colony

Read Text, Christian History, *pages 150A, 150B, 150C, 150D; 245–248*

The parent colonies
". . . The two provinces of Virginia and New England form a regular and connected story. The former in the south, and the latter in the north, may be considered as the original and parent colonies, in imitation of which and under whose shelter, all the others have been successively planted and reared."

The great stage was set for Christian America to begin to take shape as events in the Chain of Christianity began to fall logically into place in the early 17th century. The irresistible forward thrust of Christian history had made an indelible mark on men's thinking during the period known as the Reformation. It released anew "the principle of individuality, or of true spiritual freedom" as men again had access to the Word and could discover Scriptural authority for *the liberty of the sons of God.* "*Knowledge of salvation*" brought with it renewed efforts for liberation in all fields—discovery through knowledge—and the impetus was expressed in an age of exploration and scientific achievement.

With the Bible as "the polar magnet of Revelation", men reasoned to their political rights in civil government. The shadows of the Dark Ages receded, men looked anew at "heaven and earth and all creation" and the age of scientific instrumentation appeared as men calculated their universe. But greater by far was the force of conviction which launched the first frail barks upon the waters of religious and civil independence, and which sparked the onward westward momentum of Christian self-government.

The accounts of the two colonies, *Virginia* and *Plymouth*, are quite different. One was indeed characterized by human ambition for gold and gain. It brought with it

190

men seeking to satisfy their own ambition. There were serious problems which the new colony had to solve and while some of the problems which were found in Virginia were the same as those found in Plymouth—the solutions were different. The *Rights of Englishmen* and the seed of *Representative Government* came with the establishment of Virginia. It came forth with a great struggle because of the impurities in its founding. English habits, customs, even monarchial government came through Virginia in both church and state. Virginia, as many of the southern colonies, wished to mirror forth the English parliamentary system of constitutional monarchy. This conception of government eventually became transformed on the American soil. But it took a long time for the Christian influence which came to the New World to penetrate the old habits of despotism and tyranny which are attendant upon monarchy.

The story of *Plymouth* colony is the story of *Christian Liberty* and *Christian* *Self-Government* coming to be planted on these shores. The seed was tiny—50 settlers lived after the first year—and the little colony was finally swallowed up by Massachusetts. But the planting of *Plymouth* continued to grow in the local self-government of the New England colonies.

The purpose of this study is to show by comparison two aspects of self-government. One came through the system of representative government and the other travelled within the Christian conviction of the Pilgrims in 1620.

The Establishment of Virginia

Read Text, Christian History, *pages 150A–175*

Motives and Authorization. Elizabeth's charter to Gilbert 1578. An important document for future colonization. It implies that monarchy can transfer the *Rights of Englishmen* to new territories. Page 151. The search for external treasure. Page 153.

Financing and Settlement. With the planting of Virginia came the determination of Englishmen to have their rights—hence their property—respected and reckoned with. Page 155, paragraphs 2 and 3; page 156, paragraphs 1 and 2. And with Virginia came also firm adherence to English institutions—firm support of monarchy and of the established Church of England—the episcopal form of government in church and state. These in turn supported Virginia aristocracy and account for control by the great estates and the aristocratic strain of society.

Form of Government Established. Page 150C—Virginia established as a Royal Province. Page 156, paragraph 3 through page 157 to end of paragraph 2 on page 158. Captain Smith emerged as the leader of the helpless colony. Strong leadership did not develop the self-government capacity of the colonists. After Smith's departure to England anarchy followed—page 160, paragraph 1. Page 161, paragraphs 1–4, describe the providential arrival of Lord Delaware whose skilful administration reestablished the colony only to be followed by the martial law of Sir Thomas Dale. Martial law became oppressive to the colonists, accustomed to their rights as Englishmen. Thus the calling of the first legislative assembly in 1619 represented recognition of their need for greater representation in government. Page 164, paragraphs 2, 3, 4.

Monarchy Restricts Rights of Colonists. In 1624, King James dissolved the London Company, which had become a power in English politics. James attempted to frame laws for the government of the colony. Page 167, paragraphs 1, 2, 3. Charles I attempted to restrict the colonists even further and under Yardley ignored their political rights. Page 168, paragraphs 1 and 2. Finally in 1639 Berkeley was named governor of Virginia and there followed almost forty years of "mild and prudent administration." Page 169, paragraph 2.

Virginia, faithful to the last to the very monarchy which sought to restrict her rights, was finally subdued by the commonwealth. The commonwealth attempted to make the colonists dependent on the parent state and so passed laws restricting and prohibiting trade. While the colonists rankled under the restraints, their liberties were actually being legally affirmed by the Puritan party at home. The governors appointed under the commonwealth gave Virginia nine years of tranquility. Page 170, entire page through end of paragraph. Eventually, Virginia rejected the commonwealth for the support of Charles II, but it was under his rule that she suffered the most oppressive restrictions and further violations of her rights. Page 171, paragraph 2.

Rebellion Fails to Correct Oppressive Rule. Under the leadership of a political opportunist, Bacon, the longsuffering colonists attempted the violent overthrow of the government. The rebellion disintegrated with the death of Bacon and did not advance the cause of political freedom and representative government, despite the determination of the colonists to lay their grievances before their sovereign. Paragraph 2, page 173 through paragraph 2, page 175. Page 175, paragraph 3, sets forth the idea that while Virginians had the structure of English government, they had not yet embodied politically the constitutional form of government.

Individual Enterprise. Productivity is an important aspect of property. It represents individual initiative, enterprise and labor. Locke expresses this aspect of man's productivity by stating that man has "property in the free use of his faculties." Communal efforts at agriculture in James Town rewarded the idle and the improvident. The division of property permitted individual self-government and choice as to the degree of effort to be invested in one's own behalf. Page 162, paragraph 2, page 163, paragraphs 1 and 2. Self-government requires maturity of judgment and the colonists forgot moderation in the planting of tobacco.

Relations with Indians. From the first the Virginia colonists were involved in war with the natives. Smith's efforts were valiant to secure peace and obtain supplies from the Indians. The Indians observed much misconduct on the part of the settlers and in 1622 attacked Virginia colony, depleting it by one-fourth. The settlers retaliated. Page 165, paragraphs 1 and 2.

Family Life. Unlike the Pilgrims who migrated to the New World largely in family units and often as church congregations, the Virginians came as single adventurers or colonists. Most of them considered themselves as "sojourners in a land to which they were not attached by the tender ties of a family and children." In an effort to remedy this the company sent out a large number of young women "of humble birth indeed, but of unexceptional character." By encouraging the establishment of families many heretofore thoughtless adventurers became substantial citizens with a vested interest in the future of a country which they began to consider as their own. Page 163, last paragraph.

Virginia and Representative Government. April 1606 James I by Charter created the London and Plymouth companies and gave them separate territorial jurisdictions. This document marks England's claim to colonize America between the 34th and 45th parallels of latitude. The charter guaranteed that the colonists should enjoy the rights and privileges of Englishmen, page 150C. Charter of Ordinance, July 24, 1619 issued by the company to the planters, "gave a legal and permanent form to the government of the colony." Page 164, paragraph 3. "The government of the colony was in imitation of Great Britain."

Thus Virginia colony transplanted the seed of representative government from England. At first the colonists were content to maintain their rights as rights belonging to them because they were Englishmen. Later, when they more fully understood these rights to belong to them as men, they were able to modify the structure of government which they had imported with them from the Mother Country, and to adapt it to their new conceptions of liberty—*"the glorious liberty of the children of God"*—Romans 8:21. It was through the descendents of the early settlers of Virginia that the most intelligent and most eloquent pleas were voiced stating unequivocally that men are *"endowed by their Creator with certain unalienable rights"* and that the purpose of government is "to secure these rights."

The rights of
Englishmen

A Study of Virginia Colony

What might have helped the early efforts of colonization to succeed?

Could Elizabeth guarantee the *rights* of Englishmen to new settlements in America?

193

What qualities of leadership did Captain Smith display?

How could the Colonists have gained the respect of the Indians?

Why was tobacco a dangerous success to Virginia?

What steps were taken in 1619 to give the Virginians more self-government?

Summarize the cost to England of the colonization of Virginia in 1624.

What control did Parliament seek to impose on Virginia through the Navigation Acts?

What represented the greatest threat to the survival of Virginia?

Why did the settlers have to be forced to work?

Would slavery have been introduced into Virginia if its settlers had been more self-reliant and industrious?

Can you account for the Indians' treatment of the settlers?

What caused a suspension in the self-government of Virginia for many years?

Why was Bacon's proposed action against monarchy not representative of constitutional government?

The Plymouth Plantation

Read Text, Christian History, *pages 185–240*

Question: What can be discovered in the Plymouth Plantation which identifies America as a Christian nation?

"What could now sustaine them but ye spirite of God & his grace? May not & ought not the children of these fathers rightly say: Our fathers were Englishmen which came over this great ocean, and were ready to perish in this willderness; but they cried unto ye Lord, and he heard their voyce, and looked on their adversitie, &c. Let them therefore praise ye Lord, because he is good, & his mercies endure for ever. Yea, let them which have been redeemed of ye Lord, shew how he hath delivered them from ye hand of ye oppressour. When they wandered in ye deserte willderness out of ye way, and found no citie to dwell in, both hungrie, & thirstie, their sowle was overwhelmed in them. Let them confess before ye Lord his loving kindness, and his wonderfull works before ye sons of men."—William Bradford, *"History of Plimouth Plantation"*, Christian History, *page 203*

Pilgrims Came to Establish Congregational Form of Government. During the Reformation a portion of English Protestantism became Separatists. They withdrew from the national church instead of remaining to reform it. Their study of the Scriptures and the early apostolic church convinced them that each congregation should be local and self-governing. Pages 24–27. "The primitive churches were distinct, complete, independent, local, or, as we shall now denominate them Congregational churches . . ."—J. W. Wellman, *"Church Polity of the Pilgrims"*, Christian History, *page 270B*

"Joyned Themselves By a Covenant of the Lord". They were beginning to grasp the responsibility of individual reformation and salvation, and to recognize voluntary association as the basis of church organization and government. ". . . The society was purely voluntary, and every church so constituted was strictly independent of all others in the conduct of its worship, the admission of its members, the exercise of its discipline, the choice of its officers, and the entire management of its affairs. They were, in a word, independent republics . . ."—J. W. Wellman, *"Church Polity of the Pilgrims"*, Christian History, *page 270B*

"And that Rock was Christ". The Pilgrim settlement of Plymouth left an impression on the history of the world which cannot be effaced. The word "rock" is defined by an 1847 edition of Webster's Dictionary as "a firm or immovable foundation. It is significant that Plymouth Rock has remained associated in the thought of Americans as symbolizing a foundation which cannot be forgotten, *"and that Rock was Christ."* 1 Cor. 10:4.

Early Christians and the Pilgrims. The New Testament records the struggles, trials, and achievements of the early Christians—a record which will continue to inspire and instruct. So William Bradford's account of Plymouth Colony has remained a record for our time of the Christian establishment of our nation—a record to which we can turn with inspiration and gratitude. It fulfills America's destiny as inseparable from Christianity.

Motives for Colony. The Pilgrims were concerned that their children were being drawn away from parents and God in Holland. Page 192, the last seven lines to the end of paragraph on page 193. The Pilgrims wanted to propagate and advance the gospel of the Kingdom of Christ. Page 193, paragraph 1.

Authority for Colony. Freedom of religion was a major concern to the Pilgrims. For this reason they decided on the newly-opened New-England territory. To finance their voyage a patent was granted by the London Company from merchant investors. Later this patent proved to be of no legal value to the Pilgrims because they settled outside the territorial boundaries over which the Virginia Company had jurisdiction. Page 194, paragraph 3, page 195, paragraphs 1, 2, and 3.

Venture Capital. Pages 196 and 197 discuss the terms of the agreement. The joint stock company made each individual worth as many shares as his investment of work, stock, chattels. This investment was to determine the value of the return when the final division of capital and profits was to be made to all those entering into the agreement.

Departure. Pilgrims take leave of their beloved pastor, John Robinson, father of the Independents or congregational form of church government. Robinson sounded the keynote of the Christian basis for conduct and government. Pages 198–201.

Christian Self-Government. The Mayflower Compact—Page 204, paragraph 4; page 205, paragraph 1. This compact is an example of the formation of government by consent of individuals. It represents the application to civil government of the church covenant—the right of men to associate and covenant "in ye name of God." The Pilgrims never were able to secure a royal charter and thus their right to exist as a self-governing state always rested upon the Mayflower Compact.

Indians. The Pilgrims found an English-speaking Indian. They made a covenant or compact with the Indians which governed their relations. The Indians proved helpful in aiding them to successfully plant, and fish, and hunt.

Christian Economics. The need to increase the production of corn caused the Pilgrims to debate the drawbacks of farming community property. They decided to permit the individual to farm his own "parcell of land." The ample harvest vindicated the decision and the response of individual enterprise and individual self-respect to self-employment. The opportunity to *"work out your own salvation"* challenged Christian self-government—the desire and ability of each individual to work to his fullest capacity. Page 213. Page 218, paragraph 1.

Private enterprise or exchange by mutual agreement puts an end to famine. Exchange page 217, paragraphs 1 and 2.

Restrictive Acts Against Colonists. Pilgrims pay high interest on goods brought into colony. Standish seeks to reestablish former covenant but fails. Page 223, paragraphs 1 and 2. Once again, thrown upon their own resources, but blessed with their sustaining knowledge of God, the Pilgrims "began to rise again." They were not only "upheld and sustained, but their proceedings both honored and imitated by others." Page 224, paragraphs 1 and 2

Plans to Repay Loan. Pilgrims secure a loan in England. They make plans to repay original debt to the merchants and adventurers who financed their voyage. Each individual is to share in the repayment of the debt. Pages 225–227. Despite the mishandling of their affairs which increased their indebtedness, the Pilgrims prospered under God and were finally able to settle the debt, after 21 years of effort. Page 237, paragraph 1.

Christian Character. "Their godly carriage & Christian behavior", page 188, paragraph 3; Pilgrim character is formed, page 190, paragraph 2; the Christian challenge for character, page 193, last paragraph; Christian charity and self-reliance, page 205, paragraph 2; Pilgrims treated Mr. Weston's men well, despite Mr. Weston's un-Christian conduct to them, page 210, paragraphs 2 and 3; Christian forgiveness, page 219, paragraph 2; the Pilgrims uncover plot to discredit them. Trial. Pilgrims exercise forebearance, pages 219–221; a discussion of the persecution of "ye Divell" against the churches of Christ because they uphold the holiness and purity of Christianity, page 237.

THE CHRISTIAN PRINCIPLE OF SELF-GOVERNMENT

Pilgrims' Trials. The Pilgrims leave their native England because of their religious convictions, page 185; the difficult trip to Holland and the betrayals, pages 186–189; the difficulties of living in Holland, pages 189–193; the Pilgrims are sustained in the wilderness, pages 202–203; visitors reduce their supplies and they must ration, page 209, paragraphs 1 and 2; all help from England fails, page 210, paragraph 1; famine and food shortage, page 211, paragraphs 2 and 3; an unsuccessful attempt to thwart their success, page 214, paragraph 3; more arrivals with no provisions, page 216, paragraphs 1, 2 and 3; another plot to discredit the colony, page 219, paragraph 2 thru page 221; the mishandling of Pilgrim affairs by agents, page 231, paragraph 2 thru page 233; a discussion on why a Christian is tried and the rewards for fidelity, pages 238–240.

The Pilgrims relied on God. They lived as Christians in all their avenues of activity. In their economics they kept their agreements. They invested their labor and industry in order to become self-sustaining and free from debt and the Lord prospered their endeavors. Their government was based upon the "covenant" or compact, of the two great commandments and this self-government was expressed in Christian unity. As students of the Bible they taught their children, and this knowledge of the Word became the first practice and establishment of Christian education in the New World.

Christian self-government, property, union

Comparison of Self-Government in the Parent Colonies

Motives for Colonization. Why did Plymouth have to be more steadfast than Virginia in order to bring to fruition the motives for which the Pilgrim colony was established?

Individual Enterprise Replaces Community Effort. In which colony did initiative of individuals effect the change from group effort in farming to private enterprise? Explain the Christian principle of working for yourself.

Family Life. What part did family life play in each of the two colonies?

Relations with the Indians. What principle of Christian self-government made it possible for the settlers of Plymouth to live for many years in peace?

Intelligent Leadership. What evidence of wise leadership can you describe in each colony? Can you indicate some qualities of character which made for poor leadership?

Trials and Tribulation. What were some of the determining factors in the manner in which Virginia Colonists and Plymouth Settlers conducted themselves in times of stress and trouble?

Rights and Responsibilities. In which colony would you have the greater rights and privileges? In which colony would you have greater responsibility?

The Local Self-Government in the Colonies

The Government of the Parent Colonies: Township & County

Read Text, Christian History, *pages 16–19; 270A–282*

The churches of the first Century of Christianity were little self-governing republics and the principal voice was that of the whole body of Christians. While giving all honor and respect to the apostles who in many cases founded the particular churches, this provided no opportunity, at first, for special position in the determining of matters of concern to all the members of the congregation. Each church was independent of other local churches—their fellowship was a unity of the spirit—and not in any external organization of churches.

Opposition to a national church had been in large measure responsible for sending the Pilgrims fleeing to Holland. When they arrived on these shores they carried the seed of local self-government of church and society with them and put it into immediate practice. Their voluntary unity was carried out with respect to the independence of each local self-governing congregation and community. Their fellowship with other churches meant also non-interference with their church affairs. But they were always willing to unite their efforts and prayers to work for the advancement of a Christian enterprise. In this way the habit of self-government promoted both spheres of American government—the autonomy of the local community—its ability to take care of and manage its own affairs—and *union*—or the ability to work with other communities or colonies for purposes of mutual concern. One can see why these two spheres, which became later *The State* and *The Nation*, had to have their basis in the two Commands of our Lord.

198

In studying the chart on page 270C of *Christian History*, one can see why the Pilgrims were consistent in extending their *congregational form of government* to the society of the town. It is evident also that unless the *sovereign power* vested in the individual was understood from a Christian standpoint, it could very well become selfish and self-willed. But the Christian who accepted the *internal* government of God through Christ recognized the source of the governing power. With Paul he could state:

"For he that is called the Lord, being a servant, is the Lord's freeman: likewise also he that is called, being free, is Christ's servant." 1 Corinthians 7:22

On the following pages there are suggestions for making a comparison and a contrast between the *township* and the *county* system of government. Both of these systems contributed to our representative government as practiced in all of the colonies before the American Christian Revolution.

Township System of Government	*County System of Government*
Make-up of Population:	Make-up of Population:
Effect of soil and climate:	Effect of soil and climate:
Habit of Public Meetings:	Habit of Public Meetings:
Selectmen Chosen by:	Vestrymen Chosen by:
Business of Selectmen:	Business of Vestrymen:
Status of Schools:	Status of Schools:
Source of the Governing Power:	Source of the Governing Power:

Comparison	
Township System of Government	County System of Government

Contribution	
Township System of Government	County System of Government

Other Colonies	Variation of Parish, County, Township
Massachusetts	
New York	
Pennsylvania	
Virginia	
South Carolina	
Maryland	

American Episcopal Polity

In the southern colonies we note the influence upon the civil government of the form of church government which characterized the established Church of England which the Cavaliers brought with them. The important point here to consider is that the *sovereignty* or *power of government* remained in the external organization. As one studies the two charts 270C and 270E, it is important to note the *source* of government. While each chart shows the presence of the Bible—it is only when it is in the hands of the individual that it becomes for him his *political textbook*, and thus enables him to be the source of sovereignty. The Christian idea of man and government support sovereignty as an *internal* power—originating in the God-governed individual and expressed *externally*—politically in the principle of Christian self-government.

"The Church, when by its extension from the Old World it effected a lodgement in this country, was, in the very planting of it, endowed with the same Episcopal constitution which was inherent in the original stock out of which it grew. But, although Episcopal in its constitution, this Church was, for a long series of years— nearly two centuries—to a great extent deprived of personal contact with Episcopal government, the Church in the colonies prior to the Revolution having no resident Episcopate, and being regarded as an appendage to, or extension of, the jurisdiction of the Bishop of London. The result of this was that discipline greatly declined, while the dependence of the several congregations upon the Episcopate became almost nominal . . .

"And it was not to be wondered at, that succeeding generations should grow up with a conception of the Church hardly reaching beyond that of a number of independent congregations, each with its own Presbyter. The dependence, too, of many of these Presbyters upon the venerable Society for Propagating the Gospel, for the whole or a part of their support, and their status as missionaries of that Society, rather than as the bearers of the delegated authority of the Bishops as the chief ministers of the common flock, probably tended to obscure still further the relations of the parishes to the Episcopate, and thus to impress men more strongly with the congregational idea, which was the same, by the way, with that which underlay the administration of most of the societies of Puritan origin by which the Church was surrounded. The fact, too, that property, to such extent as it was possessed by the Church, was vested in the congregations or their trustees, helped to strengthen this congregational tendency of the colonial Church; and all these facts together predisposed it to the formation, when the time should come, of some system in which the body of the Church should act by representation, instead of adhering to the system of being governed by a simply Episcopal rule."

Middle Colony of Pennsylvania

Read Text, Christian History, *pages 262A–270*

Although Pennsylvania was established as a *proprietary* Colony (see page 150C for definition of Proprietary) William Penn's Christian conviction would not permit him to usurp the privilege of self-government which he was convinced belonged to each individual. Accordingly, he prepared a letter to the settlers in which he indicated that they would not be under the control, but only under the guidance of their Governor.

"You are at the mercy of no governor, who comes to make his fortune great; you shall

be governed by laws of your own making, and live a free, and if you will, a sober and industrious people."

Penn also clearly stated the availability of land for a small sum, allowing time for the investor to gain some return before payment was required. He also made the offer available to servants (often obligated to work for the price of their passage) when their indenture period was over. His Christian leadership was consistent throughout in every provision which he established so that each individual could become independent as he accepted the responsibility of work and self-government.

Definition: Quit-Rent (referred to on page 265): "A small rent that is payable by the tenants of most manors, whereby the tenant goes quit and free from all other services."

William Penn's many imprisonments for the right to worship as his conscience dictated led him to write *"The Great Case of Liberty of Conscience Debated"* while in Newgate Prison. His father, who had been unreconciled to his son's conversion to the Quaker persuasion, respected his integrity and left him these words, in addition to a plentiful estate:

"Son, William, let nothing in this world tempt you to wrong your conscience. So will you keep peace at home, which will be a feast to you in a day of trouble."

Penn's treaty
with the Indians

Thus we find William Penn consistent with his conviction for he refused to take advantage of the Indians who occupied the territory which the Crown enabled him to purchase. He first wrote to the native Indians, informing them of his desire to hold his possession with their consent and goodwill. This resulted in a new standard of treatment towards the Indians and it brought about relations of amity and "good neighborhood". (See illustration page 270 text.)

William Penn's
Christian colony

Penn's religious convictions and his own experience and observation of the persecution of religious dissenters from the established church, had much to do with his desire that this colony should afford true liberty of Conscience to all men. Accordingly, the year following the Fundamental Constitution of Pennsylvania, he published the Frame of Government, a law of which code held out a greater degree of religious liberty than had at that time been allowed in the world:

"All persons living in this province, who confess and acknowledge the One Almighty and Eternal God to be the Creator, Upholder, and Ruler of the world, and that hold themselves obliged in conscience to live peaceably and justly in civil society, shall in no wise be molested or prejudiced for their religious persuasion or practice, in matters of faith and worship; nor shall they be compelled at any time to frequent or maintain any religious worship, place or ministry whatsoever."

It is important to note that such toleration comes about through Christianity—
202   because only the Christian idea of man honors all men be they "Greek", "Jew",

"Barbarian", "Scythian", "bond" or "free". This is quite different from a *pluralistic* approach where all religions are equal from a secular base and the supremacy of belief over faith is acknowledged. Christianity respects each individual because it honors God and gives the supremacy to Him.

IX. But the Temperance *I plead for, is not only* Religiously, *but* Politically Good: "*'Tis the Interest of Good Government to Curb and Rebuke* Excesses: *It prevents many* Mischiefs; Luxury *brings Effeminacy, Laziness, Poverty and Misery; but* Temperance *preserves the Land. It keeps out Foreign Vanities, and improves our own Commodities: Now we are the Debtors, then they would be Debtors to us for our* Native Manufactures *. . . Wherefore it is, that we cannot but loudly call upon the Generality of the Times, and testifie, both by our Life and Abuses, if possibly any may be weaned from their Folly, and chuse the* Good Old Path of Temperance, Wisdom, Gravity, and Holiness, *the only Way to inherit the Blessings of Peace and Plenty here, and Eternal Happiness hereafter.*"

From *No Cross, No Crown.* A Discourse Shewing the *Nature* and *Discipline* of the *Holy Cross of Christ*, And that the Denial of *Self*, and the Daily Bearing of *Christ's Cross*, is the alone Way to the Rest and Kingdom of *God.* By William Penn, 1725.

True to his conviction that "any government is free to the people under it . . . where the laws rule and the people are a party to those laws", Penn set forth in 1682 a government vested in the governor and freemen, in the form of an elected provincial council, and an assembly consisting of all the freemen of the province. The laws were to originate in the elected council and the chief duty of the assembly was to approve of the legislation of that representative body. Thus in this unusual colony—established through the faith and conviction of one man—God raised up the seed of righteous government—whose purpose was "to make and establish such laws as shall best preserve true Christian and civil liberty, in opposition to all unchristian, licentious, and unjust practices, whereby God may have his due, Caesar his due, and the people their due . . ."

Penn, whose wisdom was "derived from that book of gospel statutes", recognized Christian character as the basis of good government. He states in Frame of Government of Pennsylvania, 1682: "Governments, like clocks, go from the motion men give them; and as governments are made and moved by men, so by them they are ruined too. Wherefore governments rather depend upon men, than men upon governments . . . That, therefore, which makes a good constitution, must keep it, *viz:* men of wisdom and virtue, qualities, that because they descend not with worldly inheritance, must be carefully propagated by a virtuous education of youth . . ."

In 1701 Penn signed the Charter of Privileges in which *liberty of conscience* was assured to all "who shall confess and acknowledge one Almighty God" and "live quietly under civil government" and that all who "believe in Jesus Christ" should be capable to serve the government.

Liberty of
conscience to all
who confess God

203

John Locke
"Of the Beginning of Political Societies"

Read Text, Christian History, *pages 83–91*

Christ the only
Liberator

The liberty of the individual did not begin until our Lord and Saviour appeared to redeem men from the internal tyranny of their sinful nature. Then the Chain of Christianity moved forward and Christian History recorded the appearing of civil liberty for men. Neander in his *"Memorials of Christian Life"*, 1845, writes of the following leavening influence of Christianity:

"Christianity always operated outwards from within: it effected no violent revolutions, like the self-will which follows not God's ways with patient resignation, but wishes to effect those changes at once by an army of flesh which can only succeed under God's guidance in gradual development. But when Christianity had penetrated deeper on all sides into the life of humanity, a relation must naturally fall of itself which is opposed to the Christian universal philanthropy, and to the ideas spread by Christianity respecting the equal destiny and dignity of all men as created in the image of God, and called to rule over nature."

One of the important arguments which men had to think through was whether kings had a "divine right" to rule men, and whether monarchy was hereditary. Especially with the appearing of the Bible in the 16th and 17th centuries men began to search Scripture to determine their political rights, and to learn the form of Christian government.

The importance
of individual
consent

One fact was evident in the study of the Old Testament and the New. The Mosaic Code had been established for the government of a nation. The gospel of Jesus Christ began with the government of individuals. While both the law and the gospel were needed in a society, Christianity demanded an internal commitment of heart, mind, feelings, *"bringing into captivity every thought to the obedience of Christ"*. Thus *individual consent* played an important part in becoming a Christian. It was much more than abject submission; it was an open profession and confession. Thus while men might live in a community where the Christian influence pervaded its laws and institutions, an individual did not become a part of Christianity until the individual embraced it and received it by active consent.

"But as many as received him, to them gave he power to become the sons of God, even to them that believe on his name." John 1:12

In his Second Essay *"Of Civil Government"*, John Locke, the Christian Philosopher of the American Revolution, deals with the beginning of government among
men in society. Challenging the supremacy of "the divine right of kings" to rule

over men, he begins the explanation of sovereignty in the individual—the power of
government as beginning in men born free.

Let us first identify some of the propositions which Locke is setting forth:

Men are Naturally Free

"*Men being, as has been said, by Nature, all free, equal, and independent, no one can
be put out of this Estate, and subjected to the political Power of another, without his
own Consent.*" Page 83:95

Governments Began by Consent

"*But to conclude, Reason being plain on our side, that Men are naturally Free, and the
Examples of History shewing, that the* Governments *of the* World, *that were begun in
Peace, had their beginning laid on that Foundation, and were* made by the Consent
of the People; *There can be little room for doubt, either where the Right is, or what
has been the Opinion, or Practice of Mankind, about the* first erecting of Governments." Page 85:104

Sufficient Declaration of Consent

"Every Man *being, as had been shewed*, naturally free, *and nothing being able to put
him into Subjection to any earthly Power, but only his own* Consent, *it is to be consider'd, what shall be understood to be a* sufficient Declaration *of a Man's* Consent,
to make him subject *to the laws of any Government.*" Page 90:119

Express Promise and Compact

"*Nothing can make any Man so, but his actually entering into it by positive Engagement, and express Promise and Compact. This is that, which I think, concerning the
beginning of political Societies, and that* Consent which makes any one a Member *of
any Commonwealth.*" Page 91:122

Mayflower Compact an Example of Express Consent

Read Text, Christian History, *pages 149–150*

Locke makes some very profound distinctions between what he terms *tacit
consent* and *express consent*. The word *tacit* means "silent", and it implies not making any outward expression or profession of one's position. It is evident that in many
cases it would be possible to *agree* to something by not making any opposition to

it—and thereby giving "tacit consent". Perhaps, because it requires more moral and political courage, and because it is the Christian way, Locke regarded the individual who had not made *express promise and compact* to accept the laws and government under which he wished to lived, as not really a member of the society in which he lived. He discusses this point on page 90.

The Mayflower Compact which is recognized as the first document of American Self-Government, was a Christian document. By their *express consent*, and by the signing of this document, the Pilgrims established themselves as a "single covenanted body of Christians, united for civil as well as spiritual purposes".

Consent represents the active, responsible ingredient of Christian self-government. It cannot be passive. But it begins within as the individual Christian accepts or receives Christ and recognizes that *"the government is upon his shoulder"*.

Majority Rule Can Be a Tyrant

On page 83, John Locke discusses the consequences of "Men's uniting into Commonwealths, and putting themselves under Government."

"The Majority Have a Right to Act"

"When any number of Men have so consented to make one Community or Government, *they are thereby presently incorporated, and make* one *Body politick, wherein the Majority have a Right to act and conclude the rest." Page 83:95*

"To Submit to the Determination of the Majority"

"And thus every Man, by consenting with others to make one Body Politick under one Government, puts himself under an Obligation, to every one of that Society, to submit to the determination of the Majority, *and to be concluded by it; or else this* original Compact, *whereby he with others incorporates into* one Society, *would signifie nothing, and be no Compact, if he be left Free, and under no other Ties, than he was in before in the State of Nature." Page 83:97*

Why the Founding Fathers Chose a Republic

Felix Morley,
*The Power in
the People*

"The men who established this Republic thought continually of 'posterity'. . . . The constant aim, as one of them wrote, was to 'lay a foundation for after ages to understand their liberty as men and Christians.' For this purpose, said William Penn, 'we put the power in the people.'

"To put the power in the people implies faith. It implies that the component individuals are, for the most part, already endowed with self-control. This Republic is grounded in the belief that the individual can govern himself. On the validity of that belief it will stand—or fall.

"As our title implies, we seek to examine this dual power—that which the people possess as individuals and that which has been entrusted to them as citizens of this republic . . .

"Some national governments, like that of Russia, have either inherited or acquired unlimited power over their subjects. Other governments, like that of Great Britain, have developed so as to respond to the will of a parliamentary majority, no matter where that may lead. The American system does not fall into either of these classifications. It was designed to prevent usurpation of absolute power by any individual; by any group; or by the spokesmen of the people to whom, as a whole, so much was given . . .

"The United States correctly designated, is neither a dictatorship, nor a complete political democracy, but a federal republic . . .

The United States is a federal republic

"The word 'republic', however, is one of many political terms that we must learn to use more precisely, if there is to be any meeting of minds on the ideas that such words were designed to convey. Long before the autocrats of the present Russian regime described the Soviet Union as a federation of republics, Madison had commented on 'the extreme inaccuracy with which the term has been used in political disquisitions.' So, in the issue of *The Federalist* . . . 'the master builder of the Constitution' reasoned that a republic has:

'. . . *a government which derives all of its powers directly or indirectly from the great body of the people, and is administered by persons holding their offices during pleasure, for a limited period, or during good behaviour. It is* essential *to such a government that it be derived from the great body of Society, not from an inconsiderable proportion, or a favored class of it . . . It is* sufficient *for such a government that the persons administering it be appointed either directly or indirectly, by the people; and that they hold their appointments by either of the tenures just specified . . .*"

"A republic, therefore, must have a truly representative government . . . On the other hand, this new government must be strong enough to preserve 'the rights of the minority,' continuously jeopardized 'in all cases where a majority are united by a common interest or passion.'

A republic must have a representative government

"Madison chose his words with an accuracy and delicacy in which modern political discussion is shockingly deficient. An elastic federal republic, democratic in form but carefully safeguarded against the 'inconveniences' of democracy, was what he sought and what actually was established for the United States . . .

"Underlying the whole plan, in Madison's memorable words, is 'that honorable determination. . . . to rest all our political experiments on the capacity of mankind for self-government.' Of recent years it has been increasingly assumed that Americans are no longer capable of governing themselves. In view of conditions that have everywhere followed the destruction of self-government, a restoration of this faith would seem to be not only honorable, but actually essential for survival."

The following point is essential to understand in learning why we are a federated Republic—and thus represent *each* individual at all times, regardless of whether he agrees or disagrees with the action of the majority. His position is not eliminated by the majority overruling him. In a democracy, as in Athens, mob-rule often exercised as much tyranny as did autocrats or kings. The Christian idea of man and government protects and preserves the rights of each individual by the balance of the two commandments—Love for God, for Principles of Right, and love or respect for one's fellowman. Again, this is an internal aspect of Christian self-government, expressed externally in government which benefits all—the minority as well as the majority.

Restraints Upon Majority Rule

Thomas M.
Cooley, LL.D.,
*The General
Principles of
Constitutional
Law in the
United States
of America*
"Government in the United States and in the several States, in all its grades, is representative; the body of the people performing very few acts directly, except that of adopting the Constitution. When they act directly, the result of their will must be ascertained by such preponderating vote as the law shall prescribe. This may be a majority vote, or it may be merely the vote in which the largest number of electors agree. In determining upon a majority or plurality, those only are counted who actually participated in the election, except in a few cases where by some constitutional provision an actual majority of all the electors is required.

"American government is frequently spoken of as a government based on faith in majorities, and the machinery of election as being provided merely to ascertain what the will of the majority is. But the government is never handed over to the absolute control of the majority, and many precautions are taken to prevent its expressing exclusively their will:—

1. In the Constitution many permanent rules are prescribed which control the majority absolutely, and which cannot be changed except by the slow process of constitutional amendment.
2. The times and methods of election of legislative and executive officers are so contrived that in different branches of the government the majority of one period will be restrained and checked by the majority of another, and it is scarcely possible that any considerable minority shall not have its representatives, and be entitled to be heard through them in the legislature, in ways that shall at least hold the majority to due accountability for their conduct and measures. It must often be the case that one house of the legislature will represent the views of a popular majority, and the other those of a minority only; but for all purposes of enacting laws, the latter has as much authority as the former.
3. The electoral system is so contrived that the President is sometimes chosen by a minority of the people; but unless a majority is overwhelming, he may generally defeat its measures by his veto.

4. All the safeguards which under kingly government were ever imposed against the tyrannical power of rulers are incorporated in the bills of rights in the American constitution as absolute limitations laid on the power of the majority for the protection of the liberty, property, privileges, and immunities of the minority, and of every individual citizen; and the judiciary is given a power to enforce these limitations, irrespective of the will or control of the legislature, such as it has never possessed in any other country. So far then from the government being based on unlimited confidence in majorities, a profound distrust of the discretion, equity, and justice of their rule is made evident in many precautions and checks, and the majority is in fact trusted with power only so far as is absolutely essential to the working of republican institutions."

America's Heritage of Christian Character

Key to the Third Principle

Dr. Augustus Neander,
Memorials of a
Christian Life

"The work which I now publish in an amended form, was undertaken from a desire to excite and cherish in the minds of persons who were not devoted to the study of theology as a science, a consciousness of the unity of that Christian Spirit which has been in action through every age of the church, and which connects us with all that has flowed from the operation of the Holy Spirit since its first effusion —to awaken an interest for everything which has proceeded from this Spirit—to let testimonies drawn from actual life, speak for general edification and instruction —and to lead to a recognition at once of the Unity of that Spirit, and of the variety that exists in its forms of manifestation . . .

"Christianity could not have taken a firm hold on human nature, if it had not penetrated it by its divine power, and thus verified itself to be indeed that which alone can satisfy the higher necessities of the inner man. This divine power of the gospel revealed itself to the heathen in the lives of Christians, which 'showed forth the virtues of him who had called them out of darkness into his marvellous light, and enabled them to walk as the children of God, in the midst of a perverse generation, among whom they shone as lights in the world.' . . .

"They saw Christians meet death in the confidence of their faith with the greatest firmness and cheerfulness, oftentimes amidst extreme tortures . . . Many asked, what gives men such energy to do and suffer everything on account of their convictions, in an age of such abject weakness, when we see all things bending before earthly power? Whoever proposed this question endeavoured to make himself acquainted with Christianity; and the consequence was, that the inquirer became captivated with the divine doctrine.

210   "As Christianity brought into consciousness the same image of God in all men, set

free the development of humanity from the narrow bounds of the state, subordinating all to the same level, and destroyed the ancient stand-point of state religion, so also ideas of religious freedom and the rights of conscience, which were unknown to the ancient world, were first diffused abroad by Christianity. The Christian apologists were the first who testified of these new ideas brought to light by Christianity. 'It is,' says Tertullian to the Roman Proconsul Scapula, 'one of the rights of man, and belongs to the natural freedom of every one, to worship according to his convictions, and the religion of one can neither injure nor profit others. But it is not religion to employ force in religion; for religion must be voluntary, and received without compulsion. Sacrifices are desired only from free hearts. If you force us to sacrifice you will give nothing to your gods, for they will not desire any forced sacrifices' . . .

"But the Roman statesmen desired only a blind obedience; they knew not how to understand the enthusiasm with which the Christians would rather surrender their earthly life than do anything against their conscience; nor could they respect the rights of that which in its nature must be the freest thing in man—the religious convictions of the individual. In this firmness of the Christians they saw nothing but blind fanaticism, criminal disobedience, men who met death and excruciating tortures with composure, rather than utter a few words, or perform some ceremonies, must have appeared very strange and suspicious. 'Such hardihood of soul,' it might be said, 'suited the heroic times of the ancient republic, but not this age of peace and refined sensibility.'

"In their conduct towards the government and the laws, the Christians distinguished themselves in contrast with the immoral practices which had gained ground in the times of despotism. In a time when the inclination of self-interest to evade the laws in secret was combined with the timorousness of a slavish spirit, the Christian set the example of the conscientious observance of the laws for God's sake, and of unbending mental freedom, which, as it only obeyed the rulers of the world as placed in their office by God, so no power on earth could force to obey when anything was required that contradicted the divine laws . . .

"As the whole life of the Christian, from the beginning to the end, is a conflict with the world and the powers of darkness, a conflict within and without, the kingdom of God in this world must appear as militant, and must make its way by conflict; so that often, in Holy Writ, the calling of the Christian is compared to that of the military life, and the Christian is represented as the soldier of his Lord. This image was very clear and familiar to the first Christians. Though Christians, in later ages, may have been led to forget the nature of their calling as one of conflict, amidst external tranquillity and prosperity, yet in primitive times their entire outward condition served to remind them of the spiritual warfare; for the church found itself on all sides in conflict with the heathen world, and the public profession made by Christians compelled them to take a share in this conflict. Christians rejoiced to consider themselves as the soldiers of God and Christ (*milites Dei et Christi*), against the hostile powers of darkness, against everything which appeared to them as belonging to the kingdom of Satan, against the service of sin and of false gods . . . To this comparison of the Christian with the military profession, the beautiful words refer in the epistle of Ignatius to Polycarp: 'Strive to please Him in whose service you are fighting, for from him you will receive the pay. Let none of you prove deserters.' "

Christian Life

Dr. Augustus
Neander,
*General History
of the Christian
Religion and
Church*

"Christianity, since it first entered into human nature, has operated, wherever it has struck root, with the same divine power for sanctification; and this divine power cannot be weakened by the lapse of ages. In this respect, therefore, the period of the first appearance of Christianity could have no advantage over any of the following ages of the Christian church. There was but one peculiarity of this first period, viz. that the change wrought by Christianity, in the consciousness and life of those in whom it was produced, could not fail to be more strongly marked by the contrast it presented with what they had previously been, as pagans . . .

"The contrast between Christianity and paganism, which was so strongly marked in the life, contributed to preserve the Christian consciousness and life more pure, and to guard it against many a debasing mixture. But here, also, what proved to some the means of awakening many Christian virtues, and in general served to promote the Christian temper of mind, became to others a source of self-deception; —to those, namely, who fancied that by a stern rejection of every thing pagan, they had quite satisfied the requisitions of Christianity and made out of this an opus operatum;—when they were thus led to conceive of the warfare with the world in too outward a sense, and on this account the more easily overlooked the inner conflict with the inward world; and spiritual pride, uncharitable fanaticism fastened at the root of their religion . . .

"That which our Lord himself, in his last interview with his disciples, described as the test by which his disciples might be distinguished,—as the mark of their fellowship with him and the Father in heaven . . . namely, that they loved one another,—precisely this constituted the prominent mark, plain and striking to the pagans themselves, of the first Christian fellowship . . . It was this . . . which, in a cold and selfish age, struck the pagans with wonder,—to behold men of different countries, ranks, relations, stages of culture, so intimately bound together,—to see the stranger who came into a city, and by his letter of recognition (his epistola formata) made himself known to the Christians of the place as a brother beyond suspicion, finding at once among those to whom he was personally unknown, all manner of brotherly sympathy and protection.

"The care of providing for the support and maintenance of strangers, of the poor, the sick, the old, of widows and orphans, and of those in prison on account of their faith, devolved on the whole church. This was one of the main purposes for which the collection of voluntary contributions in the assemblies convened for public worship, was instituted; and the charity of individuals, moreover, led them to emulate each other in the same good work. In particular, it was considered as belonging to the office of the Christian matron to provide for the poor, for the brethren languishing in prison, to show hospitality to strangers . . .

"Nor did the active brotherly love of each community confine itself to what transpired in its own immediate circle, but extended itself also to the wants of the Christian communities in distant lands. On urgent occasions of this kind, the bishops made arrangements for special collections. They appointed fasts; so that what was saved, even by the poorest of the flock, from their daily food, might help to supply the common wants . . .

"That from which such works took the impress of a truly Christian character, was indeed nothing else than the temper—which here expresses itself—of Christian love simply following the impulse from within. This Christian character was no longer present in its purity, when the charitable action had reference to an outward end; when it was converted into a ground of merit before God, into a means for extinguishing sin . . . In proportion as the reference to Christ, which the habit already noticed, of confounding the church with a set of outward forms, had no tendency to encourage, was forgotten, in the same proportion rose the estimate which men placed on their own doings, and on the merit of good works . . .

"In times of public calamity, the contrast was strikingly displayed between the cowardly selfishness of the pagans and the self-sacrificing brotherly love of the Christians . . . But with the heathen it was quite otherwise; those who showed the first symptoms of the disease, they drove from them; they fled from their dearest friends. The half-dead they cast into the streets, and left the dead unburied, making it their chief care to avoid the contagion, which however in spite of every possible precaution they could hardly escape . . .

"Again, Christianity, from its nature, must pronounce sentence of condemnation against all ungodliness, but at the same time appropriate to itself all purely human relations and arrangements, consecrating and ennobling, instead of annihilating them . . . That religion which aimed nowhere to produce violent and convulsive changes from without, but led to reforms by beginning in the first place within, —whose peculiar character it was to operate positively rather than negatively,—to displace and destroy no faster than it substituted something better . . .

"Among those social relations which were alien to the nature of Christianity, and which Christianity found existing at the time of its first propagation, belonged *slavery* . . . But Christianity brought about that change in the consciousness of humanity, from which a dissolution of this whole relation, though it could not be immediately effected, yet by virtue of the consequences resulting from that change, must eventually take place. This effect Christianity produced, first by the facts of which it was a witness; and next by the ideas which, by occasion of these facts, it set in circulation. By Christ, the Saviour, belonging to all mankind, the antagonisms among men resulting from sin were annulled; by him the original oneness was restored. These facts must now continue to operate in transforming the life of mankind. Masters as well as servants were obliged to acknowledge themselves the servants of sin, and to receive in the same manner, as a gift of God's free grace, their deliverance from this common bondage,—the *true, the highest freedom*. Servants and masters, if they had become believers, were brought together under the same bond of an heavenly union, destined for immortality; they became brethren in Christ, in whom there is neither bond nor free, members of one body, baptized into one spirit, heirs of the same heavenly inheritance. Servants often became teachers of their masters in the gospel after having practically exhibited before them the loftiness of a divine life, which must express itself even under the most constraining of relations, and shine forth the more conspicuously by the contrast . . .

"Yet Christianity nowhere began with outward revolutions and changes, which, in all cases where they have not been prepared from within, and are not based upon conviction, fail of their salutary ends. The new creation to which Christianity gave birth, was in all respects an inward one, from which the outward effects gradually and therefore more surely and healthfully, unfolded themselves to their full extent. It gave servants first the true, inward freedom, without which the outward and earthly freedom is a mere show, and which, wherever it exists, can be cramped by no earthly bond, no earthly yoke. The apostle Paul says, 'He that is called in the Lord, being a servant, is the Lord's freeman.' . . .

Christian
marriage and
womanhood
"If the ascetic tendency was but a transient moment of excess on one side in the development of the Christian life; we see on the other hand, from the first, in that which presents the strongest contrast to it, in the ennobled family relation, the power of the Christian principle of life in its healthy development. And this grand effect resulted first from the fact that the true import of marriage was realized by Christianity;—its import as the harmonious union of two individuals separated by sex, in a higher spiritual oneness of life, by the communication of a divine life destined to reconcile all antitheses. Connected with this, was the fact, that wherever Christianity found entrance, the equal dignity and worth of the female sex, as possessing a nature created in the image of God and allied to the divine no less than the male, was brought distinctly before the consciousness; and that the sex was invested with the rights belonging to it—in opposition to the principle of the ancient world, particularly in the East, where the woman was placed in an altogether subordinate relation to the man . . .

"It was required of the Christian mistress of a family, that by the sobriety of her whole demeanor, by the decency and simplicity of her dress, she should show the spirit that ruled within, and thus let her very appearance shine as a light, in an age characterized by excessive display, luxury and corruption of manners . . .

"Adhering strictly to that religious and moral point of view in which the marriage relation was first presented to Christianity, many believed that where there was no union of hearts by the bond of religion, where there was rather disunion in regard to the highest concerns of the inward life, the true significancy of marriage could not be realized. Hence they discountenanced all marriage relation between Christians and pagans . . .

"The soul of the whole Christian life was considered to be *prayer* . . . '*Prayer is the bulwark of faith*.' (Tertullian) . . . We recognize here a mode of thinking grounded in the essence of primitive Christianity, intimately connected with the consciousness of the universal Christian priesthood, which distinguishes the Christian standing ground as well from the pagan as from the Jewish,—the view of prayer as an act embracing the *whole* life,—making the entire Christian life a continuous prayer. In this reference, Origen says in his exposition of the Lord's prayer: 'We ought not to think that a set of words has been taught us which we are to repeat at certain stated seasons for prayer. If we duly understand what was said in regard to the duty of 'praying without ceasing', then our whole life—if we do thus pray without ceasing—must express 'Our Father which art in heaven;' and we being thrones of God, inasmuch as the kingdom of God has its seat in all who bear the image of the Man from heaven, and have thus become heavenly themselves.' "

Faith and Steadfastness

Read Text, Christian History, *pages 182–240*

The following experiences illustrate the qualities of *faith* and *steadfastness* and other qualities of Christian Character. This selection is intended as a suggestion of the possibilities for the study of this wondrous record of the Christian character of these Pilgrims. Most important for the Christian of today is the recognition that the character of the Christian stemming from the first century of Christianity and lived in America's first century of Christian History are applicable for all times and circumstances.

Like the stories of the Bible which grow deeper in meaning to us as we read and re-read them, so the chronicle of Plymouth should be studied by every grade until the fulness of its inspiration becomes a firm part of our knowledge and understanding of America.

This third principle of America's Christian History will be presented through Bradford's account of these worthy Christians. Each grade may read it with particular qualities of Christian character to observe in the life of the Pilgrims. Each teacher may follow both interest and inspiration in further expanding its possibilities for teaching America's Christian History.

One of the areas which has been sadly overlooked is the area of providing *models of Christian character* for even the youngest to observe. We are willing to spend many hours preparing models of many things which our students study—*examples*   215 in arithmetic, pictures on the bulletin boards—and many other visual displays for the classroom. It is much harder to provide models of character—but that is an area which needs to be spelled out in great detail and with loving care if we expect to weave lives pleasing to God. The qualities of character need to be exercised in honest encounters with the world and in this way they are strengthened from within. Much can be taught and much can be learned from the courageous story of our Pilgrims as they considered themselves "stepping stones" for those who would come after. Their adventures were sometimes exciting—sometimes they had just "daily dullness"—but the real thrill comes from perceiving the qualities which enabled them to "stay firm" for, of those who lived the first year, *not one went back.* And those who lived—lived to a wonderful age in the Lord: "God, it seems, would have all men to behold and observe such mercies and works of his providence as these are towards his people".

Read Text, Christian History, *pages 185–207*

America's heritage of Christian Character is beautifully detailed in William Bradford's *History 'of Plimoth Plantation'*. This record in all its purity is preserved for us in this narrative of the first years of the Pilgrims on this continent. It is a brave testament of their trials and their tribulations—but more of their faith and endurance, and their steadfastness. This is an account which should be cherished by Christians in America of whatever generation. It is truly the "Christian heritage" of their Pilgrim and Puritan forefathers who carried the seed of Christian life and Christian character and Christian government into all the activities of this first Christian settlement on our shores.

American Christian Character

Escape from England to Holland

TRIALS & TRIBULATIONS	FAITH & STEADFASTNESS
"Being thus constrained to leave their native soyle and countrie, their lands & livings, and all their freinds & famillier acquaintance"	*"But these things did not dismay them . . . for their desires were sett on ye ways of God & to injoye his ordinances"*
"for though they could not stay, yet were ye not suffered to goe . . . ye ports & havens were shut against them"	
"faine to seek secrete means of conveance"	
"& give exterordinarie rates for their passages"	

"yet were they often times betrayed (many of them)"

"ye poore men which were gott abord, were in great distress for their wives and children"

"endured a fearfull storme at sea, being 14 days"

"all gatt over at length"

"ye Lords power & mercie appeared in ther recoverie"

"with no small rejoycing"

Sojourn in Holland

TRIALS & TRIBULATIONS

"strange & uncouth language"
"differente maners & customes"
"povertie coming upon them like an armed man"

"their remooval to Leyden"
"not so beneficiall for their outward means of living"
"they fell to such trads & imployments as they best could"

"some of their adversaries did . . . cast out slanders against them"
"& had rather driven them out"
"many of them weer poore"

"saw them so painfull & dilligent in their callings"

FAITH & STEADFASTNESS

"yet by Gods assistance they prevailed and got ye victorie"

"valewing peace & their spirituall comforte above any other riches whatsoever"

"the Dutch . . . would trust them"
"they had found by experience how carfull they were to keep their word"

"they would strive to gett their custome, and to imploy them above others"

Reasons for Removal from Holland

TRIALS & TRIBULATIONS

"they saw & found by experience the hardnes of ye place & countrie"

"many of their children . . . were drawn away by evill examples"

FAITH & STEADFASTNESS

"ye people generally bore all these difficulties very cherfully & with a resolute courage"

"a great hope & inward zeall . . . for ye propagating & advancing ye gospell of ye kingdom of Christ in those remote parts of ye world"

217

"the place they had thoughts on was some of those vast & unpeopled countries of America"

"caused many fears & doubts amongst them selves"

"ye dangers were greate"

"ye difficulties were many"

"such attempts were not to be made and undertaken without good ground & reasons; not rashly or lightly as many have done for curiositie or hope of gaine, &c."

"all great & honorable actions are accompanied with great difficulties, and must be both enterprised and overcome with answerable courages"

"but not desperate"

"but not invincible"

"all of them through ye help of God, by fortitude and patience, might either be borne, or overcome"

"Of Their Voiage"

TRIALS & TRIBULATIONS

"incountred many times with crosse winds, and mette with many feirce stormes"
"ye shipe was shroundly shaken and her upper works made very leakie" and *"one of the maine beames in ye midd ships was bowed & craked"*

"mutterings . . . rather to returne then to cast them selves into a desperate & inevitable perill"

FAITH & STEADFASTNESS

"What could now sustaine them but ye spirite of God & his grace?"
"Let them confess before ye Lord his loving kindness, and his wonderfull works before ye sons of men"

"So they comited them selves to ye will of God, & resolved to proseede"

Arrived at Cap-Codd

TRIALS & TRIBULATIONS

"Some discontents & murmerings"
"mutinous speeches & carriages"

"in 2 or 3 moneths time halfe of their company dyed, espetialy in Jan: and February, being in depth of winter, & wanting houses and other comforts"

"being infected with ye scurvie & other diseases"

FAITH & STEADFASTNESS

"confirmed Mr. John Carter (a man godly & well approved amongst them) their Governour for that year"

"ther was but 6. or 7. sound persons, who . . . spared no pains, night nor day, but with abundance of toyle and hazard of their owne health, fetched them woode, made them fires, drest their meat, made their beads, washed their lothsome cloaths, cloathed & uncloathed them"

218

"of 100. & odd persons, scarce 50. remained"

"all this while ye Indians came skulking about them"

"Once they stoale away their tools"

"he came againe & 5. more with him, & they brought againe all ye tooles that were stolen away before, and made way for ye coming of their great Sachem, called Massasoyt"

"about 4. or 5. days after came with the cheefe of his freinds & other attendance, with the aforesaid Squanto"

"a rare example & worthy to be remembered . . . tow of these 7. were Mr. William Brewster, ther reverend Elder, & Myles Standish, ther Captein & military comander"

"ye 16. of March a certaine Indian came bouldly amongst them, and spoke to them in broken English"

"He became profitable to them in aquainting them with many things concerning ye state of ye cuntry" *"His name was Samaset"*

"With whome, after frendly entertainment, & some gifts given him, they made a peace with him (which hath now continued this 24. years)"

"But it was ye Lord which upheld them, and had beforehand prepared them; many having long borne ye yoake, yea from their youth"

Continue to the End of Bradford's History

Continue the documentation of the Pilgrim character as it faced up to the innumerable *trials & tribulations* with *faith, steadfastness,* and other *Christian virtues.*

As you conclude this study of American Christian character and read Bradford's summary of God's marvellous providence towards his people, consider what may be required of American Christians again as they face up to the individual demands upon their own Christian character—particularly in the government of their own households.

Brotherly Love and Christian Care

Read Text, Christian History, *pages 182–240*

As the Pilgrims were about to leave for the New World, their faithful pastor, who had shepherded the flock in Leyden, wrote them a farewell letter. In this letter to his "Lovinge Christian friends" Mr. Robinson instructed them in their conduct as

Christians. The following statements set the standard for their *brotherly love and Christian care.* Christian History: *pages 198–201*

1. *"And first, as we are daly to renew our repentance with our God, espetially for our sines known, and generally for our unknowne trespasses . . .*
2. *"Now next after this heavenly peace with God & our owne consciences, we are carefully to provide for peace with all men what in us lieth, espetially with our associats . . .*
3. *"But besids these, ther are diverse motives provoking you above others to great care & conscience this way: As first you are many of you strangers, as to ye persons, so to ye infirmities one of another, & so stand in neede of more watchfullness this way . . .*
4. *"And if taking of offence causlesly or easilie at mens doings be so carefuly to be avoyded, how much more heed is to be taken yt we do not take offence at God him selfe, which yet we certainly doe so ofte as we doe murmure at his providence in our crosses, or beare impatiently shuch afflictions as wherewith he pleaseth to visit us . . .*
5. *"And as men are carfull not to have a new house shaken with any violence before it be well setled & ye parts firmly knite, so be you, I beseech you, brethren, much more carfull, yt the house of God which you are, and are to be, be not shaken with un-necessarie novelties or other oppositions at ye first setling thereof."*

Paul the apostle also sets the standard for Christian conduct toward others:

"Brethren, if a man be overtaken in a fault, ye which are spiritual, restore such an one in the spirit of meekness: considering thyself, lest thou also be tempted. Bear ye one another's burdens, and so fulfil the law of Christ. For if a man think himself to be something, when he is nothing, he deceiveth himself. But let every man prove his own work, and then shall he have rejoicing in himself alone, and not in another. For every man shall bear his own burden." Galatians 6:1–5

Brotherly Love and Christian Care

Describe the first winter at Cap Codd.	How did the peace treaty with the Indians show Christian character?
God sent Squanto to the Pilgrims. How did he help them to help themselves?	What careful steps did the Pilgrims take against the winter threat of hunger?
What hardship did the newcomers put on the Pilgrims?	How did the Pilgrims treat the newcomers with Mr. Cushman?
Describe the character of Mr. Weston.	How did the Pilgrims regard Mr. Weston?
Why were Mr. Weston's men so unruly? What finally happened to them?	Why wouldn't the Pilgrims take anything from Mr. Weston's men—either food or supplies?

What was the "occasion beyond all expectation" which the Lord sent them?

Describe the character of Mr. John Lyford, the minister who was sent over to the Pilgrims.

In what way were the Pilgrims "*wise as serpents*" in uncovering the plot and obtaining the evidence?

When Mr. Edward Winslow went to England and discovered that the Colony had new debts because of Allerton's mismanagement—what did the colony plan to do?

How do you account for the fact that the Pilgrims lived to such a ripe old age?

Why did the boasted strength of Mr. Weston's men fail them?

In what way did Lyford and Oldom take advantage of the Pilgrims?

How did the Pilgrims treat the culprits? Did they make their families suffer for their sins?

Did God help the Pilgrims in this new discouragement?

Why is this chronicle of the sufferings, trials and temptations of the Pilgrims important to all of us?

Diligence and Industry

Read Text, Christian History, *pages 182–240*

Among those qualities which enabled the Pilgrims to successfully plant *Christian Liberty* on these shores were those qualities of individual enterprise—*diligence* and *industry*.

Today the character of socialism is succeeding in subtracting these qualities from our nation, changing us from God-fearing, Christ-honoring, self-reliant Christians, to insecure, dependent, frightened Americans. Thus we are unable to face with courage and resourcefulness the tasks which every generation must solve individually—or fail collectively. God set man appointed tasks to fulfill. He cannot turn his own stewardship over to another. We cannot continue to turn to the state to supply us with all our needs. This is no test of our faith. This is no honor to God.

Grateful we are that we can turn to this record of courage and resolution which our Pilgrim forebears set down in their living testimony. We see the many problems which they had to solve. But while the problems were great—the real challenge was the challenge to individual character. Could a Christian challenge an environment which was unfriendly, bleak, and afforded him little and could he shape that environment to God's purpose—because of the faith and the determination within

The character of socialism

221

him not to fail? It was not a question of external conditions—but a challenge to the internal commitment of each individual Pilgrim.

Not all of the Pilgrims were upright, forthright and Christian in their behavior. But many were. And it is to this ever-living record that we now turn to study what it takes to establish and maintain Christian Liberty and what constitutes *diligence* and *industry*.

Some Definitions

Diligence: To love earnestly; to choose.

1. Steady application in business of any kind; constant effort to accomplish what is undertaken; exertion of body or mind, without unnecessary delay or sloth; due attention; industry; assiduity. *Diligence* is the philosopher's stone, that turns everything to gold.
2. Care; heed; heedfulness.
   "*Keep thy heart with all diligence.*" Prov. 4:23
   "*Brethren, give diligence to make your calling and election sure*"—2 Pet. 1:10

Industry: Opposed to *sloth* and *idleness*.

An *Election Sermon* preached in 1741 by William Williams, Pastor of the church in Weston, Province of the Massachusetts-Bay, further defines *The Vertue of the People:*

Christian character

"What are the means of a people's strength? In their *moral* and *social* vertues: These are the visible Beauty of a People and very much their Strength. I shall Instance in the following:

1. Their *Industry* & *Diligence* in the Business of their several Callings. Man was made for Action and Imployment; even in *Innocency* he must not live in Idleness. And the present State, to which the all-wise Governour of the World hath subjected Mankind, admits of a vast variety of Employments conductive to the Benefit, Support and Comfort of Men. And in the *Christian Institution* such stress is laid upon Mens Diligence in some *lawful Calling*, that they *who will not work* and with quietness eat their own Bread, are judg'd unworthy to *eat* at *all*. Tho' the like Degrees are not required of all.

"The slothful in the Commonwealth are like *Drones* in the Hive and deserve to be thrust out. The slothful is Brother to him that is a great waster. *Drowsiness* shall cloath a Man with Rags. Prov. 18:9 . . . I have observed in particular *Towns*, more than once, that a *few leading Men by their Diligence* and discretion, by their Example & Happy Influence; have put a new Face upon Things, and the Wealth of the Place been much increased. Industry with Prudence and Discretion makes flourishing families, and these a prosperous & flourishing Commonwealth or Kingdom, whereas the idle and negligent serve only to cumber the Ground, are common *Nuisances*, neither serve God, themselves, nor others.

222

2. *Frugality* is another Vertue, not a little contributing to the Strength of a People: Which is a prudent regulating their Expences in their Tables, Furniture, Cloathing, and other Occasions. This is one of the Branches of *Moral Prudence*."

Diligence and Industry

Challenges to the Pilgrims	How the Pilgrims Answered
Poverty in Holland.	
Wild & savage wilderness of Cape Cod.	
The first winter.	
Squanto offers help.	
A ship (the Fortune) arrives with trinkets for trade.	
Second Winter approaches with little food supplies.	
Weston's men arrive. Food shortage continues.	
How to raise more corn?	
Why are all men equal—but all men are not as good as one another?	
Why did individual farming begin to reduce general want and famine?	
Why was the ship's carpenter a more honest worker than the salt maker?	
What did the Pilgrims do after Captain Standish returned from England with his discouraging report?	
Although the Colony suffered as a result of Allerton's mismanagement —how did it benefit them?	

223

Liberty of Conscience

Read Text, Christian History, *pages 182–240*

English Separatists. "So many therefore of these proffessors as saw ye evill of these things, in thes parts, and whose harts ye Lord had touched wth heavenly Zeale for his trueth, they shooke off this yoake of anti-christian bondage, and as ye Lords free people, joyned them selves (by a covenant of the Lord) into a church estate, in ye felowship of ye gospell, to walke in all his wayes, make known or to be made known unto them, according to their best endeavours, whatsoever it should cost them, the Lord assisting them." *Christian History:* Page 185

Relate the "cost" to these English Puritans who would not remain in the Church of England, but shook off this "anti-Christian" yoke and covenanted with those with whom they could have fellowship "in the gospell".

Comfort and Liberty. ". . . yet, alass, they admitted of bondage, with danger of conscience, rather than to indure these hardships . . ." *Christian History;* Page 192

Why is it not possible to compromise with "liberty of conscience"? What happened to those English who could not part with the comforts of home? Were they able to maintain "liberty of conscience"?

Liberty in Religion. Why was it so important to the Pilgrims to settle where they could have "liberty in Religion"? *Christian History:* Pages 194, 195

The Governor Opens Some Letters in Good Conscience. Who was convicted by his own actions when the Governor asked Lyford if he had done "evill to open his letters"? *Christian History:* Pages 219–221

The Pilgrims and the Debt. The Pilgrims experienced many injustices with their business affairs—far more than men require today before they declare themselves in bankruptcy. Why was it consistent with the Pilgrim Christian Character to repay the debt or investment which had been made to help them come to America—even though it took many years of their lives—and a considerable amount of all they produced in trade and farming? *Christian History:* Pages 223–240

Read Text, Christian History, *pages 241–244*

Effect of the Pilgrims on the Puritans. "The religious despotism which so despotically ruled the Bay Colony often exerted a malign influence on the comparatively liberal Plymouth; but the Independency of the latter not only survived, but extended itself until Congregationalism became the 'standing order,' even in Massachusetts and its child Connecticut . . . so that after two generations of rivalry the more genial spirit of the Pilgrims should supplant the bigoted sternness of the Puritans."

224

"Conscience is the Most Sacred of all Property"

Key to the Fourth Principle

"Of Property in General"

"There is nothing which so generally strikes the imagination and engages the affections of mankind as the *right of property*, or that sole and despotic dominion which one man claims and exercises over the external things of the world, in total exclusion of the right of any other individual in the universe.

"In the beginning of the world, we are informed by Holy Writ, the All-bountiful Creator gave to man 'dominion over all the earth, and over the fish of the sea, and over the fowl of the air, and over every living thing that moveth upon the earth.' This is the only true and solid foundation of man's dominion over external things. The earth, therefore, and all things therein are the general property of all mankind, exclusive of other beings, from the immediate gift of the Creator. And, while the earth continued bare of inhabitants, it is reasonable to suppose that all was in common among them, and that every one took from the public stock to his own use such things as his immediate necessities required.

"These general notions of property were then sufficient to answer all the purposes of human life, and might perhaps still have answered them, had it been possible for mankind to have remained in a state of primeval simplicity; as may be collected from the manners of many American nations when first discovered by the Europeans themselves Not that this *communion of goods* seems ever to have been applicable, even in the earliest stages, to aught but the *substance* of the thing; nor could it be extended to the *use* of it. For by the law of nature and reason, he who first began to use it acquired therein a kind of transient property that lasted so long as he was using it, and no longer; or, to speak with greater precision, the *right* of possession continued for the same time only that the *act* of possession lasted. Thus the ground was in common, and no part of it was the permanent property of

Marshall D. Ewell, *A Review of Blackstone's Commentaries*

Use and ownership of property

225

any man in particular. Yet, whoever was in the occupation of any determined spot of it, for rest, for shade, or the like, acquired for the time a sort of ownership, from which it would have been unjust and contrary to the law of nature to have driven him by force; but the instant that he quitted the use or occupation of it, another might seize it without injustice. Thus also a vine or other tree might be said to be in common, as all men were equally entitled to its produce; and yet any private individual might gain the sole property of the fruit which he had gathered for his own repast.

"But when mankind increased in number, craft, and ambition, it became necessary to entertain conceptions of *more permanent dominion*, and to appropriate to individuals, not the immediate *use* only, but the very *substance* of the thing to be used. Otherwise innumerable tumults must have arisen, and the good order of the world be continually broken and disturbed, while a variety of persons were striving who should get the first occupation of the same thing, or disputing which of them had actually gained it. As human life also grew more and more refined, abundance of conveniences were devised to render it more easy, commodious, and agreeable, as habitations for shelter and safety, and raiment for warmth and decency. But no man would be at the trouble to provide either, so long as he had only an usufructuary property in them, which was to cease the instant that he quitted possession,—if, as soon as he walked out of his tent or pulled off his garment, the next stranger who came by would have a right to inhabit the one and to wear the other.

A property in
every man's
house

In the case of *habitations* in particular, it was natural to observe that even the brute creation, to whom everything else was in common, maintained a kind of permanent property in their dwellings, especially for the protection of their young,—that the birds of the air had nests and the beasts of the field had caverns, the invasion of which they esteemed a very flagrant injustice, and would sacrifice their lives to preserve them. Hence a property was soon established in every man's house and homestall, which seem to have been originally mere temporary huts or movable cabins, suited to the design of Providence for more speedily peopling the earth, and suited to the wandering life of their owners, before any extensive property in the soil or ground was established . . .

"As the world by degrees grew more populous, it daily became more difficult to find out new spots to inhabit without encroaching upon former occupants, and, by constantly occupying the same individual spot, the fruits of the earth were consumed and its spontaneous produce destroyed without any provision for future supply or succession. It therefore became necessary to pursue some regular method of providing a constant subsistence, and this necessity produced, or at least promoted and encouraged, *the art of agriculture*. And the art of agriculture, by a regular connection and consequence, introduced and established the idea of a more permanent property in the soil than had hitherto been received and adopted. It was clear that the earth would not produce her fruits in sufficient quantities without the assistance of tillage; but who would be at the pains of tilling it if another might watch an opportunity to seize upon and enjoy the product of his industry, art, and labor? Had not, therefore, a separate property in lands as well as movables been vested in some individuals, the world must have continued a forest, and men have been mere animals of prey, which, according to some philosophers, is the genuine state of nature. Whereas now,—so graciously has Providence interwoven our duty and our happiness together,—the result of this very necessity has been the ennobling of the human species, by giving it opportunities of improving its *rational* faculties, as well as of exerting its *natural*. *Necessity begat property;* and in order to insure that property, recourse was had to civil society, which brought along with it a long train of inseparable concomitants; states, government, laws, punishments, and the public exercise of religious duties. Thus connected together, it was found that a part only of society was sufficient to provide by their manual labor for the necessary subsistence of all, and leisure was given to others to cultivate the human mind, to invent useful arts, and to lay the foundations of science.

"The only question remaining is, *How this property became actually vested*, or what it is that gave a man an exclusive right to retain in a permanent manner that specific *land* which before belonged generally to everybody, but particularly to nobody. *And as we before observed that occupancy gave the right to the temporary use of the soil, so it is agreed upon all hands that occupancy gave also the original right to the permanent property in the substance of the earth itself*, which excludes every one else but the owner from the use of it . . .

Separate property and individual responsibility

"And thus the legislature of England has universally promoted the grand ends of civil society, the peace and security of individuals, by steadily pursuing that wise and orderly *maxim, of assigning to everything capable of ownership a legal and determinate owner*."

"Because Ye Belong to Christ"

While the discussion of Blackstone about *external property* indicates the appearing of the distinctiveness of individual ownership and responsibility, these rights cannot be respected if their *internal* aspect is not clearly identified.

How does the Christian regard *property?* Do we not belong to God? Did He not create us for His own use and glory?

"Even every one that is called by my name: for I have created him for my glory, I have formed him; yea I have made him." Isaiah 43:7

"Thou art worthy, O Lord, to receive glory and honour and power: for thou has created all things, and for thy pleasure they are and were created." Revelation 4:11

And even as Paul reminds us that *"we are His workmanship"* we discover that the writings of John Locke, also studied by the generations of Christians who were concerned with self-government, contain a statement based upon Paul:

227

"For Men being all the Workmanship of one Omnipotent, and infinitely wise Maker: All the Servants of one Sovereign Master, sent into the World by his Order, and about his Business, they are his Property, whose Workmanship they are, made to last during his, not one anothers Pleasure . . ." Christian History, page 58:6

The American Colonists regarded *themselves* as God's property—because "man has a Property in his own Person"—and that person belongs to God. We are all His Workmanship—we are made for His glory.

The most explicit summary of the founding fathers' conception of property is found in the writings of James Madison educated as a theologian, but used of God to direct the writing of the Constitution. Madison indicates the *external* and *internal* meaning of property. He lists as external "property, land, merchandise, or money." As that more important property, the internal, he lists man's property "in his opinions and the free communication of them. He has a property of peculiar value in his religious opinions, and in the profession and practice dictated by them . . . He has an equal property in the free use of his faculties, and the free choice of the objects on which to employ them . . . Conscience is the most sacred of all property."

Thus we can see the Christian inheritance of property—from the first century when "liberty of conscience" became more important to men than their very lives. We remember the Pilgrims fleeing from England, rather than submit to *infringement* of their rights of conscience. And here we find the founding fathers reminding us that "we have a property" in our rights—and that the right to conscience is the most important. As we were reminded in the writings of Neander, liberty of conscience did not exist until Christianity appeared in the world. With its appearing the individual became important—and his most sacred possession was his conscience.

In our study of America's Christian History this important concept of *property* is basic to the recognition of its Christian foundation. Those who know that men are endowed by God to their real estate can see that whatever external goods and possessions an individual may have—their real value is dependent upon his conscientious use of them. Thus the Christian accepts stewardship of what God gives him. Again we turn to Scripture for instruction in the matter of stewardship and we find our Lord admonishing his servants to put whatever he has entrusted into their care into active service in His vineyard. To be *productive* for the Lord, and to be *fruitful* in the work which He gives us to do—to be faithful stewards—profitable unto righteousness.

In the 1856 *Webster's American Dictionary of the English Language*, the definition of *unprofitable* is of interest:

UNPROFITABLE: *"Unprofitable (from the parable of the talents) as Misimproving talents —bringing no glory to God: as an unprofitable servant."*

Just as the Christian values the talents which God has placed in trust with him, and just as he works for their productive fruition in our Lord's service, so he carefully guards the use and disposal of his property. Today much concern is expressed about "property rights" and the infringement upon individual or private enterprise. But the first invasion of property rights occurs *internally* when the individual *consents* to the *disposal* or *use* or *mis-use* of his *opinions*, his *religious convictions*, and his *faculties*. Often this consent is *tacit consent*. As you recall, John Locke differentiated between *express consent* and *tacit consent*. The word *tacit* means:

TACIT: "*Silent; implied, but not expressed. Tacit consent is consent by silence, or not interposing an objection.*

"*So we say, a tacit agreement or covenant of men to live under a particular government, when no objection or opposition is made; a tacit surrender of a part of our natural rights.*"

Thus the surrender of an individual or a nation can occur by *silence*, or by making *no objection*. Christianity, unlike any other religion, requires an *active confession* of faith, an *active acceptance* of Jesus Christ as Lord and Saviour. So a Christian also must *refuse*, through whatever duly constituted means are at his disposal, to permit his rights of conscience, his convictions, or, indeed, his very faculties, and talents, to be used contrary to what he knows to be good and true, and in accord with the laws of God. *Consent* is one's title to the property of conscience. And as John Locke reminds us only *express consent* makes one "a member of any Commonwealth". So only *express refusal* to have one's property used for purposes which do not support righteous government can make one truly faithful to the stewardship of conscience.

Surrender by silence

Paul gives us a tremendous statement concerning *conscience*.

"*And herein do I exercise myself, to have always a conscience void of offence toward God, and toward men.*" Acts 24:16

The early dictionaries, always a tool for education, contained a powerful definition of *conscience* which includes the three powers of government—basic to Christian self-government.

Conscience basic to Christian self-government

CONSCIENCE: *The principle within us, which decides on the lawfulness or unlawfulness of our own actions and affections, and instantly approves or condemns them.*

Conscience is first occupied in ascertaining *our duty (legislative), before we proceed to* action *(executive), then in* judging *of our actions when performed (judicial).*

Only an individual truly Christ-governed can be *conscientious*. The law referred to here is the *Law of God*—the internal government of God through Christ in the heart, the mind and the affections of each individual.

Read Text, Christian History, *page 248A*, Madison.

Man is God's Property

I Am God's Property

God made me for His purpose
He fashioned me to be
An image for His glory,
Almighty Father He.

I am God's Workmanship—my *hands*, my *feet*, my *voice*, my *lips*, everything that God made can glorify God. I can be "about my Father's business" every day, in everything I do—at home, at school—everywhere.

"Take My Life and Let It Be"

"Take my life, and let it be
Consecrated, Lord, to Thee;
Take my hands, and let them move
At the impulse of Thy love,
At the impulse of Thy love.

"Take my feet, and let them be
Swift and beautiful for Thee;
Take my voice, and let me sing,
Always, only, for my King,
Always, only, for my King.

"Take my lips, and let them be
Filled with messages for Thee;
Take my silver and my gold,
Not a mite would I with-hold.
Not a mite would I with-hold.

"Take my moments and my days,
Let them flow in end-less praise;
Take my intellect, and use
Ev-ry power as Thou shalt choose,
Ev-ry power as Thou shalt choose."

Read The Bible, *Matthew 25:14–30*

"His lord said unto him, Well done, thou good and faithful servant: thou hast been faithful over a few things, I will make thee ruler over many things: enter thou into the joy of thy lord."

"Moreover it is required in stewards, that a man be found faithful." 1 Corinthians 4:2

"For ye are bought with a price: therefore glorify God in your body, and in your spirit, which are God's." 1 Corinthians 6:20

What Has God Entrusted Into My Care?

230　*Stewardship at Home.* My family—and my responsibilities at home.

Loving, obeying, respecting my parents—accepting their authority and their counsel, guidance as God leads them to "train" me up "in the way" I should go.

Stewardship at School. Loving, obeying, and *respecting* my teachers—and accepting their authority, their teaching, and their counsel, as God leads them.

Loving my work which God has given me to do. Learning about God's world and the wonder and glory of all that He has done.

Stewardship at Church. Loving, obeying, and *honoring* my pastor and my Sunday School teachers, whom God has entrusted with the work of Gospel ministry. Loving our blessed Lord and Saviour with all my heart, and soul, and mind.

Respecting Property Rights

John Locke states, page 64:27, of *Christian History*

"Every man has a Property *in his own* Person"

John Locke also states that one has an individual responsibility to preserve oneself, and also a responsibility towards the preservation of the rights of others. Note, however, the importance he puts on *self-preservation*. This does not come in competition with the Christian duty to sacrifice for others. One's first duty is to take care of the property which God has entrusted to us—our own person—our bodies as well as our hearts and minds. If we do this we can then better preserve and help our fellow man.

A duty to preserve oneself

"Every one as he is bound to preserve himself, and not to quit his Station wilfully, so by the like reason, when his own Preservation comes not in Competition, ought he, as much as he can, to preserve the rest of Mankind, and may not unless it be to do Justice on an Offender, take away, or impair the Life, or what tends to the Preservation of the Life, the Liberty, Health, Limb, or Goods of another."

On the same page 58, paragraph #5, Locke discusses "that Obligation to mutual Love amongst Men". This must begin by valuing and respecting one's own person, rights, and property.

Learning to Respect the Rights of Others

There are many daily opportunities to learn the stewardship of one's own person —the care, cleanliness, and proper attention to one's appearance, one's conduct and treatment of oneself.

There are also many good opportunities to learn the same respect for fellow-students. Learning to consider one's person as *property* begins to build the concept of respect for the rights of oneself and others—so basic to our form of government. It begins in the simple attitudes cultivated in the Christian home and the Christian church which can be consistently learned—with patience.

Rioting, mob action, property damage to life, limb, liberty and estate, would not occur today, if we had been teaching *property* rights from a righteous standpoint— from the Christian approach of the *stewardship of God's property*. It begins on the local level of—*oneself*. As each individual learns to be Christianly self-governed and learns to be "*faithful over a few things*"—then more opportunities will be entrusted to our care. We will be raising up a new generation of Christian leadership in our land.

Consent is My Title to Conscience

As each student begins to learn the importance of Christian self-government, and of the responsibility which each one has to be faithful stewards of God's property —*oneself*, this becomes true Christian government. As Christian educators, parents, pastors, much effort is made to teach right and wrong from the Word of God. This begins to make each student aware of *conscience*. The consideration here, in relation to property, is that *Consenting* to do that which is right or that which is wrong is basic to Christian self-government. In our times we have replaced individual responsibility for right or wrong with psychological justification. But as Christians we recognize that it begins as soon as an individual learns what is right and what is wrong. This will be tested many times. If each student thinks of being a faithful steward to his *conscience*, he can learn that it is essentially *consenting*. Each one *consents* to do right or do wrong. Thus I give my *consent* to do what I know is right. But I will not give my *consent* to doing that which is wrong and will jeopardize my *sacred conscience*. My *consent* is my title to keeping conscience in God's will.

"Of Property"– John Locke

Read Text, Christian History, *pages 63–70*

God Gave the World to All Mankind

232 "*God, when he gave the World in common to all Mankind, commanded Man also to*

*labour, and the Penury of his Condition required it of him. God and his Reason com-
manded him to subdue the Earth, i.e. improve it for the Benefit of Life, and therein lay
out something upon it that was his own, his Labour.* He that in Obedience to this Command of God, subdued, tilled and sowed any part of it, thereby annexed to it something
that was his Property, *which another had no Title to, nor could without Injury take
from him." Page 65:32*

"The Great Foundation of Property"

*"From all which it is evident, that though the things of Nature are given in common,
yet Man by being Master of himself, and* Proprietor of his own Person, and the
Actions or Labour of it, had still in himself the great Foundation of *Property; and
that which made up the great part of what he applyed to the Support or Comfort of his
Being, when Invention and Arts, had improved the conveniencies of Life; was perfectly
his own, and did not belong in common to others." Page 69:44*

The Title to Property

*"Though the Earth, and all inferior Creatures be common to all Men, yet every Man
has a* Property *in his own* Person: *This no Body has any right to but himself. The*
Labour *of his Body, and the Work of his Hands, we may say, are properly his. Whatsoever then he removes out of the State that Nature hath provided, and left in it, he hath
mixed his* Labour *with, and joyned to it something that is his own, and thereby makes
it his* Property. *It being by him removed from the Common State Nature hath placed
it in, it hath by this* Labour *something annexed to it, that excludes the common Right of
other Men." Page 64:27*

"To the Use of the Industrious and Rational"

*"God gave the World to Men in common; but since he gave it them for their Benefit, and
the greatest conveniencies of Life they were capable to draw from it, it cannot be supposed
he meant it should always remain common and uncultivated. He gave it to the use of
the industrious and rational, (and* Labour *was to be* his Title *to it;) not to the Fancy or
Covetousness of the Quarrelsome and Contentious." Pages 65–66:34*

"The Measure of Property"

"Nature has well set the measure of Property by the extent of Mens Labour *and the
Conveniencies of Life . . . Before the appropriation of Land, he who gathered as much
of the wild Fruit, killed, caught, or tamed, as many of the Beasts, as he could; he that
so imployed his Pains about any of the spontaneous Products of Nature, as any way to
alter them, from the state which Nature put them in, by placing any of his* Labour *on
them, did thereby* acquire a Propriety *in them: But if they perished, in his Possession,*

233

without their due Use; if the Fruits rotted, or the Venison putrified, before he could spend it, he offended against the common Law of Nature, and was liable to be punished; he invaded his Neighbour's share, for he had no Right, farther than his Use *called for any of them, and they might serve to afford him Conveniencies of Life." Page 66:36, 37*

The idea of *property* became transformed through Christianity from the idea of mere *external* possession of things, territory, and other people, to what a man possesses *internally.*

In Luke 12, the parable of the rich man who built greater and greater barns to contain all his fruits and goods, brought forth some admonitions from our Lord:

"And he said unto them, Take heed, and beware of covetousness: for a man's life consisteth not in the abundance of the things which he possesseth . . . So is he that layeth up treasure for himself, and is not rich toward God."

John Locke in his study of *Property* from a Christian standpoint, stated that man is God's property, and that man has a *"Property* in his own *Person"*. As he considered the question of concern to all men—ownership of the land—he concluded that the land had value only as the individual invested his own industry and effort. Thus each individual who put forth effort had title in proportion to his Labour or individual enterprise.

We might use the example of the learning of a subject in school as an illustration of this principle which Locke is setting forth. God has given the knowledge contained in this subject to all of us—you might say it's our common possession. Yet no one actually has title to it—can prove that he owns it. If any student makes the effort to learn the subject—he acquires title to what he learns. This effort on his part hasn't in the least diminished the amount of the subject which we all still have in common. It's still there. But the student who made the effort to learn the subject does have a title to something which no-one can take from him and which he would not have had if he had not added or invested his own effort. He has property rights in the subject.

As we examine the Word of God prayerfully we can find many instances of God giving man the *opportunity* to take possession of what God has provided for man. But some effort is required on the part of each individual to acquire individual rights to what God has freely provided to all mankind. While God gives both seed and harvest, opportunity for individual enterprise is also given.

"I have planted, Apollos watered; but God gave the increase. So then neither is he that planteth any thing, neither he that watereth; but God that gave the increase. Now he that planteth and he that watereth are one: and every man shall receive his own reward according to his own labour. For we are labourers together with God: ye are God's husbandry, ye are God's building." 1 Corinthians 3:6–9

What should be "the measure of property"? This question John Locke sets forth

in a manner which is Christian, just and right. The measure is not how much one wants—but how much one *needs*. This idea is expressed in the New Testament as *sufficiency*.

"And God is able to make all grace abound toward you; that ye, always having all sufficiency in all things, may abound to every good work . . . Now he that ministereth seed to the sower both minister bread for your food, and multiply your seed sown, and increase the fruits of your righteousness." II Corinthians 9:8, 10

"And he said unto his disciples, Therefore I say unto you, Take no thought for your life, what ye shall eat; neither for the body, what ye shall put on . . . For all these things do the nations of the world seek after: and your Father knoweth that ye have need of these things." Luke 12:22, 30

Today we have forgotten the habit of *faith* and we live largely by *fear*. Locke saw each individual not coveting more than he could reasonably *use*. He also saw the habit of *not wasting substance*. For this was an offence against the Law of God.

Living through faith

Concern with the *"things really useful* to the life of Man, such as food, led men to barter or exchange those things which spoiled for other things which would not decay in and of themselves.

"Gold, Silver and Diamonds, are things, that Fancy or Agreement hath put the Value on, more than real Use, and the necessary support of Life."

Thus men could extend the use of property by not permitting anything to go to waste, and by storing up *durable representatives* of food and other perishables.

"If he would give his Nuts for a piece of Metal, pleased with its Colour; or exchange his Sheep for Shells, or Wooll for a sparkling Peble or a Diamond, and keep those by him all his Life, he invaded not the Right of others, he might heap up as much of these durable things as he pleased, the exceeding of the bounds of *his* just Property *not lying in the largeness of his Possession, but the perishing of any thing uselessly in it. And thus* came in the use of Money, *some lasting thing that Men might keep without spoiling, and that by mutual Consent Men would take in exchange for the truly useful, but perishable supports of Life."* Page 69:46

Gold value

It is important to note the inference here again—that while Gold, Silver, Diamonds, were rare enough to be used as *representatives* of *useful* things, it was only in what they represented—the food and other supports to man's life—that they were useful to man. The "sparkling Peble" or "Diamond" was only a "Fancy", not something "truly useful" in and of itself. When man lost sight of the purpose for which Gold was originally used—so much corn, fruits, wool, etc.—then he began to hoard it for itself—placing the value *externally*. The real value of anything must be placed *"where neither moth nor rust doth corrupt, and where thieves do not break through nor steal: for where your treasure is, there will your heart be also."* Matthew 6:20, 21

235

The *consent* of men to put a value on *external* money, brought about the accumulation of larger possessions. As long as the money remained as a *representative* of the "useful things" it did not deceive man. But when we forget that real value has to be *internal* first—then we lose sight of that which makes the real *foundation of property*. John Locke reminds us that the land, in and of itself, is only of value as the individual invests his talent, his time, his industry, his effort, to make it productive. Thus the gold is always *within* the people of a nation. It is their ability to be "rich toward God" that represents the *gold of Christian character*—the coin that belongs to God—not Caesar.

Life, Liberty, and Property

"The Blessings of Liberty"

<pre>
</pre>

Felix Morley,
*The Power in
the People*

"An attempt to clarify what we mean by 'liberty' does not deprive us of the emotional values surrounding this noun . . . On the contrary, the opening lines of Byron's famous sonnet may helpfully be recalled for their distinction between the spiritual aspiration of liberty and the physical condition of freedom:

> '*Eternal Spirit of the chainless Mind
> Brightest in dungeons, Liberty, thou art!*'

"Liberty" and
"Freedom"

"Yet the words 'liberty' and 'freedom' have long been used almost interchangeably . . . 'Freedom' is pre-eminently a noun descriptive of status or condition. The suffix 'dom' is the same as that found in 'kingdom', 'officialdom,' or 'Christendom.' . . . Ability to reason is not implied in the term 'freedom,' as in the case of 'liberty.' . . . Even oysters may be said to have freedom. But they will never have liberty.

"That is because the oyster does not possess the power to discriminate, which is one of the two essential ingredients of liberty . . . We speak of giving a caged bird its 'freedom,' or of setting it 'at liberty.' For 'at liberty' means that the bird must now decide whither it shall fly, whereas it will have freedom even if it merely flutters from the open cage to the ground and cowers there . . .

"Mere freedom of choice undoubtedly places its possessor 'at liberty.' But to reach the essence of liberty, and certainly to secure its blessings in co-operative living, choice must be exercised in conformity with moral principles. There must be a sense of personal responsibility, of self-restraint, and therefore of self-government . . .

236   "When the founders spoke of the blessings of liberty, they did not discount the

value of freedom. But it is apparent to any student of the period that they generally used the word 'liberty' to convey a sense of individual responsibility which the alternative noun 'freedom' does not imply. The blessings of freedom may be of very questionable value. Those of liberty, properly understood, are priceless . . .

"That the condition of freedom can be maintained only by the divinely implanted urge for liberty was fully understood when the Republic was launched . . . The blessings of liberty, which political government may safeguard or destroy but can never itself provide, are therefore intimately connected with personal belief in, and practice of, Christian doctrine. As Paul told the Corinthians also: "Where the Spirit of the Lord is, there is liberty."

The Preservation of Property

Read Text, Christian History, *page 91:124; pages 248A, 261*

This statement of John Locke so well expressed the Colonists' conception of the purpose of government that it was found ringing through their writings and their expositions on the subject.

It had taken sixteen hundred and twenty years for the appearing of Christian Liberty expressed politically by the Pilgrims. What they knew reversed the course of history and, eventually, it was beautifully phrased in our Declaration of Independence: men "*are endowed by their Creator with certain unalienable Rights, that among these are Life, Liberty, and the Pursuit of Happiness—That to secure these Rights, Governments are instituted among Men . . .*"

Property Rights—the rights to life and liberty—vested in the individual by God —and not granted, extended or provided—by the structure of government. *Secured yes*, but *provided no!*

Government does not give men "rights"

The experience and study of the Founding Fathers of our nation convinced them that they were going to be very sure of a political structure of government which would *secure* these *rights* to be preserved as part of the *sacred property* of man— God-Granted.

A "Property in One's Rights"

Read Text, Christian History, *pages 321, 365–370*

This famous paper—the most explicit expression of the "Property of One's Rights"—was widely circulated. Define the following principles as they were expressed in the three categories of:

	Men	*Christians*	*Subjects*
Source of rights: Purpose of civil government: Liberty depends on: Does one have a right to defend one's rights?			

Why did the colonists consider Roman Catholics *politically subversive?*

Would the same reasoning apply to Communists in the United States today?

No Taxation Without Representation

Read Text, Christian History, *page 95:138*

"Men *therefore* in Society having Property, *they have such a right to the Goods, which by the Law of the Community are theirs, that no Body hath a right to take their Substance or any part of it from them, without their own Consent; without this they have no Property at all. For I have truly no* Property *in that, which another can by right take from me, when he pleases against my Consent.*"

Read Text, Christian History, *pages 13, 15, 38*

The English or Teutonic method of representative government is described as *federalism*. This needs to be identified in terms of the government of the United States.

Felix Morley,
*Freedom and
Federalism*

"The United States, as the name implies, are a union of sovereign States, federal in nature. Certain characteristics herewith ennumerated, are common to all federations. First and foremost, federalism involves dispersion of political power. There will, of course, be some delegation of overriding authority to the general or central government. This requires the establishment of a national capital, the presence of which itself distinguishes a federation from a mere league or alliance of independent sovereignties. The seating of the central government is the material reflection of the process of federation, whereby the component parts—while reserving certain powers to themselves—have permanently surrendered some prerogatives of sovereignty to a common national pool.

238   "This division of sovereignty between the central government and the constituent

states must be defined. In consequence, a constitution is prerequisite to any federation, and it is in practice necessary that this should be a written contract so that both the state and central governments may have reasonably precise understanding of their respective functions and authority . . .

"Flexibility is an outstanding asset of the federal form of government. By the device of keeping certain governmental powers under strictly local control, people with great diversities may be encouraged to unite under one flag . . .

"The great overriding advantage of the federal system is that it operates to avert the dangers inherent in government by remote control. The essence of federalism is reservation of control over local affairs to the localities themselves, the argument for which becomes stronger if the federation embraces a large area, with strong climatic or cultural differences among the various states therein. One justifying assumption for such a loose-knit system is that citizens as a body are both interested in, and for the most part competent to handle, local problems. When that assumption is valid there is little doubt that federalism, despite its disadvantages serves admirably to foster freedom without the sacrifice of order."

Advantage of the federal system

Read Text, Christian History, *pages 249–257*

The first American Constitution of Connecticut specifically embodies the representative principle—designed to preserve the rights and property of the people —through individual sovereignty.

Read Text, Christian History, *pages 297–339*

This period describes the steps Britain took to inaugurate a system of internal taxation which "was an assertion by parliament of the right to tax the colonies by a body in which they were not represented". The consequences were directly the result of the Colonists' clear understanding of the principles of *representation*, *property* and *rights* and of the degree to which these principles were being infringed, and usurped by the British ministry. Identify the principal invasions of the *property rights* of the Colonists by the action of the British Parliament, which finally culminated in the patriots of Boston refusing to let tea be landed in Boston:

Action of British Ministry	*Specific Property Rights Invaded*	*Action of American Colonists*

239

The Christian Form of Our Government

Key to the Fifth Principle

It is a common error among Christians to state that neither our *form* of government nor our nation is Christian, because the majority of its population are not born-again Christians. They doubt that the Constitution was formed as a Christian document because they believe that the Founding Fathers were not all Christians.

The determining factor as to whether our nation is a Christian nation, and as to whether the Constitution is a Christian document is—not whether Christians *formed* the Constitution—but whether *the form is Christian*. The basis for judgment is the Bible.

To understand the American Christian Constitution as the Christian form of government, it is necessary to consider its two spheres—the *spirit* and the *letter*—the *internal* and the *external*. Both spheres must be active in order that the Constitution function to preserve the basic republican spirit of individual liberty. Today we still have the *letter* of the Constitution. That is, we still go through most of the legal processes of the *structure* of the Constitution in enacting legislation, and in the executive and judicial branches. But the *spirit* which was intended and understood by our Founding Fathers is missing—and has been for the last one hundred years. That *spirit* was the Christian foundation of our Constitution—the Faith of our Fathers—and as our nation has fallen away from its foundations—the essence of that faith—our Constitution has become a hollow shell.

In 1799, Dr. Jedidiah Morse preached an election sermon, referred to on pages IV and V of the *Preface to Christian History*. Dr. Morse reminds us that it is "to the kindly influence of Christianity we owe that degree of civil freedom, and political and social happiness which mankind now enjoy." He continues with a warning, concerning the atheism of the French Revolution. Timely for his day, it has even

240

more significance for our times—"that all efforts made to destroy the foundations of our holy religion, ultimately tend to the subversion also of our political freedom and happiness. Whenever the pillars of Christianity shall be overthrown, our present republican forms of government, and all the blessings which flow from them, must fall with them."

The *spirit* and the *letter* of our Constitution can also be described as the *nature and essence* and the *structure and framework*. There is a Biblical basis for both.

The *nature and essence* of our Constitution—the *internal* or *spirit*—includes: *property, Christian self-government,* and *union.* Two of these aspects we have already indicated as having an internal, Christian basis in our consideration in the foregoing lessons of *Christian self-government* and *property.* We shall deal with *Biblical Christian unity* in the last principle.

The *structure and framework*—the *external*—or *letter*—of our Constitution includes:

The Principle of Representation
The Separation of Powers
The Dual Form of Our Government

We shall consider these three aspects of our Constitution in their Christian form and origin.

The Biblical basis
of Representation

We often hear it explained that ours is a representative government. Where does the principle of representation come from and what are the qualifications for one to be a representative?

In the first chapter of the book of *Deuteronomy* we are told that Moses was instructed by the Lord God to:

"Take you wise men, and understanding, and known among your tribes, and I will make them rulers over you . . . captains over thousands, and captains over hundreds, and captains over fifties, and captains over tens, and officers among your tribes."

Our first written
constitution

We find that this was the text chosen by the Rev. Thomas Hooker, May 31, 1638, for a lecture leading the way to the *First written constitution in America*—that of *Connecticut.* Excerpts from the *Fundamental Orders of Connecticut* can be found on pages 253–257 of *Christian History.* On page 250 of *Christian History* can be found Dr. Hooker's development of the political principles of representative government taken from the text in Deuteronomy:

I "That the choice of public magistrates belongs unto the people by God's own allowance.

II "The privilege of election which belongs unto the people, therefore, must not be exercised according to their humors, but according to the blessed will and law of God.

III "They who have power to appoint officers and magistrates, it is their power, also, to set the bounds of the power and place unto which they call them . . .

"Eight months later, the fundamental laws embodying these principles for the first time in human history, were 'sentenced, ordered, and decreed'. It is impossible not to recognize the Master hand."

The separation of the powers of government—more commonly known as the *three branches of government*—legislative, executive, and judicial, we take very much for granted. But where did the principle of the separation of powers originate? Turning to *Isaiah* 33:22 we find these words:

"*For the Lord is our judge, the Lord is our lawgiver, the Lord is our king . . .*"

These three governmental actions are accepted in the New Testament wherein Jesus Christ is recognized as the *Judge* and *King*, and God as the *Lawgiver*. It is because our forefathers understood that they were under the authority of God through Christ, that they *embodied* these three characteristics of individual action in their respective spheres of government—*local, state* and *national.*

When the individual Christian prays to know and do God's will he, figuratively, *legislates, executes,* and *judges.* Thus he literally fulfills the three functions of government by carrying out God's purpose in his life.

Can we expect these three governmental actions to operate correctly if we, as individual Christians, do not know the source from which they were derived, and what was their purpose? In our ignorance today we are tempted to believe that the power of the judicial, executive, and legislative branches of our government resides in those individuals who *staff* these offices. Yet, upon consideration of the Biblical base and purpose, we can see that the power or control resides *not in the staffing but in the electorate which these offices represent.* It resides in each individual Christian as he allows Christ to rule his life.

Seldom today do we hear mentioned one of the most unique aspects of our Constitution—our dual form of government—the *state* and the *nation.* This refers to the *national-federal* structure of our Constitution. There is not a country today on the face of the globe that embodies this Christian principle of government—and we ourselves have allowed it to deteriorate.

The Biblical base of the dual form of our government is the two commands of our Lord when asked by the lawyer which is the greatest commandment of them all?

"*Jesus said unto him, Thou shalt love the Lord thy God with all thy heart, and with all thy soul, and with all thy mind. This is the first and great commandment. And the second is like unto it, Thou shalt love thy neighbour as thyself. On these two commandments hang all the law and the prophets.*" Matthew 22:37-40

Our *national* sense, as *Americans*, is predicated upon our willingness to be God-governed—the first commandment. This is the basis for Christian Self-Government.

Our *federal* sense, as Californians, Washingtonians, Oregonians, etc., is predicated upon the second commandment.

242 The individual's relation to God and to man are hereby stated, and for the

Christian, there must be consistency in his behavior—whether he is dealing with one neighbor—or two hundred million.

This statement by John Ponet, written in 1556, and quoted in the works of John Adams, states the principle of the dual form of our government:

"This rule is the Law of Nature *. . . set further in writing in the decaloge or ten commandments: and after reduced by Christ our saveour into these two wordes: Thou shalt love thy lorde God above all things, and thy neighbour as thy self. The latter part whereof he also thus expoundeth: What so ever ye will that men doo unto you, doo ye even so to them. In this lawe is comprehended all justice, the perfit way to serve and glorifie God, and the right meane to rule every man particularly, and all men generally: and the only staye to mayntayne every commonwealth. This is the touchstone to try every manes doinges (be he King or beggar) whether they be good or evil. Bi this all menes laws be discerned, whether they be juste or unjuste, godly or wicked."* John Ponet, "A Short Treatise of Politike Pouur", 1556

The Christian Idea of Man and Government

It is important to plant the seeds of our Christian form of government early in the student's experience to learn how these principles function. The classroom provides many wonderful, natural opportunities.

The concept of having someone represent, or re-present us, is one which begins in the Old Testament, which we have referred to in our discussion of the *Fifth Principle*. In the beginning of the development of political government it was recognized that although everyone took part in the lawmaking function of government, every single person could not take the time to go to the place where the lawmaking body was meeting. So it was decided to choose someone to stand-in-the-place-of, or represent, a certain number of individuals. In this way members of a local community took turns being the lawmaking body and taking an active part in making decisions which affected all the other non-present individuals. They were representing the interests of themselves and of those who were not present and who had chosen them to stand in their place—as though they were there.

Our colonists were very explicit to instruct those individuals to whom they had delegated the power of representation. They indicated how these representatives should vote on many important matters. They were also very sure of electing men of integrity—who could also stand for their own integrity and character.

Whenever the teacher in the classroom sends someone to the office, or on an errand, for the class, this individual becomes, in effect, the *representative* of the class. While the teacher very often *appoints* these individuals, when there is time

243

to do so, it would be instructive to *choose* or *elect* representatives and to determine what their job of representation is. Evaluation of how individuals perform their errands of representation might help students to see how important such opportunities are for *responsible action*. There might also be opportunities for the teacher to relate these simple classroom activities to the periodic elections which are held locally, and for state and national offices.

Many classrooms have special weekly assignments for such tasks or responsibilities as 1) cleaning blackboards after school 2) simple housekeeping tasks such as straightening up bookcases, desks, etc. 3) responsibility for playground equipment—taking out or bringing in balls, bats, etc. Here again there are opportunities for taking time to elect different members of the class to these jobs or offices and learning how to *select* and evaluate how they carry out their elected positions.

Class-room government can also begin by electing officers to perform weekly or monthly governmental functions which involve decisions affecting every member of the class.

This principle of the separation of the powers of government into its three parts—legislative or lawmaking, executive or putting law into action, and judicial, deciding whether law is in accordance with our Constitution, can be taught as *individual action*.

Legislating or
planning action

When we contemplate doing any action—we are, in essence, *legislating* or *planning how* we will perform this action. For example, the child who is starting to walk home from school plans which route he will take. He may decide to walk on the sidewalks, cross the highway with the traffic light, and go home in an orderly manner. Or, he or she, may decide to cut across several front yards, scoot across the highway when there are no cars, regardless of the light, and go home any old way. This planning, which seems often unconscious, can be made to become *conscious action* for the purpose of helping students learn that each individual is governed in some way. Either he or she is governed by the laws of God and of man —or he is lawless. So whenever one contemplates action—this is one's *legislative function*. Just how an individual plans any action is, in effect, his lawmaking function.

Executing or
doing the action

Putting plans into action and *doing the action*, or executing the plan, becomes our *executive function*. Again, a good executive carries out the laws and does not make up laws to govern his own behavior. In this function particularly, we have many opportunities to instruct our students in the need for each one to determine if actions are in accordance with God's laws. As we *review* action already taken, or contemplate action which we propose to take, this becomes our *Judicial* or judging function. A Christian has the Bible as God's law upon which to base his judgment of action. As an American citizen he has the laws of the local community, the laws of the state, and the laws of the nation upon which to base his action. As the Constitution is the law of the land, in the same way the Bible is the law of the individual.

Judicial or
judging the
action

244   The chart on page 270C is a useful illustration for primary students to look at for

they can clearly see that the Pilgrim in this picture is consulting his Bible to instruct him how to govern himself in both church and society.

The two commandments of our Lord are the basis of our dual form of government. How one acts as an American—the first commandment—represents one's duty to God. The second commandment is the basis of the relation of the individual states to each other—our relation to our neighbor. These two aspects of our Constitutional form of government can be taught in the classroom activities. The individual might consider his first relation to his school—and his second to his fellow-students. He would let the two commandments found in the New Testament be his guide to these two aspects of his action. In this way he would be learning the dual form of his own individual Christian self-government.

The Law and the Gospel as the Basis of Our Government

"Where the Spirit of the Lord is, There is Liberty." 2 Cor. 3:17

Read Text, Christian History, *Dedication Page, I*

This page is dedicated to "the Christian principle upon which this nation is founded". Where can we find the record of the Law and the Gospel upon our nation?

Read Text, Christian History, *pages 182–183*

Here we find reference to the Pilgrims and the Puritans who brought the Christian principle to these shores. Remember, the Puritan held to the *letter* of the Old Testament. The Pilgrim, on the other hand, lived the New Testament precepts and permitted others to do so also.

Read Text, Christian History, *pages 28A, 28B, 25–28*

When Wickliffe first translated the Bible into English he began the Reformation. This was the impetus which, by opening the Bible to the individual, launched the recognition of evangelical liberty and political liberty. As the Pilgrims found evidence in Scripture for the local self-governing church of the New Testament, they were impelled to break with the centralized Church of England and to count the cost of liberty of conscience.

Read Text, Christian History, *pages 245–248*

This review of the importance of Plymouth and of the influence of Bible-loving and Bible-living Christians helps us remember the beginnings of our nation. The rock upon which the Pilgrims founded their laws, their institutions, and their hope, was the Rock, Christ.

Read Text, Christian History, *pages 248B–252*

The first American Constitution was founded on the Word of God and became an important link in the Chain of Christianity.

Read Text, Christian History, *page 375, second paragraph*

This Order of Congress, directing the Committee of Commerce to import 20,000 copies of the Bible, is an important indication of the recognition by the patriots that they could not fight a Revolution without the Bible. They called it their *political textbook*.

The Founding Fathers of our nation were well aware that in order to keep our Christian Liberty—we must have "true and useful knowledge". To this end they established schools—schools so that each student could, first of all, learn to read the Word of God. They knew that "the Old Deluder", Satan, was the enemy of liberty—and therefore it was imperative that each Christian know the Word of God in order to keep free from sin and evil.

Jedidiah Morse, one of the early Christian ministers and educators in America, wrote in 1795:

"On the early and proper education of children depend, in a great measure, their own happiness, that of their parents, their country, and posterity. The continuance and security of true Religion, and of civil liberty, among any people, must result from their being enlightened by true and useful knowledge. The foundation of this knowledge is laid in Schools and Families, where its rudiments are, or should be taught."

Read Text, Christian History, *page 240B*

The foundation of Harvard College, as were other colleges, was for the glory of God—not of man. The whole purpose of education, at every level, was to "lay Christ in the bottome, as the only foundation of all sound knowledge and Learning"

Read Text, Christian History, *pages 405–410*

The Declaration of Independence, Washington's Farewell Address, and the Constitution of the United States, should be studied by the youth of our country, as their *"political scriptures."*

Our forefathers were convinced that one of the best deterrents to tyranny was a knowledge of history. The individual who knew history would know the price which must be paid for liberty. Furthermore, a knowledge of history would reveal how important is the character of men, and of the need to safeguard Liberty with Virtue!

Emma Willard, a pioneer Christian educator, and a student and author of American History, felt that the study of our American history was vital to maintaining our republic.

Most important of all, Emma Willard discerned that Christian principles formed the foundation of all true education. "Moral improvement is the true end of the intellectual", she said, and when instructing young teachers, she admonished them to "bring God into all subjects", that their pupils might begin to see His wonderful government of the universe in all its aspects.

A Government Resting on Moral Principles

Read Text, Christian History, *page 47*

" 'Dominion', said Wickliffe, 'belongs to grace'; meaning, as I believe, that the feudal government, which rests on the sword, should yield to a government resting on moral principles."

A government resting upon God's laws

While, it is true, we are a government of *laws* and not a government of *men*, still it is men and women, who constitute a nation, and who in turn become its leaders. And so, a government resting on moral principles must be supported by true Christian virtue and morality in its people.

Read Text, Christian History, *page 364B*

As one reads John Locke's famous definition of Liberty—not Licence—and sees these reflections in the writings of Samuel Adams, it is not hard to realize why the Founding Father generation knew that a government must be founded on moral principles and that these principles must be expressed in the lives of its citizens.

Liberty not licence

"He therefore is the truest friend to the liberty of his country who tries most to promote its virtue, and who, so far as his power and influence extend, will not suffer a man to be chosen into any office of power and trust who is not a wise and virtuous man. . . . The sum of all is, if we would most truly enjoy this gift of Heaven, let us become a virtuous people . . ."

Read Text, Christian History, *pages 396–397*

The qualities of a good ruler are also the qualities of those who are governed in a republic.

Read Text, Christian History, *pages 416–417*

Here is defined briefly some of the qualities of George Washington, whom God   247 raised up to lead the thirteen colonies in a seven years war for their liberation from tyranny.

Read Text, Christian History *page XIV, second paragraph.*

The Pulpit and American Independence

"The writer of these letters, then a chaplain in the Leacock battalion, many of whom were members of his congregation, was afterward the revered pastor of the old church at Freehold, New Jersey, wherein William Tennent had preached. He was also chaplain at Valley Forge, to which place he repaired with every male member of his congregation; for in those days politics were preached in the pulpits, and men were led to action on the side of freedom by faithful pastors. The eminent General Muhlenberg was one of this stamp. When the war for independence was kindling, he was a clergyman in Virginia, and at the close of 1775, he concluded a sermon with the words of Scripture: "There is a time for all things—a time to preach and a time to pray;" but those times, he said, had passed away; and then, in a voice that sounded like a trumpet-blast through the church, he exclaimed: "There is a time to *fight*, and that time has now come' ". Then laying aside his sacerdotal gown, he stood before his flock in the full uniform of a Virginia colonel. He ordered the drums to be beaten at the church door for recruits; and almost the entire male audience, capable of bearing arms, joined his standard. Nearly three hundred men enlisted under his banner on that day."

Patriotic clergy "*What Can the Righteous Do?*" This question was mightily answered in the courage and integrity of the American clergy—north, south, and in the middle colonies—both before, during and after the American Christian Revolution. For 150 years prior to the revolution the men of foresight and conviction in the American pulpit preached the principles of Christian government. They contributed much to the righteous government of the times and to the clear understanding of the principles of the Christian form of our government.

Read Text, Christian History, *pages 372–390*

The Political Sermons contained in the pages referred to above represent a fine understanding of Christian government. Many of these pastors realized that some of their brethren of the cloth frowned on their forthright stand for preaching against the political evils of the time and for taking such an active part in the struggle for independence. But the men who express their ideas here so forcefully, are representative of a large number of Christian Ministers who saw their duty to God and their country in a clear light of fundamental Christianity. Sincere and devoted to

248

God, these men could not shut their eyes to the stirring challenges of the times —and they considered it their Christian duty to use their talents, given to them of God, to defend Christian Liberty from its enemies within and without.

An example of the attitude of the clergy during our Revolutionary period can also be found in the following quotation from the Reverend John Witherspoon, a member of the Continental Congress, in his Fast Day sermon of May 17, 1776—a Fast Day called for by Congress:

"Upon the whole, I beseech you to make a wise improvement of the present threatening aspect of public affairs and to remember that your duty to God, to your country, to your families, and to yourselves is the same. True religion is nothing else but an inward temper and outward conduct suited to your state and circumstance in Providence at any time. And as peace with God and conformity to Him, adds to the sweetness of created comforts while we possess them, so in times of difficulty and trial, it is in the man of piety and inward principle that we may expect to find the *uncorrupted patriot*, the *useful citizen*, and the *invincible soldier*,—God grant that in America *true religion* and *civil liberty* may be *inseparable*, and the unjust attempts to destroy the one, may in the issue tend to the support and establishment of both."

The "uncorrupted patriot"

249

How the Seed of Local Self-Government is Planted

Key to the Sixth Principle

Read Text, Christian History, *pages 147–150*

The seed of Christian self-government, born in the first century of Christianity, came to these shores with the tiny settlement of the Mayflower Pilgrims.

"Our popular government lay in embryo on board the Mayflower, all environed with its only possible preservatives, popular intelligence and popular virtue."

Webster defines American government

The word "popular" as defined in *Webster's* first American Dictionary means "pertaining to the common people", which refers to a government "of the people" as opposed to the divine right of kings theory of government.

The Republican form of government depends upon the principles contained in the Holy Scriptures. Our foundations were Christian and in order to maintain the republicanism of Christianity we must be a God-fearing, Christ-honoring nation. Emma Willard reminds us of the obligation of each individual American:

"The government of the United States is acknowledged by the wise and good of other nations, to be the most free, impartial, and righteous government of the world; but all agree, that for such a government to be sustained many years, the principles of truth and righteousness, taught in the Holy Scriptures, must be practised. The rulers must govern in the fear of God, and the people obey the laws."

The external threat to our nation will never be so great as the challenge within. That challenge is a challenge to the integrity of individual Christian self-government. Samuel Adams sounded the warning note in 1779:

250

"*A general Dissolution of Principles and Manners will more surely overthrow the Liberties of America than the whole Force of the Common Enemy. While the People are virtuous they cannot be subdued; but when once they lose their Virtue they will be ready to surrender their Liberties to the first external or internal Invader . . . If Virtue and Knowledge are diffused among the People, they will never be enslaved. This will be their great Security.*"

Read Text, Christian History, *page XIV*

Samuel Adams—*The Father of the Revolution*—reminds us that the art of self-government is learned through "the study and practice of the exalted virtues of the Christian system . . ."

Paul defines *virtue:* as "*the righteousness of God and our Saviour* Jesus Christ." He admonishes us to "*add to your faith virtue; and to virtue knowledge . . . knowledge of our Lord* Jesus Christ." 2 Peter: 1:5, 8.

The Father of the Revolution

The leaders of the American Christian Revolution have long been obscured or misrepresented in their efforts to set forth the basis of the conflict. Since the decline of Christian leadership in America—leadership and morality have often been divorced and the pages of our glorious history effaced in the effort to impute to the Founding Fathers the motives and methods of a period not animated by Christian virtues.

The Christian
character of our
Founding
Fathers

Read Text, Christian History, *pages 396–397*

But the shining lights of the past cannot be extinguished when, once again, we examine our history with the light of Christianity. Of Samuel Adams much has been written and the attempt has been to categorize him as a political propagandist, rabble rouser and atheist. Nothing could be farther from the truth and his works praise him and bear evidence to the contrary. He is characterized by the eminent American historian, George Bancroft, as follows. The time May, 1764, at the period when the British Parliament had just passed the Stamp Act:

"*Before it was known that the bill had passed, the alarm was given in Boston, at its town-meeting in May 1764, by Samuel Adams, a native of the place, a provincial states-man of a clear and logical mind, which, throughout a long life, imparted consistency to his public conduct. His will resembled well-tempered steel, which may ply, but will not break. Bred as a Calvinist of the strictest sect, his riper judgment confirmed him in his creed. On church government he adhered to the Congregational forms, as most friendly to civil and religious liberty; was a member of the church; and the austere purity of his life witnessed the sincerity of his profession. Evening and morning his house was a house of prayer; and no one more revered the Christian sabbath. He was a tender husband, an affectionate parent, and could vividly enjoy conversation with friends; but the walls of his modest mansion never witnessed anything inconsistent with the discipline of the man whose desire for his birthplace was that 'Boston might become a Christian Sparta.' "*

The Father of
the Revolution

Samuel Adams won his title, *The Father of the Revolution*, because he not only understood the issues of the controversy with England, but because he stood forth in defense of the colonists' rights. Only a Christian could understand the sources of conflict between the British Parliament and the colonists. It was more than an economic or political struggle, although there were both economic and political elements involved. In the beginning it was the assertion of the rights of Englishmen as these rights had been granted throughout English history. But, more than this, it was the reasoning of Americans, such as Samuel Adams, that the rights of the colonists were Christian rights as documented in the New Testament.

"Jefferson says that Samuel Adams was constantly holding caucuses of distinguished men, in which the measures to be pursued were generally determined upon . . . He ascribed great influence to Samuel Adams in promoting the Revolution. His labors in the cause had been for years so unremitting, that it may be justly said of him, 'His feet were ever in the stirrup, his lance ever in its rest.' "—Christian History, *Page 351*

Samuel Adams'
essay on liberty

At the age of 28 years, writing in the year 1750, Samuel Adams had already perceived that man's political liberty relates to spiritual freedom under the law of God. Like Paul he recognized that sin enslaves man and does not permit him to be "subject to no other control" and "commanded by no other power than the laws and ordinances of the great Creator of all things."

In Romans 7:22–23, Paul writes:

"For I delight in the law of God after the inward man: But I see another law in my members, warring against the law of my mind, and bringing me into captivity to the law of sin which is in my members."

Deliverance comes only through Christ.

"For the law of the Spirit of life in Christ Jesus hath made me free from the law of sin and death." Romans 8:2

Samuel Adams discusses liberty—*Christian History*, page 364B

In 1772, Samuel Adams wrote his famous *Rights of the Colonists*, which represented the "most systematic presentation of the American cause." Adams' phrases in this paper are colored by his own study of the great Christian philosopher of an earlier century, John Locke. Locke's clarification of the rights of man had helped to establish the reason and logic which overthrew the infallibility of the doctrine of

252

the "divine right of kings." Locke states that "a State of Liberty" is not "a State of Licence." He describes the "State of perfect Freedom" as "the State of Nature" in which all men may "order their Actions, and dispose of their possessions and Persons as they see fit." But this state is subject to the "Law of Nature" which governs it. Locke describes this "Law of Nature" as the active preservation of the sovereign rights of each individual. He defines the "Law of Nature" in the following words:

The Law of Nature

"*The* State of Nature *has a Law of Nature to govern it, which obliges everyone: And Reason, which is that Law, teaches all Mankind, who will but consult it, that being all* equal and independent, *no one ought to harm another in his Life, Health, Liberty, or Possessions. For Men being all the Workmanship of one Omnipotent, and infinitely wise Maker: All the Servants of One Sovereign Master, sent into the World by his Order, and about his Business, they are his Property, whose Workmanship they are, made to last during his, not one anothers Pleasure: And being furnished with like Faculties, sharing all in one Community of Nature, there cannot be supposed any such* Subordination *among us, that may authorize us to destroy one another, as if we were made for one another's Uses, as the inferior ranks of Creatures are for ours.*"—Christian History, *Page 58; 6*

Men, Christians, Subjects

On pages 365–370 Adams' treatise on *Rights of the Colonists* is divided into three sections—"Rights of the Colonists as Men," "The Rights of the Colonists as Christians," and "The Rights of the Colonists as Subjects." In his first section he defines the rights of the Colonists as Men in these words:

"*Among the natural rights of the Colonists are these: First, a right to life; Secondly, to liberty; Thirdly, to property; together with the right to support and defend them in the best manner they can.*"—Christian History, *Page 365*

Echoing Locke's argument of "Liberty under Law", Samuel Adams develops, step by step, his basic premise:

"*The natural liberty of man is to be free from any superior power on earth, and not to be under the will or legislative authority of man, but only to have the law of nature for his rule.*"—Christian History, *Page 366*

Liberty is an individual responsibility, Adams asserts, which the individual can never surrender because the right to freedom is a gift from God. Read page 367, paragraph "Liberty is a Responsibility."

In his "The Rights of the Colonists as Christians" Samuel Adams states the source of these rights:

"*These may be best understood by reading and carefully studying the institutes of the great Law Giver and Head of the Christian Church, which are to be found clearly written and promulgated in the New Testament.*"—Christian History, *Page 367*

253

The "rights" of the Colonists as Christian men culminate in their rights as subjects, and it is here that Adams delivers the consequences of a government based
upon "unalienable Rights":

*"The absolute rights of Englishmen and all freemen, in or out of civil society, are
principally personal security, personal liberty, and private property."*—Christian
History, *Page 368*

*"Thirdly, the supreme power cannot justly take from any man any part of his property,
without his consent in person or by his representative."*—Christian History, *Page 369*

In 1764 Samuel Adams had worded the first public denial of the right of the
British Parliament to tax the Colonists. Now, in 1772, he raises the question which
is to form the Christian basis of protest of the rights of the Colonists. This question
is not an economic question, nor is it alone a political question. It touches upon
the sanctity and sovereignty of the individual whose rights are God-granted.
Governments only exist to "insure" these rights and thus an infringement of *one*
of the rights of man constitutes a threat to *all* of his rights:

See definition of property, by James Madison, Christian History, *Page 248A*

Samuel Adams states the case for America's sure defense—as true now as then:

*"May every citizen in the army and in the country, have a proper sense of the Deity
upon his mind, and an impression of that declaration recorded in the Bible, 'Him that
honoreth me, I will honor, but he that despiseth me shall be lightly esteemed.'—'God
helpeth those who help themselves,' says an eminent writer. Perhaps the sentiment is
better expressed in holy writ, where, when we are bid to work out our own salvation, we
are told that 'It is God who worketh in us.' It seems to be the Divine Constitution, that
success shall generally crown virtuous exertions."*

Samuel Adams was unceasing in his efforts to promote the course of independence.
His concern was to educate his fellow Colonists to reason out their political con-
victions from the standpoint of their Christian rights. He knew that, in the tradition
of freemen, they must *discuss, dispute,* and *debate* the implications of their position.
Thus it was largely through his tireless efforts that he brought into being the
Committees of Correspondence and kept them functioning through the years prior
to the revolution. It was particularly through his own vigorous participation in the
Boston Town Meeting that he encouraged public discussion as well as private
correspondence as a means of self-education. Samuel Adams stands as a challenging
reminder to us all that faith can indeed be embodied in works. And as the words
of the Declaration of Independence resound down the years we can remember that
"the price of liberty is eternal vigilance." Because the American Revolution is a
254 Christian revolution for individual freedom—or salvation—it is never over.

Samuel Adams – Christian Patriot

If one looks into the life of Samuel Adams, one is immediately struck by the fact that it is characterized more by its *expression* of Christian character, than by the *profession* of those qualities. Samuel Adams was, like his namesake, Samuel of old, a man whose *life* was the full testimony of his convictions. There are many parallels between these two Samuels who were raised up of God to give leadership to other men.

Samuel Adams' mother and father did much to shape his interests and his character:

"The mother of Samuel Adams was a woman of severe religious principles, and she early imbued her children with reverence for the Christian virtues which she practised. To the scrupulous attention of his parents to devotional subjects must have been greatly due the religious turn of mind which was a prevailing trait throughout the life of the son."

William V. Wells, *The Life and Public Services of Samuel Adams*

His family life after marriage was known for its Christian spirit of purity and simplicity, frugality and devotion to the principles of Christian liberty. Above all was his absolutely selfless devotion to the service of his country. This was expressed in the tireless activity of his efforts to write, to debate, to encourage the understanding and practice of self-government at the local level of each individual community and each individual colony. Samuel Adams was a hard worker. He never sought a political office for personal benefit but served from the early years simply as a man of integrity and conviction and willingness to sacrifice all—if need be, for the principles of justice and liberty. His standards of Christian morality as qualification for political office were exemplified in his own devotion to Christ and country and the consistency of his conduct in everything he undertook.

A consistent Christian character

Despite the ties which bound the colonies to England, the time finally came when, despite all affection for the brethren in England, America had to take her stand against tyranny. Writing in 1773, Samuel Adams wrote:

The break with England

". . . still there is the great and perpetual law of self-preservation, to which every natural person or corporate body hath an inherent right to recur. This being the law of the Creator, no human law can be of force against it . . ." Page 282A, Text, Christian History

Early in 1775 it was evident that the British were considering attempts to subdue the colonists. For some time "the Committees of Safety and Supplies, upon information sent to Samuel Adams, energetically engaged in removing cannon, ammunition, and provisions to places of security." These "places of security" were the little towns and communities in the neighborhood of Boston. Samuel Adams and his friend, John Hancock, were concerned about the rumors that the British were

255

going to attempt to seize their precious supplies of food and ammunition hidden away in the country. So they left Boston and went to Lexington where they remained several days in the house of the Rev. Jonas Clark.

But what Samuel Adams and John Hancock did not realize was that they themselves were in personal danger. For the orders of the British were to capture them as leaders of the opposition to England.

Paul Revere had agreed to give the signal to the colonists across the Charles River by placing a lantern in the North Church Steeple.

William V. Wells,
*The Life and
Public Services of
Samuel Adams*

"If the British went out by water, he would display two lanterns in the North Church Steeple, and if by land, one, as a signal that the news might be conveyed to Lexington, should the communication with the peninsula be cut off. Having instructed a friend to that effect, he was rowed across Charles River. It was the young flood, the ship was winding, and the moon rising. Landing in Charlestown, Revere found that his signal had been understood. He then took horse, and rode towards Lexington.

Paul Revere's ride

"After several adventures on the way, in which he narrowly escaped capture, he reached the house of Mr. Clark about midnight, and gave the alarm. He was just in time to elude the vigilance of the British in Boston; for Earl Percy, having accidentally ascertained that the secret was out, gave orders to allow no person to leave the town. Revere found the family at rest, and a guard of eight men stationed at the house, for the protection of Adams and Hancock. He rode up, and requested admittance, but the Sargeant replied that the family before retiring had desired that they might not be disturbed by any noise about the house. 'Noise!' replied Revere, 'you'll have noise enough before long. The Regulars are coming out.' He was then admitted.

"About one o'clock on the morning of the 19th, the militia were mustered on the green near the meeting-house, and messengers sent for additional information. By two o'clock the countrymen numbered one hundred and thirty. The guns were loaded with powder and ball in the presence of Adams, Hancock, and Clark. One of the messengers returning with the report that no troops could be seen, and the weather being chilly, the men were dismissed with orders to appear again at the beat of drum . . .

British troops
arrive at
Lexington

"Colonel Smith had marched his column but a few miles, when the ringing of bells and firing of guns satisfied him that the country was alarmed. He immediately detached six companies of light infantry, under command of Major Pitcairn, with orders to press forward, and secure the two bridges at Concord, while he sent back for reinforcements. By capturing those whom he met upon the road, Pitcairn prevented the news of his approach from going before him, until he came within a mile and a half of Lexington meeting-house, when a horseman, who had succeeded in eluding the troops, galloped into the village. Then, about seventy towns-people assembled as the drums beat, and at the sound the British halted to load. The advance guard and grenadiers then hurried forward at double quick, and when within five or six rods of the Provincials, Pitcairn shouted, 'Disperse, ye villains!

256

ye rebels, disperse! Lay down your arms! Why don't you lay down your arms and disperse?' Most of the minute-men, undecided whether to fire or retreat, stood motionless, having been ordered by their commander not to fire first. Some were joining the ranks, and others leaving them, when Pitcairn in a loud voice gave the word to fire, at the same time discharging his pistol. The order was obeyed at first by a few guns, which did no execution, and immediately after by a deadly discharge from the whole British force. A few of the militia, no longer hesitating, returned the fire, but without serious effect. Parker, seeing the utter disparity of forces, ordered his men to disperse. The Regulars continued their fire while any of the militia remained in sight, killing eight and wounding ten. The village green, where this event took place, has been aptly termed by the historian, 'a field of murder, not of battle.'

"A few farmers had assembled, willing to defend their homes, but determined not to commence hostilities, and unsuspicious of the sudden onslaught. The firing was soon over, and the royal troops remained masters of the field; but the sacrifice of that little band revolutionized a world. It was the first scene in the drama which was to carry with it the destinies of mankind.

"Adams and Hancock, as the soldiers made their appearance, were persuaded to retire to the adjacent village of Woburn, their safety being regarded as of utmost importance. Passing through the fields, while the sunlight glistened in the dew of the fresh spring morning, Adams felt his soul swell with uncontrollable joy as he contemplated the mighty future, and with prophetic utterance of his country's dawning independence, he exclaimed, 'O! what a glorious morning is this!' . . .

"Everett in his Concord Address, in 1825, investing it in his own beautiful language, says: 'That memorable exclamation, than which nothing more generous, nothing more sublime, can be found in the records of Grecian or Roman heroism.' And in the graphic picture by Bancroft: 'Heedless of his own danger, Samuel Adams, with the voice of a prophet, exclaimed, "O! what a glorious morning is this!" for he saw that his country's independence was rapidly hastening on, and, like Columbus in the tempest, knew that the storm did but bear him the more swiftly towards the undiscovered world.'"

Patriotic Letters – Committees of Correspondence

These words have a special meaning for Christian Liberty, because they indicate the importance of *ideas* in overcoming tyranny.

One of the great concerns in Sam Adams' heart was for the colonies to be united "not by external bonds, but by the vital force of distinctive ideas and principles". He particularly wanted the colonists to be "united in constitutional principles". 257

His concern was not like the concern today for information on the latest *issues* or the latest acts of tyranny upon individual liberty. It was a harder task to *educate in principles* than in *issues*, but Sam Adams knew that education in constitutional principles would result in *lawful* action—while a lack of such knowledge might result in riot and rebellion.

In 1772 Samuel Adams proposed *Committees of Correspondence*, in an educational effort to unite the colonies in knowledge, sentiment and purpose. His idea was for each town to express itself and to write to other towns. Thus town by town, and colony by colony, each individual could not only become informed and educated, but could inform and educate others. "If each town would declare its sense of these matters, I am persuaded our enemies would not have it in their power to divide

us." But it takes a long time to educate in matters which require thought and consideration. Not all of the colonies responded, and if it had not been for Samuel Adams' great faith in the cause of independence, and of the efforts of many individuals who contributed time and a great amount of energy, the project might have failed. But there were many hearts that kindled with devotion. They recognized the time approaching when these colonies would need to be united to resist the constant encroachment upon liberty and freedom. They felt "that they were acting not merely for their country, but for humanity."

Committees of Correspondence

Page 318, last par. Who was Sam Adams?

Page 319, 2nd par. To what right did Sam Adams appeal?

Page 320, 1st par. What method did Sam Adams propose?

Page 321, 2nd par. Who composed the committee in Boston?

Page 322, 1st par. How did Sam Adams encourage the patriots?

Page 322, 1st par. What Christian sentiments were expressed?

Page 322, 2nd par. Which town was the first to inaugurate a committee?

Page 323, 1st par. What did Massachusetts hope would happen?

Page 324. How did Virginia patriots respond to Massachusetts?

Page 325, 2nd par. How many colonies acted, how many did not?

Page 326, last par. Why was Boston the leader in political education?

Pages 327–328. Why did the colonies shun the English tea?

Pages 329–330. What did the patriots of Boston decide to do about the tea ships?

Pages 331–332. Why didn't the patriots smash up the tea ship when they dumped the tea overboard?

Page 333, 1st par. Did the other ports let the tea ships land?

Page 333, 2nd par. Why did Sam Adams feel that now the colonies were united?

Page 334, 2nd par. How did England propose to deal with Boston?

Page 335, 2nd par. How was the Act to close Boston port received in the colonies?

Page 336, 2nd par. How did Virginia respond?

Page 335, 3rd par. How did the committees of correspondence function?

Page 336, 1st par. How did New England respond?

Page 338, last par. What Christian encouragement was given to Boston patriots?

The American Colonies Practice
Self-Government for 150 Years

Read Text, Christian History, *pages 149–150*

For America the first seed of Christian self-government was the *Mayflower Compact* of 1620—when the Pilgrims covenanted "to frame, enact, and obey such just and equal laws as from time to time should be thought most meet for the general good of the colony."

Read Text, Christian History, *page 282A*

In the years that followed 1620 the Colonists learned Christian self-government, and practiced its principles for some 150 years prior to the war for independence. What follows is a summary of some of the challenges to that self-government by the British Crown. It reveals how the colonies deliberated and considered how they should conduct themselves as colonies of the Mother country. "In a word, they aimed to preserve their liberties and also to preserve their union with Great Britain." This was the test and it required patience and forebearance to oppose and not merely resist the encroachments upon their liberties. But the lessons learned here became the training ground for the United States of America. This enabled the colonies to conduct a seven years' war—five years of which was without a national government—dependent upon the individual government of each colony. Describe the reasoning of the Colonists.

In a letter to Arthur Lee, Samuel Adams wrote in 1773: ". . . Every art and every instrument was made use of to prevent the meetings of the towns in the country, but to no purpose. It is no wonder that a message calculated to promote a correspondence and free communication among the people should awaken their apprehensions, for they well knew it must detect their falsehood . . ."

Self-government
requires
responsible
action

The Practice of Local Self-Government

Liberty Under Law

Read Text, Christian History, *pages 27–28*

"The tendency of the true Gospel principles is to bring the most absolute despotism under the limits of law."

Because their love of liberty was first evangelical liberty, second political liberty, the Pilgrim Separatists, in fleeing from the despotism of a centralized church did not reject a government of laws. But they recognized that law must spring from an *internal conviction* rather than derive its sanction from the force of *external control*.

Samuel Adams, writing of Liberty at the age of 28, speaks of "this gift of Heaven"; text, 364B.

"The perfection of liberty therefore, in a state of nature, is for every man to be free from any external force, and to perform such actions as in his own mind and conscience he judges to be rightest; which liberty no man can truly possess whose mind is enthralled by irregular and inordinate passions; since it is no great privilege to be free from external violence if the dictates of the mind are controlled by a force within, which exerts itself above reason."

Liberty is internal

When the Townshend Acts were enacted against the Colonists, part of a long series of restrictive and afflictive acts, there was a storm of agitation. At this time some of our wisest leaders reminded the Colonists that our redress must be in keeping with the principles which we loved and espoused. "American liberty must be entirely of American fabric." Among those who denounced riotous action was James Otis, who reminded the colonists:

Constitutional methods for redress

". . . no possible circumstances, though ever so oppressive, could be supposed sufficient to justify private tumults and disorders, either to their consciences before God, or legally before men."

It was believed sincerely by the patriots, as it had been by the Pilgrims, that "Our cause is a cause of the highest dignity; it is nothing less than to maintain the liberty with which Heaven itself has made us free . . . We have constitutional methods of seeking redress, and they are the best methods."

Read Text, Christian History, *pages 327–346A*

The culmination of ten years of petition and opposition finally resulted in Britain's attack upon the militia at Lexington and Concord. Then opposition became resistance and the Colonists had to choose between slavery and submission or liberty, perhaps with death.

The Christian Principle
of American Political Union

Key to the Seventh Principle

At the end of the ten-year period, from 1764–1774, when the Boston Port Bill was enforced against Massachusetts, and the *external* circulation from foreign and domestic trade was cut off, the *internal* flow of Christian support blossomed into independence. The colonies were not yet a nation, but there was stirring evidence that the Christian Character of these people, their education in Biblical principles, their consciousness of Christian constitutional principles, was a mighty force for Christian unity.

Boston Port Bill
enforced It is significant to note that the day the Boston Port Bill was enforced, June 1st, 1774, was appointed to be a *"day of humiliation, fasting and prayer* throughout the colonies to seek the divine direction and aid, in that critical and gloomy juncture of affairs." These Fast Days were frequent "at the commencement of hostilities and during the whole progress of the war . . . They were considered by the people, as an humble appeal to Heaven for the justness of their cause, and designated to manifest their dependence on the GOD OF HOSTS for aid and success in maintaining it against their hostile brethren." So wrote Jedidiah Morse, as he attributed the patriotism and piety of the clergy a factor of immense importance in attaining our liberation from England.

What was the response to Boston's punishment? Would the 20 years which Samuel Adams and others had spent in the education of the colonists as to their political rights and responsibilities have meaning in this darkest hour of oppression?

"The colonies had grown up under constitutions of government so different, there was so great a variety of religions, they were composed of so many different nations, their customs, manners and habits had so little resemblance, and their intercourse had been so rare, and their knowledge of each other so imperfect, that

262

to unite them in the same principles in theory, and the same system of action, was certainly a very difficult enterprise. The complete accomplishment of it, in so short a time and by such simple means, was, perhaps, a singular example in the history of mankind—Thirteen clocks were made to strike together; a perfection of mechanism which no artist had ever before effected."

Within the space of two months, for the first time in Christian history, three million people achieved Biblical Christian Unity. As the support flowed in to the town of Boston, the colonies found themselves united both in the cause of Liberty and in the *"unity of Spirit."* Thus there was achieved in the seventeen hundred years of Christianity—a unique event which revealed the Chain of Christianity and its inseparability from America.

Boston Patriots and the Tea Act

Read Text, Christian History, *pages 327–339*

There are two important aspects to note in this tea experience which are not commonly taught:

1. It was a matter of *property*—internal property—the property of *consent*—a basic principle of Christian Self-Government.

    "For what Property have I in that, which another may by right take, when he pleases to himself?"

2. The act of throwing out the tea was not in the category of the *destruction of property* which we see so rampant where there is evidence of lawlessness.

    "No other property was injured; no person was harmed; no tea was allowed to be carried away."

As a matter of historical note, Benjamin Franklin's first proposition for negotiations in 1775 in regard to the misunderstandings between Great Britain and America was "the tea destroyed to be paid for." Our American Christian colonists respected property—the destruction of it in this case had been the only solution for removing the tea ships from their harbor.

Repayment of tea offered.

The action taken at this time was done in the tradition of honorable men who will not submit to that which is *against conscience*. As one wrote:

"They did not rise up against the paltry duty because they were poor and could not pay, but because they were free and would not submit to wrong."

The action taken by the Boston Patriots brought down upon them the cruel economic strangulation of the Boston Port Bill. But instead of isolating Boston, it

263

had the effect of uniting all the colonies for the first time in their history. Within two months the flow of Christian support and unity of purpose had cemented together the thirteen colonies in a manner which all their efforts at unification had never achieved. This was the true Biblical Christian unity, produced by voluntary support on the part of the many communities and tiny towns and cities all over America. They were united in a cause which they felt to be God-ordained. "Stand firm, and let your intrepid courage show to the world that you are Christians." From every colony flowed gifts of food, money and other needed commodities. From every heart recognizing the importance of Boston's stand there was fellowship and determination not to surrender their "glorious liberty" to the control of tyranny.

Boston Port is Closed –
A Day of Fasting and Prayer

Read Text, Christian History, *pages 327–346A*

Jedidiah Morse,
*Annals of the
American
Revolution* "No sooner did the news of the destruction of the tea reach Great Britain, than Parliament determined to crush that devoted town. On the king's laying the American paper before them, a bill was brought in and passed to 'discontinue the lading and discharging, landing and shipping of goods, wares and merchandizes at the town of Boston, or within the harbor.'

"This act, passed March 25, 1774, and called *The Boston Port Bill*, threw the inhabitants into the greatest consternation. The town of Boston passed a resolution, expressing their sense of this oppressive measure, and a desire that all the colonies would concur to stop all importations from Great Britain. Most of the colonies entered into spirited resolutions, on this occasion, to unite with Massachusetts in a firm opposition to the unconstitutional measures of the Parliament. The first of June, the day on which the Port Bill was to take place, was appointed to be kept as a day of humiliation, fasting and prayer throughout the colonies, to seek the divine direction and aid, in that critical and gloomy juncture of affairs.

"It ought here to be observed, that this rational and pious custom of observing fasts in times of distress and impending danger, and of celebrating days of public thanksgiving, after having received special tokens of divine favor, has ever prevailed in New-England since its first settlement, and in some parts of other states. These public supplications and acknowledgements to Heaven, at the commencement of hostilities, and during the whole progress of the war, were more frequent than usual, and were attended with uncommon fervour and solemnity. They were considered by the people, as an humble appeal to Heaven for the justness of their

264

cause, and designed to manifest their dependence on the GOD OF HOSTS for aid and success in maintaining it against their hostile brethren. The prayers and public discourses of the clergy, as has already been suggested, who were friends to their suffering country, (and there were few who were not) breathed the spirit of patriotism; and as their piety and integrity had generally secured to them the confidence of the people, they had great influence and success in encouraging them to engage in its defence. In this way, that class of citizens aided the cause of their country; and to their pious exertions, under the GREAT ARBITER of human affairs, has been justly ascribed no inconsiderable share of the success and victory that crowned the American arms."

The history of the founding of the United States of America is a Christian history because its government was established upon the unique form of government evolved by Christianity—namely, self-government.

Self-government is predicated upon the Rights of Man. These rights, by the colonists' own statement are Christian Rights:

"We hold these Truths to be self-evident, that all Men are created equal, that they are endowed by their Creator with certain unalienable Rights, that among these are Life, Liberty, and the Pursuit of Happiness—That to secure these Rights, Governments are instituted among Men . . ."—"A Declaration by the Representatives of the United States of America."—The Declaration of Independence, *1776*—Christian History, page *248A.*

George Bancroft, American historian of the 19th century, has spoken of Samuel Adams as, more than any other man, "the type and representative of the New England town-meeting." In tracing the development of representative government through the town-meeting one writer has said:

"The Folk-mote, the fixed, frequent, accessible meeting of the individual freemen for discussing and deciding upon public matters, had great importance in the polity of the primeval Teutons, and was transmitted by them to their English descendants. All thoughtful political writers have held it to be one of the best schools for forming the faculties of men; it must underlie every representative system in order to make that system properly effective. The ancient folk-mote, the proper primordial cell of every Anglo-Saxon body-politic, which the carelessness of the people and the encroachments of princes had caused to be much overlaid in England, reappeared with great vitality in the New England town-meeting . . .

"Throughout the thirteen colonies, the folk-mote existed in well-developed form only in the New England town-meeting; few traces of it can be found in the South; nor in the middle colonies was the case much different. At the time of the Revolution, New England stood alone in having restored a primitive liberty which had been superseded, each of her little democracies governing itself after a fashion for which there was no precedent without going back to the folk-mote of a remote day—to a time before the kings of England began to be arbitrary, and before the people became indifferent to their birth-right."

James K. Hosmer,
*American
Statesmen—
Samuel Adams*

The value of the town-meeting as a training ground in self-government cannot be overlooked—its chief value being participation and the visibility of government. It demonstrated the principle "where the law was administered, the law was made".

Read, Christian History, *pages 271–282—"Township and County"*

The art of
self-government
must be learned To Samuel Adams the "art of self-government" had to be learned and he was tireless in his efforts to publically have discussed in the town-meetings of Boston the problems and responsibilities which the Colonists faced. Involvement and participation he felt were an outgrowth of reasoning based upon information and knowledge of the principles of representative government. Thus, he, more than any other single individual took full advantage of the opportunities afforded by the town-meeting to demonstrate its effectiveness in the scheme of self-government. Bancroft has stated that "American freedom was more prepared by courageous counsel than successful war" and the Anglo-Saxon tradition of individuals cogitating and discussing public matters has never been so gloriously evident as in the town-meeting. Samuel Adams recognized unity among the Colonists depended upon "mind meeting mind" and he knew that if they were united in principle then the threat of superior retaliation would not move a determination firm in its adherence to its inherent rights. This oneness of mind and purpose was the greatest single instrument possessed by the Colonists in their resistance to usurpation of their rights. Adams recognized that efforts would be made to prevent this:

". . . *Every art and every instrument was made use of to prevent the meetings of the towns in the country, but to no purpose. It is no wonder that a measure calculated to promote a correspondence and free communication among the people should awaken their apprehensions; for they well knew it must detect their falsehood . . ."*—Christian History, *Page 282B*

" *'Let associations and combinations be everywhere set up to consult and recover our just rights.' This suggestion . . . Samuel Adams proceeded to put at once in practice, setting on foot one of the most memorable schemes with which his name is associated."* —James K. Hosmer, *"American Statesmen—Samuel Adams"*, *page 196.*

The purpose of the Committees of Correspondence was to promote union both among the Colonists and among men in England who were of the same mind, and united in constitutional principles.

Read page 320, paragraph 1 through page 323, top of page.

But personal leadership alone could not accomplish the desired union. The cause needed something to catch the public imagination. The Tea Act of 1773 supplied the necessary fuel for igniting the righteous indignation of the Colonists. After the object of arbitrary taxation had been dumped into Boston Harbor the issue became a living one!

The Cement of American Union

Read Text, Christian History, *pages 16, 17*

It was from the churches of the New Testament that the Pilgrims derived their ideas of Christian Unity.

"Individuals and families, drawn toward each other by their common trust in Jesus the Christ, and their common interest in the good news concerning the kingdom of God, became a community united, not by external bonds, but by the vital force of distinctive ideas and principles."

Unity in Christ

Bradford relates on page 185 of his history of Plymouth Plantation, that the story of Plymouth began when "they shooke off this yoke of anti-Christian bondage, and as ye Lords free people, joyned them selves (by a covenant of the Lord into a church estate, in ye felowship of ye gospell, to walke in all his wayes . . . And that it cost them something this ensewing historie will declare."

Read Text, Christian History, *pages 249–252*

This "Charter of public rule" was "far in advance of anything the world had ever seen." Again the Christian principle of government was extended to the civil affairs of the colony by "mutual covenant".

Read Text, Christian History, *pages 334–339*

Beneath the diversity of the colonies was that "unity of the spirit" which united them. For one hundred and fifty years they had been practicing the principles of Christian Self-Government. They knew that their rights and liberties were of God and not of man and therefore they were united in this conviction. All of their Christian history had borne out this conviction.

Unity with
diversity

Read Text, Christian History, *pages 346B–364*

The representatives of the *"United States of America"* declared it necessary to *"dissolve the Political Bands which have connected them"* to the mother country, and to publically declare themselves to be *"free and independent States." "We mutually pledge to each other . . ."*

"Till we all come in the unity of the faith, and of the knowledge of the Son of God . . ."
Ephesians 4:13
"Where the Spirit of the Lord is, there is liberty." II Corinthians 3:17
"Stand fast therefore in the liberty wherewith Christ hath made us free, and be not entangled again with the yoke of bondage." Galatians 5:1

267

American Unity is Christian Unity

Page 327. England seeks to remedy its loss of the American trade in tea, by making it "duty free".

Page 328. The tea scheme was an attempt to establish the right of parliament to tax the colonies and to establish a monopoly on tea for the East-India Company. The Colonists were never so well informed as to their rights.

Page 329. American patriots begin to hold meetings aware that the tea ships were en route to four ports.

Page 330. The committees of correspondence circularize the issues between the colonies and Great Britain. Boston patriots prevent unloading of tea.

Pages 331–2. The tea is quietly dumped into Boston Harbor.

Page 333. Great unity of spirit among the colonies. Hope to see an American congress grows out of the movement.

Page 334. England decides to punish America. Massachusetts singled out for punishment.

Page 335. Passage of the Boston Port Bill promotes rapid and widespread dissent throughout the colonies.

Page 336. All New England pledges aid. Virginia House of Burgesses observes day of prayer.

Page 337. British men-of-war close Boston Harbor. All Colonies deeply moved, June 1, 1774.

Page 338. English regiments occupy Boston. Contributions pour into Boston from the other colonies and from hundreds of localities. The word is: "Stand firm, and let your intrepid courage show to the world that you are Christians."

Page 339. Evidence of American unity —a unity which flowed from individual recognition of the invasion of rights which had consequence for every citizen —a union based upon the Christian tradition of voluntary association—the Pilgrim ideal of a "single covenanted body of Christians, united for civil as well as spiritual purposes."

Appendix

Special Study Projects

A. *For Class Discussion*

1. Discuss Christianity's influence upon American life, i.e., the use of the Bible to pledge one's support of the Constitution when assuming public office; prayer to open sessions of Congress, the Supreme Court, etc.; the observance of the Sabbath by most places of business; the inscription upon our coins "*In God we Trust*." What evidences do you find that Christianity is a major influence in many areas of American life, customs, institutions, etc.?

2. What is the Christian significance of our American flag? See page 371, *Christian History*. The magazine *Ideals* has a special issue on American flags and their historical significance.

3. What songs about America have a Christian basis?

4. What stories in the Bible show us the importance of learning how to be self-governed? Christian self-government means being obedient to God's commands, listening to the "*still small voice*," being courageous and learning to be self-reliant and responsible. Joseph in Egypt, Samuel in the temple, Daniel in the lion's den, David and Goliath, and Ruth, all exemplify self-government. There are many others in our Book of books.

5. What Christian rights are found written into the Constitution? Why are they written into our Constitution? Which law is the first law of the land?

6. The Bible teaches us that we are free when we know and obey God's law. Jesus said that all the law was summed up in the commandments. What laws do we have in our community which are based upon the commandments? Who makes the laws in our community? Can they ever be changed? Does the passing of a law make men good?

7. It is only because we are a Christian nation that we have religious freedom. Christianity is inclusive and permits each individual to worship as he pleases. If this nation were founded upon any other religion there would be no religious freedom. Christianity honors each individual. The Christian idea of man states that in the eye of God, all men are equal.

B. *For Class Reports*

1. Why is the Christian idea of man and government America's greatest defense against Communism? See pages 1 and 2.

2. Give some specific examples from your own community of how a productive individual can create prosperity for himself and thus for the community, refuting the idea that the community must provide for the welfare of the individual. See page 6. "Individual benefit", and "Minimum of governmental interference."

3. The Greek republics were independent of each other and found unity for the purposes of defense difficult. The Roman republic, on the other hand, was highly centralized and achieved the unification of the whole Mediterranean world. Why did neither of these pagan republics truly achieve representative self-government or union? What did Christianity contribute as the basis of our government which achieves both these strands—local self-government and unity?

4. Trace the links, or steps, in the lives of Calvin and Luther which led up to their recognition that salvation cannot be granted by king or pope, but must come through individual redemption in Christ. How does this relate to Christian self-government?

5. What were the greatest advances for the Christian in the King James translation of the Bible? What connection did this translation have with American Christian education?

6. Trace a specific right of Englishmen through the Magna Charta, the Petition of Rights, the English Bill of Rights to the Declaration of Independence.

7. Can you list the specific rights which the colonists declared in the Declaration had been invaded by England? (Page 346B)

8. To what theory of government does the statement "consent of the governed" refer in the Declaration of Independence? What is the Christian background of this kind of government? Where did we first see it evidenced in a written statement of government?

C. *Special Program Projects*

Thanksgiving Program of the Plymouth Plantation

Thanksgiving is the only truly American holiday. It is significant that its Christian basis has particular reference to our nation's founding. It has been customary to commemorate this holiday with school programs reminding us of the circumstances surrounding our first Christian settlement.

Thanksgiving Day Programs should be a part of every American Christian home, every American Christian church, and every American Christian school for the Christian History of America begins with the story of this small remnant of primitive Christians—the Pilgrims—and of their efforts to carry out CHRIST HIS STORY in their lives as they labored for His glory in this new land.

With the fine record by William Bradford appearing in *Christian History*, pages 185–240, there is an abundance of factual material from which to draw the main strands which characterize this colony and which form the basis of our nation.

The following outline suggests some particular *themes* which might become the basis of a Thanksgiving Day Program:

271

Planning a Thanksgiving Day Program About the Pilgrims

	Main Themes	Characters	Sequence of Events	Places
1	Oppressed non-conforming Puritans become Separatists. (Pages 23–27)	William Brewster William Bradford	"New church formed in houses of Separatists" (Page 26)	Scrooby
2	Become fugitives from persecution. Separatists become Pilgrims. (Pages 26–27; 185–189)	John Robinson (Pastor)	Flee to Holland. Betrayals	Amsterdam
3	Pilgrims wish to keep free from contention in Church in Amsterdam. Move to Leyden. Dutch see evidence of Pilgrim Character. (Pages 189–191)	Separatists (described Page 27)	"Removaal to Leyden". The move not to their business advantage.	Leyden
4	Pilgrims decide to leave Holland. Reasons: (Pages 191–194) a) Protect children from anti-Christian influences b) Propagate the Gospel of Christ c) Seek to settle where they may have freedom of religion.		Request Patent of Merchants in England. New England offered for settlement.	London
5	Plans for the voyage to New World. Set up stock company with merchants. Changes in original agreements. (Pages 194–197)	Mr. Weston (Agent)	"Day of humiliation" depart Holland to sail from England.	South Hampton
6	Mayflower Compact drawn up. First article of self-government. Officers elected. (Pages 204–205)	Strangers, Mutineers, Pilgrims John Carter (Gov.)	Establish their first foundation of government	"Cape Codd"
7	The landing in a desolate wilderness. Winter hardships. Not one Pilgrim went back. Firm reliance on God sustains them. (Pages 201–206)	Samaset Massasoyt Squanto Captain Miles Standish	First winter in wilderness. Half colony perish. Help and assist each other. Outstanding Christian leaders in Rev. Brewster and Miles Standish. Indians help them get established.	"Cape Codd"

Planning a Thanksgiving Day Program
About the Pilgrims

	Main Themes	Characters	Sequence of Events	Places
8	New arrivals without provisions. Help from England fails. Pilgrims turn to their religion for help and comfort. Food rationing and famine. (Pages 208–210)	Pilgrims visitors Mr. Cushman	Arrival of ships eagerly anticipated for the help promised from England.	Plymouth Plantation
9	Mr. Weston's unruly settlers, having not God nor self-government, fall into want and moral degradation. (Pages 210–212)		Weston's men are fed, housed, cared for by Pilgrims.	
10	How to raise more corn? Turn from communal farming to private enterprise. Ample harvest. (Pages 213, 217, 218) The market. (Page 217) Bargain and exchange by mutual agreement. Barter. (Page 218)		End of communism and collectivism. Beginning of the free market.	
11	Oldom and Liford start faction. Plot to discredit colony uncovered. Trial. (Pages 219–223)	Oldom Liford	The wise and Christian conduct of the Pilgrims in this effort to discredit them in England.	England
12	Christian Economics. The whole story of the Pilgrim's long struggle in their efforts to repay their original patent. (Pages 223–240)	Miles Standish Allerton Winslow	The Pilgrims prosper under God. They use their talents to become self-reliant and free.	
13	Covenant with Indians as compared with experience of Virginia colony. (Pages 206–207)	Massasoyt Squanto	The compact form of self-government—by voluntary association is successful for 24 years.	
14	How Christian character was their mainstay through all trials. (Pages 237–240)		The Pilgrims glorify God by living their Christianity like the early Christians.	

Planning a New England Town Meeting

The New England town meeting was an important function in the development of representative government. In New England the town meeting often became the primary assembly, or legislative and executive body of the township. The local government of the town was conducted under the eyes of the people, and the people directly governed themselves. The political training of the New England town meeting has proven itself of inestimable educational value in the practice of self-government. The arguments and debates on matters of public concern, the clarification of political rights, the reasoning of the principles of government were a vital part of the fabric and life of many townships. The records show the fierce pride of New Englanders in their right of self-government as displayed in the town meeting. Actually, the history of New England is written in the archives of these township reports and a study of the voluminous pages, painfully inscribed, reveal the spirit, tenacity and love of this public arena of representative government in which the Christian rights of man were woven into the warp and woof of daily living. *Christian History*, pages 271–276

Participating in a New England Town Meeting

This lesson is designed to encourage both a study of the principles and actions of the American Revolution and to give some experience to students in the conducting of a town meeting. The outline which follows may suggest to the teacher some approaches to the kinds of meetings which were held during a particular period just prior to the writing of the Declaration of Independence. It would also be possible, after students can see how public matters are debated and acted upon, to take some current issues which are of local concern. These local concerns could be debated from the standpoint of the principles outlined below.

Place:
Any township in New England

Location:
The meetinghouse

Purpose of Meeting:
To discuss the resolutions of Lord North that Parliament subsidize the importation of British tea into the colonies.

Arguments and Debates:

The opposition to these measures might be argued on the following basis:

1. "Rights of the Colonists as Men." Samuel Adams, pages 365–367.
2. "Rights of the Colonists as Christians." Samuel Adams, pages 367–368.
3. "The Rights of the Colonists as Subjects." Samuel Adams, pages 368–70.
4. John Locke on "The fundamental law of property." Page 95, paragraph 138. Also marginal note, page 328.

Action Resulting from Debates:

1. Patriots resolve to "support the common liberties of America." They vote the tea shall not be landed.
2. Patriots vote to pledge their support to the port towns in their resolve not to let the tea enter.
3. Boston patriots plan the dumping of the tea into Boston Harbor. This plan is carefully planned. No other property is to be harmed. Custom officers will be warned to stay out of the way. The matter is one of liberty and law.

Purpose of Meeting:

To discuss the Boston Port Bill, passed by England to punish Boston for the Boston Tea Party.

Action Resulting from Debates: (outside Boston)

1. Reading of a circular from Sam Adams and the Boston Town meeting "promising to suffer for America with fortitude, but confessing that singly they must find their trial too severe." The circular asks for support of other colonies.
2. The town meeting passes resolves against the Boston Port Bill.
3. Resolve in support of Boston's courageous stand against oppression.
4. Aid pledged to Boston. Individual citizens vote to send food, wood, livestock, money, ammunition, etc.
5. Meeting votes to break off trade relations with Britain until Boston Port shall be re-opened.
6. A day of "*humiliation and prayer*" is voted.
7. It is recommended that a congress of the colonies be formed.

Action Resulting from Debates: (in Boston)

1. Call on sister colonies for support.
2. Resolves passed not to resist by any physical or military act, the arrival and encampment of English regiments.
3. Resolve to muffle and toll bells from morning to night.

275

4. Resolve to keep flags at half-mast.
5. Resolve to continue every effort to inform the populace of their grievances, of their rights, or opportunities to resist the efforts of their oppressors to bring them to submission. In short the Boston patriots resolved to continue all political activity.
6. To pray daily to God for fortitude and strength.

What Identifies America as a Christian Nation?

Christian Character

America's heritage of character comes from the first century of Chritianity. This seed of *Christian Character* was planted by the Pilgrims of Plymouth Plantation. The story of their struggle during the ten years in which *not one went back* is a story of courage, faith and steadfastness.

From the Pilgrims, the Puritans and the Patriots, Americans have a heritage of *Christian Character*—a character which sustained them through all the long years of a seven years' war with England for their independence. It was only when we as a nation began to "fall away" that we also forgot our American Christian Character and our American Christian Constitution.

References:

Plymouth: Spirit of the First Settlement Pages 245–248
The Pilgrim wanted individual liberty Page 182
The significance of Pilgrim endurance Pages 182–183
Christian Morality in leadership Pages 396–397

Christian Self-Government

The word "consent" characterizes the individual's commitment to Christ. Entering into the commands and accepting the "covenant" of the Lord the individual Christian is self-governed.

"This is the covenant that I will make with them after those days, saith the Lord, I will put my laws into their hearts, and in their minds will I write them" Hebrews 10:16.

276

In discussing the relationship between the church covenant and the Mayflower Compact, the first document of the right of self-government in America, written by the Pilgrims, the following comment is useful:

"Behind the compact lie the Puritan beliefs in the word of God as a higher law, the establishment of the higher law in written documents, and the formation of government by the consent of individuals." Andrew C. McLaughlin, "The Foundations of American Constitutionalism"—1932.

Every aspect of an individual's life is expressed by his degree of self-government. How an individual is governed from within is always outwardly expressed. Our individual obedience to the Law of God indicates our ability to be self-governing Christians in every avenue into which our Christian citizenship carries us.

Christian Economics

Christian economics is characterized by initiative, industry, and individuality. It is manifested as the productive quality of the active Christian who in being busy about His Father's business glorifies the Creator. Christianity has the dual aspect of promise and fulfillment—the mountaintop respite and the marketplace realization. It is both *"the still small voice"* of conscience as well as the *"loaves and fishes"* of human need. Christian Economics is characterized throughout by *integrity*, *justice*, and *sufficiency* in every enterprise. Webster characterizes *integrity* as follows:

"INTEGRITY comprehends the whole moral character, but has a special reference to uprightness in mutual dealings, transfers of property, and agencies for others." (Webster, *1856 ed.*)

Webster also states in part what *economy* is:

"ECONOMY includes also a prudent management of all the means by which property is saved or accumulated; a judicious application of time, of labor, and of the instruments of labor."

Christian economics is the basis of private enterprise in our country. It is more characterized as being *productive* and *fruitful* in the Word than being characterized as for *profit* alone. But being productive and fruitful and glorifying God in every activity brings abundance and success.

Paul admonishes Timothy to seek certification from God:

"Study to shew thyself approved unto God, a workman that needeth not to be ashamed, rightly dividing the word of truth."—2 Timothy 2:15

277

The Master, commenting upon the servants and their use of the talents given unto them states that the "unprofitable" servant be cast into outer darkness. Webster defines this as: "Misproving talents; bringing no glory to God; as an *unprofitable* servant. Matt. 25. Not useful to others."

In describing the American people, Charles Bancroft, on page 6 of the text, states:

"Our people are busy using their liberties and energies, each for his individual benefit, as is quite right and proper; since the welfare of individuals makes the prosperity of the community. But a government left to take care of itself is prone to do that work only too well. We have done well and wisely in important crises; but a more intelligent and constant watchfulness over the ordinary course of public affairs would have been still better . . .

" 'Knowledge is power,' when wisely applied; and a more accurate acquaintance with their government and its history will enable American citizens to mould it more wisely still, to correct all defects of administration, and to speedily reach that minimum of governmental interference with the efforts and interests of the citizens which shall give them fullest liberty consistent with security and surrender the whole round of human life, as completely as possible to the beneficent action of natural law."

John Locke discusses *property* in his essay, pages 63–70 in the text. He states that God has given the world to men to use for their support and comfort and that by appropriating it for his wants man invests his labor and thus acquires title to that which he needs. But being governed by Reason each will respect the rights of all men to his "Life, Health, Liberty, or Possessions."

The notable example of Christian Economics occurred in Plymouth when individual enterprise replaced the communal system of cooperative farming in the colony. The individual Pilgrim, being liberated to *"work out his own salvation,"* then became self-governing in directing his own initiative and industry and investing his own labor and efforts. His efforts in his own behalf could only benefit the community. Thus, once again, self-reliance and independence prove themselves to be more mutually beneficial to all than group enterprise and interdependence. As each individual assumes his own responsibility and becomes economically self-sufficient he *is* the welfare of the community instead of being dependent upon community welfare for his sufficiency. *"Our sufficiency is of God"* indeed when being productive in His behalf and for His glory. See Bradford's Report, pages 217, 218.

References: Jamestown divides property for farming Page 162; Definitions of *Property* Page 248A; Consent is property (Samuel Adams) Page 38; Chief end of government is preservation of property, paragraph 124 Page 91

Christian Education

278 American Christian education was the foundation of our nation's great growth,

progress and success. The rise of the individual in our country and his freedom to conduct his affairs in the manner of his own choosing was the direct outcome of the expression in American life of "the Christian idea of man."

The colonists brought with them a tradition of Biblical scholarship and the fruition of the Reformation—the Scriptures in English. And with their Bibles they brought a determination to continue the individual study and practice of the Christian verities contained therein. Because of their sincere desire to teach their children to read the Scriptures they established schools. Their colleges were the culmination of the need for an enlightened ministry.

Historically American education had for its basis both a sound Christian foundation and a curriculum which had both academic and literary excellence.

References: Samuel Adams on education (2nd paragraph) Page XIV; Founding of Harvard college Page 240B; John Locke on education Pages 398–404; Emma Willard *Study of American History*, Fundamentals in Education Pages 405–407; Harvard college—library Pages 372–373; Check *Index* for other references on *education*

Christian Unity

"For as the body is one, and hath many members, and all the members of that one body, being many, are one body; so also is Christ."—I Cor. 12:12

Frothingham, in discussing the two great elements which run through our history, local self-government and national union makes the following statement:

"I do not purpose to study the Why of the E Pluribus Unum: but an order of facts that seem to show the How it came to pass,—a class of events that mark the continuous blending of Diversity and Unity in the formation of the public opinion, that evolved The One from the many; or, how the United States came to be the United States, free from the benumbing influences of centralization on the one hand, and from the fatal dangers of disintegration on the other.

"At every state in the progress towards this result, the two main elements of the national life are found acting in harmony. It may be useful to preface the narrative by a glance at the origin and progress of the Idea of Local Self-Government, which developed into the State, and at the Idea of Union, which developed into the nation."—Christian History, *Page 149*

Without the Christian foundation upon the Rock, Christ, it would look as though many came together to form one. But Paul is explicit in this point, and it is one which has consequence for our nation:

"For by one Spirit are we all baptized into one body, whether we be Jews or Gentiles,   279

whether we be bond or free; and have been all made to drink into one Spirit." 1 Cor. 12:13

"*But now are they many members, yet but one body.*" 1 Cor. 12:20

"*Now ye are the body of Christ, and members in particular.*" 1 Cor. 12:27

"*There is one body, and one Spirit, even as ye are called in one hope of your calling.*" Ephesians 4:4

Because we are one in Christ our Nation is expressed as the Union of the many members—or States. Thus it has a spiritual basis upon the Rock, Christ—"*and the gates of hell shall not prevail against it.*"

References: Christian unity in early primitive churches Pages 16–17; Robinson's letter to Pilgrims on relations with others Page 199; Unity of colonies after Boston tea incident Page 333; The colonies rally to support of Boston Pages 338–339; Union must be predicated upon liberty Page 346A

The Life and Testimony of Noah Webster

Chauncey A. Goodrich, Professor in Yale College, Editor

IT is natural for those who make frequent use of a work like this, to desire some knowledge of the author's life, and especially of that long course of intellectual labor, by which he contributed so largely to the literary treasures of our language. To gratify this desire is the object of the present Memoir. A brief outline will be given of the leading occurrences of his life, with particular reference to the occasions which called forth the principal productions of his pen. The materials of this sketch were obtained from Dr. Webster himself.

Noah Webster was born in Hartford, Connecticut, about three miles from the center of the city, on the 16th of October, 1758. His father was a respectable farmer and justice of the peace, and was a descendant, in the fourth generation, of John Webster, one of the first settlers of Hartford, who was a magistrate, or member of the colonial council from its first formation, and, at a subsequent period, governor of Connecticut. His mother was a descendant of William Bradford, the second governor of the Plymouth colony. The family was remarkable for longevity. His father died at the advanced age of nearly ninety-two. He and one of his brothers lived considerably beyond the age of eighty. His remaining brother died in his eightieth year; and of his two sisters, one was advanced beyond seventy, and the other had nearly reached the same age, at the period of their death.

Mr. Webster commenced the study of the classics, in the year 1772, under the instruction of the clergyman of the parish, the Rev. Nathan Perkins, D.D., and in 1774 was admitted a member of Yale College. The war of the revolution, com-

280

mencing the next year, interrupted the regular attendance of the students on their usual exercises, and deprived them of no small part of the advantages of a collegiate course of instruction. In his Junior year, when the western part of New England was thrown into confusion by General Burgoyne's expedition from Canada, Mr. Webster volunteered his services under the command of his father, who was captain in the *alarm list*, a body comprising those of the militia who were above forty-five years of age, and who were called into the field only on pressing emergencies. In that campaign, all the males of the family, four in number, were in the army at the same time. Notwithstanding the interruption of his studies by these causes, Mr. Webster graduated with reputation in 1778.

THE LIFE AND TESTIMONY OF NOAH WEBSTER

Webster admitted to Yale College, 1774

The class to which he belonged produced an unusual number of men who were afterward distinguished in public life. Among these may be mentioned Joel Barlow, author of the Columbiad, and minister of the United States to the court of France; Oliver Wolcott, secretary of the treasury of the United States under the administration of Washington, and subsequently governor of the State of Connecticut; Uriah Tracy, a distinguished member of the senate of the United States; Stephen Jacob, chief justice, and Noah Smith, associate judge, of the Supreme Court of Vermont; Zephaniah Swift, chief justice, and Ashur Miller, associate judge, of the Supreme Court of Connecticut; besides a number of others who were either members of Congress, or among the leaders of our great political parties, at the commencement of the present century.

The period at which Mr. Webster entered upon life, was an unpropitious one for a young man to be cast upon the world without property. The country was impoverished by the war to a degree of which it is difficult, at the present day, to form any just conception; there was no prospect of peace; the issue of the contest was felt, by the most sanguine, to be extremely doubtful; and the practice of the law, which Mr. Webster intended to pursue, was in a great measure set aside by the general calamity. It was under these circumstances that, on his return from the Commencement when he graduated, his father gave him an eight dollar bill of the Continental currency, (then worth about four dollars in silver,) and told him that he must thenceforth rely on his own exertions for support. As a means of immediate subsistence, he resorted to the instruction of a school, and during the summer of 1779, resided at Hartford, Connecticut, in the family of Mr., afterward Chief Justice, Ellsworth. An intimate friendship was thus formed between these two gentlemen, which was interrupted only by the death of the chief justice.

Webster resides with Chief Justice Ellsworth, 1779

Not having the means of obtaining a regular education for the bar, Mr. Webster, at the suggestion of a distinguished counselor of his acquaintance, determined to pursue the study of the law in the intervals of his regular employment, without the aid of an instructor; and, having presented himself for examination, at the expiration of two years, was admitted to practice in the year 1781. As he had no encouragement to open an office, in the existing state of the country, he resumed the business of instruction, and taught a classical school, in 1782, at Goshen, in Orange county, New York. Here, in a desponding state of mind, created by the unsettled condition of things at the close of the war, and the gloomy prospects for business, he undertook an employment which gave a complexion to his whole future life. This was the compilation of books for the instruction of youth in schools. Having prepared the first draught of an elementary treatise of this kind, he made a journey to Philadelphia in the autumn of the same year, and, after exhibiting a specimen of the work to several members of Congress, among whom was Mr. Madison, and to the Rev. S. S. Smith, D.D., at that time a professor, and afterward president, of the college at Princeton, he was encouraged by their approbation to prosecute his design. Accordingly, in the winter following, he revised what he had written, and, leaving Goshen in 1783, he returned to Hartford, where he published his *"First Part of a Grammatical Institute of the English Language."* The second and third parts were published in the years immediately following. These works, comprising a Spelling Book, an English Grammar, and a compilation for reading, were the first books of the kind published in the United States. They were gradually introduced into most of the schools of our country; and to so great an extent has the Spelling Book been used, that, during the twenty years in which he was employed in compiling his American Dictionary, the entire support of his family was derived from the profits of this work, at a premium for copyright of less than a cent a copy. About twenty-four millions of this book have been published, down to the present year, 1847, in the different forms which it assumed under the revision of the author; and its popularity has gone on continually increasing. The demand for some years past, has averaged about one million copies a year. To its influence, probably, more than to any other cause, are we indebted for that remarkable uniformity of pronunciation in our country, which is so often spoken of with surprise by English travelers.

In entering thus early on his literary career, Mr. Webster did not confine himself to the publication of his own works. At a period when nothing had as yet been done to perpetuate the memorials of our early history, he led the way in this important branch of literary effort, by the publication of that highly valuable and characteristic work, Governor Winthrop's Journal. Having learnt that a manuscript copy was in possession of Governor Trumbull, of Connecticut, he caused it to be transcribed, at his own expense, by the governor's private secretary, and risked more than the amount of his whole property in its publication. The sale never remunerated him for the expenses thus incurred.

At the period of Mr. Webster's return to Hartford, in 1783, the state was agitated by violent dissensions, on the subject of a grant made by Congress to the army, of half pay for life, which was afterward commuted for a grant of full pay for five years beyond their term of service. To this grant it was strongly objected, that, if the army had suffered by the reduced value of the bills in which they were paid, the country at large had sustained an equal loss by the depreciation of the currency, and by other causes. So strong was the excitement on this subject, that public meetings were held throughout the state, to prevent the laws of Congress from being carried into effect; and at length a convention met at Middletown with the same

design, at which two thirds of the towns in Connecticut were represented. In this state of things, Mr. Webster, though only twenty-five years of age, came forward to vindicate the measures of Congress, and wrote a series of papers on the subject, under the signature of *Honorius*, which were published in the Connecticut Courant, and read extensively throughout the state. The effect was great. At the next election, in April, 1784, a large majority of the legislature were supporters of Congress in their measures. So highly were Mr. Webster's services appreciated on this occasion, that he received the thanks of Governor Trumbull in person, and was publicly declared, by a member of the council, to have "done more to allay popular discontent, and support the authority of Congress at this crisis, than any other man."

These occurrences in his native state, together with the distress and stagnation of business in the whole country, resulting from the want of power in Congress to carry its measures into effect, and to secure to the people the benefits of a stable government, convinced Mr. Webster, that the old confederation, after the dangers of the war were past, was utterly inadequate to the necessities of the people. He therefore published a pamphlet, in the winter of 1784-5, entitled "*Sketches of American Policy*," in which, after treating of the general principles of government, he endeavored to prove that it was absolutely necessary, for the welfare and safety of the United States, to establish a new system of government, *which should act not on the states, but directly on individuals, and vest in Congress full power to carry its laws into effect.* Being on a journey to the Southern States, in May, 1785, he went to Mount Vernon, and presented a copy of this pamphlet to General Washington. It contained, the writer believes, the first distinct proposal, made through the medium of the press, for a new constitution of the United States.

One object of Mr. Webster's journey to the south was, to petition the state legislatures for the enactment of a law securing to authors an exclusive right to the publication of their writings. In this he succeeded to a considerable extent; and the public attention was thus called to a provision for the support of American literature, which was rendered more effectual by a general copyright law, enacted by Congress soon after the formation of our government. At a much later period, (in the years 1830-31,) Mr. Webster passed a winter at Washington, with the single view of endeavoring to procure an alteration of the existing law, which should *extend* the term of copyright, and thus give a more ample reward to the labors of our artists and literary men. In this design he succeeded; and an act was passed more liberal in its provisions than the former law, though less so than the laws of some European governments on this subject.

On his return from the south, Mr. Webster spent the summer of 1785 at Baltimore, and employed his time in preparing a course of lectures on the English language, which were delivered, during the year 1786, in the principal Atlantic cities, and were published in 1789, in an octavo volume, with the title of "*Dissertations on the English Language.*"

The year 1787 was spent by Mr. Webster at Philadelphia, as superintendent of an Episcopal academy. The convention which framed the present constitution of the United States were in session at Philadelphia during a part of this year; and when their labors were closed, Mr. Webster was solicited by Mr. Fitzsimmons, one of the members, to give the aid of his pen in recommending the new system of government to the people. He accordingly wrote a pamphlet on this subject, entitled an *"Examination of the Leading Principles of the Federal Constitution."*

In 1788, Mr. Webster attempted to establish a periodical in New York, and for one year published the *"American Magazine,"* which, however, failed of success; as did also an attempt to combine the efforts of other gentlemen in a similar undertaking. The country was not yet prepared for such a work.

Webster practices law in Hartford, 1789

In 1789, when the prospects of business became more encouraging, after the adoption of the new constitution, Mr. Webster settled himself at Hartford in the practice of the law. Here he formed or renewed an acquaintance with a number of young men just entering upon life, who were ardently devoted, like himself, to literary pursuits. Among these may be mentioned his two classmates, Barlow and Wolcott; Trumbull, author of McFingal; Richard Alsop; Dr. Lemuel Hopkins; and, though somewhat older, the Rev. Nathan Strong, pastor of the First Congregational Church, who, in common with the three last mentioned, was highly distinguished for the penetration of his intellect and the keenness of his wit. The incessant contact of such minds, at the forming period of their progress, had great influence on the literary habits of them all, in after life. It gave them a solid and manly cast of thought, a simplicity of taste, a directness of statement, a freedom from all affectation and exuberance of imagery or diction, which are often best acquired by the salutary use of ridicule, in the action and reaction on each other of keen and penetrating minds. It had, likewise, a powerful influence on the social circles in which they moved; and the biographer of Governor Wolcott has justly remarked, that at this time "few cities in the Union could boast of a more cultivated or intelligent society than Hartford, whether men or women."

Webster marries, 1789

In the autumn of the same year, encouraged by the prospect of increasing business, Mr. Webster married the daughter of William Greenleaf, Esq., of Boston, a lady of a highly cultivated intellect, and of great elegance and grace of manners. His friend Trumbull speaks of this event in one of his letters to Wolcott, who was then at New York, in his characteristic vein of humor. "Webster has returned, and brought with him a very pretty wife. I wish him success; but I doubt, in the present decay of business in our profession, whether his profits will enable him to keep up the style he sets out with. I fear he will breakfast upon Institutes, dine upon Dissertations, and go to bed supperless." The result, however, was more favorable than it appeared in the sportive anticipations of Trumbull. Mr. Webster found his business profitable, and continually increasing, during his residence of some years in the practice of the law at Hartford.

This employment he was induced to relinquish, in 1793, by an interesting crisis in public affairs. General Washington's celebrated *proclamation of neutrality*, rendered necessary by the efforts of the French minister, Genet, to raise troops in our country for the invasion of Louisiana, and to fit out privateers against nations at peace with the United States, had called forth the most bitter reproaches of the partisans of France; and it was even doubtful, for a time, whether the unbounded popularity of the *Father of his Country* could repress the public effervescence in favor of embarking in the wars of the French revolution. In this state of things, Mr. Webster was strongly solicited to give the support of his pen to the measures of the administration, by establishing a daily paper in the city of New York. Though conscious of the sacrifice of personal ease which he was called upon to make, he was so strongly impressed with the dangers of the crisis, and so entirely devoted to the principles of Washington, that he did not hesitate to accede to the proposal. Removing his family to New York, in November, 1793, he commenced a daily paper, under the title of the *Minerva*, and afterward a semi-weekly paper, with that of the *Herald*, names which were subsequently changed to those of the *Commercial Advertiser*, and *New York Spectator*. This was the first example of a paper for the country, composed of the columns of a daily paper, without recomposition—a practice which has now become very common. In addition to his labors as sole editor of these papers, Mr. Webster published, in the year 1794, a pamphlet which had a very extensive circulation, entitled "*The Revolution in France.*"

The publication of the treaty negotiated with Great Britain by Mr. Jay, in 1795, aroused an opposition to its ratification of so violent a nature, as to stagger for a time the firmness of Washington, and to threaten civil commotions. Mr. Webster, in common with General Hamilton and some of the ablest men of the country, came out in vindication of the treaty. Under the signature of *Curtius*, he published a series of papers, which were very extensively reprinted throughout the country, and afterward collected by a bookseller of Philadelphia in a pamphlet form. Of these, ten were contributed by himself, and two by Mr., afterward Chancellor, Kent. As an evidence of their effect, it may not be improper to state, that Mr. Rufus King expressed his opinion to Mr. Jay, that the essays of *Curtius* had contributed more than any other papers of the same kind, to allay the discontent and opposition to the treaty; assigning as a reason, that they were peculiarly well adapted to the understanding of the people at large.

When Mr. Webster resided in New York, the yellow fever prevailed at different times in most of our large Atlantic cities; and a controversy arose among the physicians of Philadelphia and New York, on the question whether it was introduced by infection, or generated on the spot. The subject interested Mr. Webster deeply, and led him into a laborious investigation of the history of pestilential diseases at every period of the world. The facts which he collected, with the inferences to which he was led, were embodied in a work of two volumes, octavo, which, in 1799, was published both in this country and in England. This work has always been considered as a valuable repository of facts; and during the prevalence of the Asiatic cholera in the year 1832, the theories of the author seemed to receive so much confirmation, as to excite a more than ordinary interest in the work, both in Europe and America.

During the wars which were excited by the French revolution, the power assumed

285

by the belligerents to blockade their enemies' ports by proclamation, and the multiplied seizures of American vessels bound to such ports, produced various discussions respecting the rights of neutral nations in time of war. These discussions induced Mr. Webster to examine the subject historically; and, in 1802, he published a treatise full of minute information and able reasoning on the subject. A gentleman of competent abilities, who said he had read all that he could find on that subject, in the English, French, German, and Italian languages, declared that he considered this treatise as the best he had seen. The same year, he also published "*Historical Notices of the Origin and State of Banking Institutions and Insurance Offices*," which was republished in Philadelphia by one Humphrey, without giving credit to the author; and a part of which, taken from this reprint, was incorporated into the Philadelphia edition of Rees's Cyclopedia.

At this time, Mr. Webster resided at New Haven, to which place he had removed in the spring of 1798. For a short period after his departure from New York, he wrote for the papers mentioned above, which, although placed under the care of another editor, continued for a time to be his property. He very soon succeeded, however, in disposing of his interest in them, and from that time devoted himself entirely to literary pursuits.

In the year 1807, Mr. Webster published "*A Philosophical and Practical Grammar of the English Language.*" This was a highly original work, the result of many years of diligent investigation. The author's views may be gathered from the motto on the title page, taken from Lord Bacon's Aphorisms,—"Antisthenes, being asked what learning was most necessary, replied, 'To unlearn that which is *naught.*' " He considered our English Grammars as objectionable in one important respect, namely, that of being too much conformed to those of the Latin and Greek languages in their nomenclature and classification. True philosophy, he maintained, requires us to arrange things, and give them names, according to their real nature. But our language is rude and irregular, in comparison with those of the ancients. It can not be reduced to the same orderly system. The several parts of it can not be brought under the same names and classifications. We need, therefore, a nomenclature of our own, in some important particulars. Thus the word *pronoun* properly denotes a *substitute* for a noun. But, in many cases, words of this class are substitutes for clauses, or parts of sentences, and not for single nouns. There are also other words, not ordinarily ranged among pronouns, which act equally as substitutes, that is, perform the office of pronouns. Mr. Webster, therefore, proposed to lay aside the word *pronoun*, and apply the term *substitute* to this whole class, as describing their true office. Other changes were proposed, of the same nature, and for the same reasons. No one, who examines the subject with attention, can doubt the advantages of Mr. Webster's nomenclature, in itself considered. It enabled him to give an analysis of sentences, and to explain constructions, in a manner incomparably superior to that of the ordinary systems. His intimate acquaintance with the sources of our language prepared him to account, in the most satisfactory manner, for many puzzling forms of expression. Still, the prejudice against a change of nomenclature is so great, that this work has been far less known than it ought to be. It contains much valuable matter found in no other work, and is believed to be the most truly philosophical Grammar which we have of the English language.

After publishing his Grammar, Mr. Webster entered, in the same year, (1807,) on the great work of his life, which he had contemplated for a long period,—that of preparing a new and complete Dictionary of the English language. As preliminary to this, he had published, in 1806, a dictionary in the octavo form, containing a large number of words not to be found in any similar work, with the definitions corrected throughout, though necessarily expressed in very brief terms. From this time, his reading was turned more or less directly to this object. A number of years were spent in collecting words which had not been introduced into the English dictionaries; in discriminating with exactness the various senses of all the words in our language, and adding those significations which they had recently received. Some estimate may be formed of the labor bestowed on this part of the work, from the fact that *"The American Dictionary of the English Language"* contained, in the first edition, twelve thousand words, and between thirty and forty thousand definitions, which are not to be found in any preceding work. The number has been swelled, by subsequent additions, to about thirty thousand new words. Seventy years had elapsed since the first publication of Johnson's Dictionary; and scarcely a single improvement had been attempted in the various editions through which it had passed, or the numerous compilations to which it had given rise, except by the addition of a few words to the vocabulary. Yet in this period the English mind was putting itself forth in every direction, with an accuracy of research and a fertility of invention which are without a parallel in any other stage of its history. A complete revolution had taken place in almost every branch of physical science; new departments had been created, new principles developed, new modes of classification and description adopted. The political changes which so signally marked that period, the excitement of feeling and conflict of opinion resulting from the American and French revolutions, and the numerous modifications which followed in the institutions of society, had also left a deep impress on the language of politics, law, and general literature. Under these circumstances, to make a defining dictionary adapted to the present state of our language, was to produce an entirely *new work*; and how well Mr. Webster executed the task, will appear from the decision of men best qualified to judge, both in this country and in Europe, who have declared that his improvements upon Johnson, are even greater than Johnson himself made on those who preceded him. Still more labor, however, was bestowed on another part of the work, viz., the etymology of our leading terms. In this subject, Mr. Webster had always felt a lively interest, as presenting one of the most curious exhibitions of the progress of the human mind. But it was not till he had advanced considerably in the work as originally commenced, that he found how indispensable a knowledge of the true derivation of words is, to an exact development of their various meanings. At this point, therefore, he suspended his labors on the defining part of the Dictionary, and devoted a number of years to an inquiry into the origin of our

287

language, and its connection with those of other countries. In the course of these researches, he examined the vocabularies of twenty of the principal languages of the world, and made a synopsis of the most important words in each; arranging them under the same radical letters, with a translation of their significations, and references from one to another, when the senses are the same or similar. He was thus enabled to discover the real or probable affinities between the different languages, and, in many instances, to discover the primary, physical idea of an original word, from which the secondary senses have branched forth. Being thus furnished with a clew to guide him among the numerous, and often apparently inconsistent, significations of our most important words, he resumed his labors on the defining part of the Dictionary, and was able to give order and consistency to much that had before appeared confused and contradictory. The results of his inquiries into the origin and filiation of languages, were embodied in a work, about half the size of the American Dictionary, entitled "*A Synopsis of Words in Twenty Languages.*" This, owing to the expense of the undertaking, has not yet been published; though its principal results, so far as our language is concerned, are briefly given in tracing the etymology of our leading terms.

During the progress of these labors, Mr. Webster, finding his resources inadequate to the support of his family at New Haven, removed, in 1812, to Amherst, a pleasant country town within eight miles of Northampton, Massachusetts. Here he entered, with his characteristic ardor, into the literary and social interests of the people among whom he was placed. His extensive library, which was open to all, and his elevated tone of thought and conversation, had naturally a powerful influence on the habits and feelings of a small and secluded population. It was owing, in part, probably, to his removal to this town, that an academy was there established, which is now among the most flourishing seminaries of our land. A question having soon after arisen respecting the removal of Williams College from a remote part of the state to some more central position, Mr. Webster entered warmly into the design of procuring its establishment at Amherst, as one of the most beautiful and appropriate locations in New England. Though the removal did not take place, so strong an interest on the subject was awakened in Amherst and the neighboring towns, that a new college was soon after founded there, in the establishment of which Mr. Webster, as president of its first board of trustees, had great influence, both by his direct exertions to secure it patronage, and by the impulse which he had given to the cause of education in that part of the state.

In 1822, Mr. Webster returned with his family to New Haven, and, in 1823, received the degree of LL.D. from Yale College. Having nearly completed his Dictionary, he resolved on a voyage to Europe, with a view to perfect the work by consulting literary men abroad, and by examining some standard authors, to which he could not gain access in this country. He accordingly sailed for France in June, 1824, and spent two months at Paris in consulting several rare works in the *Bibliothèque du Roi*, and then went to England, where he remained till May, 1825. He spent about eight months at the University of Cambridge, where he had free access to the public libraries; and there he finished *"The American Dictionary."* He afterward visited London, Oxford, and some of the other principal cities of England, and in June returned to this country. This visit to England gave him an opportunity to become acquainted with literary men and literary institutions in that country, and to learn the real state of the English language there.

Soon after Dr. Webster returned to this country, the necessary arrangements were made for the publication of the work. An edition of twenty-five hundred copies was printed in this country, at the close of 1828, which was followed by an edition of three thousand in England, under the superintendence of E. H. Barker, Esq., editor of the *Thesaurus Græcæ Linguæ* of Henry Stephens. With the publication of the American Dictionary, at the age of seventy, Dr. Webster considered the labors of his literary life as brought, in a great measure, to a close. He revised a few of his earlier works for publication, and particularly his *"History of the United States,"* a book designed for the higher classes of schools, for youth who are acquiring a taste for history, and for men of business who have not time to peruse larger treatises.

In 1840, Dr. Webster published a second edition of the American Dictionary, consisting of three thousand copies, in two volumes, royal octavo. The improvements consisted chiefly in the addition of a number of thousand words to the vocabulary, the correction of definitions in several of the sciences, in conformity with later discoveries and classifications, and the introduction and explanation of many phrases from foreign languages, and of foreign terms used in books of music.

In 1843, he published *"A Collection of Papers on Political, Literary, and Moral Subjects,"* in one volume, octavo. This was composed chiefly of tracts and disquisitions, which had been published at an earlier period of his life, either in the form of pamphlets, or of papers read before literary and philosophical societies, and printed among their Transactions. It contains his *"Observations on the French Revolution,"* his *"Essay on the Rights of Neutral Nations,"* and the papers signed *Curtius,* in vindication of Mr. Jay's treaty with Great Britain. To these is added an elaborate dissertation *"On the supposed Change in the Temperature of Winter,"* which was read before the Connecticut Academy of Arts and Sciences, in the year 1799. In this he controverts the opinion which has generally prevailed, that the temperature of the winter season, in northern latitudes, has suffered a material change, and become warmer in modern than it was in ancient times. The subject was one which required very great minuteness and extent of historical research, and this paper contains the result of a series of investigations, which had been carried on, in conjunction with the author's other pursuits, for a period of more than ten years. Many of the facts which it presents are of a very curious and striking nature. There is, probably, no other treatise which exhibits the historical evidence on this subject with so much fullness and accuracy. In addition to this, the volume contains a number of other papers of an interesting character, and the whole collection forms a truly valuable record of the author's earlier labors.

In thus tracing the principal events of Dr. Webster's life, we have reached the commencement of the year in which he died; and it may here be proper to pause for a moment, and consider some of those qualities and habits of mind, which prepared him for this long course of public service and literary labor. The leading traits in the character of Dr. Webster were enterprise, self-reliance, and indomitable perseverance. He was naturally of a sanguine temperament; and the circumstances under which he entered on the active duties of life, were eminently suited to strengthen the original tendencies of his nature. Our country was just struggling into national existence. The public mind was full of ardor, energy, and expectation.

Webster's
associations
with our
Founding
Fathers

His early associates were men of powerful intellect, who were engaged, to a great extent, in laying the foundations of our government, and who have stamped the impress of their genius on the institutions of their country. As the advocate of the Federal Constitution, and a strenuous supporter of Washington's administration, he was brought into habits of the closest intimacy with Alexander Hamilton, John Jay, Oliver Wolcott, Timothy Pickering, and the other great men on whom Washington relied for counsel and aid in organizing the new government. The journal which he established at New York was their organ of communication with the public, in the great commerical emporium of the United States. He was thus placed on terms of constant and confidential intercourse with the leading members of the cabinet, and the prominent supporters of Washington throughout the country. While he had their respect as a ready and energetic writer, he enjoyed their counsel, imparted with the utmost freedom, as to the manner in which he might best conduct the defense of their common principles. The natural result, especially on a mind constituted like his, was the formation of all his habits of thought and action, into a resemblance to theirs. Energy, self-reliance, fearlessness, the resolute defense of whatever he thought right and useful, the strong hope of ultimate success,—these became the great elements of his intellectual character. He carried them with him, at a subsequent period, into all his literary pursuits, and they sustained him under the pressure of difficulties which would have crushed the spirit of almost any other man.

Webster indexes
and preserves all
his acquired
knowledge

One of the habits which Dr. Webster formed in this early course of training, was that of arranging all his acquired knowledge in the most exact order, and keeping the elements of progressive thought continually within his reach. Although his memory was uncommonly quick and tenacious, he saw, as the editor of a daily journal, how idle and unsafe it is, to rely on mere recollection for the immense mass of materials which a public writer must have ever at command. He learnt, therefore, to preserve *documents* of all kinds with the utmost care. All that he had ever written, all that had been written against him, every thing that he met with in newspapers or periodicals which seemed likely to be of use at any future period, was carefully laid aside in its appropriate place, and was ready at a moment's warning. He had also a particular mark by which he denoted, in every work he read, all the new words, or new senses of words, which came under his observation. He filled the margin of his books with notes and comments containing corrections of errors, a comparison of dates, or references to corresponding passages in other works,

until his whole library became a kind of *Index Rerum*, to which he could refer at once for every thing he had read.

Another habit which resulted in part from his early pursuits, was that of carrying on numerous and diversified employments at the same time. To men of the present generation, Dr. Webster is known chiefly as a learned philologist; and the natural inference would be, that he spent his whole life among his books, and chiefly in devotion to a single class of studies. The fact, however, was far otherwise. Though he was always a close student,—reading, thinking, and writing at every period of his life,—he never withdrew himself from the active employments of society. After his first removal to New Haven, he was for a number of years one of the aldermen of the city, and judge of one of the state courts. He also frequently represented that town in the legislature of the state. During his residence at Amherst, he was called, in repeated instances, to discharge similar duties, and spent a part of several winters at Boston as a member of the General Court. He entered with zeal into all the interests of the town and county where he lived, in schools and academies, its agriculture and mechanic arts, its advance in taste and refinement. He gave freely of his time, his counsel, and the efforts of his pen, when requested, in public addresses, or through the medium of the press, for the promotion of every kind of social improvement. Equally large and diversified was the range of his intellectual pursuits. There was hardly any department of literature which he had not explored with lively interest, at some period of his life. He wrote on a greater variety of topics than perhaps any other author of the United States;—on the foundations of government, the laws of nations, the rights of neutrals, the science of banking, the history of his country, the progress of diseases, and the variations of climate; on agriculture, commerce, education, morals, religion, and the great means of national advancement, in addition to the principal theme of his life, philology and grammar. Such was the activity of his mind, and the delight he found in new acquisitions, that a *change* of employment was all the relief he needed from the weariness of protracted study. The refreshment which others seek in journeys, or the entire suspension of intellectual effort, he found, during most of his life, in the stimulus afforded by some new and exciting object of pursuit. Mental exertion was the native element of his soul; and it is not too much to say, that another instance of such long-continued literary toil, such steady, unfaltering industry, can hardly be found in the annals of our country.

The last of those mental habits which will now be traced, was that of original investigation, of thorough and penetrating research. The period at which Dr. Webster came forward in public life was one, to an uncommon extent, in which every important subject was discussed in its *principles*. It was a period when the foundations of our civil polity were laid, and when such men as Hamilton, Madison, and Jay, became "the expounders of the constitution," and the advocates of the new government. All things conspired to make the discussions of that day masterly exhibitions of reasoning and profound investigation,—the character of the men engaged, the conflict of great principles, and the weighty interests suspended on the issue. Dr. Webster for some years took a large share in these discussions, both

Webster carried on numerous and diversified employments at the same time

Webster's habit of original investigation and thorough research in pamphlets and through the journal which he conducted. The habits which he thus formed went with him into all the literary pursuits of his subsequent life. They made him a bold, original thinker,—thorough in all his investigations, and fearless in proclaiming the results. He had no deference for authority, except as sustained by argument. He was no copyist, no mere compiler. Every thing he wrote, from a chapter in "The Prompter," to his "Introduction to the American Dictionary," bore the same impress of original thought, personal observation, and independent inquiry.

It is unnecessary to say how perfectly these habits were adapted to prepare Dr. Webster for the leading employment of his life, the production of the American Dictionary. Nothing but his eager pursuit of every kind of knowledge, and his exact system in bringing all that he had ever read completely under his command, could have enabled him to give in his first edition more than twelve thousand words and forty thousand definitions, which could then be found in no other similar work. Nothing but his passion for original investigation prevented him from building, like Todd, on the foundation of Johnson, or arranging Horne Tooke's etymologies, like Richardson, with some additions and improvements, under their proper heads in a dictionary. But, commencing with the Diversions of Purley as the starting-point of his researches, he was led by the character of his mind to widen continually the field of his inquiries. He passed from the western languages to the eastern, in tracing the affinities of his native tongue. He established some of those great principles which have made etymology a science, and led the way in that brilliant career of investigation, by which the German philologists are throwing so clear a light on the origin and filiation of the principal languages of the globe. But into these studies he would never have entered, nor even thought of attempting such a work as an original dictionary of the English language, except under the impulse of those other traits,—that sanguine temperament, that spirit of self-reliance, that fearless determination to carry out every thing that he thought useful and true, to its utmost limits,—which were spoken of above, as forming the master principle of his character. It is difficult to conceive, at the present day, how rash and hopeless such an undertaking then appeared, on the part of any citizen of the United States. It was much as though we should now hear of a similar design by one of the settlers of New Holland. He was assailed with a storm of ridicule at home and abroad; and even his best friends, while they admired his constancy, and were fully convinced of his erudition, had strong fears that he was engaged in a fruitless effort,—that he would never have justice done him, in bringing his work before the world under such adverse circumstances. Nothing, plainly, but uncommon ardor, boldness, and self-confidence, could have sustained him under the pressure of these difficulties. But such qualities, it must be confessed, notwithstanding all the support they afford, are not without their disadvantages. They often lead to the adoption of hasty opinions, especially in new and intricate inquiries. Of this Dr. Webster was aware. He saw reason to change his views on many points, as he widened the sphere of his knowledge. In such cases, he retracted his former statements with the utmost frankness; for he had not a particle of that pride of opinion which makes men so often ashamed to confess an error, even when they have seen and abandoned it. This ardor of mind is apt, also, to lead men into a strength and confidence of statement which may wear at times the aspect of dogmatism. If Dr. Webster should be thought by any one to have erred in this respect, the error, it should be remembered, was one of temperament,—the almost necessary result of that bold, self-relying spirit, without which no man could have undertaken, much less have carried through, the Herculean task of preparing the American Dictionary. Those, however, who knew him best, can testify, that his strength of statement, however great it might be, was never the result of arrogance or presumption. He spoke from the mere frankness of his nature; he practiced no reserve; he used none of that cautious phraseology with which most men conceal their feelings, or guard against misconstruction. He was an ardent lover of truth, and he spoke of the discoveries which he believed himself to have made, much as he would have spoken of the same discoveries when made by others. He was aware that there must be many things in a book like this, especially on a science so imperfect in its development as etymology, which would not stand the test of time. But he never doubted, even in the darkest seasons of discouragement and obloquy, that he could at last produce such a work, that the world "should not willingly let it die." The decision of the public verified his anticipations, and freed him from the charge of presumption. Three very large editions, at a high price, have already been exhausted in this country and England. The demand is still increasing on both sides of the Atlantic; and the author might well be gratified to learn, that a gentleman who asked, some years since, at one of the principal bookselling establishments of London, for the best English dictionary on their shelves, had this work handed to him, with the remark, "That, sir, is the only *real* dictionary which we have of our language, though it was prepared by an American."

In his social habits, Dr. Webster was distinguished by dignified ease, affability, and politeness. He was punctilious in his observance of all the nicer properties of life. There was nothing that annoyed him more, or on which he remarked with greater keenness, than any violation of the established rules of decorum, any disposition to meddle with the concerns of others, or to encroach on the sanctity of those rights and feelings, which, as they can not be protected by law, must owe their security to delicacy of sentiment in an enlightened community. He had an uncommon degree of refinement in all his thoughts and feelings. Never, in his most sportive or unguarded moments, did any sentiment escape him which was coarse or vulgar. He had, in this respect, almost a feminine purity of mind. It might be truly said of him, as was remarked concerning one of his distinguished contemporaries in public life, that he was never known to utter an expression which might not have been used with entire freedom in the most refined female society. In his pecuniary transactions, he was acknowledged by all to be not only just, but liberal. It was a principle with him, for life, never to be in debt. Every thing was paid for at the time of purchase. In all his dealings and social intercourse, he was remarkably direct, frank, and open. He had but one character, and that was "known and read of all

Webster had but
one character
"known and read
of all men"

293

men." Whatever faults might be imputed to him, no one ever suspected him of double dealing; no one ever thought he was capable of a mean or dishonorable action.

In the discharge of his domestic duties, Dr. Webster was watchful, consistent, and firm. Though immersed in study, he kept in his hands the entire control of his family arrangements, down to the minutest particulars. Every thing was reduced to exact system; all moved on with perfect regularity and order, for *method* was the presiding principle of his life. In the government of his children there was but one rule, and that was instantaneous and entire obedience. This was insisted upon as *right*,—as, in the nature of things, due by a child to a parent. He did not rest his claim on any explanations, or on showing that the thing required was reasonable or beneficial. While he endeavored to make it clear to his children that he sought their happiness in whatever he required, he commanded as one having *authority*, and he enforced his commands to the utmost, as a duty which he owed equally to his children and to God, who had placed them under his control. He felt that, on this subject, there had been a gradual letting down of the tone of public sentiment, which was much to be deplored. Many, in breaking away from the sternness of Puritan discipline, have gone to the opposite extreme. They have virtually abandoned the exercise of parental authority, and endeavored to regulate the conduct of their children by reasoning and persuasion,—by the mere presentation of motives, and not by the enforcement of commands. If such persons succeed, as they rarely do, in preserving any thing like a comfortable state of subordination in their families, they fail at least in the accomplishment of one great end for which their offspring were committed to their care. They send forth their children into life, without any of those habits of submission to lawful authority which are essential to the character of a good citizen and a useful member of society. In the intellectual training of his children, on the other hand, Dr. Webster had much less of system and complicated machinery, than many are disposed to adopt. His great principle was not to overdo, —to let nature have free scope, and to leave the development of the mind, within certain limits, to the operation of awakened curiosity directed to its proper objects. He therefore threw open his extensive library to his children at an early period of their lives, and said, in the words of Cotton Mather, "Read, and you will know."

He felt that children should learn to acquire knowledge by severe effort; that the prevailing disposition to make every thing easy is unphilosophical and wrong; that the great object of early training is to form the mind into a capacity of surmounting intellectual difficulties of any and every kind. In his view, also, the young have much to learn in early life, the use of which they can not then comprehend. They must learn it by rote, particularly the spelling of so complicated a language as ours; and all those systems which lead forward children no faster than they can understand and apply every word they spell, he considered as radically erroneous. He wished, on the contrary, at this early period of ready memory and limited comprehension, to store the mind with many things which would afterward be found of indispensable use; things which are learnt with the utmost reluctance, or rather, in most cases, are not learnt at all, in the more advanced stages of intellectual progress. He felt that there must necessarily be much of drudgery in the formation of a thoroughly educated mind. He thought it wise, therefore, to commence those tasks which it involves, from the earliest period at which the youthful intellect can endure them. Upon these principles he constructed his Spelling Book, and other works for the use of children. He designed to make them instructive, and not mere books of amusement. Whether his views were incorrect or unphilosophical, the public will judge.

In respect to religion, Dr. Webster was a firm believer, during a large part of his life, in the great distinctive doctrines of our Puritan ancestors, whose character he always regarded with the highest veneration. There was a period, however, from the time of his leaving college to the age of forty, when he had doubts as to some of those doctrines, and rested in a different system. Soon after he graduated, being uncertain what business to attempt or by what means he could obtain subsistence, he felt his mind greatly perplexed, and almost overwhelmed with gloomy apprehensions. In this state, as he afterward informed a friend, he read Johnson's Rambler with unusual interest; and, in closing the last volume, he made a firm resolution to pursue a course of virtue through life; and to perform every moral and social duty with scrupulous exactness. To this he added a settled belief in the inspiration of the Scriptures and the governing providence of God, connected with highly reverential views of the divine character and perfections. Here he rested, placing his chief reliance for salvation on a faithful discharge of all the relative duties of life, though not to the entire exclusion of dependence on the merits of the Redeemer. In this state of mind he remained, though with some misgiving and frequent fluctuations of feeling, to the winter of 1807–8. At that time, there was a season of general religious interest at New Haven, under the ministry of the Rev. Moses Stuart, now a professor in the Andover Theological Seminary. To this Dr. Webster's attention was first directed, by observing an unusual degree of tenderness and solemnity of feeling in all the adult members of his family. He was thus led to reconsider his former views, and inquire, with an earnestness which he had never felt before, into the nature of personal religion, and the true ground of man's acceptance with God. He had now to decide not for himself only, but, to a certain extent, for others, whose spiritual interests were committed to his charge. Under a sense of this responsibility, he took up the study of the Bible with painful solicitude. As he advanced, the objections which he had formerly entertained against the humbling doctrines of the gospel, were wholly removed. He felt their truth in his own experience. He felt that salvation *must* be wholly of grace. He felt constrained, as he afterward told a friend, to cast himself down before God, confess his sins, implore pardon through the merits of the Redeemer, and there to make his vows of entire obedience to the commands and devotion to the service of his Maker. With his characteristic promptitude, he instantly made known to his family the feelings which he entertained. He called them together the next morning, and told them, with deep emotion, that, while he had aimed at the faithful discharge of all his

295

duties as their parent and head, he had neglected one of the most important, that of family prayer. After reading the Scriptures, he led them, with deep solemnity, to the throne of grace, and from that time continued the practice, with the liveliest interest, to the period of his death. He made a public profession of religion in April, 1808. His two oldest daughters united with him in the act, and another, only twelve years of age, was soon added to the number.

In his religious feelings, Dr. Webster was remarkably equable and cheerful. He had a very strong sense of the providence of God, as extending to the minutest concerns of life. In this he found a source of continual support and consolation, under the severe labors and numerous trials which he had to endure. To the same divine hand he habitually referred all his enjoyments; and it was known to his family, that he rarely, if ever, took the slightest refreshment, of any kind, even between meals, without a momentary pause, and a silent tribute of thanks to God as the giver. He made the Scriptures his daily study. After the completion of his Dictionary, especially, they were always lying on his table, and he probably read them more than all other books. He felt, from that time, that the labors of his life were ended, and that little else remained but to prepare for death. With a grateful sense of past mercies, a cheering consciousness of present support, and an animating hope of future blessedness, he waited with patience until his appointed change should come.

During the spring of 1843, Dr. Webster revised the Appendix of his Dictionary, and added some hundreds of words. He completed the printing of it about the middle of May. It was the closing act of his life. His hand rested, in its last labors, on the volume which he had commenced thirty-six years before. Within a few days, in calling on a number of friends in different parts of the town, he walked, during one afternoon, between two and three miles. The day was chilly, and immediately after his return, he was seized with faintness and a severe oppression on his lungs. An attack of peripneumony followed, which, though not alarming at first, took a sudden turn after four or five days, with fearful indications of a fatal result. It soon became necessary to inform him that he was in imminent danger. He received the communication with surprise, but with entire composure. His health had been so good, and every bodily function so perfect in its exercise, that he undoubtedly expected to live some years longer. But though suddenly called, he was completely ready. He gave some characteristic directions as to the disposal of his body after death. He spoke of his long life as one of uniform enjoyment, because filled up at every stage with active labors for some valuable end. He expressed his entire resignation to the will of God, and his unshaken trust in the atoning blood of the Redeemer. It was an interesting coincidence, that his former pastor, the Rev. Mr. Stuart, who received him to the church thirty-five years before, had just arrived at New Haven on a visit to his friends. He called immediately; and the interview brought into affecting comparison the beginning and the end of that long period of consecration to the service of Christ. The same hopes which had cheered the vigor of manhood, were now shedding a softened light over the decay and sufferings of age. "I know in whom I have believed,"—such was the solemn and affecting testi-

AN AMERICAN
DICTIONARY OF
THE ENGLISH
LANGUAGE

"I know in whom
I have believed",
1843

mony which he gave to his friend, while the hand of death was upon him,—"I know in whom I have believed, and that He is able to keep that which I have committed to him against that day." Thus, without one doubt, one fear, he resigned his soul into the hands of his Maker, and died on the 28th day of May, 1843, in the eighty-fifth year of his age.

In his person, Dr. Webster was tall, and somewhat slender, remarkably erect throughout life, and moving, even in his advanced years, with a light and elastic step.

Dr. Webster's widow survived him more than four years, and died on the 25th day of June, 1847, in the eighty-second year of her age. He had seven children who arrived at maturity,—one son, William G. Webster, Esq., who resides at New Haven, and six daughters. Of these, the oldest is married to the Hon. William W. Ellsworth, of Hartford, late governor, and now judge of the Supreme Court of Connecticut; the second to the author of this sketch; the third, now deceased, was first married to Edward Cobb, Esq., of Portland, Maine, and afterward to the Rev. Professor Fowler, of Amherst, Mass.; the fourth, also deceased, was married to Horatio Southgate, Esq., of Portland, Maine, and left at her death a daughter, who was adopted by Dr. Webster, and is now married to Henry Trowbridge, Jun., Esq., of New Haven; the fifth is married to the Rev. Henry Jones, of Bridgeport, Conn.; and the sixth remains unmarried, in the family of her brother.

In conclusion, it may be said that the name of *Noah Webster*, from the wide circulation of some of his works, is known familiarly to a greater number of the inhabitants of the United States, than the name, probably, of any other individual except the *Father of his Country*. Whatever influence he thus acquired was used at all times to promote the best interests of his fellow-men. His books, though read by millions, have made no man worse. To multitudes they have been of lasting benefit, not only by the course of early training they have furnished, but by those precepts of wisdom and virtue with which almost every page is stored.

August, 1847.

An American Dictionary of the English Language

In the year 1783, just at the close of the Revolution, I published an elementary book for facilitating the acquisition of our vernacular tongue, and for correcting a vicious pronunciation, which prevailed extensively among the common people of this country. Soon after the publication of that work, I believe in the following year, that learned and respectable scholar, the *Rev. Dr. Goodrich*, of Durham, one of the trustees of Yale College, suggested to me the propriety and expediency of my compiling a Dictionary, which should complete a system for the instruction of the citizens of this country in the language. At that time, I could not indulge the thought, much less the hope, of undertaking such a work; as I was neither qualified by research, nor had I the means of support, during the execution of the work, had I been disposed to undertake it. For many years, therefore, though I considered such a work as very desirable, yet it appeared to me impracticable; as I was under the necessity of devoting my time to other occupations for obtaining subsistence.

About thirty-five years ago, I began to think of attempting the compilation of a Dictionary. I was induced to this undertaking, not more by the suggestion of friends, than by my own experience of the want of such a work, while reading modern books of science. In this pursuit, I found almost insuperable difficulties, from the want of a dictionary, for explaining many new words, which recent discoveries in the physical sciences had introduced into use. To remedy this defect in part, I published my *Compendious Dictionary* in 1806; and soon after made preparations for undertaking a larger work.

My original design did not extend to an investigation of the origin and progress of our language, much less of other languages. I limited my views to the correcting of certain errors in the best English dictionaries, and to the supplying of words in which they are deficient. But after writing through two letters of the alphabet, I determined to change my plan. I found myself embarrassed at every step, for want of a knowledge of the origin of words, which *Johnson, Bailey, Junius, Skinner,* and some other authors, do not afford the means of obtaining. Then, laying aside my manuscripts, and all books treating of language, except lexicons and dictionaries, I endeavored, by a diligent comparison of words having the same or cognate radical letters, in about twenty languages, to obtain a more correct knowledge of the primary sense of original words, of the affinities between the English and many other languages, and thus to enable myself to trace words to their source.

I had not pursued this course more than three or four years, before I discovered that I had to unlearn a great deal that I had spent years in learning, and that it was necessary for me to go back to the first rudiments of a branch of erudition which I had before cultivated, as I had supposed, with success.

I spent ten years in this comparison of radical words, and in forming a *Synopsis of the principal Words in twenty Languages, arranged in Classes under their primary Elements or Letters.* The result has been to open what are to me new views of language, and to unfold what appear to be the genuine principles on which these languages are constructed.

After completing this *Synopsis,* I proceeded to correct what I had written of the Dictionary, and to complete the remaining part of the work. But before I had finished it, I determined on a voyage to Europe, with the view of obtaining some books and some assistance which I wanted; of learning the real state of the pronunciation of our language in England, as well as the general state of philology in that country; and of attempting to bring about some agreement or coincidence of opinions, in regard to unsettled points in pronunciation and grammatical construction. In some of these objects I failed; in others, my designs were answered.

It is not only important, but in a degree necessary, that the people of this country should have an *American Dictionary of the English Language;* for, although the body of the language is the same as in England, and it is desirable to perpetuate that sameness, yet some differences must exist. Language is the expression of ideas; and if the people of one country can not preserve an identity of ideas, they can not retain an identity of language. Now, an identity of ideas depends materially upon a sameness of things or objects with which the people of the two countries are conversant. But in no two portions of the earth, remote from each other, can such identity be found. Even physical objects must be different. But the principal differences between the people of this country and of all others, arise from different forms of government, different laws, institutions, and customs. Thus the practice of *hawking* and *hunting,* the institution of *heraldry,* and the *feudal system* of England originated terms which formed, and some of which now form, a necessary part of the language of that country; but, in the United States, many of these terms are no part of our present language,—and they can not be, for the things which they express do not exist in this country. They can be known to us only as obsolete or as foreign words. On the other hand, the institutions in this country which are new and peculiar, give rise to new terms or to new applications of old terms, unknown to the people of England; which can not be explained by them, and which will not be inserted in their dictionaries, unless copied from ours. Thus the terms *land-office; land-warrant; location of land; consociation* of churches; *regent* of a university; *intendant* of a city; *plantation, selectmen, senate, congress, court, assembly, escheat,* &c., are either words not belonging to the language of England, or they are applied to things in this country which do not exist in that. No person in this country will be satisfied with the English definitions of the words *congress, senate,* and *assembly, court,* &c.; for although these are words used in England, yet they are applied in this country to express ideas which they do not express in that country. With our present constitutions of government, *escheat* can never have its feudal sense in the United States.

But this is not all. In many cases, the nature of our governments, and of our civil institutions, requires an appropriate language in the definition of words, even when the words express the same thing as in England. Thus the English dictionaries inform us that a *justice* is one deputed by the *king* to do right by way of judgment —he is a *lord* by his office—justices of the peace are appointed by the *king's commission*—language which is inaccurate in respect to this officer in the United States. So *constitutionally* is defined, by *Chalmers, legally;* but in this country the distinction between *constitution* and *law* requires a different definition. In the United States, a *plantation* is a very different thing from what it is in England. The word *marshal,* in this country, has one important application unknown in England, or in Europe.

A great number of words in our language require to be defined in a phraseology accommodated to the condition and institutions of the people in these States, and the people of England must look to an *American Dictionary* for a correct understanding of such terms.

The necessity, therefore, of a dictionary suited to the people of the United States is obvious; and I should suppose that, this fact being admitted, there could be no difference of opinion as to the *time* when such a work ought to be substituted for English dictionaries.

There are many other considerations of a public nature, which serve to justify this attempt to furnish an American work which shall be a guide to the youth of the United States. Most of these are too obvious to require illustration.

One consideration, however, which is dictated by my own feelings, but which, I trust, will meet with approbation in corresponding feelings in my fellow-citizens, ought not to be passed in silence; it is this:—"The chief glory of a nation," says Dr. Johnson, "arises from its authors." With this opinion deeply impressed on my mind, I have the same ambition which actuated that great man, when he expressed a wish to give celebrity to *Bacon*, to *Hooker*, to *Milton*, and to *Boyle*.

I do not indeed expect to add celebrity to the names of *Franklin*, *Washington*, *Adams*, *Jay*, *Madison*, *Marshall*, *Ramsay*, *Dwight*, *Smith*, *Trumbull*, *Hamilton*, *Belknap*, *Ames*, *Mason*, *Kent*, *Hare*, *Silliman*, *Cleaveland*, *Walsh*, *Irving*, and many other Americans distinguished by their writings or by their science; but it is with pride and satisfaction that I can place them, as authorities, on the same page with those of *Boyle*, *Hooker*, *Milton*, *Dryden*, *Addison*, *Ray*, *Milner*, *Cowper*, *Davy*, *Thomson*, and *Jameson*.

A life devoted to reading and to an investigation of the origin and principles of our vernacular language, and especially a particular examination of the best English writers, with a view to a comparison of their style and phraseology with those of the best American writers, and with our colloquial usage, enables me to affirm, with confidence, that the genuine English idiom is as well preserved by the unmixed English of this country, as it is by the best *English* writers. Examples to prove this fact will be found in the *Introduction* to this work. It is true that many of our writers have neglected to cultivate taste, and the embellishments of style; but even these have written the language in its genuine *idiom*. In this respect, *Franklin* and *Washington*, whose language is their hereditary mother tongue, unsophisticated by modern grammar, present as pure models of genuine English as *Addison* or *Swift*. But I may go further, and affirm, with truth, that our country has produced some of the best models of composition. The style of President *Smith*; of the authors of the *Federalist*; of Mr. *Ames*; of Dr. *Mason*; of Mr. *Harper*; of Chancellor *Kent*; [the prose] of Mr. *Barlow*; of Dr. *Channing*; of *Washington Irving*; of the legal decisions of the Supreme Court of the United States; of the reports of legal decisions in some of the particular states; and many other writings; in purity, in elegance, and in technical precision, is equaled only by that of the best British authors, and surpassed by that of no English compositions of a similar kind.

The United States commenced their existence under circumstances wholly novel and unexampled in the history of nations. They commenced with civilization, with learning, with science, with constitutions of free government, and with that best gift of God to man, the Christian religion. Their population is now equal to that of England; in arts and sciences, our citizens are very little behind the most enlightened people on earth; in some respects, they have no superiors; and our language, within two centuries, will be spoken by more people in this country than any other language on earth, except the Chinese, in Asia; and even that may not be an exception.

It has been my aim in this work, now offered to my fellow-citizens, to ascertain the true principles of the language, in its orthography and structure; to purify it from some palpable errors, and reduce the number of its anomalies, thus giving it more regularity and consistency in its forms, both of words and sentences; and in this manner to furnish a standard of our vernacular tongue, which we shall not be ashamed to bequeath to *five hundred millions of people*, who are destined to occupy, and I hope to adorn, the vast territory within our jurisdiction.

If the language can be improved in regularity, so as to be more easily acquired by our own citizens and by foreigners, and thus be rendered a more useful instrument for the propagation of science, arts, civilization, and Christianity;—if it can be rescued from the mischievous influence of sciolists, and that dabbling spirit of innovation, which is perpetually disturbing its settled usages and filling it with anomalies;—if, in short, our vernacular language can be redeemed from corruptions, and our philology and literature from degradation; it would be a source of great satisfaction to me to be one among the instruments of promoting these valuable objects. If this object can not be effected, and my wishes and hopes are to be frustrated, my labor will be lost, and this work must sink into oblivion.

This Dictionary, like all others of the kind, must be left, in some degree, imperfect; for what individual is competent to trace to their source, and define in all their various applications, popular, scientific, and technical, *seventy* or *eighty thousand* words! It satisfies my mind that I have done all that my health, my talents, and my pecuniary means, would enable me to accomplish. I present it to my fellow-citizens, not with frigid indifference, but with my ardent wishes for their improvement and their happiness; and for the continued increase of the wealth, the learning, the moral and religious elevation of character, and the glory, of my country.

To that great and benevolent Being, who, during the preparation of this work, has sustained a feeble constitution, amidst obstacles and toils, disappointments, infirmities, and depression; who has borne me and my manuscripts in safety across the Atlantic, and given me strength and resolution to bring the work to a close, I would present the tribute of my most grateful acknowledgments. And if the talent which he intrusted to my care, has not been put to the most profitable use in his service, I hope it has not been "kept laid up in a napkin," and that any misapplication of it may be graciously forgiven.

Noah Webster.

New Haven., 1828

Part

IV

A Study Program for the Christian Home
the Christian Church, the Christian School

Christian History
Study Course

Contents

Explanation of Study Course

This study course for *Christian History of the Constitution of the United States of America* has been arranged into *Eight Lessons* which make it possible to study the book in sequence—but—at the same time to take related principles and concepts at once, extensively, into the text.

The first six lessons have Seven Parts or Steps, and they have been designed to establish the habit of focusing study upon the *principles* of America's *Christian History of the Constitution.*

Step One: Concepts for Observation. This step introduces some basic principles to be identified and considered.

Step Two: Reading for "Leading Ideas". This step gives specific purpose for the reading of the Text, *Christian History.*

Step Three: Reading Assignment. This step contains the sequential assignment through the text. Combined with Step Five almost the entire text is covered during the Course.

Step Four: Questions for Invention. This step encourages the student to re-phrase the *principles* for discussion, to make a "new application" of the principles.

Step Five: Study of Concepts. This step encourages the student to go extensively into the text, seeking to relate the principles under consideration to their further historical development and significance.

Step Six: Original Thought. This step is designed to challenge some original response to the principles and ideas focused in the lesson and to enable each individual to relate America's *Christian History* to himself.

Step Seven: What Identifies America as a Christian Nation? This final step encourages the identification of America's individual function in the *Chain of Christianity.*

Lesson Seven, *A Biblical-Political Index to John Locke* is designed to introduce the student to the study of John Locke as the Founding Fathers studied him—in the light of the HOLY SCRIPTURES. This section is not extensive—it is introductory—in the hope of encouraging each individual to begin to Bible-base all of the philosophers of *Christian History.*

Lesson Eight, *The Colonists Act on the Christian Principles of Self-Government, Property, and Union,* represents the consequence of these Christian Principles historically as the Colonists maintained their position upon the clear identification of *principles* and therefore were able to detect the infraction and usurpation of their fundamental liberties.

The Christian Idea of Man and Government

Lesson One

Step One: Concepts for Observation

In this step we identify some basic principles to be learned in this lesson. These are quoted from the text, *Christian History*. The purpose is to fix them clearly in thought as we study so that we may see how these Christian principles were applied by the American colonists in the establishment of Christianity's republican form of government.

The Christian Idea of Man

"Christianity then appeared with its central doctrine, that man was created in the Divine image, and destined for immortality; pronouncing, that, in the eye of God, all men are equal. This asserted for the individual an independent value." Christian History, page 2

The Purpose of Government

"It occasioned the great inference, that man is superior to the State, which ought to be fashioned for his use."

". . . the idea that the State ought to exist for man; that justice, protection, and the common good, ought to be the aim of government . . ." Christian History, page 2

"And tis' not without Reason, that he seeks out, and is willing to joyn in Society with others, who are already united, or have a Mind to unite, for the mutual Preservation of their Lives, Liberties and Estates, which I call by the general Name, Property."

306 *John Locke*, Christian History, *248A*

"We hold these Truths to be self-evident, that all Men are created equal, that they are endowed by their Creator with certain unalienable Rights, that among these are Life, Liberty, and the Pursuit of Happiness—That to secure these Rights, Governments are instituted among Men . . ." Declaration of Independence, Christian History, *248A*

Step Two: Reading for "Leading Ideas"

Here are some ideas which "lead" us into the Christian History of our country.

1. The conception of the pagan or socialist state rests upon an un-Christian conception of man. What is it? What effect does this conception of man have upon the form of government which results from this premise?

2. Why is America identified with the "principle of individuality"? Without a Christian basis what becomes of the "principle of individuality"?

Step Three: Reading Assignment

Read pages 1 and 2 of Text, Christian History

Step Four: Questions for Invention

Part of the Webster, 1856 definition of the word "invention" is *"To find out something new"*. An aspect of *invention* is *devise* and this word is defined in part as *"to think,* divide or share, *to talk* or *interchange thoughts."* A further aspect of *invent* is to *contrive* or, by definition, "to form in the mind by *new combinations of ideas, new applications of principles,* or *new arrangement of parts."*

This section is designed to aid the student of *Christian History* to apply the Christian constitutional principles in each lesson to questions relating to man in society. A basic Christian premise here is that society is the *effect* or result of the degree to which God's laws are being lived and practiced by men.

The purpose of this section is to help each student think actively about his own relationship to Christian government.

1. The pagan or socialist state claims to exist to promote the welfare of its citizens. What is the Christian concept of welfare and why is it in conflict with the pagan conception?
   Reference: See page 6 of *Christian History*, paragraphs 2 and 3, beginning *"Our people are busy . . ."*

307

2. What did the pagan state regard of value in the individual? What does Christianity regard of value in the individual?

3. What are the *"civic virtues"* which are taught today? In what ways do they relate the individual to the state?

4. Why is monarchy a pagan idea of government?

5. What particularly significant words does Frothingham use to describe the effect of paganism upon the *mental climate*? What effect does the concentration of power in the state, rather than in the individual, have upon discovery, exploration and invention?

6. In what ways was the Reformation a rebirth of *"true spiritual freedom"*?

7. What specific factors in Christianity make it *"the basis of the good, permanent, and progressive in modern civilization"*?

8. Why did Milton and Locke carefully define the Rights of Man as existing before civil government? See page XIII, paragraph 5.

9. If the state does not bring into being man's Rights, what is the purpose for the existence of government?

10. On page 58 of *Christian History*, paragraph 6, beginning line 8, Locke describes man as God's property, basing this concept upon Scripture, Ephesians 2:10:

   "For we are his workmanship, created in Christ Jesus unto good works, which God hath before ordained that we should walk in them."

If the end of government is the preservation of property why does Locke put the responsibility for this goal upon the individual?

Step Five: Study of Concepts

In this step we expand and enlarge our background of the concepts being observed and build them into their historical Christian significance in the development of our country.

The Christian Idea of Man and Government will be studied throughout this Text, *Christian History of the Constitution*, in relation to the following terms:

Sovereignty of the Individual
Representative Government
Church Government

    Episcopal form of government
    Presbyterian form of government } American Constitutional Government
    Congregational form of government

Local Self-Government
308 *Republican Form of Government*

Each of these terms has its basis or premise in the Christian Idea of Man and Government and will be directly related to the development of the founding and establishment of our American Christian Constitutional form of government. Those who wish to relate these terms to our present lesson are urged to use the *Index*. They will be dealt with in future lessons.

Step Six: Original Thought

The suggestions in this step are to guide students of *Christian History* to raise their own concerns and interests relating to each lesson. The original thought of each student is important and significant and the form of the individual production may also reflect the uniqueness and distinction of each contributor. Each one is encouraged to regard his own reflections about the lesson as most valuable and important to understanding his American Christian heritage and its significance to one's daily life.

The following quotation appears in Emma Willard's article "Study of American History" on page 405 of *Christian History*.

"Each individual is to himself the centre of his own world; and the more intimately he connects his knowledge with himself, the better will it be remembered, and the more effectually can it be rendered in after life subservient to his purposes . . ."

In our study of the Christian concepts upon which our nation is founded we shall continue to discover the individual nature of Christian self-government. We can take possession of our own Christian history of America by taking the same steps which the Pilgrims and colonists took as they clarified their conception of government over a one-hundred-and-fifty-year period. We, too, can turn, as they did, to a study of the Bible, for at the end of this 150 years they were able to establish a God-based government because they understood the Christian idea of man and government. We, too, must become Pilgrims, wroughting out our Christianity in every phase of our living—in our economy, our society, our education—evidencing Christian self-government, and as a way of educating ourselves. We must live our Christian character, in every avenue of our life practice.

In the study of *Christian History of the Constitution* each individual can reconstruct his Christian past and build his Christian present by identifying the areas in which the Christian idea of man and Christian self-government may be active. There is no phase of American life wherein Christian principles cannot enter in.

Each student of *Christian History* may ask himself or herself the following:

"Where in my home life, my school life or my business life, can I apply the principles of the Christian idea of man and government?"

309

Step Seven: What Identifies America as a Christian Nation?

Each lesson will be concluded by a brief review of the relationship of America to Christianity. America's divine destiny will be identified and the importance of her present history to every Christian American. Just as the Founding Father generation related the Bible to government, as they did to every aspect of life, so we must again "*search the Scriptures*" for our direction and purpose in present history.

Where can you find indications in the text for the following statements:

1. America has a divine destiny to bring forth Christianity's form of government. (See lesson, pages 1 and 2, and also pages 27 and 28, *Christian History*)
2. The Christian idea of man makes the State exist for Christian man.
3. John Milton and John Locke based their work on political liberty upon Christianity and prepared the way for the appearance of these rights in our American Christian form of government.

The Chain of Christianity Moves Westward

Lesson Two

Step One: Concepts for Observation

Each Continent has a Special Role in Christian History

"*The conclusion is irresistible - - that the entire globe is a grand organism, every feature of which is the outgrowth of a definite plan of the all-wise Creator for the edification of the human family, and the manifestation of his own glory.*" Christian History, page 5

America's Government a Model of Christian Rights

"*There may be no literal copy or close formal imitation; but there is little doubt that the spirit and true sense of our Declaration of Independence will finally mould the structure and control the workings of all governments . . .*" Christian History, page 6

Independence and Self-Reliance are Christian Concepts

"*Our people are busy using their liberties and energies, each for his individual benefit, as is quite right and proper; since the welfare of individuals makes the prosperity of the community.*" Christian History, page 6

God-governed men Base their Freedom and Equality on the Christian "Obligation to Mutual Love"

"*The State of Nature has a Law of Nature to govern it, which obliges every one: And Reason, which is that Law, teaches all Mankind, who will but consult it, that no one ought to harm another in his Life, Health, Liberty or Possessions . . .*" John Locke, Christian History, page 58:6

311

The Christian Idea of Man Moves Westward

"In this way a continuous growth has been secured that impresses on advancing culture the same unity, from first to last, that we see in the growth and mental development of the individual man." Christian History, page 7

The American System of Self-Government Ennobles Manhood

". . . So America adopts the children of all lands only to return a manhood ennobled by a sense of its own dignity through the practice of a system of self-government which improves the condition and promotes the interest of each while it produces harm to none." Christian History, page 8

America's Christian Colonial Policy

"America, then, will colonize Ideas, extensively, when her institutions are thoroughly matured." Christian History, page 9

Step Two: Reading for "Leading Ideas"

Consider the following statements before reading the assignment:

We can either interpret history as the story of autonomous man striving for progress and achievement, or we can see God's plan at work, moving men and nations towards salvation through CHRIST.

Each link of Christianity's Chain on page 6A of *Christian History* promoted the Christian idea of man and government as Christianity moved westward. Greece and Rome each contributed ideas which later became established upon a Christian basis and appeared in our American form of government. What aspect of man's political development came from Greece? Upon what was the Roman structure of government based?

What did mankind have to recognize before the Chain of Christianity could come to the continent of America? All of the advances of mankind could not bring about permanent liberty and political freedom until there was the willingness to accept what had been stated in the first century of Christianity.

Step Three: Reading Assignment

312 *Read pages 3–9 of Text*, Christian History

Step Four: Questions for Invention

1. The United Nations' Declaration of Human Rights sets forth the rights, privileges and benefits which all people should receive. Contrast this premise with the statement on page 248A from the Declaration of Independence. What was the source of the *human rights* referred to on page 5 of the text? Are *"rights"* human? What is the "living rock" upon which America is founded?

2. One meaning of the word "secure" is, "To insure, as property." Locke uses the word "preservation", a meaning of which is "To uphold; to sustain." Why is it economically more beneficial for the community if the individual sustains his own Life and Liberty, his own "Pursuit of Happiness"? When does "Welfare" become the largest item on County, State and National budgets?

3. Why does the Law of Nature, which Locke calls "the Will of God", begin with *"self-preservation"* as the first step to fulfilling the *"Obligation to mutual Love amongst Men"*? What is the Scriptural basis for this concept? Why does the Welfare State trespass the Commandments?

4. The history of the world has been evaluated in terms of the freedom and progress of individual man. Why is spiritual freedom a condition of man's progress? See the first links in the Chain of Christianity on page 6A. What is the foundation stone of all law and government?

5. Greece and Rome have always been regarded as the highest civilizations which man ever produced. Account for their failure to perpetuate themselves.

6. The interest of the Greeks and Romans in both the intellectual and political life of man had in it one fatal omission which is basic to republican government and was clearly represented in "the profound yet simple precepts of Jesus Christ." What was this primary concern which Calvin made the basis of his civil government?

7. Guyot, page 4 of *Christian History* states that "America seems destined to furnish the most complete expression of the Christian civilization." Bancroft on page 8 of *Christian History*, after enumerating the peoples of the world who have come to New and Free America speaks of the *"common contributions of character, energy and activity to the support and enlargement of a common country."* After reading Guyot, the geographer, page 4, and Bancroft, the historian, pages 8 and 9, is there agreement as to what constitutes the greatness of America? What is the source of America's great progress and wealth? Was the *unity* and *brotherhood* to which these writers refer the *result* of American geography and due to the structure of the continent, or was there another factor which was the "common ground"?

8. Why does self-government *ennoble manhood*? See quotations of John Locke and James Wilson on page 282A.

9. What ideas has America *"colonized"* and where may they be seen in other parts of the world?

313

10. Does America need to look outside herself for that which will stimulate the growth of her economy, the extension of her science, the enhancement of her self-government, the promotion of individual progress? What is the great resource she has always had at hand by which she may, in the words of Bancroft, page 9, *"reconstruct herself within herself"?*

Step Five: Study of Concepts

A leading concept in this lesson is the flowering and ennobling of manhood in the Christian setting of America. The Chain of Christianity culminating on these shores in the Christian idea of man and government brought forth a freer, fuller development of the individual. America became the *"promised land"* of individual freedom and opportunity and drew many who recognized that man had inherent rights which were a divine inheritance from the Creator. Here on this continent these rights were to be wrought upon the anvil of self-government as men learned that understanding *internal* government as the government of man by God, through CHRIST, the *external* government becomes representative of the *internal* and produces the conditions which insure or *secure* the rights already belonging to man.

Individualism which is not born of Christianity represents autonomous man whose history originates biologically and terminates environmentally. Man as Christianity brings him forth is God-governed, through CHRIST, but his success depends upon individual responsibility, individual effort, individual achievement. Truly, *"work out your own salvation"* is an American Christian tradition. It is the basis of our American way of life, producing the self-reliance and independence which enables men and women to live rich, productive lives.

The following references enlarge our understanding of the historical importance of the concepts in this lesson.

"A Degree of Freedom in the Individual". American commonwealth based upon the Christian element of intelligent self-direction. Read pages 148–150

"The American Imbued with a Spirit of Individual Freedom". The individual creates "his own proper sphere of action as the unit of a free State". Protests of the Colonists of 1760 against foreign control. Read pages 292 through paragraph on top of page 293

"The American Mind Alert to Natural Rights and Constitutional Law". England's Declaratory Resolves challenged the Whig Principles of Republicanism based upon "the Christian idea of man". Read pages 298–302 to end of section

The Colonists Carry Out Their Convictions in Economics. "Patriots use and wear American manufactures". Fundamental differences between England and America

314

upon the application of the "rights of Englishmen". Read pages 313–315 to end of section

Boston Platform of Christian Civil Rights. Samuel Adams defines the rights of the Colonists as men, Christians and subjects with faith that "the cause would make friends". Read page 321 to top of page 323

"The Christian Idea Moulding American Institutions". "This people . . . were animated by a love of liberty and a spirit of personal independence unknown to the great body of the people of Europe". Read page 344 main paragraph

"Colonists Envision a Country Founded on 'The Christian Idea of Man' ". The Christian geography of America was its inspiration in the shaping and founding of a republic. Read page 348, last paragraph to page 349, end of second paragraph

Christian Principles of the Declaration of Independence. The Christian idea of man accepted as the basis of political institutions. Read page 359, last paragraph

Step Six: Original Thought

The following quotation from page 94:135 of *Christian History* is from John Locke's discussion "Of the Extent of Legislative Power":

"Thus the Law of Nature stands as an Eternal Rule to all Men, Legislators, *as well as others. The* Rules *that they make for other Men's Actions must, as well as their own, and other Men's Actions, be conformable to the Law of Nature, i.e. to the Will of God. of which that is a Declaration, and the* Fundamental Law of Nature Being the Preservation of Mankind, *no Human Sanction can be good, or valid against it"*.

Bancroft speaks on page 6 of "the beneficent action of natural law" to which American citizens can "surrender the whole round of human life" when they have learned how to achieve "that minimum of governmental interference with the efforts and interests of the citizens".

Describe the functioning of our economy, our education and our cultural arts if left to the *"beneficient action of natural law"*—*"the Will of God"*.

The Christian idea of man and government as revealed in the first century culminated in America where the individual under God became the sovereign, or governor of his own affairs, including the establishment of government. This freedom and independence was only achieved through Christianity and only in this country has it ever so truly related the independence of the individual to independence through government.

"The self-government which developed and is recognized in the Republic is not simply a   315

custom, in the units termed municipalities or States, of managing their local affairs; but a degree of freedom in the individual to engage in the various pursuits of life, unrecognized elsewhere at the period when the Republic was formed, and yet unknown where centralization prevails . . ." Christian History, page *149*

As you study the Chain of Christianity on page 6A of the text, *Christian History*, what do you consider were some particularly *significant contributions* which brought about this fulfillment of Christian self-government in America?

Step Seven: What Identifies America as a Christian Nation?

Can you support the following statements from the text of this lesson?

1. The American continent was designed to play a role of Christian unity in the "definite plan of the all-wise Creator".
2. America *ennobles manhood* through Christian self-government.
3. The Chain of Christianity has moved westward through history to culminate in "New and Free America".

The Principle of Representation

Lesson Three

Step One: Concepts to Be Observed

"The Oriental Method of Nation-Making"

"... conquest without incorporation. *A tribe grows to national dimensions by conquering and annexing its neighbors, without admitting them to a share in its political life.*" Christian History, *page 11*

"The Roman Method of Nation-Making"

"... conquest with incorporation, but without representation. *The secret of Rome's wonderful strength lay in the fact that she incorporated the vanquished peoples into her own body politic.*" Christian History, *page 12*

"The English Method of Nation-Making"

"*it contains* the principle of representation. *For this reason, though like all nation-making it was in its early stages attended with war and conquest, it nevertheless does does not necessarily require war and conquest in order to be put into operation. Of the other two methods war was an essential part.*" Christian History, *page 13*

"No Taxation Without Representation"

"*The fundamental principles of political freedom is 'no taxation without representation'; you must not take a farthing of my money without consulting my wishes as to the use that shall be made of it.*" Christian History, *page 15*

Man is God's Property

"For Men being all the Workmanship of one Omnipotent, and infinitely wise Maker: All the Servants of one Sovereign Master, sent into the World by his Order, and about his Business, they are his Property, whose Workmanship they are, made to last during his, not one anothers Pleasure." John Locke, Christian History, *page 58*

The "End of Government is the Preservation of Property"

"The great and chief End *therefore, of Mens uniting into Commonwealths, and putting themselves under Government,* is the Preservation of their Property." Christian History, *page 91, paragraph 124.* John Locke

"Man has a *Property* in his Own *Person*"

"Though the Earth, and all inferior Creatures be common to all Men, yet every Man has a Property *in his own* Person: *This no body has any right to but himself. The* Labour *of his Body, and the* Work *of his Hands, we may say, are properly his. Whatsoever then he removes out of the State that Nature hath provided, and left it in, he hath mixed his* Labour *with, and joyned to it something that is his own, and thereby makes it his* Property." Christian History, *page 64, paragraph 27.* John Locke

The Property of My Consent

"Men *therefore* in Society having Property, *they have such a right to the Goods, which by the Law of the Community are theirs, that no Body hath a right to take their Substance or any part of it from them without their own Consent; without this they have no* Property at all. *For I have truly no* Property *in that, which another can by right take from me, when he pleases, against my Consent."* Christian History, *page 95, paragraph 138.* John Locke

Step Two: Reading for "Leading Ideas"

"The Freedom *then of Man, and Liberty of acting according to his own Will, is* grounded on *his having Reason, which is able to instruct him in that* Law *he is to govern himself by, and make him know how far he is left to the* Freedom *of his own Will. To turn him loose to an unrestrain'd Liberty, before he has Reason to guide him, is not the allowing him the privilege of his Nature to be Free; but to thrust him out amongst Brutes, and abandon him to a State as wretched, and as much beneath that of a Man, as theirs."* Christian History, *page 73, paragraph 63.* John Locke

318   The primitive, pagan methods of building nations reflected a lack of knowledge of

man. Mankind had little regard for the individual—for the property of his person or his rights. Christianity brought knowledge of SALVATION and a new appreciation for the individual and his equality before God. As this understanding of "the right to freedom being the gift of God Almighty" became known its effect was felt.

Christ Jesus said, *"Ye shall know the truth, and the truth shall make you free."* As men came to know themselves through CHRIST as created in the Divine image, the spirit of independence and liberty began to assert itself in the world.

As the Roman Empire united the Mediterranean world what evidence of the *leaven* of the Christian idea of man and government made itself felt as it permeated the "whole vast structure"? What factor became more important than *"the glory that was Greece and the grandeur that was Rome"*?

To "achieve national unity on a grand scale, without weakening the sense of personal and local independence" is to identify the *"centre of power"*. What is man's *"centre of power"* under Christianity and how is it expressed as government?

Step Three: Reading Assignment

Read pages 10 through 15 and top of page 16 in Text, Christian History of the Constitution

Step Four: Questions for Invention

1. Fiske's statement on page 10 of the text, Christian History, conveys a valuable description of the *"political art"*:

   "Skill in the political art is the fruit of the ages of intellectual and moral discipline . . ."

This description of the art needed to build nations is worthy of consideration. Why is the Christian needed to play a significant role in the field of political leadership? Does *politics* come to have a new significance when regarded as a political art based upon *Christian principles*?

2. Why does Fiske put such stress upon *individual conduct* in his reference to the study of the political history of "nation-making"?

3. The Oriental method of nation-making consisted of an alliance of closely related tribes who used their alliance to conquer and enslave neighboring peoples. What parallels of *"conquest by annexation"* have we seen in the modern world? Why does enslavement violate the basic Christian concepts of property as stated by John Locke?

4. The Roman method of nation-making broke down "the ancient barriers of

religion, speech, and custom" and brought large numbers of differing peoples together to share the "material and spiritual benefits of Roman civilization". Why did the Roman Empire resemble the structure of the United Nations? In what ways does the United Nations violate the foundations "of a common Christendom, furnished with a common stock of ideas concerning man's relation to God and the world, and acknowledging a common standard of right and wrong"?

5. While Roman citizenship seemed to raise "human life to a much higher plane" what seeds of the Dark Ages were actually being planted? What basic principle was constantly being violated by this "One World" government?

6. An individual is not truly "represented" in a government in which he has no part. Thus, except for the ruling classes in Rome, all other men had no voice in the laws that governed them. What was the Roman concept of power which enabled them to extend Roman rule at a distance from the central source of power?

7. What is the difference between the Greek concept of a union of federated city-states and the Roman concept of the union of many nations and peoples under one Empire?

8. Unity from the *top down* or centralization absorbs the political life of the parts. Unity "*of the spirit*" creates a responsible and self-respecting citizenry and permits growth of the parts thus strengthening the whole. Why is America a unique and outstanding example of *federation*? What is the dual aspect of American government?

9. As "the servants of one Sovereign Master, sent into the World by his Order, and about his Business" men are God's representatives. Why does the Christian idea of man and government bring about a demand for representative government? Why does monarchy deny God's government through Christ?

10. Primary assemblies do not generally carry the representative principle far enough. How did England carry the Teutonic idea farther?

11. The *fundamental principle of representation* rests upon the Christian concept of the rights and equality of each individual before God. These "rights" are man's chief property and men unite to preserve their property under representative government—government which represents each man equally. Therefore man's rights, his person, his property cannot be taken from him without his consent—either personally given or through a representative of his voice. What is the basis for the Christian's active participation in government as found in tracing *consent* or *agreement* through Scripture?

12. When we permit the state to "*seize upon the fruits of other people's labor*" through excessive taxation we are permitting the growth of a "superior caste" in our society—those supported by the funds of the state—funds which represent "fruits of other people's labor". This "oppresses with frightful cruelty" those who create the *productivity* of our economy by their "labor"—the investment of their property—time, talents or "talents". It further saps the *initiative*

and *energy* of those living on the "fruits" of other people's toil "in what has been aptly termed Oriental luxury . . ." Freedom from slavery—be that freedom political or economic—demands the same *vigilance* it requires to be a Christian. The *"work of the Lord cannot be done by the listless or the slothful."* Why is taxation *without* representation un-Christian?

Step Five: Study of Concepts

Liberty brings Responsibility. One of the great differences between a *republic* and a *democracy* lies in the concept of *individual responsibility* rather than *collective responsibility.* In a democracy *concensus* is of primary concern. In a republic concern for the *representation* of *differing* positions is safeguarded. In a further study of the subject of representative government watch for individual responsibility.

Montesquieu on Representative Government. Read 138 for comment on Montesquieu's work, *"Laws: Indestructible Foundation Grounded in Christianity."*

Read pages 134–136 to marginal note *"Judiciary least"*. These pages give the background of representative government and discuss the "representatives". Note particularly last paragraph on page 135.

John Locke on Equal and Proportionate Representation. Read pages 100 and 101, paragraphs 157 and 158.

This reminds us of the marginal note in our lesson on page 15 *"Eternal Vigilance is the Price of Liberty"*. Also on the same page the admonition *"the work of the Lord cannot be done by the listless or the slothful"*, reminds us that representative government begins with Christian self-government, the government of Christianity.

Connecticut Republic—Early Model for the United States of America. Read pages 252–257. The development of a Christian republic and the representative system devised to preserve the rights of the people. Note especially section #8 in the "Fundamental Orders of Connecticut" discussing the choosing of deputies or representatives of the people. Also, note section #11, wherein is set forth *"proportionate taxation with equal representation"*.

Locke on the "Power to Lay and Levy Taxes on the People". Read page 96, paragraph 140, "The Fundamental Law of Property".

The Little Government of the Town Shares in Making Up the Great Government of the State. Read page 275, middle paragraph beginning "We have seen what a great part taxation plays in the business of government . . ."

John Locke on the Original Right of Representation in Government. Read pages 91, 92, Chapter IX, "Of the Ends of Political Society and Government".

Step Six: Original Thought

The problem of delegating the responsibility and power of government has always been a problem. Moses first encountered it when he sat to judge the people and he discovered that he could not fulfill all the demands upon his time. It was then that Jethro, Moses' father-in-law, advised him to delegate some of the responsibility of government to qualified men:

"Moreover thou shalt provide out of all the people able men, such as fear God, men of truth, hating covetousness; and place such over them, to be rulers of thousands, and rulers of hundreds, rulers of fifties, and rulers of tens: And let them judge the people at all seasons: and it shall be, that every great matter they shall bring unto thee, but every small matter they shall judge: so shall it be easier for thyself, and they shall bear the burden with thee." Exodus 18:21, 22.

The government of a nation rests upon the *qualities of character* which *represent* us. Individual citizens choose (elect) the men and women who will represent them at every level of *"representative"* government. One meaning of *represent* is *"to stand in the place of"*. Thus, in essence, we are electing representatives who will stand in our place for us because our time and commitments may not permit us to be in the exact spot where certain aspects of government are being transacted. But we are there because our representatives are standing in our place for us. How important then for us to choose those who will stand for us—as us.

This problem of qualification for public office has always been a concern to Christians in America. For 150 years before the American Revolution our men of the pulpit discussed the principles of government and the moral qualifications requisite for leadership. There are many notable passages by the clergy of Christian America in the pages of *Christian History*. These may be found on pages 372–390.

Here are some specific references to the qualities of a good ruler: Read page 379 first paragraph beginning on page 379. Read pages 396–397 *"Christian Morality in Leadership"*. Read page 416, beginning, "America has furnished to the world the character of Washington . . ." through page 417. Read page 205, second paragraph beginning on the page, to end on page 206—a discussion of the Pilgrim character under hardship.

How Can a Christian Today Bear Witness to Christ in Government?

1. Discuss or write how you would represent the government of God through CHRIST if you were a representative elected to stand for your fellow Christians. How would you choose someone to *stand for you*—to represent you?
2. Discuss or write an account of good government from the Scriptures and give special consideration to the specific *qualities of character* which were in evidence.

Step Seven: What Identifies America as a Christian Nation?

1. Man is God's property (Locke page 58, par. 6) and the end of government is the preservation of property. See page 248A, *Declaration*.
2. "No taxation without representation". No one has a right to my property without my consent. The Christian covenant becomes the basis of representative government. See page 204, *"The Mayflower Compact"*.
3. Christian morality is the basis of public office and Christians must select carefully only those men and women who represent the highest Christian virtues to re-present them. (See page 364B, *Samuel Adams Writes on Liberty:* Year 1750–Age 28)

The Republicanism
of Christianity

Lesson Four

Step One: Concepts to Be Observed

Christian Unity

"*In the beginning, Christianity was simply Gospel. Ecclesiastical organization was not the cause, but the effect of life. Churches were constituted by the spontaneous association of believers. Individuals and families, drawn toward each other by their common trust in Jesus the Christ, and their common interest in the good news concerning the kingdom of God, became a community united, not by external bonds, but by the vital force of distinctive ideas and principles.*" Christian History, *page 16*

The Primitive Church a Local Institution

"*Each local church was complete in itself, and was held responsible to Christ for its own character, and the character of those whom it retained in its fellowship . . .*" Christian History, *page 17*

Separation of Church and State

"*The men of the new party, instead of remaining in the Church of England to reform it, boldly withdrew themselves from that ecclesiastico-political organization, denouncing that and all other so-called national churches as institutions unknown to the law and mind of Christ.*" Christian History, *pages 23, 24*

The Puritan Separatist Becomes a Pilgrim

324 "*All had gained the intelligence that comes from the diligent study of the Bible, and all*

were honest and earnest believers in the Christ of the New Testament. Such were the men and the women who were thus driven out of their native England, yet hunted and intercepted in their flight, as if they were criminals escaping from justice. Why did they suffer the spoiling of their goods, arrest, imprisonment, exile? . . . They had caught from the Bible the idea of a church independent alike of the pope and the queen, independent of Parliament as well as of prelates, and dependent only on Christ. It was their mission to work out and organize that idea . . ." Christian History, *page 27*

The Republicanism of Christianity

"Our own De Witt Clinton said, 'Christianity, in its essence, its doctrines, and its forms, is republican' . . ." Christian History, *page 28*

Step Two: Reading for "Leading Ideas"

According to historians of the New Testament, the churches of the first century of Christianity were local self-governing churches with a bond of union which sprang from their unity with CHRIST. Within one hundred years the organization and government of the churches had changed from *congregational* to *episcopal*. Christian healing, widely practiced during the first century, began to be replaced by dependence upon external methods.

". . . *The society was purely voluntary, and every church so constituted was strictly independent of all others in the conduct of its worship, the admission of its members, the exercise of its discipline, the choice of its officers, and the entire management of its affairs. They were, in a word, independent republics . . ."* (Church Polity of the Pilgrims, Christian History, *page 270B*)

As the problems of growth increased the churches departed from "the simplicity that is in Christ" and "the principle of equality and fraternity began to be superseded by the spirit of authority and subordination".

The English Reformation was an attempt to recover primitive Gospel. It brought about a recognition that "voluntary conformity to the rules and principles given in the New Testament" could come about by individuals accepting the responsibility for personal reformation "*under the guidance of the Scriptures*". This led eventually to the refusal of some Christians to accept a national or state church. The attempt to purify this national church led to the separation of some "*conscientious objectors*" from the organized national church to a reorganized local church where the preaching of individual repentance brought about a revival of enthusiasm for primitive gospel and Christian behavior. Those who took this step and who would not conform to the national church organization were persecuted.

325

From primitive Christianity the Pilgrims learned their idea of the completeness and independence of the local church body. For this idea they were driven from their native land and came, at last, to these shores to found the great governing principle of Christianity—Christian self-government, which became the basis of our American Constitutional government.

Step Three: Reading Assignment

Read pages 16–28 of Text, Christian History

Step Four: Questions for Invention

1. What does the New Testament reveal of the constitution or general fundamental principles of government—the polity—of the primitive churches?

    "Were the whole Christian world to revert back to the original model, how far more simple, uniform, and beautiful would the church appear, and how far more agreeable to the ecclesiastical polity instituted by the holy apostles". 1783—Ezra Stiles, *President of Yale College*

2. What united the first Christians? What form did their union take?
3. Ecclesiastical organization in the beginning of Christianity was the *effect* not the *cause* of Christian unity so spontaneous and so vital was the conviction of the believers. The increase of the *external* bonds of Christian unity seemed to diminish the *internal* spark and vital force. What form of government keeps the internal and external church in balance?
4. The Christian commonwealth was a local republic. Each member accepted the responsibility to govern himself according to the teachings of Christ Jesus. What caused the change in the republican form of church government and when did the "self-governing Christian assemblies" permit the "transfer of power" from the individual to a group or ecclesiastical hierarchy?

    ". . . The principal voice was that of the people, or of the whole body of Christians; for even the apostles themselves inculcated, by their example, that nothing of any moment was to be done or determined on but with the knowledge and consent of the brotherhood. The assembled people elected their own rulers and teachers, or by their free consent received such as were nominated to them . . . In a word, the people did every thing that is proper for those in whom the supreme power of the community is vested . . . Among all the members of the church, of whatever class or condition, there was the most perfect equality" page 270B, Christian History

326

5. The early church did not protect itself from the loss of its local independence and liberty. What are the arguments, used throughout history, which enable power to accumulate in the hands of the few to govern the many?

6. Why would the individual churches have kept their local autonomy if they had been "*distributed*" rather than "*divided*" into a "plurality of assemblies"?

7. Why was the extending of the mother church from its administration of one city church to include all believers in the suburbs the beginning of an ecclesiastical monarchy?

8. How many years did it take before Protestantism proclaimed again the independence of the local church as a self-governing republic, united to the universal church in bonds of faith, hope and charity?

9. Frothingham on page 1 of *Christian History*, characterizes the Reformation as "the assertion of the principle of individuality, or of true spiritual freedom". Why was the recovery of "the primitive Gospel" a key to political freedom?

10. How did Puritanism arise in England? What was the position of the Puritans towards church government? Why is monarchy an episcopal form of government?

11. What part did "*freedom of conscience*" play in dividing the Puritans into two positions regarding church reformation?

12. Cartwright's lectures on "church government as given in the Scriptures" defined the Church-State wherein the church government and the civil government are controlled by the same authority. When government or sovereignty begins from "*the top down*" power is centralized and the freedom of the individual becomes dependent upon those who can make decisions affecting him and with whom he has no voice or influence. When government begins from the "*grass roots*"—with sovereignty in the individual—then government becomes representative of all equally. Why was the assumption upon which Cartwright based his theory that "an independent Christian nation is an independent Christian church" false?

13. What caused men to doubt that the National Church was not in accord with Scriptural church polity? What position did the new party of men take in regard to the State or National Church?

14. What effect did the recognition of "*individual responsibility to God*" have upon the lives of men? Did this recognition come to them by government proclamation or through reform legislation? How did the Word of God reach these individuals?

15. After the Puritans determined that the Church of England was "a positively anti-Christian institution" what steps did they take to separate themselves and reform or re-establish "churches according to the mind of Christ"?

16. Why is the "church that is in the house of William Brewster" called the "germ of New England"?

17. What was the most outstanding quality of the Puritan Separatists which they had in common with each other and which made them uncommon in their clear

convictions?

18. In what ways were the Pilgrims like the Christians of the first century? Why were they willing to go into exile?

19. The Christian idea of man declaring that "all are equal in the sight of God" is the foundation of republican government. Why do Gospel principles "prepare the people to govern themselves"? What does 'Lords over God's heritage' mean?

20. Why is government which operates "with the knowledge and consent of those govered" truly Christian and truly republican? In what important decision did the first Christian brethren participate? What did their participation mean?

21. What examples do Mosheim and Neander provide that the early church acted upon the basis of individual covenant or consent of the governed?

Step Five: Study of Concepts

1. The congregational form of government is based upon the Christian idea of man. (See page 2 of *Christian History*) The equality of all men before God puts equal responsibility for government in each individual. The concept "the State ought to exist for man" puts the source of government in each individual. See *Christian History*, pages 270B and 270C, numbers 1 and 7.

2. The congregational form of government is based upon the Christian pattern of *individual covenant* and *voluntary consent* of the governed. See *Christian History*, pages 270B and 270C, numbers 2 and 4.

3. In New England the congregational form of government of the church brought forth the congregational form of government of the civil society. By representing one individual completely, the state represents equally all men and the sanctity of the individual is recognized as the basis of government. See *Christian History*, pages 270B and 270C, numbers 2, 4, 8, 10, 11, and 12.

4. Congregational government begins from the bottom up—from the "*grass roots*" and derives its sovereignty from the individual. It is *republican* rather than *democratic* in that it is government which is *representative of every individual*, rather than of a *majority*. See *Christian History*, pages 270B and 270C, numbers 4, 10, 13, and 14.

Episcopal Form of Government

1. The definition of Episcopal form of government:
". . . In church government supreme authority resides in a body of bishops, and not in any individual . . ." See *Christian History*, pages 270D and 270E, numbers 1, 2, and 3.

2. Representation is appointive from the top down, rather than elective from the

bottom up. See *Christian History*, pages 270D and 270E, numbers 4, 7, and 12.

3. Sovereignty resides in centralization of authority in a structure called the "*state*," which determines the greatest good for the greatest number. The individual is represented as a *part* of the whole—rather than the completeness of each individual, expressed by every individual, wholly represented by the state. See *Christian History*, pages 270D and 270E, numbers 1 and 6.

4. The government of Virginia imaged forth English constitutional form of monarchy. ". . . The Virginians were Royalists in their sympathies, and firm supporters of Church and State". The county system of Virginia represented the unit of representation for the national government at the local level. See *Christian History*, pages 270D and 270E, numbers 5, 9, 10, 11, and 12.

Locke on Christian Unity—"The Law of Nature, i.e. The Will of God Obligates". Locke describes the Law of Nature as the foundation of individual sovereignty and equality, "Wherein all the Power and Jurisdiction is Reciprocal, no one having more than another". Locke includes Hooker's comment upon equality as being the "Foundation of that Obligation to mutual Love amongst Men," on which he builds the duties they owe one another. Read *Christian History*, page 58, paragraphs 4 and 5. Locke refers to the Law of Nature as the Will of God on page 94, line 20.

American Christian Unity—England Punishes and the Colonies Unite. Read *Christian History*, pages 335–339, Boston Port Bill.

The Pilgrim Wanted Individual Liberty. Read *Christian History*, page 182, first paragraph.

The Growth of Self-Government and Republicanism in the Colonies. Read *Christian History*, page 288, last paragraph through first sentence of last paragraph, page 289.

Locke Lays the Axe at the Argument That Monarchy is Divine. Read *Christian History*, page 88, paragraph 112.

Step Six: Original Thought

1. The following quotation appears on pages 2 and 302 of Volume II of *Christian History* entitled "*Self-Government with Union*", compiled by Verna M. Hall.

"He gives them (the disciples) a bond of union, by which they should always be linked to Him and to each other in the principle of love. The followers of great Teachers and Rabbis had their distinctive marks. Here was the distinctive Christian Mark, which all men should be able to read. It is instructive that the characteristic mark of Christianity should thus be asserted by its Founder to consist, not in any formulary or signs, but in the love which asserts the brotherhood of man. The apolo-

329

gists of the first centuries delighted in appealing to the striking fact of the common love of Christians, which was a new thing in the history of mankind; and while the Church has sometimes forgotten the characteristic, the world never has. By their love for each other, for mankind, for God, is it known or denied that men who call themselves Christians are really Christ's disciples."

Write a short sketch or tell about three people who you believe bear the Christian Mark. How can this mark be read—or made visible to others? What qualities do these people express and how are these qualities known? Would you care to describe your own efforts to bear the Christian Mark?

2. Can you think of at least three areas in which you have a *"unity of common ideas and principles"* with other individuals? What is accomplished by working with those who think and feel as you do about something?

3. What advantages are there to keeping any group of organized individuals local and independent? How does increased organization often change *"independence"* to *"dependence"*?

4. Today the state and national government have stepped into the life of the individual to help him solve many of his problems.
   When do you think the individual should let an organized agency or a governmental department perform a service for him? Does a Christian have a moral obligation to take responsible action for specific activities of his own life? What happens to the local self-government of the individual when he relinquishes, or gives up, local control of his life in some areas.

5. How can the following statement be applied as a *yardstick* to you as an individual in your evaluation of your own freedom and effective self-government?

"No organization that takes any thing away from the completeness of a local church, or in any degree forms a complement to it, or to its authority, has any warrant in Scripture." (Christian History, *page 270B*)

Step Seven: What Identifies America as a Christian Nation?

1. The Pilgrims established a republican form of church and civil government patterned after their recovery of the Primitive Gospel, but each separate and complete.

2. "The Pilgrim wanted liberty for himself and his wife and little ones, and for his brethren, to walk with God in a Christian life as the rules and motives of such a life were revealed to him from God's Word. For that he went into exile; for that he crossed the ocean; for that he made his home in a wilderness." (Page 182, *Christian History*)

3. The Boston Port Bill, designed to punish Boston for the Tea Party, served to

move all of the sister colonies to unite in a spirit of resistance to an invasion of their own Christian rights. It brought forth a spirit of Christian unity which came from the *"unity of common ideas and principles."* It evoked both spiritual support and material aid; also a recognition of a common aggressor.

The conviction of the Pilgrims that they were "instruments" in the Hands of God persisted throughout our history as Christians of different generations took up the challenge of Christian liberty. This inward conviction is the true patriotism which will stand for God and country and know the principles of that patriotism.

Samuel Adams, writing as Vindex, in the Boston Gazette, June 12, 1780, says: "The people of this country were not driven to take up arms, they did it voluntarily in defence of their liberty. They properly considered themselves as called by God, and warranted by Him, to encounter every hazard in the common cause of Man."

The Bible in English

Lesson Five

Step One: Concepts to Be Observed

The Wycliffe Bible—1380

"Wycliffe's Teutonic love of truth, of freedom and of independence . . . moved him to give his countrymen the open Scripture as their best safeguard and protection . . . and it was the development of the English language into a literary medium of expression . . . which first made a people's Bible possible . . . And if Wycliffe represents a new movement in our literature, so too does he represent a new departure in our religious history. For the rise of Lollardy, in so far as it was a religious movement, marks the earliest break in the . . . continuity of Latin Christianity in England." Christian History, *page 29*

The Tyndale Bible—1526

"Tyndale is the true father of our present English Bible . . . It has been estimated that, of Tyndale's work as above specified, our Bibles retain at the present day something like eighty per cent, in the Old Testament, and ninety per cent, in the New. If this estimate may be accepted no grander tribute could be paid to the industry, scholarship, and genius of the pioneer whose indomitable resolution enabled him to persevere in labours prolonged through twelve long years of exile from the land that in his own words he so 'loved and longed for' with the practical certainty of a violent death staring him all the while in the face." Christian History, *page 30*

The Great Bible—1539

332 *"Within twelve months of the martyrdom of its author at Vilvorde, (Tyndale) the*

translation which 'either with glosses (marginal notes) or without' had been denounced, abused, and burnt at St. Paul's, was now, under its assumed name (the Matthew Bible) formerly approved by the King's grace, and published, together with Coverdale's Bible, under the shelter of a royal proclamation and license . . . In April 1539, the first edition of this magnificent specimen of the art of printing was ready for publication." Christian History, *page 31*

The Genevan Bible—1559

"In many ways this edition formed a new departure and offered new attractions. Especially was this the case with regard to bulk . . . In the place of the heavy black letters to which the readers had been accustomed, there appeared the clear Roman type with which our modern press has made us familiar. The division of the chapters into verses . . . has undeniable advantages." Christian History, *page 32*

The King James Bible—1611

"In 1611 the Authorized Version, a folio volume in black-letter type, was issued to the public. It had no notes, and the interpretation of it was therefore left perfectly free . . . The predominance of Saxon words in this version is very remarkable. As compared with Latin words they actually constitute some nine-tenths of it . . . In the Lord's Prayer no less than fifty-nine words out of sixty-five are of Saxon origin . . . They had ready to hand the rich results of nearly a century of diligent and unintermittent labour in the field of Biblical study. The great lines which were to be followed had long since been marked out by Wycliffe, Tyndale, and Coverdale, while useful side-lights could be derived from the Latin and modern translations above enumerated." Christian History, *pages 35-36*

Step Two: Reading for "Leading Ideas"

It is difficult today to realize that there was ever a time when the BIBLE—our HOLY SCRIPTURES—was not available to everyone. That is why this is one of the greatest stories ever told in Christian History. So precious were the words and the teachings of CHRIST JESUS that although they were spoken in a decaying language the providence of God brought them forth:

"How beautiful upon the mountains are the feet of him that bringeth good tidings, that publisheth peace; that bringeth good tidings of good, that publisheth salvation; that saith unto Zion, Thy God reigneth!" Isaiah 52:7

CHRIST JESUS was confident that his words would be perpetuated so that the message of SALVATION might be read by all mankind. He said:

333

"Heaven and earth shall pass away: but my words shall not pass away." Luke 21:33

The story of how our Scriptures were translated into English is one all Christians should know. For only Christian love could have brought forth the Word and made it available to the individual. Despite persecution, imprisonment and martyrdom the efforts of those devoted men of God did indeed bring to us today the Book of books. The following pages tell the story of the man whose life work with the Scriptures contributed so much to making the word available to each one of us.

J. H. Merle
D'Aubigne,
*History of the
Reformation
in Europe*

The Martyrdom of William Tyndale. "The Holy Scriptures, translated, studied, circulated, and preached since the fourteenth century by Wycliffe and his disciples, became in the sixteenth century, by the publication of Erasmus's Testament, and the translations of Tyndale and Coverdale, the powerful instrument of a real evangelical revival, and created the scriptural reformation . . .

"Most of the reformers, Luther, Zwingle, Calvin, Knox, and others have acquired that name by their preachings, their writings, their struggles, and their actions. It is not so with the principal reformer of England: all his activity was concentrated in the Holy Scriptures . . .

"One man, desirous of reviving the Church of Christ in England, had made the translation of the Holy Scriptures the work of his life. Tyndale had been forced to leave his country; but he had left it only to prepare seed which, borne on the wings of the wind, was to change the wildernesses of Great Britain into a fruitful garden.

"Tyndale . . . was in prison at Vilvorde, near Brussels. In vain was he girt around with the thick walls of that huge fortress. Tyndale was free. 'There is the captivity and bondage,' he could say, 'whence Christ delivered us, redeemed and loosed us. His blood, his death, his patience in suffering rebukes and wrongs, his prayers and fastings, his meekness and fulfilling of the uttermost point of the law broke the bonds of Satan, wherein we were so strait bound.' Thus Tyndale was as truly free at Vilvorde, as Paul had been at Rome. He felt pressed to accomplish a vow made many years before. 'If God preserves my life', he had said, 'I will cause a boy that driveth a plow to know more of the Scriptures than the pope.' True Christianity shows itself by the attention it gives to Christ's little ones. It was time for Tyndale to keep his promise. He occupied his prison hours in preparing for the humble dwellers in the Gloucestershire villages and the surrounding counties, an edition of the Bible in which he employed the language and orthography used in that part of England . . .

"At that time there lived at Antwerp, as chaplain to the English merchants in that city, a young man from the county of Warwick, named Rogers, who had been educated at Cambridge, and was a little more than thirty years old. Rogers was learned, but submissive to the Romish traditions. Tyndale having made his acquaintance, asked him to help in translating the Holy Scriptures, and Rogers caught joyfully at the opportunity of employing his Greek and Hebrew. Close and constant contact with the Word of God gradually effected in him that great transformation, that total renewal of the man which is the object of redemption. 'I have found the true light in the Gospel,' he said one day to Tyndale . . . From that hour Tyndale received from Rogers the help which he had formerly received from John Fryth, that pious martyr, whose example Rogers was to follow by enduring the first under Mary, the punishment of fire. The Holy Scriptures have been written in English with the blood of martyrs—if we may so speak—the blood of Fryth, Tyndale, and Rogers: it is a crown of glory for that translation. At the moment of Tyndale's perfidious arrest, Rogers had fortunately saved the manuscript of the Old Testament, and now resolved to delay the printing no longer. When the news of this reached the Reformer in his cell at Vilvorde, it cast a gleam of light upon his latter days and filled his heart with joy. The *whole Bible*,—that was the legacy which the dying Tyndale desired to leave to his fellow-countrymen. He took pleasure in his gloomy dungeon in following with his mind's eye that divine Scripture from city to city and from cottage to cottage; his imagination pictured to him the struggles it would have to go through, and also its victories . . .

"We do not know for certain in what city Rogers printed the great English folio Bible. Hamburg, Antwerp, Marburg, Lubeck, and even Paris have been named. Extraordinary precautions were required to prevent the persecutors from entering the house where men had the boldness to print the Word of God, and from breaking the printing-presses. Tyndale had the great comfort of knowing that the whole Bible was going to be published, and that prophets, apostles, and Christ himself would speak by it after his death . . .

"This man, so active, so learned, and so truly great, whose works circulated far and wide with so much power, had at the same time within him a pure and beneficent light—the love of God and of man—which shed its mild rays on all around him. The depth of his faith, the charm of his conversation, the uprightness of his conduct, touched those who came near him. The jailer liked to bring him his food, in order to talk with him, and his young daughter often accompanied him and listened eagerly to the words of the pious Englishman. Tyndale spoke of Jesus Christ; it seemed to him that the riches of the divine Spirit were about to transform Christendom . . . The jailer, his daughter, and other members of their house were converted to the Gospel by Tyndale's life and doctrine. However dark the machinations of his enemies, they could not obscure the divine light kindled in his heart, and which *shone before men*. There was an invincible power in this Christian man. Full of hope in the final victory of Jesus Christ, he courageously trampled under foot tribulations, trials, and death itself. He believed in the victory of the Word. 'I am bound like a malefactor,' he said, 'but the Word of God is not bound.' The bitterness of his last days was changed into great peace and divine sweetness . . .

"Friday, the 6th of October, 1536 was the day that terminated the miserable but glorious life of the reformer . . . On arriving at the scene of punishment, the reformer found a numerous crowd assembled. The government had wished to show the people the punishment of a heretic, but they only witnessed the triumph of a

335

martyr. Tyndale was calm. 'I call God to record,' he could say, 'that I have never altered, against the voice of my conscience, one syllable of his Word. Nor would do this day, if all the pleasures, honors, and riches of the earth might be given me.' The joy of hope filled his heart: yet one painful idea took possession of him. Dying far from his country, abandoned by his king, he felt saddened at the thought of that prince, who had already persecuted so many of God's servants, and who remained obstinately rebellious against that divine light which everywhere shone around him. Tyndale would not have that soul perish through carelessness. His charity buried all the faults of the monarch: he prayed that those sins might be blotted out from before the face of God; he would have saved Henry VIII at any cost. While the executioner was fastening him to the post the reformer exclaimed in a loud and suppliant voice: 'Lord, open the king of England's eyes!' They were his last words. Instantly afterwards he was strangled, and flames consumed the martyr's body. His last cry was wafted to the British Isles, and repeated in every assembly of Christians. A great death crowned a great life. 'Such,' says the old chronicler, John Foxe, 'such is the story of that true servant and martyr of God, William Tyndale, who, for his notable pains and travail, may well be called the *Apostle of England in this our later Age.*'

"His fellow-countrymen profited by the work of his life. As early as 1526 more than twenty editions of Tyndale's New Testament had been circulated over the kingdom, and others had followed them. It was like a mighty river continually bearing new waters to the sea. Did the reformer's death dry them up suddenly? No. A greater work still was to be accomplished: the entire Bible was ready. But could it be circulated? The king had refused his consent to the circulation of Coverdale's Bible; would he not do the same with this, and with greater reason? . . .

"Henry ran over the book: Tyndale's name was not in it, and the dedication to his Majesty was very well written. The King regarding (and not without reason) Holy Scripture as the most powerful engine to destroy the papal system, and believing that this translation would help him to emancipate England from the Romish domination, came to an unexpected resolution: he authorized the sale and the reading of the Bible throughout the kingdom . . .

"For centuries the English people had been waiting for such a permission, even from before the time of Wycliffe: and accordingly the Bible circulated widely. The impetuosity with which the living waters rushed forth, carrying with them everything they met in their course, was like the sudden opening of a huge floodgate. This great event, more important than divorces, treaties, and wars, was the conquest of England by the Reformation. 'It was a wonderful thing to see,' says an old historian. Whoever possessed the means bought the book and read it or had it read to him by others. Aged persons learnt their letters in order to study the Holy Scriptures of God. In many places there were meetings for reading; poor people clubbed their savings together and purchased a Bible, and then in some remote corner of the church they modestly formed a circle, and read the Holy Book between them . . .

"In all the towns and villages of Tyndale's country the holy pages were opened, and the delighted readers found therein those treasures of peace and joy which the martyr had known. Many cried out with him, 'We know that this Word is from God, as we know that fire burns; not because any one has told us, but because a Divine fire consumes our hearts. O the brightness of the face of Moses! O the splendor of the glory of Jesus Christ, which no veil conceals! O the inward power of the Divine word, which compels us with so much sweetness, to love and to do! O the temple of God within us, in which the Son of God dwells!' Tyndale had desired to see the world on fire by his Master's Word, and that fire was kindled."

As you study this lesson think about its relationship to the Christian founding of America. Why could our nation have not been founded without the Scriptures in English?

Step Three: Reading Assignment

Read, pages 28A through page 36 Text, Christian History

Step Four: Questions for Invention

1. Why was Wycliffe called "*the morning-star of the Reformation*"?
2. Superstition, fear, ignorance, sin kept men from religious and political liberty during the Dark Ages. The ages were dark because the Scriptures were closed to man. Only the priesthood had access to the Holy Word of God. Why did Wycliffe feel that the Scriptures would give men "*freedom*"? What kind of freedom?
3. Just as primitive Christianity brought a new way of life for men to live and love, so Wycliffe believed that men needed to study the Gospel to know how to live a Christian life. In what language was the Bible written in his time? Who owned the Bibles then in existence?
4. What political events caused a change in the language of England? Why would constant war with France tend to develop English patriotism?
5. As English became the language of the people, Wycliffe crowned it as a literary language with his translation of the Scripture from Latin into English. Not only was this an important step for the development of English literature, but also religiously it represented a most important step towards the Reformation. Name this step. Why was it like "*reform without tarrying for any*"?
6. Tyndale improved the Wycliffe Bible in what significant ways? How much of his work do we find in today's Bible?

337

7. Although the work of William Tyndale had been condemned how did it actually get into print? What was the name of this publication?

8. In 1538 the members of a church could find *"one boke of the whole Bible"*. Where was this Bible kept? Why was it chained? What was its size? Who used it?

9. What made the Genevan Bible easier to read than earlier editions? What particular feature was of great significance to those who wanted to be Bible owners?

10. The Genevan Bible increased the habit of Bible reading. What other books were being read at the time? What did they have in common with each other? What specific evidence is offered here to show that the Bible, the Word of God, was the basis of education? Why is it probable that the greatest writers of England were educated from the Bible?

11. The Hampton Court Conference of 1604 actually met to settle what Puritan petition? What was the outcome of this conference?

12. What evidence of Christian unity did the new translation bring about?

13. Who was chosen to work on the new translation? What was their first qualification? When were experts to be consulted? How were the less important clergy to contribute to the translation?

14. How long a time was spent in producing the Authorized Version? What was particularly significant for the individual Bible student in this translation? Why is this translation significantly an English translation?

Step Five: Study of Concepts

The beginnings of our American History were made by God-fearing men and women who regarded themselves as *"chosen soldiers of Christ"* whose work here was to lay *"the everlasting foundations of God's kingdom upon earth"*. Such men and women were profound students of the Scriptures and, in fact, related every act and activity of their lives to a Biblical base. Read page 391, *Christian History*.

"The Bible, The Great Political Text-Book of the Patriots". Read page 413, second paragraph, through the third paragraph on page 414, describing the Bible as the source book of government of the colonists.

In 1777 Congress authorized the importation of 20,000 copies of the Bible. Read page 375, the paragraph with marginal note *"Remarks by Thornton"*.

The Story of the First American Bible Printed in the United States. The following quotations are from the book entitled, *The Bible of the Revolution*, An Essay Concerning It by Robert R. Dearden, Jr. and Douglas S. Watson. Printed by Edwin & Robert Grabhorn for John Howell, San Francisco, 1930.

"The Bible of the Revolution is a national document, and the printing of the
Scriptures for the first time in our mother tongue in America by Robert Aitken

in Philadelphia is part of our national history.

"Seven years before Thomas Jefferson put into words the thoughts of freedom-loving Americans, Robert Aitken had come from his native Dalkeith in Scotland to settle in Philadelphia. There he set up as a bookseller and there he began the publication of 'The Pennsylvania Magazine', to which Thomas Paine often contributed, and which so ardently espoused the cause of liberty that Robert Aitken narrowly escaped arrest and subsequent detention in the British prison hulk then anchored in New York harbor.

"Before the rupture with the mother country, the Colonies had depended largely for their literature upon England, and entirely so for their Bibles in their native tongue. The Revolutionary War stopped importation, and at length the situation reached such an acute stage that the Chaplain of Congress, the Rev. Patrick Allison, D.D., placed before that body a petition praying for immediate relief. The memorial was assigned to a special committee which weighed the matter with great care, and on September 11, 1777, it reported:

". . . *that the use of the Bible is so universal and its importance so great that your committee refer the above to the consideration of Congress, and if Congress shall not think it expedient to order the importation of types and paper, the Committee recommend that Congress will order the Committee of Congress to import 20,000 Bibles from Holland, Scotland, or elsewhere, into the different parts of the States of the Union.*

"*Whereupon it was resolved accordingly to direct said Committee to import 20,000 copies of the Bible . . .*

"During the session in the fall of 1780 the demand for Bibles, and the difficulty of procuring them, was again before the Congress. Under date of October 26th, James McLene introduced the following motion, which was seconded by John Hanson, respecting the printing of the Old and New Testaments:

"*Resolved that it be recommended to such of the States who may think it convenient for them that they take proper measures to procure one or more new and correct editions of the Old and New Testament to be printed and that such states regulate their printers by law so as to secure effectually the said books from being misprinted.*

Congress recommends the states to print Testaments

"This motion which in McLene's handwriting was by order of the Congress referred to a committee.

". . . Revolutionary America without Bibles presented an impossible situation. In no country in the world was the Good Book then so relied upon. Faith in Divine Providence and the consolation and guidance of Holy Writ were necessary to all patriots in the struggle for Liberty.

Revolutionary America without Bibles

"Robert Aitken knew this, and he recognized the plight of the people of the new-born Nation who found themselves without Bibles in the English tongue. A Testament was better than no Bible at all, and during the agitation he quietly set to

339

work upon the printing of one . . .

"We may imagine Robert Aitken stealing off from his work to pass a pleasant half hour in the Coffee House where patriots from all of the Thirteen States were wont to gather. There he would rub shoulders with Signers of the Declaration of Independence: there he would talk of his fondest desire; the printing of the entire Bible in English.

"He must have received many words of encouragement, for on January 21, 1781, he had presented to the Congress a petition announcing his determination, which was duly referred to a committee of which the Rev. John Witherspoon, and Thomas McKean, both Signers, were members.

"Aitken had not only asked Congressional sanction of his great work, but had pleaded for support. What form that support was to take may be gleaned from the Committee's report which follows, is dated September 12, 1782:

"The Committee to whom was referred a Memorial of Robert Aitken, Printer, dated 21st January, 1781, respecting an edition of the Holy Scripture, report, That Mr. Aitken has, at a great expense, now finished an American edition of the Holy Scriptures in English; that the Committee have from time to time attended to his progress in the work; that they also recommended it to the two chaplains of Congress to examine and give their opinion of the execution, who have accordingly reported thereon; the recommendation and report being as follows:

"*Philadelphia, 1st September, 1782*

Reverend Gentlemen:

"*Our knowledge of your piety and public spirit leads us without apology to recommend to your particular attention the edition of the Holy Scriptures published by Mr. Aitken. He undertook this expensive work at a time when, from the circumstances of the war, an English edition of the Bible could not be imported, nor any opinion formed how long the obstruction might continue. On this account particularly he deserves applause and encouragement. We therefore wish you, Reverend Gentlemen, to examine the execution of the work, and if approved, to give it the sanction of your judgment, and the weight of your recommendation.*

"*We are, with very great respect, your most obedient humble servants.*

*James Duane
Chairman, in behalf of a
Committee of Congress on
Mr. Aitken's Memorial*

Reverend Doct. White & Revd. Mr. Duffield,
Chaplains of the United States in Congress assembled.
The Chaplain's Report

"Gentlemen

"Agreeably to your desire we have paid attention to Mr. Robert Aitken's impression *"Witnesses of the
demand for this
invaluable book"*
of the Holy Scriptures of the Old and New Testament. Having selected and examined
a variety of passages throughout the work, we are of opinion that it is executed with great
accuracy as to the sense and with as few grammatical and typographical errors as could
be expected in an undertaking of such magnitude. Being ourselves witnesses of the
demand for this invaluable book, we rejoice in the present prospect of a supply; hoping
that it will prove as advantageous as it is honorable to the gentleman who has exerted
himself to furnish it at the evident risk of his private fortune. We are, Gentlemen, Your
very respectful and humble servants,

William White
George Duffield

Philadelphia, September 10th, 1782
Honorable James Duane, Esq., Chairman, and the other
Honorable Gentlemen of the Committee of Congress
on Mr. Aitken's Memorial

"The favorable action of the Congress upon the report of the Committee charged with The Bible of the
examining into the Memorial presented by Robert Aitken may be read in the certificate Revolution
which was printed by the publisher and bound into all copies of The Bible of the Revo-
lution.

"Whereupon, Resolved,
"That the United States in Congress assembled highly approve the pious and laudable
undertaking of Mr. Aitken, as subservient to the interest of religion, as well as an in-
stance of the progress of arts in this country, and being satisfied from the above report
of his care and accuracy in the execution of the work, they recommend this edition of the
Bible to the inhabitants of the United States, and hereby authorize him to publish this
recommendation in the manner he shall think proper.

Cha. Thomson, Secy.

"The attesting signature is that of Charles Thomson, the Secretary to the Congress. The First
American Bible
"Thus was the Bible of the Revolution, now one of the world's rarest books, in English
printed by Robert Aitken in 1782 with the approval of Congress. It was entirely
American . . .

"Thirty two copies of Robert Aitken's great work are known to be in existence. Of
these but two are owned in England, and of the rest all are, as they should be, in
American possession, largely in the safe-keeping of our great libraries and historical
societies."

Step Six: Original Thought

How can *we* use the Bible as a *"political text-book"*?

Find the Biblical basis for the following political terms: *Self-government*, *Property*, *Union*

Is the word *freedom* found in the Bible?

Is there a significant point to be observed in the fact that today a word commonly used in political circles is *freedom*, not *liberty*?

What is the *cause* of freedom?

How does Locke establish the Biblical basis for *property?*

How can *unity* be considered the *cause of union?*

Step Seven: What Identifies America as a Christian Nation?

1. "The Puritan Separatist becomes a Pilgrim". See pages 26, 27.

   "They had caught from the Bible the idea of a church independent alike of the pope and the queen, independent of Parliament as well as of prelates, and dependent only on Christ. It was their mission to work out and organize that idea . . ."

2. "The Bible, the great political text-book of the patriots" pages 413, 414.

   "The Bible came with them. And it is not to be doubted, that to the free and universal reading of the Bible, in that age, men were much indebted for right views of civil liberty."

3. The Bible the basis of all government and legislation. See pages 270C and 270E

   The Bible as the source of the Ten Commandments and Christianity shown as being the basis of the governments of the parent colonies, New England and Virginia.

Christian Rights and English Law

Lesson Six

Step One: Concepts to Be Observed

"Where the Spirit of the Lord is, There is Liberty"

"*For he that is called in the Lord, being a servant, is the Lord's freeman: likewise also he that is called, being free, is Christ's servant.*" 1 Corinthians 7:22

Government by Compact or Consent of the Governed

"*This* Legislative *is not only the* Supream Power *of the Commonwealth, but sacred and unalterable in the hands where the Community have once placed it; nor can any Edict of any Body else in what form soever conceived, or by what Power soever backed, have the force and obligation of a* Law, *which has not its* Sanction from *that* Legislative, *which the publick has chosen and appointed. For without this the Law could not have that, which is absolutely necessary to its being a* Law, the Consent of the Society, *over whom no Body can have a Power to make Laws, but by their own Consent and by Authority received from them* . . ." John Locke, Christian History, *page 93:134*

"The Fundamental Law of Property"

"The Supream Power cannot take *from any Man any part of his* Property *without his own Consent. For the preservation of Property being the end of Government, and that for which Men enter into Society, it necessarily supposes and requires, that the People should* have Property . . . Men *therefore* in Society Having Property, *they have such a right to the Goods, which by the Law of the Community are theirs, that no Body hath a right to take their Substance or any part of it from them, without their own* 343

Consent; without this they have no Property *at all. For I have truly no* Property *in that which another can by right take from me, when he pleases against my Consent."* John Locke, Christian History, *page 95:138*

"No Taxation without Representation"

"For if anyone shall claim a Power to Lay *and* Levy Taxes *on the People, by his own Authority, and without such consent of the People, he thereby invades the* Fundamental Law of Property, *and subverts the end of Government. For what Property have I in that, which another may by right take, when he pleases to himself?"* John Locke, Christian History, *page 96:140*

Men are "Endowed by their Creator with Certain Unalienable Rights"

"We hold these Truths to be self-evident, that all Men are created equal, that they are endowed by their Creator with certain unalienable Rights, that among these are Life, Liberty, and the Pursuit of Happiness—That to secure these Rights, Governments are instituted among Men . . ." From the Declaration of Independence, 1776, *Christian History, page 248A*

Step Two: Reading for "Leading Ideas"

Magna Charta—1215

America's Christian establishment as a nation enabled her to do something which no other nation had ever been able to do—namely to identify the Rights of man as God-given and God-granted. This enabled America to set forth these rights and to establish Christianity's form of government—Christian Self-Government—which is government predicated upon liberty under law and which represents the rights and liberties of each individual under the law. This is the culmination of the Christian idea of man and government.

England did much to establish the rights of the individual as law. But these rights had to be *granted* by monarchy to its citizens. America established a Christian precedent by being the first nation to define the rights of the individual as *God-granted* and thus as the sacred *property* of the individual—the *preservation and protection* of this property was defined as *the chief end of government.*

As we read the Magna Charta today with its many strange sounding terms we can begin to see the thread of individual liberty running through. In order to appreciate what a victory the Magna Charta was we need to glimpse Feudal England of the time of King John.

344

"Magna Charta was the culmination of a protest against the arbitrary rule of King John, who was using governmental powers which had been established by the great builders of the English nation, William the Conqueror, Henry I, and Henry II, for selfish and tyrannical purposes. In general, these abuses took the pattern of increasing customary feudal obligations and decreasing established feudal rights and privileges. The barons were forced to pay taxes above the usual rate, and their right to hold court for their tenants was restricted. The king exerted pressure in order to influence church elections. The merchants of London were burdened by heavy taxes, and their trading privileges were curtailed. To a limited extent even the lowest of King John's subjects suffered because his confiscation of church property destroyed the only available source of poor relief . . .

Richard L. Perry,
Editor, *Sources of
Our Liberties*

"The final crisis of the reign began . . . when John sought to revive the war with the king of France. The barons refused to follow their king to battle, and John prepared to march against them to compel obedience. The barons rallied around Stephen Langton, who produced in their midst a copy of Henry I's Charter of Liberties. The barons then resolved to fight for those liberties 'even unto death' . . . John's last hope of success disappeared when the merchants of London turned against him and opened the gates to the insurgents. With only a small band of supporters remaining, John at last agreed to meet the demands of the barons. The dramatic meeting occurred on June 15, 1215 at Runnymede, along the banks of the Thames . . . The articles presented by the barons were agreed to and sealed, and during the next few days copies of Magna Charta were drawn up in final form and sealed by the King." *Sources of Our Liberties*, edited by Richard L. Perry, 1959, American Bar Foundation, Chicago, Illinois

John Locke reminds us that under the "Law of Nature . . . i.e. the Will of God" "no one ought to harm another in his Life, Health, Liberty, or Possessions". Why this consideration of each other?

Now after centuries of permitting only certain individuals in a society to have protection of *body* and *property*, the Magna Charta sets forth certain rights which are to belong to every "*freeman*". This doesn't cover everyone who lives in the kingdom yet, but it is a big step forward.

The most important clauses of the Magna Charta can be traced down through our own Bill of Rights. What do these terms mean to you?

a) the protection of the *writ of habeas corpus*

b) the rights of *trial by jury*

c) the guarantee that no person can be deprived of life, liberty or property without *due process of law*

The following Old English terms found in the Magna Charta need some definition:

"No scutage or aid shall be imposed in our kingdom" (page 39, *Christian History*). 345

A *scutage* was a money payment in lieu of knight's service. An *aid* was a grant by the tenant to his lord in times of distress.

"*A freeman shall not be* amerced *for a small offence*" (page 39). A *freeman* shall not be *fined* for a small offence.

"*and for a great crime according to the heinousness of it*" (page 39). And for a great offence he shall be fined *in proportion* to the *magnitude* of the offence.

"*And a villein shall be amerced after the same manner*" (page 39). A *villein*, in feudal terms, was one who held land in tenure from the lord of the manor.

"*Wainage*" refers to agricultural instruments, "*amerciaments*" means "fines"

"*No constable shall distrain any knight*" (page 39), *distrain* means "require"

"*No freeman shall be taken or imprisoned, or disseised*" (page 40), *disseised* means dispossessed

"*contenement*" means "freehold" or "unit of land"

Petition of Right—1628

Richard L. Perry,
Editor, *Sources of
Our Liberties*

"By recourse to ancient principles of the English constitution, the Petition of Right announced important restrictions upon government by prerogative as practiced by Charles I (1625–49) in violation of the principles of individual liberty. It struck at prerogative taxation, which was the power of the king to exact taxes without the consent of Parliament; it provided that prisoners committed at the king's command should be freed on bail before trial; it declared illegal the quartering of troops in private houses; and it forbade the trial of civilians under the martial law. Parliament presented the grievances of the people in the form of a petition to the king, asserting that no more was asked than the observance of existing laws. Although no change in the law was intended, several important points were clarified by the document. Once the royal assent had been secured, these points became established as part of the law of the land.

"The Petition of Right was 'the first of those great constitutional documents since Magna Charta, which safeguard the liberties of the people by securing the supremacy of the law.' It has also been called 'the second Great Charter of the liberties of England' and 'the first great official interpretation of Magna Charta since the time of Edward III.' . . .

"A petition of right was a request by the individual that the benefit of the law be allowed to him in cases where it was alleged that the king's prerogative had overridden the law. It was distinguished from a petition of grace, which was presented to the king in Parliament praying for an alteration of the law in a particular case."

346

"The Bill of Rights, enacted December 16, 1689, established in statutory form the provisions of the Declaration of Rights. The Declaration had been agreed to by Parliament on February 12, 1689, and was presented to William and Mary the next day, when they were proclaimed king and queen of England . . .

Richard L. Perry,
Editor, *Sources of
Our Liberties*

"These documents asserted the supremacy of Parliament over the claimed divine right of kings. The royal prerogative was sharply curtailed, and even the possession of the crown became a statutory right, not a hereditary right. Toleration for Protestant dissenters was assured, and a number of individual liberties, insisted upon as among the rights of the subject, were given formal recognition as part of the law of the land . . .

"The Bill of Rights of 1689 was the direct ancestor of the bills of rights adopted by the states at the time of the American Revolution and of the first ten amendments to the Constitution of the United States. Many of its provisions directly affected the form and content of specific provisions found in those documents under which the liberties of the citizen of the United States are protected even today."
Sources of Our Liberties, American Bar Foundation

Step Three: Reading Assignment

Pages 37–47 in Text, Christian History

Step Four: Questions for Invention

1. In Feudal England the king, as the supreme head of the government, possessed the superior rights and privileges, these belonging in lesser and descending degree to his noblemen. In the Magna Charta the barons are checking the uncontrolled power of the king to take their property or their person for his own use without their consent. What clauses in the Magna Charta are the basis for *"no taxation without representation"*?
2. What exceptions to "no taxation without representation" does the king make?
3. How can the beginnings of representative government be seen in the manner in which the general council of the king is called?
4. What elements of self-government do we see emerging in regard to the City of London?
5. Which statement in the Magna Charta means that Christian justice shall be observed in regard to punishment? Why was this necessary?
6. Which statement protects the individual's property by protecting his means of

livelihood or productivity?

7. How does the Magna Charta indicate a concern of government for what Locke calls the *"Fundamental Law of Property"*?

8. What statement in the Magna Charta indicates a recognition that the person, or body, or an individual is property and as such has rights?

9. What kinds of action on the part of the constable or bailiff requires the consent of the individual?

10. What provision is made for a freeman to recover his rights if he feels he has been deprived unjustly?

11. Why is judgment by one's peers a form of local self-government?

12. What safeguard did the barons demand from the king to secure their hard-fought rights?

13. Over four hundred years passed after Magna Charta before Englishmen again had to remind the throne that there were certain principles of individual liberty which were sacred and which they demanded that parliament, as representing all of the people, protect. Why was the occasion of this petition such a moving one for these Englishmen?

14. What similar rights are set forth in the Petition of Right which you found in the Magna Charta?

15. What new rights are set forth in the Petition of Right?

16. What statements in the Petition of Right indicate that all of the king's subjects not just freemen, are being protected by the laws of the land as represented by Parliament? Why is this concept closer to the Christian idea of man and government?

17. Upon what basis is it declared that the king's subjects have these rights and freedoms?

18. In what way was Parliament fulfilling Locke's concept of the *Legislative* as the *"Supream Power"* of the Commonwealth"?

19. Compare the Magna Charta, the Petition of Right and the English Bill of Rights. What big change in the *tone* of these declarations of rights do you note from the first statement in the Magna Charta through that of the English Bill of Rights?

20. On June 12, 1776, three weeks before the Declaration of Independence was signed, the Virginia Convention, meeting in Williamsburg, adopted a declaration of rights. It contains such phrases as "That all men are by nature equally free and independent, and have certain inherent rights . . ." This declaration was one of the most important forerunners of the first ten amendments—our Federal Bill of Rights.

The following provisions for individual liberty and property rights are found in the American Bill of Rights as contained in the first ten Amendments to the Constitution of the United States of America. Trace these rights from their appearance in the English documents. How is Locke's concept of the "end of government" as "the preservation of property" carried out to a fuller degree?

The American Bill of Rights

Article I

Freedom of Religion, of Speech, of the Press, and Right of Petition. "Congress shall make no law respecting an establishment of religion, or prohibiting the free exercise thereof; or abridging the freedom of speech, or of the press; or the right of the people peaceably to assemble, and to petition the Government for a redress of grievances."

Article II

Right of People to Bear Arms and not to be Infringed. "A well regulated Militia, being necessary to the security of a free State, the right of the people to keep and bear Arms, shall not be infringed by law."

Article III

Quartering of Troops. "No Soldier shall, in time of peace be quartered in any house, without the consent of the Owner, nor in time of war, but in a manner to be prescribed by law."

Article IV

Persons and House to be Secure from Unreasonable Searches and Seizures. "The right of the people to be secure in their persons, houses, papers, and effects, against unreasonable searches and seizures, shall not be violated, and no Warrant shall issue, but upon probable cause, supported by Oath or affirmation, and particularly describing the place to be searched, and the persons or things to be seized."

Article V

Trials for Crime—Just Compensation for Private Property Taken for Public Use. "No person shall be held to answer for a capital, or otherwise infamous crime, unless on a presentment of indictment of a Grand Jury, except in cases arising in the land or naval forces, or in the Militia, when in actual service, in time of War or public danger; nor shall any person be subject for the same offence to be twice put in jeopardy of life or limb; nor shall be compelled in any criminal case to be a witness against himself, nor be deprived of life, liberty, or property, without due process of law; nor shall private property be taken for public use without just compensation."

Article VI

Civil Rights in Trials for Crimes Enumerated. "In all criminal prosecutions, the accused shall enjoy the right to a speedy and public trial, by an impartial jury of the State and district wherein the crime shall have been committed, which district shall have been previously ascertained by law, and to be informed of the nature and cause of the accusation; to be confronted with the witnesses against him; to have compulsory process for obtaining witnesses in his favor, and to have the Assistance of Counsel for his defense."

Article VII

Preservation of Right of Trial by Jury. "In suits at common law, where the value in controversy shall exceed twenty dollars, the right of trial by jury shall be preserved, and no fact tried by a jury, shall be otherwise re-examined in any Court of the United States, than according to the rules of the common law."

Article VIII

Excessive Bail, Fines and Punishments Prohibited. "Excessive bail shall not be required, nor excessive fines imposed, nor cruel and unusual punishments inflicted."

Article IX

Reserved Right of People. "The enumeration in the Constitution, of certain rights, shall not be construed to deny or disparage others retained by the people."

Article X

Powers Not Delegated, Reserved to States and People Respectively. "The powers not delegated to the United States by the Constitution, nor prohibited by it to the States, are reserved to the States respectively, or to the people."

Step Five: Study of Concepts

Read page 248A, *Christian History*. *"Life, Liberty and Property"*. Madison's statement on property indicates that the *whole of man is his property*. It calls to mind the statement in Ephesians 2:10 indicating that man is God's *"workmanship"*, God's property, *"created in Christ Jesus unto good works."*

The First American Constitution—Connecticut—1638. Read pages 249–257. Closely based upon the Bible and the Christian form of government by *covenant* consent, this constitution indicates that the colonists recognized *"the origin of all civil authority as derived under God from the agreement and covenant of the whole body of the governed."*

350

Massachusetts Body of Liberties—1641. Read pages 257–261. Again we see Christianity as the source and protection of those *"fundamental principles relating to the sacredness of life, liberty, property, and reputation."*

Samuel Adams, 'Rights of the Colonists', November, 1772. Read pages 365–370. Adams set forth Locke's basic principle regarding *"the Law of Nature,* i.e., *"the Will of God"* as a "declaration, and the *fundamental law of Nature being the preservation of Mankind".* Adams refers back to the Magna Charta as a statement of the fundamental natural, or Christian, rights of each individual, governed by God, through CHRIST.

Step Six: Original Thought

In Madison's statement about what constitutes a man's property he makes the following statement: "No man is safe in his opinions, his person, his faculties, or his possessions. Where there is an excess of liberty . . ." Locke, on page 364, states that the law of Nature refers to a Liberty which is not a State of "Licence". Sam Adams, also on page 364, refers to "liberty which no man can truly possess whose mind is enthralled by irregular and inordinate passions; since it is no great privilege to be free from external violence if the dictates of the mind are controlled by a force within, which exerts itself above reason". He who serves the law of God is a *free man.* How can observance of God's law preserve your liberty and freedom? What does *"licence"* mean to you? Why is *"licence"* the enemy of *liberty?*

How does this statement of Samuel Adams on page 364 of *Christian History* relate to the Christian self-government of each individual? How can each of us promote the liberty of our country?

"He therefore is the truest friend to the liberty of his country who tries most to promote its virtue . . ."

What is the Legislative or law-making body of our state called? of our nation? How can we register our "consent" or lack of "consent" to the decisions of this body?

Name some current matters before our state or national legislative body which could be infringements upon our Christian rights.

Step Seven: What Identifies America as a Christian Nation?

1. ". . . that the form of civil government here established was simply an extension to the domain of secular affairs of the principles already adopted in religious matters—the mutual covenant and agreement of those associated as under God

351

the ultimate law." *Christian History*, page 250, *Comments on the Connecticut Constitution*

2. "The free fruition of such liberties Immunities and priveledges as humanitie, Civilitie, and Christianitie call for as due to every man in his place and proportion without impeachment and Infringement hath ever bene and ever will be in the tranquilitie and Stabilitie of Churches and Commonwealths. And the deniall or deprivall thereof, the disturbance if not the ruine of both." *Christian History*, page 257, *Massachusetts Body of Liberties*

3. "*The Rights of the Colonists as Christians*". "These may be best understood by reading and carefully studying the institutes of the great Law Giver and Head of the Christian Church, which are to be found clearly written and promulgated in the New Testament . . ." *Christian History*, page 367

4. "*The Rights of the Colonists as Subjects*". "First, 'The first fundamental, positive law of all commonwealths or states is establishing the legislative power. As the first fundamental natural law, also, which is to govern even the legislative power itself, is the preservation of the society.' " *Christian History*, page 368

A Biblical-Political Index to John Locke

Lesson Seven

Introduction: John Locke and the American Christian Constitution

For one hundred and fifty years prior to the American Revolution the Colonists studied the Scriptures for the authority and source of government. They regarded the Bible as their "*Political Textbook*". From the pulpit and the rostrum the clergy preached political principles based upon their studies of writers who believed that government should be *revelational of God*.

In a study entitled *The New England Clergy and the American Revolution*, Alice Baldwin indicates the degree to which the clergy educated the colonists in the Scriptural principles of government and of the quality of their knowledge and involvement in the political life of the new nation:

"*The New England clergy of the eighteenth century occupied a position of peculiar influence and power in the life of their own communities and of the several colonies . . . They were for the most part a 'learned clergy', graduates of Harvard or of Yale . . . They preached not only on Sunday but on many special occasions prescribed by the churches or ordered by the colonial assemblies, such as days of fasting and prayer and days of thinksgiving . . . The sources from which the New England ministers developed their theories may be learned partly from the quotations and foot-notes which frequently are to be found in sermons and pamphlets, partly from diaries, letters, and other documents . . . The most common source was the Bible . . . Indeed there was never a principle derived from more secular reading that was not strengthened and sanctified by the Scriptures . . .*

"*The next great source was the works of John Locke, his essays on religious toleration and human understanding as well as those on government. He was quoted by name as early as 1738, but his influence is to be seen in earlier works. Especially after 1763 the*

*references to him are numerous, not only by the more prominent ministers of the larger
towns but by those of the country villages as well."*

For many years there has been a concerted effort to separate Christians from
John Locke. He has been called a Deist, classified as a philosopher of the French
Revolution, and appropriated by the Progressive Educators. Now, through the
documentation of the *primary sources*, referred to by Miss Baldwin, the *Christian
History of the Constitution*, compiled by Verna M. Hall, reveals him as a *saved
Christian*.

In the fifth edition of *A Commonplace-Book to The Holy Bible: or the Scripture's
Sufficiency Practically Demonstrated*, by John Locke and published by the American
Tract Society, there occurs the following statement:

*"A relative having inquired of Mr. Locke what was the shortest and surest way for a
young gentleman to attain a true knowledge of the Christian religion, he replied in these
golden words: 'Let him study the Holy Scripture, especially in the New Testament.
Therein are contained the words of eternal life. It has God for its Author, Salvation for
its end, and Truth without any mixture of error for its matter.'"*

The study of the *original* volumes of John Locke reveal his extensive marginal
notes from Scripture. His Scriptural research and his political treatises were the
axe which finally cut the root of the *divine right of kings* theory of government. In
America he was widely studied and his phrases and statements can be found inter-
laced and quoted in the writings of our Founders.

John Locke, the Philosopher of the American Revolution "was admitted to Christ
Church College in 1651, when Dr. Owen, the Independent was Dean,—the same
who was thought of for the presidency of Harvard College. 'Educated,' says Sir
James, 'among the English Dissenters, during the short period of their political
ascendency, he early imbibed *the deep piety and ardent spirit of liberty which actuated
that body of men* . . . By the Independent divines, who were his instructors, our
philosopher was taught *those principles of religious liberty which they were the first
to disclose to the world.*" ("The Pulpit of the American Revolution" by John Wingate
Thornton, 1860")

The Biblical-Political Index which follows represents the challenge of John Locke
to his political descendents—Christian constitutionalists. It is presented as a guide
to what each student of American History must do so that we once again restore
the Holy Scriptures as America's "political textbook".

It is hoped that patriots, parents, preachers and teachers will compile their own
Biblical-Political Index of John Locke. This Index is not exhaustive. It covers
some major propositions Biblically Indexed from *Of Civil Government—Book II*
found in the Text, *Christian History*, pages 57–125.

A Biblical-Political Index to John Locke

CHRISTIAN
HISTORY STUDY
COURSE

The Bible
Biblical
Index

Of the State of Nature.

Christian History
Political
Index

The Bible *Biblical Index*	Of the State of Nature.	*Christian History* *Political Index*
Man's Original state Gen. 1. 26, 27 "The Lord's free-man . . . is Christ's servant" I Cor. 7:22	*Deriving "Political Power" from its "Original".* Page 58:4. "We must consider what State all Men are naturally in, and that is, a *State of perfect Freedom* to order their Actions, and dispose of their Possessions".	*The Declaration of Independence* page 248A The "free and independent man" page XIII
Christian Obligation John 15:12 ". . . as I have loved you."	*"All the Power and Jurisdiction is Reciprocal".* Page 58:4, 5. "This *Equality* of Men by Nature . . . the Foundation of that Obligation to mutual Love amongst Men. . . ."	*The Christian idea of man* page 2
Golden Rule Luke 6:31	*"The State of Nature has a Law of Nature to govern it".* Page 58:6. "No one ought to harm another in his Life, Health, Liberty, or Possessions"	Samual Adams *Rights of the Colonists* page 365
Galatians 5:13 ". . . use not liberty for an occasion to the flesh. . ."	*"A State of Liberty, yet it is not a State of Licence".* Page 58:6. "He has not Liberty to destroy himself, or so much as any Creature in his Possession . . ."	Virtue—a condition of Liberty page 364B
Ephesians 2:10 "For we are his workmanship. . ."	*Man created as the Property of God.* Page 58:6. "All the Servants of one Sovereign Master, sent into the World by his Order, and about his Business, they are his Property, whose Workmanship they are. . . ."	*Life, Liberty & Property* page 248A
Acts 24:16 "a conscience void of offence toward God, and toward men."	*Preservation of Law and Property in Every Man's Hands.* Page 58:7. "The *Execution* of the Law of Nature is . . . put into every Man's Hands, whereby every one has a Right to punish the Transgressors of that Law . . ."	"*Conscience* is the most sacred of all Property"
I Peter 1:18, 19 Redeemed "with the precious blood of Christ"	*A Transgressor Consents not to be Ruled by the Law.* Page 59:8. "In transgressing the Law of Nature, the Offender declares himself to live by another Rule . . . and so he becomes dangerous to Mankind, the Tye . . . being slighted and broken by him . . ."	*John Locke* "Over whom no Body can have a Power to make Laws, but by their own Consent . . ." page 93:134
Exodus Chap. 20 The Ten Commandments *The Pentateuch* Mosaic Law	*Punishment of Crime is the Right of Self-Preservation.* Page 59:10, 11. "The damnified Person has this Power of appropriating to himself, the Goods or Service of the Offender, *by Right of Self-Preservation*, as every Man	*Magna Charta* pages 38–41 *Bill of Rights* pages 44–47

The Bible
Biblical
Index

Christian History
Political
Index

A BIBLICAL
POLITICAL
INDEX TO
JOHN LOCKE

has a Power to punish the Crime, to prevent its being committed again, *by the Right he has of Preserving all Mankind . . ."*

1 Peter 3:15
"Be ready always to give an answer to every man that asketh you a reason of the hope that is in you."

Man in the State of Nature is Answerable to Mankind. Page 60:13. *"In the State of Nature, every one has the Executive Power* of the Law of Nature . . . And if he that judges, judges amiss in his own, or any other Case, he is answerable for it to the rest of Mankind."

John Locke
"The *Federative Power"* of the Commonwealth page 97:146, 147

Romans 2:14, 15
"These, having not the law, are a law unto themselves"

All Men are Naturally in the State of Nature. Page 61:14, 15. "That all Men are naturally in that State, and remain so, till by their own Consents they make themselves Members of some politick Society . . ."

"That to secure these Rights, Governments are instituted among men . . ."
page 248A

Of the State of War.

"The carnal mind is enmity against God"
Romans 8:6, 7

"The *State of War* is a state of *Enmity* and *Destruction:* And therefore declaring by Word or Action, not a passionate and hasty, but a sedate settled Design, upon another Man's Life, *puts him in a State of War* with him . . ."

Monarchy
royal prerogative enmity vs. constitutional rights page 295: 2, 3

"The Lord . . . forsaketh not his saints . . . but the seed of the wicked shall be cut off."
Psalms 37:28

"For *by the fundamental Law of Nature, Man being to be preserved,* as much as possible, when all cannot be preserved, the safety of the Innocent is to be preferred: And one may destroy a Man who makes War upon him, or has discovered an Enmity to his being, for the same Reason, that he may kill a *Woolf* or a *Lion;* . . . and so may be treated as Beasts of Prey . . ."

"Which imagine *mischief in their hearts . . .* preserve me from the violent man: who have purposed to overthrow my goings"
Psalms 140:2,4

"for no body can desire to *have me in his absolute Power,* unless it be to compel me by force to that, which is against the Right of my Freedom, *i.e.* make me a Slave. To be free from such force is the only security of my Preservation; and reason bids me look on him, as an Enemy to my Preservation, who would take away that *Freedom,* which is the fence to it".

The American Declaration of Independence
page 346B

357

CHRISTIAN
HISTORY STUDY
COURSE

The Bible
Biblical
Index

Christian History
Political
Index

"... Shall not the Judge of all the earth do right?"
Genesis 18:25

"Want of a common Judge with Authority, puts all Men in a State of Nature: Force without Right, upon a Man's Person, makes a state of War, both where there is, and is not, a common Judge."

"thou doest me wrong to war against me"
Judges 11:27

"To avoid this *state of War* (wherein there is no Appeal but to Heaven, and wherein every the least Difference is apt to end, where there is no Authority to decide between the Contenders) is one great *reason of Men's putting themselves into Society*, and quitting the State of Nature."

"is willing to joyn in Society with others ... for the mutual *Preservation* of their ... *Property*"
page 91:123

Acts 24:16
"a conscience void of offence toward God, and toward men."

"Where there is no Judge on Earth, the Appeal lies to God in Heaven. That Question then cannot mean, who shall judge? whether another hath put himself in a *State of War* with me, and whether I may as *Jephtha* did, *appeal to Heaven* in it? Of that I myself can only be Judge in my own Conscience, as I will answer it at the great Day, to the supream Judge of all Men."

"Conscience is the most sacred of all property"
page 248A

Of Slavery.

Galations 5:1
"Stand fast ... in the liberty wherewith Christ hath made us free"

"The *Natural Liberty* of Man is to be free from any superior Power on Earth, and not to be under the Will or legislative Authority of Man, but to have only the Law of Nature for his Rule.

Christian Self-Government
"As Christians, we have Jesus the Messiah for our King, and are under the Law reveal'd by him in the Gospel"

"We ... were never in bondage to any man"

"Whosoever committeth sin is the servant of sin"
John 8:33, 34

"But *Freedom of Men under Government*, is, to have a standing Rule to live by, common to every one of that Society, and made by the legislative Power erected in it; a Liberty to follow my own Will in all things, where that Rule prescribes not; and not to be subject to the inconstant, uncertain, unknown, arbitrary Will of another Man:"

John Locke, page XIII

Algernon Sidney pages 128–130

The Bible
Biblical
Index

Christian History
Political
Index

A BIBLICAL-
POLITICAL
INDEX TO
JOHN LOCKE

Galatians 4:30,31
"Cast out the bond woman and her son . . . we are not children of the bond woman, but of the free"

"For a Man, not having the Power of his own Life, *cannot*, by Compact, or his own Consent, *enslave himself* to any one, nor put himself under the absolute, arbitrary Power of another, to take away his Life, when he pleases."

Samuel Adams
"The right to freedom being the gift of God Almighty, it is not in the power of man to alienate this gift and voluntarily become a slave."
page 367

Of the Beginning of Political Societies.

The Ten Commandments
Duties to Man
Exodus 20:12-17

"The only Way whereby any . . . puts on the Bonds of Civil Society". Page 83:95. "The only Way whereby any one devests himself of his natural Liberty, and puts on the *Bonds of Civil Society* is by agreeing with other Men to joyn and unite into a Community . . . and make *one Body politick*, wherein the *Majority* have a Right to act and conclude the rest . . ."

Voluntary Association
"individuals joined together in church and society"
pages 270B, 270C

Second Commandment of Our Lord
Matthew 22:39

"So every one is bound by that consent". Page 83:96. "For when any number of Men have, by consent of every individual, made a *Community*, they have thereby made that *Community* one Body, . . . and so everyone is bound by that consent to be concluded by the *Majority* . . ."

"Puts himself under an Obligation, to every one of that Society". Page 83:97. "And thus every Man, . . . puts himself under an Obligation, to every one of that Society, to submit to the determination of the *Majority*, and to be concluded by it; or else this *original Compact*, whereby he with others incorporates into *one Society*, would signifie nothing . . ."

Mayflower Compact
pages 150,204, 205

"Thou shalt love thy neighbor as thyself"

"The consent of the Majority shall . . . conclude every individual". Page 83:98. "For if the *consent of the Majority* shall not, in Reason be received, as *the act of the whole*, and conclude every individual; nothing but

The Representative Principle
pages 96:140; 135

359

CHRISTIAN
HISTORY STUDY
COURSE

The Bible
Biblical
Index

Christian History
Political
Index

the consent of every individual can make any thing to be the act of the whole . . . For where the *majority* cannot conclude the rest, there they cannot act as one Body, and consequently will be immediately dissolved again."

The *"new covenant"*

The Beginning of Political Society. Page 84:99. "And thus that, which begins and actually *constitutes any Political Society*, is nothing but the consent of any number of Freemen capable of a majority to unite and incorporate into such a Society. And this is that, and that only, which did, or could give beginning to any *lawful Government* in the World."

The Fundamental Orders of Conn. "The choice of public magistrates belongs to the people by God's own allowance" page 250

Hebrews 8:10 ". . . I will put my laws into their mind, and write them in their hearts"

Search into the "Original" of Government. Page 84:101, 102. "By consent were all *equal*, till by the same consent they set Rulers over themselves. So that their *Politick Societies* all *began* from a voluntary Union, and the mutual agreement of Men freely acting in the choice of their Governors, and forms of Government."

"Abraham our father as pertaining to the flesh" *Romans 4:1*

"The law was our schoolmaster to bring us unto Christ" *Galatians 3:24*

Paternalism Traced. Page 85:105, 107. "Government commonly began in the Father . . . He was the fittest to be trusted . . . and the Custom of obeying him, in their Childhood, made it easier to submit to him . . . The Father's Government of the Childhood of those sprung from him, having accustomed them to the *Rule of one Man* . . . it was no wonder that they should pitch upon, and naturally run into that Form of Government, which . . . by Experience, they had found both easie and safe . . ."

John Locke "Of Paternal Power" pages 70–77 No "absolute Arbitrary Dominion of the Father". page 73:64

1 Samuel 8:18, 19 "And ye shall cry out in that day because of your king which ye shall have chosen"

The "Golden Age" corrupted by "vain Ambition". Page 87:111. . . . "Men found it necessary to examine more carefully *the Original* and Rights *of Government;* and to find out ways to *restrain the Exorbitances*, and *prevent the Abuses* of that Power, which they having entrusted in another's Hands only for their own Good they found was made use of to hurt them."

Samuel Adams "The Rights of the Colonists as Men, Christians, and Subjects" pages 365–370

"Nay; but we will have a king over us"

Monarchy Originally Chosen by Free Men. Page 88:112. ". . . as far as we have any Light from History, we have reason to conclude, that all peaceful beginnings of *Government* have been *laid in the Consent of the People.*"

Ephesians 2:12 ". . . ye were without Christ, being aliens"

"By being born under any Government" are we *"naturally Subjects to it"?* Pages 88, 89: 115–117. "For there are no Examples so frequent in History . . . as those of Men withdrawing themselves, and their Obedience, from the Jurisdiction they were born under, . . . and *setting up new Governments* in other Places . . . The Son cannot ordinarily enjoy the Possession of his Father, but under the same Terms his Father did: by becoming a member of the Society; whereby he puts himself presently under the Government, he finds there established . . ."

Ephesians 2:19–22 "Now therefore ye are no more strangers and foreigners, but fellow citizens with the saints, and of the household of God."

"Governments . . . claim no Power over the Son because of the Father". Page 89:118. *"A Child is born a Subject of no Country or Government.* He is under his Father's Tuition and Authority, till he comes to Age of Discretion; and then he is a Freeman, at Liberty what Government he will put himself under; what Body Politick he will unite himself to . . ."

"What shall I do to inherit eternal life?" *Luke 18:18*

"What shall be a . . . sufficient Declaration of a Man's Consent"? Page 90:119–122. *"Tacit Consent".* "But submitting to the Laws of any Country, living quietly, and enjoying Privileges and Protection under them, *makes not a Man a Member of that Society . . ."*

"On these two commandments hang all the law and the prophets" *Matthew 22:40*

"Express Promise and Compact". "To be *Subjects or Members of that Commonwealth.* Nothing can make any Man so, but his actually entering into it by positive Engagement, and express Promise and Compact. This is that, which I think, concerning the beginning of political Societies, and that *Consent which makes any one a Member* of any Commonwealth."

361

CHRISTIAN
HISTORY STUDY
COURSE

The Bible
Biblical
Index

Christian History
Political
Index

"Of the Ends of Political Society and Government."

Life
John 17:3
"And this is life eternal, that they might know thee the only true God, and Jesus Christ, whom thou hast sent"

"The end and purpose of Government". Page 91:124. "The great and *chief End* therefore, of Mens uniting into Commonwealths, and putting themselves under Government, *is the Preservation of their Property* . . . Lives, Liberties and Estates".

Declaration of Independence
". . . to secure these Rights, Governments are instituted among Men."
page 346B

Liberty
2 Cor. 3:17
"Where the Spirit of the Lord is, there is liberty"

Estate
Jude 6
"The angels which kept not their first estate . . ."

"In the state of Nature there are many things wanting". Page 91:124–126.

First, There wants an *establish'd*, settled, known *Law*, received and allowed by common Consent to be the Standard of right and wrong, and the common Measure to decide all Controversies between them" . . .

Secondly, In the state of Nature there wants *a known and indifferent Judge*, with Authority to determine all Differences according to the established Law" . . .

Thirdly, In the state of Nature there often wants *Power* to back and support the Sentence when right, and to *give* it due *Execution*."

Christ
"and the government shall be upon his shoulder"
Isaiah 9:6

"The better to preserve himself his Liberty and Property". Page 92:131.

"But though Men when they enter into Society, give up the Equality, Liberty, and Executive Power they had in the State of Nature, into the hands of the Society . . . yet it being only with an intention in every one the better to preserve himself his Liberty and Property . . . the Power of the Society, or *Legislative* constituted by them, can *never be suppos'd to extend farther than the common good;* but is obliged to secure every ones Property, by providing against those three defects above mentioned, that made the State of Nature so unsafe and uneasie."

James Madison
"Where an excess of power prevails, property of no sort is duly respected. No man is safe in his opinions, his person, his faculties, or his possessions."
page 248A

The Colonists Act on the Christian Principles of Self-Government, Property, Union 1643-1776

Lesson Eight

Read Text, *Christian History*, pages 282A–364A. This section represents the historical development of the Christian Constitutional Principles of *Property*, *Self-Government and Union*, as carried out by the Colonists in their understanding of government, and which led to their final severance of ties with Great Britain, in order to maintain their God-endowed rights of *life*, *liberty*, *property* through Christian Self-Government.

Self-Government

The Colonists Establish Government with Liberty
British Commission Created to Regulate Internal Affairs of New England—Mass. Defends Its Right of Self-Government. Text, *Christian History*, pages 285–287.

The Twelve Colonies Govern Their Own Local Affairs. Text, *Christian History*, pages 288, 289.

British Ministry Checks Growth of Republicanism. Text, *Christian History*, pages 289–290.

Great Britain Treats Colonies as Aliens and Rivals. Text, *Christian History*, page 291, last paragraph.

Self-Government and Property
Right to labor
Habeas Corpus
Jury Trial
Popular Representation
Free Press

Self-Government Promotes Principle of Individual Freedom. Text, *Christian History*, page 292.

Colonists Aimed to Preserve their Liberties and their Union with Great Britain. Text, *Christian History*, pages 293–295.

363

THE COLONISTS
ACT ON THE
CHRISTIAN
PRINCIPLES OF
SELF-
GOVERNMENT,
PROPERTY,
UNION

Christian History, page 321.

*Self-Government
with Union*

Sam Adams Proposes Committees of Correspondence to Show that Colonists are United in Constitutional Principles. Text, *Christian History*, pages 320–322.

Patriotic Letters—The Press. Text, *Christian History*, pages 322–323.

*Property
Self-Government
Union*

A Test Case of Union 'Gaspee' Incident—Trial in England. Text, *Christian History*, pages 323–324.

Committees of National Correspondence—Unite Half of Colonies. Text, *Christian History*, page 325.

*Property
Self-Government
Union*

Right to Trial by Jury Attained by American Union. Text, *Christian History*, page 325.

Common Union in Stamp Act—Leadership of Massachusetts and Virginia. Text, *Christian History*, page 326.

Love of Liberty Under Law a Reigning Principle of Colonists. Text, *Christian History*, page 327.

American Christian Unity: Boston Tea Party and the Boston Port Bill. Text, *Christian History*, pages 327–339.

Union

Colonies Unite with Massachusetts Against Regulatory Acts. Text, *Christian History*, page 341.

*Property
Self-Government
Union*

Colonists Tighten Resistance in Accordance with Their Christian Duty to Resist Oppression. Text, *Christian History*, page 342.

*Property
Self-Government
Union*

Committee of Safety Formed—The Minute Men Pledge Action. Text, *Christian History*, page 343.

Lexington and Concord, April 19, 1775. Text, *Christian History*, pages 345–346.

*Property
Self-Government*

An Appeal to Arms and to Almighty God—Patrick Henry, "Give me Liberty, or give me death". Text, *Christian History*, page 346A.

Union

The Declaration of Independence, July 4, 1776. Text, *Christian History*, page 346B.

Independence from England. Text, Christian History, page 348.

Union

America founded on the Christian Idea of Man and Government. Text, *Christian History*, pages 348–349.

Property

Washington Unfurls the Flag of the United Colonies. Text, *Christian History*, page 351.

Self-Government *The Effort to Achieve Unanimity of the Colonies through their Voice in the Local Assemblies.* Text, *Christian History*, pages 352–359.

Property
Self-Government *Principles of the Declaration of Independence.* Text, *Christian History*, page 359.
Union

Epilogue

"*And the Lord said unto Samuel, Hearken unto the voice of the people in all that they say unto thee: for they have not rejected thee, but they have rejected me, that I should not reign over them . . . Nevertheless the people refused to obey the voice of Samuel; and they said, Nay; but we will have a king over us; that we also may be like all the nations . . ."
I Samuel 8:7, 19, 20*

"*Then Peter and the other apostles answered and said, We ought to obey God rather than men . . . and when they had called the apostles, and beaten them, they commanded that they should not speak in the name of Jesus, and let them go. And they departed from the presence of the council, rejoicing that they were counted worthy to suffer shame for his name. And daily in the temple, and in every house, they ceased not to teach and preach Jesus Christ." Acts 5:29, 40–42*

Index to Bible Quotations and References

Prepared by James and Barbara Rose

New Testament

Bibliography

BIBLIOGRAPHY

A

Adams, Amos, Rev.
Pastor First Church of Roxbury
General Fast Day Sermon, April 6, 1769

Appleton, Rev. Nathanial, A.M.
Election Sermon, May 26, 1742
Massachusetts Bay

B

Baldwin, Alice M.
The New England Clergy and the American Revolution
Frederick Ungar Pub. Co., New York, 1928

Bancroft, George
History of the United States of America
D. Appleton & Co., 1886

C

Conybeare, Rev. W. J. and Howson, Rev. J. S.
The Life and Epistles of St. Paul
S. S. Scranton & Co., Hartford, 1855

Cooley, Thomas M., LL.D.
The General Principles of Constitutional Law in the United States of America
Little, Brown, & Co., Boston, 1898

D

D'Aubigne, J. H. Merle
History of the Reformation in Europe in the Time of Calvin
Robert Carter and Bros., New York, 1867

Dearden, Jr., Robert R. and Watson, Douglas S.
The Bible of the Revolution
John Howell, San Francisco, 1930

de Tocqueville, Alexis
American Institutions and their Influence
A. S. Barnes & Co., New York, 1851

E

Ewell, Marshall D, LL.D.
A Review of Blackstone's Commentaries
Mathew Bender & Co., Albany, N. Y., 1915

F

Frothingham, Richard
The Rise of the Republic of the United States
Little, Brown & Co., Boston, 1873

G

Gregg, David, D.D.
Makers of the American Republic, A Series of Patriotic Lectures
E. B. Treat, New York, 1896

Guyot, Arnold
The Earth and Man: Lectures on Comparative Physical Geography, in its Relation to the History of Mankind
Gould and Lincoln, Boston, 1852

Guyot, Arnold
Physical Geography
Ivison, Blakeman & Co., New York, 1885

H

Hoffman, David
A Course of Legal Study
Joseph Neal, Baltimore, 1836

Hosmer, James K.
American Statesmen—Samuel Adams
Houghton, Mifflin & Co., Boston, 1891

I

Ingram, Rev. T. Robert
The World Under God's Law, Criminal Aspects of the Welfare State
St. Thomas Press—1962
Houston, Texas

L

Lechler, Prof. Gotthard Victor
John Wycliffe and His English Precursors
The Religious Tract Society, London, 1904

Linn, Rev. William
The Blessings of America
Tammany Society, or Columbian Order
New York, 1791

Lossing, Benson J.
Washington and the American Republic, 1870

M

Magoon, E. L.
Orators of the American Revolution
C. Scribner, New York, 1857

McLaughlin, Andrew C.
The Foundations of American Constitutionalism
Fawcett Publications, Greenwich, Conn., 1961

More, Hannah
The Works of Hannah More, American Edition
J. J. Woodward, Philadelphia, 1830

Morley, Dr. Felix
Freedom and Federalism
Regnery Company, 1959

Morley, Dr. Felix
The Power in the People
D. Van Nostrand Company, 1949

Morse, Jedidiah
Annals of the American Revolution
Hartford, 1824

N

Neander, Dr. Augustus
General History of the Christian Religion and Church
Houghton, Mifflin & Co., Boston, 1871

Neander, Augustus
Memorials of a Christian Life
Henry G. Bohn, London, 1852

P

Penn, William
No Cross, No Crown.
A Discourse Shewing the Nature and Discipline of the Holy Cross of Christ, The Seventh Edition, London, 1725

Perry, Richard L., Editor
Sources of Our Liberties
American Bar Foundation, Chicago, 1959

Phillips, Rev. S. Phillips, A.M.
The Christian Home as it is in the Sphere of Nature and the Church.
G. & F. Bill, New York, 1861

Pound, Roscoe
The Development of Constitutional Guarantees of Liberty
Yale University Press, 1957

S

Seabury, William Jones, D.D.,
An Introduction to the Study of Ecclesiastical Polity,
Crothers and Korth, New York, 1894

Sheldon, Henry C.
History of the Christian Church, 1894

Simpson, Rev. A. B., D.D.
The Holy Spirit
Christian Publications, Inc.
Harrisburg, Pa., 1896

Spindler, Dr. George D.
Education in a Transforming American Culture
Harvard Educational Review, Summer
1955

T

Townsend, Rev. L. T.
The Bible and the Nineteenth Century
Chautauqua Press, 1891

V

Veritas Foundation Staff Study
The Great Deceit, Social Pseudo-Sciences
West Sayville, New York, 1964

W

Webster, Noah
An American Dictionary of the English Language, 1856
George and Charles Merriam, Springfield, Mass.

Wells, William V.
The Life and Public Services of Samuel Adams
Little, Brown, & Co., 1865

West, Samuel, A.M.
Pastor of a Church in Dartmouth
Election Sermon, 1776, *The True Principles of Government*

Willard, Emma
History of the United States or, Republic of America
A. S. Barnes & Co., New York, 1843